The Great Powers and the International System

Systemic Theory in Empirical Perspective

Do great leaders make history, or are they compelled to act by historical circumstance? This debate has remained unresolved since Thomas Carlyle and Karl Marx framed it in the mid-19th century, yet implicit answers inform our policies and our views of history. In this book, Professor Bear F. Braumoeller argues persuasively that both perspectives are correct: leaders shape the main material and ideological forces of history that subsequently constrain and compel them. His studies of the Congress of Vienna, the interwar period, and the end of the Cold War illustrate this dynamic, and the data he marshals provide systematic evidence that leaders both shape and are constrained by the structure of the international system.

BEAR F. BRAUMOELLER is a political scientist and an Associate Professor at The Ohio State University. He has previously held faculty positions at Harvard University and the University of Illinois. His research lies at the intersection of international security, statistics, and diplomatic history, and in particular on translating the nuanced and contextual arguments of students of world politics into new statistical methods for political scientists. His work has been published in journals such as the *American Political Science Review*, the *American Journal of Political Science*, *International Organization*, *Political Analysis*, and *International Studies Quarterly*.

T0382615

Cambridge Studies in International Relations

123 The Great Powers and the International System

Systemic Theory in Empirical Perspective

EDITORS

Christian Reus-Smit
Nicholas J. Wheeler

EDITORIAL BOARD

James Der Derian, Martha Finnemore, Lene Hansen, Robert Keohane,
Rachel Kerr, Inderjeet Parmar, Jan Aart Scholte, Peter Vale,
Kees van der Pijl, Jutta Weldes, Jennifer Welsh, William Wohlforth

Cambridge Studies in International Relations is a joint initiative of Cambridge University Press and the British International Studies Association (BISA). The series will include a wide range of material, from undergraduate textbooks and surveys to research-based monographs and collaborative volumes. The aim of the series is to publish the best new scholarship in International Studies from Europe, North America, and the rest of the world.

The list of books in the series follows the index.

The Great Powers and the International System

Systemic Theory in Empirical Perspective

BEAR F. BRAUMOELLER
Ohio State University

CAMBRIDGE
UNIVERSITY PRESS

CAMBRIDGE
UNIVERSITY PRESS

University Printing House, Cambridge CB2 8BS, United Kingdom

One Liberty Plaza, 20th Floor, New York, NY 10006, USA

477 Williamstown Road, Port Melbourne, VIC 3207, Australia

314-321, 3rd Floor, Plot 3, Splendor Forum, Jasola District Centre, New Delhi-110025, India

79 Anson Road, #06-04/06, Singapore 079906

Cambridge University Press is part of the University of Cambridge.

It furthers the University's mission by disseminating knowledge in the pursuit of education, learning and research at the highest international levels of excellence.

www.cambridge.org
Information on this title: www.cambridge.org/9781107659186

© Bear F. Braumoeller 2012

This publication is in copyright. Subject to statutory exception and to the provisions of relevant collective licensing agreements, no reproduction of any part may take place without the written permission of Cambridge University Press.

First published 2012

A catalogue record for this publication is available from the British Library

Library of Congress Cataloging in Publication data
Braumoeller, Bear F.
The great powers and the international system : systemic theory in empirical perspective /
Bear F. Braumoeller, Ohio State University.
p.   cm. – (Cambridge studies in international relations)
Includes bibliographical references and index.
ISBN 978-1-107-00541-9 (hardback) – ISBN 978-1-107-65918-6 (paperback)
1. Great powers.   2. International relations – Philosophy.   3. International relations –
History.   I. Title.
JZ1310.B73   2012
327.101–dc23   2012004346

ISBN 978-1-107-00541-9 Hardback
ISBN 978-1-107-65918-6 Paperback

Cambridge University Press has no responsibility for the persistence or accuracy of URLs for external or third-party internet websites referred to in this publication, and does not guarantee that any content on such websites is, or will remain, accurate or appropriate.

To Molly
whose perseverance and grace are an inspiration

Contents

ix

Preface

The idea that the environment within which people interact has an impact on their behavior is anything but radical. Indeed, to urban architects, physicians, sociologists, economists, and policy analysts, it will seem commonplace. And because people are both aware of the impact of their environment and able to alter it, it comes as little surprise that we seek to do so: strategic placement of one-way streets eases traffic congestion, snack machines with healthier options improve diets, restructuring government subsidies alters consumer behavior. The combination of these two ideas – that environments have an impact on people's behavior and that people act to alter their environment – is the essence of systemic thinking.

This mode of thinking has made remarkably little headway in the field of international relations. We generally take key elements in the international environment as given: the balance of power, for example, is seen to be either immutable or something that changes of its own accord. Not only do we not understand how people seek, collectively, to influence the international environment within which they interact, but – almost entirely without exception – we do not even try. This is a problem because for many of us the international system is our fundamental object of study, and our understanding of the parts far outstrips our understanding of the whole. The field of astronomy would be embarrassed, and rightly so, if its most prominent academics could be grouped into "gravity theorists," "orbit theorists," "Jupiter theorists," and so on, none of whom could give a coherent account of the workings of a solar system.[1]

Objectively, there is no reason for this neglect. Clear attempts to influence the milieu within which states interact go back at least two centuries, if not earlier. European statesmen at the Congress of Vienna sought very explicitly to establish, and later to maintain, distributions of material capabilities and political ideology on the Continent that would render war less likely. Their successors, too, sought and upheld settlements that were meant, explicitly, to structure the international environment in a manner that would influence the behavior of its members in beneficial ways. In short,

---

[1] This analogy, I think, helps to explain why those few system-level studies that do exist are represented far out of proportion to their number on international relations syllabi and in bibliographies: the endeavor is seen as an important one, even if the extent of those theories' ability to explain the world has at times been unclear. At this writing, for example, Google Scholar shows nearly 3,000 citations for Alexander Wendt's *Social Theory of International Politics* and more than twice that many for Kenneth Waltz's *Theory of International Politics*.

international relations is every bit as systemic as other disciplines. Our theorizing should reflect that fact.

It is possible that scholars of international relations do little to comprehend systemic politics because our instinctive focus is on smaller-scale interactions: systemic phenomena may not attract attention, perversely, precisely because they are so monumental. To continue the example, the Vienna statesmen and their successors did not just fight wars: they also sought, on an ongoing basis (and to varying degrees), to transform the environment within which wars were fought. It is easy to focus on the wars rather than their context and in so doing not to notice that that context was neither accidental nor irrelevant to the outcome.

It is also possible that the lasting influence of the division of the field into so-called levels of analysis (Waltz 1959; Singer 1961) explains our neglect of systemic politics. Rather than just theorize – a difficult enough challenge as it is – international relations scholars typically meta-theorize, dividing reality up according to level of aggregation (individual, state, or international system as a whole, for example) before analyzing it. The historical justification for this division – Singer cited the "general sluggishness that characterizes the development of theory" in "our emerging discipline" as a result of "failing to appreciate the value of a stable point of focus" (77–78) – is now far less a concern than it was when he made these points a half-century ago. Today, it seems more likely that the greater danger lies in reflexively continuing to develop explanations within levels of analysis, a practice that degrades our ability to derive useful explanations that bridge them.

Regardless of the reason, international relations remains a subject in which, despite the signal importance of system-level variables like the balance of power, truly systemic explanations – those that explain the impact of the actors on the structure of the system and vice versa – are unbelievably scarce. This book represents my attempt to rectify that situation. It is probably worth explaining its main contributions in some depth, if only because the latter are usually much clearer to authors than to readers.

First of all, as already mentioned, **this book constructs a systemic theory of international politics.** That is, it explains international relations as a whole, not the foreign policies of individual states or groups of states. Moreover, it explains international relations not as the result of individual motivations or the interactions of pairs of states, but rather as the outcome of systemic forces – the interplay between the structure of the international system (the balance of power, for example) and the units that make it up (the individual countries, or states).

Reasonable scholars differ on the question of whether this has been accomplished before. Most, however, implicitly or explicitly concur with Wendt's (1999, 11) coding rule: a theory is systemic if it *either* explains structural outcomes *or* points to the structure of the system when explaining state behavior. As the earlier discussion makes clear, I take a systemic theory to be one that does both. By that definition, fully systemic theories of international politics are, at best, extremely rare.

In addition to constructing such a theory, **the book evaluates the systemic theory of international politics that it proposes.** Evaluating systemic theories (however defined) in a concrete and systematic manner is also extremely rare. Even their

proponents have been frustrated by the difficulty of deriving unambiguous predictions from them. This book does so in two ways. The first is a statistical analysis of a dataset that contains original data and spans nearly two centuries of Great Power interactions. The second is a set of three detailed historical case studies of critical junctures within that period that allow me to trace the theory's causal mechanisms in depth while accounting for the idiosyncrasies particular to each case.

More specifically, I design this theory to predict how active a state will be (from extremely internationalist, on one end of the spectrum, to isolationist on the other) but not anything about the specific form that that activity will take: it can predict when a state will increase its level of activity, for example, but other factors will determine whether that increase in activity will take the form of increased armaments, an alliance, or an invasion. In other work (Braumoeller 2008), I demonstrate how the theory can be combined with lower-level theories (deterrence theory and the spiral model) to predict more specific outcomes – in that case, the onset of militarized disputes.

At a preliminary presentation of the book manuscript and its findings at Northwestern University, Professor Hendryk Spruyt offered the thought-provoking comment that the argument brought us full circle, back from the deductive systemic theorizing of Waltz's (1979) *Theory of International Politics* to the inductive reasoning of Richard Rosecrance's (1963) *Action and Reaction in World Politics*. This comment stands out in my mind, in large part because it captures so much of the essence of what I have sought to do here. Each of these works strikes me as iconic, fascinating, incredibly useful... and capable of benefiting from an infusion of what the other provides. My goal was not to return completely to an inductive mode of thinking, but rather, to marry the two as effectively as possible – to construct a work that retained a rigorous deductive theoretical superstructure but evaluated that deductive theory using rich historical content.

A third point is of particular interest to scholars of international relations: **the book integrates different theories of state behavior into a single, unified explanation** and, in so doing, demonstrates that they produce more complete answers than any one of them could separately. Because parts of the theory are drawn from different traditions in the political science literature (in particular, from the study of ideas and politics, the study of domestic political institutions, and the study of power politics, or *realpolitik*), the answer to this question will have implications for the ability of scholars within those paradigms to explain international politics. As I explain later, this is new and exciting: although in the past partial theories drawn from these traditions have been compared in an ad hoc manner, they have hardly ever been integrated into a larger theory so that they can be tested against one another directly.[2]

For exactly this reason, the theory is not associated with any single theoretical paradigm, or "-ism." This is perhaps the most challenging aspect of it for traditional students of international relations, many of whom have become accustomed to dividing the literature along paradigmatic lines. The book draws on and integrates insights from scholars who would label themselves realists, rationalists, liberals, public choice

---

[2] The exception that proves the rule is Niou and Ordeshook (1994).

theorists, and constructivists, just to name a few. As I demonstrate, the end result cannot be reduced to any one of them.

This book was a very substantial undertaking.[3] Over the course of writing it, accordingly, I accumulated many debts. In fact, when I sat down to think about who to thank, I realized it was not much of an exaggeration simply to write "everyone I know." A remarkable number of colleagues have had some input into the book at some stage, and friends and family who have only an imprecise sense of what it is about have nevertheless lent essential support during the course of its completion, whether they knew it at the time or not.

The germ of what would later become the book was my doctoral dissertation at the University of Michigan, the subject of which was isolationism. In that undertaking, I incurred a long list of debts, starting with my advisor, Robert Axelrod. Bob not only provided outstanding advice but also provided me with an excellent model for how to advise my own students: letting me find my own direction and knowing how to encourage worthwhile trains of thought while curtailing less promising ones, he was the intellectual equivalent of a Bonsai master. I benefited greatly from his advice and his example.

Christopher Achen and William Zimmerman also served on the committee, and the end product was greatly enhanced by the breadth and depth of their knowledge. Each is a respected expert in his own area, but I found their comments on the project to be impressively wide-ranging and deep. They prompted me to rethink a long list of issues involving everything from the finer points of American foreign policy to the utility of a basic crosstab, for which I am immensely grateful. Paul Huth and Bradford Perkins rounded out the committee, and each not only provided excellent feedback but also showed me a platonic ideal of a committed, dedicated scholar working in a particular idiom.

Only after I received my Ph.D. did I fully realize that, in designing a rudimentary systemic theory to answer a question about states' foreign policies, I had used a sledgehammer to kill a fly. I had also written a dissertation that was begging to be substantially rewritten before publication. I am indebted to Andrew Moravcsik, now at Princeton University, who, more than anyone else, nudged me off the fence and toward redrafting the manuscript, though he may never have been aware of the fact that he did so. I co-taught the introductory graduate seminar at Harvard University with Professor Moravcsik for two years, and his perspective on the field enriched my own greatly, in particular with regard to the potential place of my own work in the larger picture.

I am also indebted to Professor Iain Johnston, still at Harvard, who helped me past one of the most difficult hurdles I faced: obtaining data. Over lunch one day I remember expressing my frustration at not being able to obtain comparable cross-national data on my quantities of greatest interest, dating back to 1815. Our discussion prompted me to consider expert surveys, which ended up costing me years and

---

[3] When I introduced draft versions of the book at talks, in fact, I told audiences that, when I took a position at an Ivy League institution, I found that my contract obliged me to commit one act of unmitigated hubris, and this was my fulfillment of that obligation.

considerable effort – but which provided the data for the few key missing variables that I needed to make the statistical analysis work.

Although he also might not realize it, Professor Jorge Dominguez at Harvard had a considerable impact on how I carried out the study. His advice with regard to papers and job talks – "Always leave them whistling a tune" – impressed upon me the importance of focusing one's message and communicating it succinctly. Unfortunately, in this manuscript in particular I seem doomed to whistle multiple tunes, but that does not obviate the importance of separating them and clarifying each, as I have attempted to do earlier and throughout.

These are just the tip of the iceberg, however, of the community of scholars, assistants, and staff who helped me immensely over the course of the book's evolution. Anne Sartori, now at Northwestern University, gave me innumerable and very valuable comments over many years and even more valuable friendship to ease the difficult times. Ted Hopf discouraged me quite effectively (and kindly) from pursuing my first dissertation idea and was equally enthusiastic about the second; later, he read the entire manuscript and provided detailed comments, as did Bob Pahre, Paul Diehl, Randy Schweller, and Daniel Verdier. Two scholars outside my field, Bruce Hannon, a geographer at the University of Illinois, and Steve Dunbar, a mathematician at Nebraska, took an interest in the model and, to my great surprise and delight, engaged me out of the blue in thoughtful discussions of its characteristics. Beth Simmons goaded me into organizing an author's conference toward the end of my time at Harvard, with a terrific team of scholars – Iain Johnston, Andrew Kydd, Bill Zimmerman (again), Allan Stam, Jake Bowers, Michael Hiscox, and Adam Berinsky – who read part or all of the manuscript and provided truly invaluable advice on how to improve it. David Atkinson, Lars-Erik Cederman, Michael Cohen, Sarah Croco, Matt Evangelista, Maria Fanis, Erik Gartzke, Hein Goemans, Rick Hall, Michael Horowitz, Paul Huth, Mark Kramer, Charles Maier, Iain McClatchie, Greg Mitrovich, Jim Morrow, Karl Mueller, Dan Reiter, David Rousseau, Erin Simpson, Nikolai Sokov, Cindy Skach, and Dina Zinnes all provided valuable feedback at one point or another. Shannon Rice and Ethan Kiczek did a terrific job of setting up the expert survey; a significant number of anonymous experts took the time to answer it; and Merve Emre, David Margolis, Jeff Rosenfeld, and Doug Stinnett provided excellent research assistance. I am grateful to all of them.

I was also fortunate to have the opportunity to present the book at various stages in its development to some outstanding audiences, all of which offered stimulating feedback as well. I am grateful to participants in seminars at Northwestern University's Department of Political Science; the Swiss Federal Institute of Technology, Zürich, Switzerland; the University of Maryland, Department of Government and Politics; the University of Wisconsin, Department of Political Science; the University of Michigan, Department of Political Science; Princeton University, Department of Politics; Rutgers University, Department of Political Science; The Ohio State University, Mershon Center; Rochester University, Department of Political Science; Columbia University, Department of Political Science International Politics Seminar; the 2006 Conference on New Macrotheoretical Approaches to International Relations; Fakultät für Soziologie, Institut für Weltgesellschaft, Bielefeld, Germany; the Junior Masters Class at

the University of Illinois at Urbana-Champaign; and annual meetings of the Peace Science Society International, the American Political Science Association, and the International Studies Association.

And finally, family. My brother Rick was invariably there when I needed him, without complaint, and given how unexpected the twists and turns in a young faculty member's life can be I ended up needing him far more than I would have thought. Looking back at our childhood, I can only imagine that our parents would be stunned. My ex-wife, Colleen Yuhn, supported and encouraged me and put up not just with the ordinary stresses and strains of married life but also with the infuriating air of distance that comes over scholars in the midst of a project that never sleeps. And my mother, Molly, to whom this book is dedicated, and who only grasped what I do in the vaguest terms but was proud of it anyway, mostly taught me, both in life and in her early death as this book was completed, about the person I want to be.

It goes without saying, given the number and quality of the supporters just listed, that any remaining errors are my own.

COLUMBUS, OH

1 | Introduction

In Thucydides' *History of the Peloponnesian War*, the author recounts an incident in which the Athenians sailed to the island of Melos, a Spartan colony, and two Athenian Generals, Cleomedes and Tisias, sent their representatives to negotiate with the Council of the Melians. What makes their dialogue especially noteworthy is the Athenians' bald statement at the onset that, in their negotiations, the Melians should not appeal to the Athenians' sense of justice, because, quite simply, "the strong do what they can and the weak suffer what they must." The sphere of power is independent of the sphere of justice, rendering the state an autonomous actor, able to pursue its own interests, limited only by its own capabilities. Millennia later, in an era in which Great Powers have given way to superpowers and nuclear weapons have magnified the disparity between strong and weak to a degree unimaginable to the Athenians, the aphorism remains familiar and seems more applicable than ever.

It is surprising, therefore, to find some of the most adroit statesmen at the helm of some of the most powerful states of the past two centuries expressing near helplessness in the face of the impersonal forces that shape world politics. No less effective a diplomat than Charles de Talleyrand-Périgord famously said that "[t]he art of statesmanship is to foresee the inevitable and to expedite its occurrence." Otto von Bismarck, architect of German unification, wrote that "[e]ven victorious wars can only be justified when they are forced upon a nation."[1] Such quotes, indicating as they do that even Great Powers often have very little freedom of action amid the overwhelming pull of international events, seem puzzling coming from statesmen famous for their ability to produce the outcomes they desired.

The tension between these two perspectives – that Great Powers are free to act, unhindered by external constraints; and that even the actions of Great Powers are dictated largely by circumstance – though rarely made explicit, divides our understanding of international relations. The overwhelming majority of explanations of Great Power behavior in history and political science are premised on one or the other. As long ago as 1841, Thomas Carlyle wrote that "the history of the world is but the biography of great men"; Karl Marx claimed a decade later that people make history, but not under circumstances of their own choosing.[2] More recently, Kenneth

---

[1] Quoted in Bernhardi (1914, 38).

[2] Carlyle's quote is verbatim, from his *Heroes and Hero-Worship;* Marx's aphorism has been distilled by time, which has done it a considerable kindness. The actual quote, from *The Eighteenth Brumaire of Louis Napoleon,* is far less succinct: "Men make their own history, but they do not make it as they

1

Waltz (1959), describing what was to become a foundational distinction in the field of international relations, wrote of "first and second image and leaders" explanations of state behavior, which look to the characteristics of states and leaders as the sources of state action, and "third image" explanations, in which "[t]he requirements of state action are . . . imposed by the circumstances in which all states exist" (160).

Although well established, this division is ill advised, because it detracts from and fragments our understanding of international politics. When astronomers have sought to understand the behavior of a planet, at least since Copernicus, they have built a model of the larger solar system that governs its motion – one in which the parts of the system both depend on and constitute the larger whole. Similarly, students of fields as diverse as medicine, agriculture, and psychology favor systemic explanations of their subject matter that provide a comprehensive understanding that a more atomistic point of view cannot. By contrast, the division in international relations between explanations that focus on context and those that emphasize state agency perpetuates an artificial distinction – artificial because the circumstances that constrain and compel state action are also produced by state action.[3] Explanations that lack an account of this reciprocal relationship cannot hope to offer a comprehensive explanation of international politics.

Conceptualizing states, not as individuals or one of a pair, but rather as one state embedded in a larger system of states, can improve our ability to understand that state's behavior. For example, as I demonstrate in Chapter 4, a focus on America's reaction to changes in the international system, rather than to characteristics or actions of the Soviet Union, makes it easier to understand what Anatoly Chernyaev called the "Lost Year"[4] – the puzzling gap between the sweeping Soviet military and ideological *démarche* of December 1988 and the accommodationist American response in November 1989. A focus on American attention to the international system helps us understand the American turn away from isolationism around the time of the fall of France; and in the 1830s, the Great Powers' focus on the ideological division of the system (between legitimist and constitutional states) explains the parallel rift that developed in their alliance structure.

Moreover, these insights also help to clarify the connections between events such as the ones just described and prior events – thereby lengthening the causal chain and expanding the scope of our understanding. In the case of the Cold War we can understand not just how the United States reacted to changes in the international system but also how, and why, the Soviets produced that change. Similarly, we can understand the forces that led the Germans prior to World War II and the Europeans prior to 1830 to produce changes in their respective systems. In each instance we can see how prior state action produced a change in the systemic context that prompts

---

please; they do not make it under self-selected circumstances, but under circumstances existing already, given and transmitted from the past."

[3] The circumstances that forced war on Bismarck, for example, would hardly have existed without him, a fact of which he was surely well aware. Indeed, as he proved with maneuvers such as his creative retransmission of the Ems Dispatch, he was not at all above provoking others to force him to fight.

[4] Chernyaev (2000, 201).

state action, which in turn produces subsequent state action: a systemic dynamic come full circle. This deeper lesson – that states, especially strong ones, produce the circumstances that subsequently compel them to act – was brought home most recently when investigations following the September 11 attacks on the World Trade Center and the Pentagon led to the suggestion that the radical Islamic group responsible and the regime that sheltered them had both benefitted from American support of the anticommunist insurgency in Afghanistan in the 1980s.[5]

The goal of this book is to elaborate and test a systemic theory of international politics that is designed to provide the same holistic understanding of interstate relations that systemic perspectives provide in other fields. It is not the first such portrayal, by any means, although systemic theories remain quite rare,[6] and it is noteworthy that those few systemic theories that do exist in the international relations literature have been unusually persistent[7] – a fact that may reflect scholars' intuitive sense that thinking systemically about international politics is an important objective. The book provides an empirically and theoretically rigorous explanation of how the Great Powers simultaneously shape and are influenced by the structure of the international system. Using both statistical methods and historical case studies, it demonstrates that structural balances and Great Power actions over the past two centuries strongly support the argument.

Understanding why integrating the behavior of the states and the structure of the international system is a difficult problem, and how we can go about resolving it, requires a bit of preliminary background in the form of a foray into the agent–structure debate and its application to international relations.

The agent–structure debate

The tension between explanations based on the behavior of unconstrained agents and explanations based on the exigencies of their circumstances has manifested itself in international relations in what has come to be known as the "agent–structure debate." The question at the heart of the debate – whether to focus on people or on their circumstances when explaining political events – is among the most fundamental issues in the study of politics. I will argue that the agent–structure debate should have no victor: in the realm of international politics, each has an impact on the other, and

---

[5] The argument that the American CIA funded or trained bin Laden directly is not generally credited; the connections were most likely indirect (Coll 2004), a fact that makes their magnitude difficult to estimate. Nevertheless, even those who most categorically deny American involvement with al Qaeda (e.g., Bergen 2002) conclude that the United States channeled a substantial amount of funding to the Pakistani ISI, which preferred to fund more radical groups.

[6] There may be many reasons for the rarity of these works. Many are controversial, few as much as Waltz's – a fact that may cast a pall on systemic theorizing in general. At the same time, however, the complexity of systemic theorizing can be daunting, a fact that may in part explain the paucity of systemic theories of international relations.

[7] Waltz's seminal *Theory of International Politics*, for example, remains a staple on graduate school field seminar syllabi, despite being more than three decades old; Organski and Kugler's *War Ledger* and Gilpin's *War and Change in World Politics* are one and two years younger, respectively.

neither should be granted theoretical primacy. Before doing so, however, I discuss the meanings of the terms.

The nature of structure

First, we must understand the meaning of the word "structure." Philip Cerny, who examines structure and agency in considerable depth, defines structure as "the pattern of constraints and opportunities for action and choice."[8] Though succinct, this definition is one step removed from the one that we seek, because it conflates an explanation of what structures *do* (constrain, provide opportunities) with an explanation of what they *are* (patterns). If they are to have a causal role in the theory, this role must not already be assumed in the definition. Unfortunately, separating the two leaves us with "patterns," which is not very enlightening. Anthony Giddens conceives of structure as the "rules and resources, recursively implicated in the reproduction of social systems." Again, focusing on what structure is rather than what it does leaves us with "rules and resources," where rules are understood as things that "generate – or are the medium of the production and reproduction of – practices."[9]

An examination of existing structural theories helps to flesh out the definition a bit. Theda Skocpol's examination of social revolutions was highly critical of previous studies for their lack of appreciation of the role of structural factors. In particular, according to Skocpol, international structure (the state's position in the world economy and its level of development, as well as international military balances) and internal structure (the organizational and coercive capacity of the state) are critical factors in the revolutions that she studies.[10] Douglass C. North's seminal discussion of the role of economic structure and historical change is admirably succinct on the question of what constitutes structure: property rights, which give rise to the rules and regulations that govern society and the enforcement structures and norms that underpin them.[11] Peter Hall's discussion of institutions suggests yet another understanding: they are "the formal rules, compliance procedures, and standard operating practices that structure the relationship between individuals in various units of the polity and economy."[12] In the introduction to a volume of essays on historical institutionalism, Kathleen Thelen and Sven Steinmo survey a remarkable array of structural factors, from property rights to economic interest groups to party systems.[13]

---

[8] Cerny (1990, 4).

[9] Giddens (1979, 64, 67). Elsewhere, Giddens offers a different definition of rules as "techniques or generalizable procedures applied in the enactment/reproduction of social practices" (Giddens 1984, 21). He likens rules to mathematical formulae – though he hastens to add that "I do not mean to say that social life can be reduced to a set of mathematical principles" (20). By this reading, Giddens' conception of rules may come closer to the structures of the differential equations used later in the book to model the international system; conceived of in this sense, that aspect of structure is not only exogenous but also constant in the theory presented here. This is in keeping with established practice in international relations theory; few actors in game-theoretic models, for example, are allowed to alter the structure of the game tree that defines their available options.

[10] Skocpol (1979). On critiques of previous studies see pp. 14–24; discussions of international and internal structures can be found *passim* and are summarized especially on pp. 22–24 and 284–287.

[11] North (1981, 17–18).   [12] Hall (1986, 19).   [13] Steinmo and Thelen (1992).

What do these structural elements have in common, other than their purported effects (which, for the reasons just mentioned, are impermissible as part of the definition)? Remarkably little, save that they tend to be *distributions* of something: distributions of rules or resources, in the form of property rights or political rights or organizational capacity or coercive power or norms within society, for example. Granted, there are some structural concepts that are difficult to understand in purely distributional terms. However, many of these are either intentionally general formulations that, when applied in concrete terms, are often distributional in nature ("patterns of relationships") or are one step removed from a structural element that is distributional ("standard operating practices").[14]

If we move to the more rarified air of the international realm, the distributional nature of structure becomes more readily apparent. Historically, pride of place must go to a particular distribution: the balance of power or, more precisely, the distribution of realized military capabilities across the most powerful states in the system.[15] This distribution has been the focus of students of international politics for centuries.[16] They assert that, in some very important ways, although they often disagree on which ones, politics in a system of many Great Powers is fundamentally different from politics in a system of few. Although systematic differences in, say, the likelihood of war across different systems have been difficult to tease out,[17] the general assertion that politics is dramatically different in multipolar than in bipolar systems is hard to deny. Surely German Chancellor Otto von Bismarck's legendary political maneuvers would have

---

[14] Waltz (1979, 79–82) makes the case for the distributional nature of structure in IR theory, and Buzan, Jones, and Little (1993, 51–52) defend it and elaborate.

[15] "Realized" capabilities are those that are actual rather than potential: soldiers rather than citizens, tanks and planes rather than iron and steel, and so on. Capabilities that have yet to be realized will be referred to as "latent." See p. 42 for a more in-depth discussion. "Balance" is a notoriously ambiguous word, meaning both "distribution" and "rough equality." Ernst Haas's 1953 paper on the subject of the balance of power is quite illuminating.

[16] The most prominent works written from this systemic perspective include Waltz (1979) and Kaplan (1957); explaining polarity as outcome is Rosecrance (1963). For a general discussion see Butterfield (1966); for a remarkably lucid exposition and critique see Claude (1962). Wagner (1986) and Niou, Ordeshook, and Rose (1989) provide a foundation for the balance of power grounded in game theory. Deutsch and Singer (1964) provide a theoretical discussion of the advantages of a system of many powers rather than a system of few. Gulick (1955) is the classic historical discussion of the balance of power – although Schroeder (1994b) provides a convincing and thorough argument that balance-of-power politics did not survive the Napoleonic Wars; and Healy and Stein (1973) attempts to provide formal empirical structure with which to evaluate the proposition. Gilpin (1981) and Organski and Kugler (1980), though they depict serial unipolarity rather than a constant tendency toward multipolar balance, nevertheless emphasize the distribution of capabilities in the system – that is, they focus on *the* balance of power without claiming that *a* balance of power exists.

[17] Contrast, for example, the findings of Organski and Kugler (1980) and Mansfield (1988) with those of Thompson (1986) and Spiezio (1990) regarding the relationship between unipolarity and war: the former studies find unipolar systems to be more warlike than other sorts, whereas the latter two find them to be less so. There has historically been difficulty in assessing the relative merits of bipolar vs. multipolar systems because the correlation between bipolarity and the existence of nuclear weapons has been nearly perfect, making their effects difficult to untangle. Hopf (1991) is a remarkably creative attempt to circumvent this problem.

been far more difficult in the bipolar 1970s than they were in the multipolar 1870s: one Great Power in a world of two can hardly play its potential enemies off of one another.

As to the issue of which distribution(s) will constitute the most important element of the structure of the system, the only safe generalization seems to be that security politics has typically been greatly influenced by the distribution of *any* characteristic deemed important by the main actors. As Alexander Wendt (1999) has argued, the distribution of ideas can define an international system. One need look back no further than the Cold War to find a distribution of ideologies that provided the context for Great Power politics for nearly half a century. Raymond Aron emphasizes the causal importance of the distribution of values and principles across the international system, a quantity that he sums up succinctly with his concept of "heterogeneous" and "homogeneous" systems.[18] Karl Deutsch's international system consists primarily of communications and interaction flows; their distribution is thought to be indicative of the presence or absence of political community.[19] Immanuel Wallerstein's understanding of history is based on the distribution (in particular, the degree of centralization) of both economic and political capacity in the international system; only a discontinuity between the two, he argued, permitted the growth of capitalism.[20] Kalevi Holsti surveyed more than 300 years of Great Power conflicts and found their sources to have been quite diverse: the list includes the distribution of territory, strategic territory, state boundaries, national or religious or ethnic groups (within or across borders), commercial resources, ideology, and so on.[21] More recently, distributions of a wide range of phenomena, from temperate climate to natural resources to culture and religion, have been implicated as primary motivating causes of group or state behavior.[22] It seems that few distributions can be ruled out *a priori* as relevant elements of the structure of the international system: when, for example, the Great Powers decided in the early 17th century that possession of nutmeg was critically important, its distribution became a vital issue that touched off the Spice Wars and resulted, ultimately, in the Dutch cession of Manhattan to the British.[23]

This, then, constitutes the understanding of structure that will be used throughout the book: systemic distributions of quantities deemed most important by the states in the system in the realm of international security.

---

[18] "I call homogeneous systems those in which the states belong to the same type, obey the same conception of policy. I call heterogeneous, on the other hand, those systems in which the states are organized according to different principles and appeal to contradictory values" (Aron 1966, 100, emphasis removed).

[19] Deutsch (1966). Similarly, David Easton's research on the international system emphasized the distribution of political interactions, i.e., those relevant to a society's "authoritative allocation of values" (Easton 1965, 25). For an intriguing application of Deutsch's work on interaction flows see Nierop (1994).

[20] And, somewhat confusingly, was permitted by it; Wallerstein (1979).

[21] Holsti (1991).

[22] See Diamond (1997), Homer-Dixon (1994) and Klare (2001), and Huntington (1996), respectively.

[23] See Milton (2000). Granted, many of these distributions were at least tangentially related to wealth and power, but often much more so after they became structural distributions: nutmeg, for example, was an extremely valuable commodity, but only because it was thought to cure the plague.

Ameliorating the dilemma: reciprocity

The agent–structure debate could be resolved quite easily if the structure were outside of the agents' control. In this regard, it is important to note that all structures are not alike: some are less easily changed than others. At the extreme, agents may have very little control over the structure of the system of which they are a part. The theory of natural selection is a good example. Structures are highly immutable contexts, and the agents that are poorly adapted to them perish. The agents themselves, while they may have a substantial collective impact on some parts of their ecological niche over time, may have little if any ability to manipulate the harsh climates, mountain terrain, parched soil, access to food, etc., that govern their probability of reproduction. Under these circumstances, we really only need to understand the effects of structures on agents, because agents *can't* have any effect on structures.

In the international system, by contrast, structure is the result of purposive action by the agents: they exert control over it, though it may not conform to their wishes. Because the international system is a system of this kind, we cannot ignore either the effects of the agents or those of the structure. We must attempt to describe, in Giddens' words, "the ways in which that system, via the application of generative rules and resources, and in the context of unintended outcomes, is produced and reproduced in interaction."[24] The easy way out is unavailable to us.

Given that people have an effect on the contexts within which they interact and those contexts in turn have an effect on people, the problem is that focusing on one of these two effects typically forces the theorist to de-emphasize the other.[25] Without explaining how both of these processes occur and unfold over time, no systemic theory can be complete. Unfortunately, doing so has proven to be extremely difficult. Faced with this dilemma, political scientists have done what it is perhaps in the nature of academics to do: they have taken sides.

On one side, researchers focus on the actions of states and statesmen (the agents) and downplay or ignore the circumstances in which they find themselves.[26] A surfeit of studies that fit this description can be found in the political science literature; they focus on characteristics of decision makers, the behavioral implications of the internal characteristics of states, and so on. At the same time, the proliferation of

---

[24] Giddens (1979, 66).

[25] For "focusing on" one might reasonably read "implicitly or explicitly asserting the ontological priority of." See Wendt (1987) and Dessler (1989) for review and discussion of the debate. Waltz views his theory as being entirely structural, in that the distribution of capabilities within the system influences outcomes and an individual state's activity is irrelevant. Dessler's 1989 critique of Waltz's theory, simply put, is precisely the reverse: all of the action is the result of purposive state activity, and that activity presupposes the existence of the system – the context within which action takes place.

[26] For an argument in favor of focusing on the role of statesmen in history, see Byman and Pollack (2001). The emphasis on dispositional rather than situational factors as causes of behavior is not entirely surprising; research (e.g., Rosenberg and Wolfsfeld 1977) suggests that, although actors tend to explain their actions in situational terms, observers tend to explain them in dispositional ones, and academics tend overwhelmingly to be observers of rather than participants in the political process.

data-gathering endeavors like the Correlates of War project, the Polity project, and so on, which focus on national and sub-national attributes, has ensured an emphasis on actors rather than contexts in the quantitative international relations literature.[27]

Another group of scholars, however, has chosen to seek the source of history not within those entities but rather in the environment within which they interact (structure). Neorealism, an extension of the classical political realism of such authors as Hans Morgenthau and George Kennan, is the most prominent example: its proponents argue that the most important determinant of the behavior of states is not their internal nature but their external environment, in particular, the distribution of power in the international system.

Neoliberals have also chosen to focus on the environment within which states interact but have emphasized different aspects of it – the distribution of authority in the form of international political institutions,[28] the role of economic processes and information flows, and so forth. Still other scholars, whose collective theoretical breadth defies any common label save "ideationalists," have focused on the social structure of the international system, that is, the distribution of ideas that comprise the identities of the states within it.[29]

Few approaches attempt to combine structure and agency in a manner that reflects both the contribution of each to political outcomes and the ability of each to influence the other. Rational choice theory[30] does not inherently contain any role for structure beyond the rather minimal sense implied by the interaction of the agents (what Wendt calls "micro-structure," or interaction structure).[31] In fact, rational choice theory's ability to explain similar behavior in such diverse structural settings as the

---

[27] For example, Geller and Singer (1998), a volume devoted to a review of statistical studies of the sources of war, devotes two pages to studies that examine the effects of changes in distributions of capabilities across the system (121–122).

[28] "Institution" is a broad term meant to encompass any of a number of multi-state deliberative entities that both result from and facilitate cooperation. The North Atlantic Treaty Organization and the United Nations are prominent examples; the International Telecommunications Union is a less prominent but more venerable one.

[29] Here see esp. Wendt (1999, ch. 6).

[30] Rational choice theory, which (confusingly enough) is almost entirely a methodology rather than a theory (for treatment as a method, see Rasmusen 1989; for treatment as a theory, see Morrow 1994; and for a seminal example of waffling see Von Neumann and Morgenstern 1944, ch. 1), has its roots in the economics literature but has become quite popular in political science due, I think, to its impressive analytical rigor and ability to produce intriguing and often counterintuitive conclusions. In general, the method involves describing the actors in a given situation, their possible actions and the associated outcomes, the actors' utility functions (which imply some utility or disutility for each possible outcome), and what each of the actors knows and does not know about the situation. Rational choice theory is of no inherent use in specifying what each of these elements will consist of, just as statistical methods like linear regression are of no help in specifying which variables should be included in a test. In both cases, this is the role of theory. (For an example of explicitly realist foundations to a game-theoretic argument see Powell (1999, 53–58).)

[31] Wendt (1999, 147–150). It should be apparent from this discussion that these "micro-structures," the contexts that arise from the mere fact that states interact, are conceptually unrelated to the structure of the international system described earlier (which more or less corresponds to Wendt's idea of "macro-structure"). Two states that are aware of one another's incentives may be unable

U.S. Senate and the trenches of World War I is often seen as a major strength.[32] Modeling the influence of agents on structures, or vice versa, though possible in principle, is underexplored: in fact, both the agents and the structural setting of their interaction are typically assumed to remain constant for the duration of the game. Moreover, rational choice theory predicts behavior "in equilibrium," that is, when no actor has an incentive to act differently; but changes in agents and structures imply that equilibration, not equilibrium, may be the phenomenon of interest in systemic theories, and therefore quite a bit of out-of-equilibrium behavior may be observed.[33]

As a result, as Richard Little has put it,

> explanations in the social sciences . . . frequently operate at one of two extremes. At one extreme, human beings are seen to be free agents with the power to maintain or transform the social systems in which they operate. At the other extreme, it is assumed that human beings are caught in the grip of social structures which they did not create and over which they have no control.[34]

The unavoidable truth is that each perspective, structural and agentic, tells part of the story. The proper response to Carlyle and Marx, in other words, is that history constrains those who make it.[35] Today's decisions take place in an environment shaped by yesterday's actions, and the results of today's decisions provide the environment for tomorrow's.

A few examples will help to illustrate the reciprocal relationship between agents and structures.

- The French Revolution, although it devolved into tyranny, nevertheless popularized the ideals of liberty, equality, and fraternity in a monarchical era. As a result European international politics after the fall of Napoleon played out in the context of the ongoing struggle between nationalism and political liberty, on the one hand, and traditional royal authority on the other. The most prominent international events and institutions from this period – the Treaty of Vienna, the Holy Alliance, the Quadruple Alliance, the various Congresses – were the results of actors attempting to resolve this struggle.
- In the early 20th century, arms races and international tensions divided Europe into two rival camps, the Triple Entente and the Triple Alliance. The diplomatic

---

to trust one another even though each could benefit from cooperation; that is the effect of micro-structure. The distribution of capabilities in the system may prompt weak states to work harder than strong ones to improve their relative positions; that is the effect of structure.

[32] Axelrod (1984). Some recent research has modeled the impact of changes in domestic institutional structure, typically either as changes in payoffs or as changes in the options available to players, though research in this vein remains "in its infancy" (Rogowski 1999, 135).

[33] The main exception to this generalization is evolutionary game theory; see Weibull (2002) for an introduction. It should be noted that these are all examples of a relatively "thin" conceptualization of structure, meaning that structure is seen as producing or constraining behavior in agents, rather than fundamentally constituting them.

[34] Buzan, Jones, and Little (1993, 103).

[35] For "history," one might just as reasonably substitute "politics," for the history discussed herein is the history *of* politics.

environment was so polarized and relations were so tense that the assassination of an obscure Austrian archduke plunged the continent into war.

• Closer to our own time, the leaders of the two superpowers often cited (and, the evidence suggests, felt genuinely compelled by) the necessities dictated by an overarching ideological struggle when making security policy during the Cold War. Their behavior in turn perpetuated the structural division that caused it. Only a radical deviation in behavior on the part of the Soviet Union in the late 1980s broke this vicious cycle.

In short, the interaction of states produces an international systemic context, or structure, and that structure subsequently defines the limits within which leaders must work as well as the opportunities that are open to them.

There are, historically, two major strands of literature on international relations that bear on the issue of the interrelation of agents and structures: general systems theory and systemic international relations theory. I turn now to an examination of each and a discussion of their potential.

Systemic traditions

A systemic approach to international politics may be somewhat alien to many readers, especially those in more empirically oriented subfields. Most present-day explanations of outcomes in the international realm proceed by examining either the characteristics of states themselves (as when, for example, a state's behavior is attributed to its ideology or its domestic structure) or the logic of interactions between pairs of states (or "dyads"). Even large-scale, aggregated statistical studies of every state in the system across many decades conceive of the relations between those states as being fundamentally dyadic in nature.[36]

The main reason to think systemically about international relations is that the international system actually *is* a system, and it acts like one.[37] In international affairs, interactions between two powers are very often colored by the possibility of third-party involvement, three-party interactions must take into account the possibility of fourth-party involvement, and so on. States and dyads cannot be neatly excised from the context that prompts their actions and analyzed in isolation from one another; moreover, the sum of a series of such analyses will fail to capture the essence of the whole system. Actions appropriate in a dyadic or triadic context may not be appropriate in a systemic one, and in a system actions may produce outcomes that can only be understood in the context of the larger picture. In short, no amount

---

[36] On this point see Croco and Teo (2005).

[37] As the concept of a system will be very important to the book, it merits explicit definition. Hedley Bull and Adam Watson define a system as a situation in which "the behaviour of each [actor] is a necessary factor in the calculations of the others" (1984, 1). Anthony Giddens, quoting Amitai Etzioni, defines a social system as "a relationship in which changes in one or more component parts initiate changes in other component parts, and these changes, in turn, produce changes in the parts in which the original changes occurred" (1979, 73). The system of states, or at least that of Great Powers, surely counts as a system by these criteria.

of sophistry, deft wielding of assumptions, or outright hand-waving can provide an adequate substitute for actually including the entire system in the analysis.[38]

Unfortunately, although much international relations scholarship has been couched in the language of systems theory, few of the tools of the latter have actually been brought to bear on the problems of analysis. For this reason, systemic thinking has yet to realize its fullest potential. A review of the international relations literature on systems and systemic theories reveals two broad traditions, each of which seems for the most part to be uninterested in the other. This fact is regrettable, because each contains some elements that could compensate for some of the shortcomings of the other.

The first broad systemic tradition in international relations theory consists primarily of research by scholars with strong backgrounds in mathematics or computer science and often a familiarity with systems theory as it is applied to other disciplines and who have an interest in applying it to the study of international relations. Perhaps because of their role in politics in the nuclear age, physicists seem particularly prone to import mathematical skills to the study of politics, often on issues like arms races.[39] The first and most extreme form of this kind of systemic theory is general systems theory, a paradigm outlined in a series of lectures by Ludwig von Bertalanffy at the University of Chicago prior to World War II but popularized only after the war.[40] General systems theory was based on the premise that one can demonstrate similarities, or "isomorphisms," between the international system (or various national political systems) and entirely different kinds of systems, such as biological or physical ones. The work of Lewis Fry Richardson, a physicist and meteorologist who applied his skills to a voluminous attempt to gain a better understanding of the sources of deadly quarrels, is perhaps the most thorough and detailed application of this approach.[41] Although its adherents believed that it held the keys to nothing less than a general theory of international conflict, applications of general systems theory to international relations theory exhibited dangerous tendencies to obsess over analogies of questionable utility. Researchers who demonstrated the existence of such analogies often had a difficult time answering a single, devastating question: "So what?" Assessments of general system theory's promise for the study of politics faded fairly quickly after its inception.[42] With rare exceptions, this variant of systems theory did not survive the 1970s.[43]

---

[38] Quite a few other characteristics, such as nonlinearity, equifinality, and the omnipresence of unintended results, have been attributed to systems; for a thorough discussion see Jervis (1997, ch. 2), and for a brief summary see e.g., Schweller (1998, 7–8). I do not consider them to be especially compelling justifications for taking a systemic approach, however, for two reasons: one, they are hardly unique to systems, so systems do not raise problems in those regards that have not already been raised elsewhere, and two, they have been dealt with in a much more satisfactory way already than have the analytical problems outlined earlier.

[39] See, e.g., Saperstein (1999).

[40] Bertalanffy (1969) is the seminal discussion.   [41] Richardson (1960).

[42] See Stephens (1972) for a discussion of the American literature and Blauberg, Sadovsky, and Yudin (1977) for a Soviet assessment. The Soviet view is noteworthy in that dialectical materialism would seem, on the surface, to be particularly amenable to a systems approach; the authors' assessment of its promise is qualified at best.

[43] McClelland (1966) is an interesting early discussion of general systems theory and international relations research; see also Harty and Modell (1991) for a retrospective.

Most of the later research in this tradition has abandoned the idea of isomorphisms and seeks to understand the international system as a system – but in its own terms. Two broad traditions have followed general systems theory: equation-based modeling (EBM) and agent-based modeling (ABM). Both have proven to be remarkably versatile tools for understanding the behavior of political systems. EBMs have been devised to model everything from the global system as a whole down to political dynamics at the substate level. Global models[44] have to a large extent fallen into disfavor following the publication of *The Limits to Growth* (Meadows et al. 1972), a spectacular book that promised abrupt global catastrophe early in the 21st century if present population, industrialization, and pollution trends continued unchecked. Subsequent criticism,[45] which focused on the sensitivity of the *Limits* model's conclusions to minor changes in the assumptions and perturbations in the parameters, alerted researchers to the fact that the uncertainty of one's conclusions grows exponentially with the number of assumptions. Perhaps as a result, emphasis in EBMs in international relations has shifted away from all-encompassing global models that include large numbers of densely interrelated variables and toward a more narrow focus on the variables and relationships of interest.[46] Although EBMs that were systemic in scope began to address topics of interest to students of international politics, such as balances of power[47] and international integration,[48] the models focused on agents and process to the near exclusion of the structure of the system and were therefore of limited relevance to systemic IR theory. This nascent, quantitative systemic tradition never sought to grapple with the agent–structure debate to the extent that its qualitative counterpart (described later) did, and in any event few examples persisted beyond the early 1990s.

Although EBMs such as Richardson's famous arms race model had been possible, at least in theory, since the invention of calculus in the mid-to-late 1600s, the spread of ABMs had to wait for intensive computing power.[49] The most prominent product of the ABM agenda to date was also one of the first: Robert Axelrod's *The Evolution of Cooperation* (1984) derived impressively general conclusions about the origins of cooperation from computer tournaments. Since that time ABMs have attracted a substantial following, though they remain underutilized in the study of international systems.[50]

---

[44] By "global models" I refer to research such as the Simulated International Processes (SIP) project, initiated at Northwestern University by Harold Guetzkow (Guetzkow and Valadez 1981), and Stuart Bremer's Simulated International Processor (SIPER) and GLOBUS projects (Bremer 1977, 1987).

[45] See, e.g., Cole, Freeman, Jahoda, and Pavitt (1973).

[46] See Gillespie, Zinnes, Tahim, Schrodt, and Rubison (1977), Li and Thompson (1978), Muncaster and Zinnes (1983), Zinnes and Muncaster (1988), and Wolfson, Puri, and Martelli (1992) for examples.

[47] Hart (1974); McDonald and Rosecrance (1985); Niou, Ordeshook, and Rose (1989).

[48] Alker (1970); Zinnes and Muncaster (1987).

[49] There is one exception to this generalization: Thomas Schelling's "neighborhood model" (1978) demonstrated that surprising conclusions could be derived from ABMs using nothing but pennies, dimes, and a chessboard.

[50] For a thorough review of recent literature see Cederman (2001).

The second systemic tradition in international relations theory is most famously exemplified by Kenneth Waltz's *Theory of International Politics* (1979), though it can arguably be dated at least to Morton Kaplan's *System and Process in International Politics* (1957).[51] It consists largely of scholars with strong international relations backgrounds who have applied language and concepts from general systems theory to the study of politics, both at the national and the international level.[52]

Unfortunately, as Barry Buzan, Charles Jones, and Richard Little point out in their 1993 discussion of Waltz's book, what passes for systemic theory in this tradition is often structural rather than systemic, meaning that it stops at the level of the structure of the international system.[53] Clearly, international politics is unique, or nearly so, in that it takes place in an anarchic realm – one in which states must interact outside of the scope of formal and regular political authority. To make this point and to explore its implications in isolation, however, is to miss a critical fact: that the politics that takes place in this anarchic realm is first and foremost the interaction of states that are themselves organized political units, and that differences in the form of states' domestic political structures can be responsible for striking differences in how they engage in international politics. To stop there, however, is to miss an equally critical fact: that politics, by its nature, is a system that establishes the means by which we as citizens pursue our goals. Systemic theories incorporate the entirety of the system; structural theories focus only on the uppermost layer and "bracket" (that is, ignore) the rest. Waltz's formulations clearly support such an interpretation, as when, on page 74, he writes that structures "limit and mold agents and agencies and point them in ways that tend toward a common quality of outcomes even though the efforts and aims of agents and agencies vary" (1979, 74). Agents play virtually no role, either in determining their own fates (except within the narrow limits afforded them by the harsh dictates of the system) or in transforming any aspect of the system within which they act.

As Alexander Wendt points out, however, another category of systemic theory in international relations exists. In addition to the Waltzean model, in which the structure of the system is the independent variable (the cause), there are also systemic theories that posit that the structure of the international system is the dependent variable (the effect):

> A theory is systemic in the first, dependent variable sense when it takes as its object of explanation patterns of state behavior at the aggregate or population level, i.e., the states system. . . . In [the second] sense, . . . a theory is considered 'systemic' (or, sometimes, 'structural') when it emphasizes the causal powers of the structure of the international system in explaining state behavior." (Wendt 1999, 11)

---

[51] Waltz would undoubtedly argue against such an assertion; he refers to his predecessors collectively as "[s]tudents of international politics who claim to follow a systems approach" (Waltz 1979, 58).

[52] Other prominent works that could be cited as examples of the latter include Jervis (1997), Knorr and Verba (1961), Rosecrance (1963), Deutsch and Singer (1964), Keohane (1984), Buzan, Jones, and Little (1993), and Wendt (1999).

[53] The distinction between system and structure is clarified later; for the moment, think of a system as being made up of both actors (or agents) and the distribution of whatever it is that defines their relationship to one another (structure).

As a description of systemic theories of international relations, the statement is an accurate one: most systemic theories have been, and continue to be, of one sort or the other.[54] Yet as Walter Carlsnaes (1992, 250) points out, this dichotomy is problematic from a prescriptive point of view: "as long as actions are explained with reference to structure, or vice versa, the independent variable in each case remains unavailable for problematization in its own right." In each kind of theory, the independent variable is known to be endogenous – in fact, is believed by other scholars to be a product of the *dependent* variable – but is treated as if it were not. In substantive terms, what that means is that neither of these approaches can ameliorate the dilemma regarding which of the two should be prioritized.[55]

Moreover, as mentioned before, theories that fall into this category are notoriously imprecise. Waltz himself writes that "[m]ost theories of international politics are so imprecise that expectations of outcomes cannot be stated in ways that would make falsification possible" (1979, 13),[56] but his version of balance-of-power theory derives the expectation that "balances of power recurrently form" (124) from the premises that states in an anarchical system "are unitary actors who, at a minimum, seek their own preservation and, at a maximum, drive for universal domination" (118). In fact, Waltz specifically argues that, "[a]ccording to the theory, balances of power tend to form whether some or all states consciously aim to establish and maintain a balance, or whether some or all states aim for universal domination" (119). It is not at all clear how the prediction follows from these premises. In fact, in the next chapter I argue that it does *not* follow unless two more assumptions are added.[57]

---

[54] Waltz clearly focuses solely on the mechanisms by which structures have an impact on the actions of agents. Robert Gilpin's (1981) theory of hegemonic rise and stagnation and A. F. K. Organski and Jacek Kugler's (1980) "power transition theory" go a long way toward specifying those same mechanisms by highlighting the role of power parity in Great Power war, and the former work also specifies the processes within nations that result in differential growth and variation in system structure, but neither specifies any sort of feedback: system–agent and agent–system processes are entirely distinct. Even Dale Copeland's "dynamic differentials theory" (2000), which is motivated in large part by a recognition of these shortcomings, fails to close the causal circle: although it improves upon Waltzean comparative statics by developing a theory of how (present and pending) changes in the structure of the international system have an impact on state behavior, little is said about the other criteria. Wendt's own systemic theory (1999), in which agents and micro-structures are mutually constitutive, is a bit difficult to fit into an independent/dependent variable framework but clearly falls into the bottom-up rather than the top-down category.

[55] The dichotomy is also problematic from the point of view of terminology, because all three kinds of theories – those in which the structure of the international system is the dependent variable, those in which the behavior of the actors is the dependent variable, and those in which *both* are dependent variables – are called "systemic" by their authors. I uphold this convention here, though it is bound to cause confusion, for lack of a more appealing alternative.

[56] "Falsification" refers to the act of disproving one or more of a theory's predictions. Clearly, I disagree with Waltz: the goal of this book is precisely to elaborate a systemic theory – i.e., a theory of international politics, in Waltz's terms – precisely enough to test it, and then to do so.

[57] The imprecision of the theory extends to the question of what does, and does not, constitute structure: Waltz argues (p. 80) that the attributes of, and interactions among, units should be left out of the definition of structure, and that we should focus on characteristics that define how states stand in relation to one another; but why it is that the distribution of one attribute – power – that

Although students of international relations have adopted the forms of systems theories by paying lip service to concepts like feedback and equilibrium, they eschew the substance by failing to specify their theories in such a way that those concepts can be meaningfully applied. Their work remains, as Weltman (1973) rather colorfully put it, an exercise in "metaphoric hypertrophy." Despite the fact that the application of mathematics to international systems was a major growth industry in the 1960s and 1970s, for example, Waltz seems either ignorant or disdainful of the entire literature, which is glaringly omitted from his *magnum opus*. Although systems theory and cybernetics are not slighted *in the abstract* – indeed, Waltz credits a handful of authors on those topics (fn., p. 40) with having influenced his thinking about a systemic theory of international politics – the authors who have actually applied them to the study of international politics are almost entirely ignored, despite the fact that Waltz is clearly aware of some of their other research. Karl Deutsch's work with J. David Singer on the subject of multipolarity is mentioned in passing, but his work on cybernetics, feedback loops, and equilibria in political systems is ignored.[58] Stuart Bremer's work with J. David Singer and John Stuckey on capabilities, uncertainty, and war is discussed, but Bremer's research involving simulated international systems – prominently published not two years before Waltz's own book – is unmentioned, despite its obvious relevance.[59] Even after the passage of two decades, Waltz's most prominent systemic critic and most outspoken realist successor[60] seem no more eager than he to engage the work of those who have applied the tools of systems theory to the analysis of international systems.

To be fair, the latter group rarely engages the former on their own terms. Although systems approaches are flexible enough to be applied to phenomena as diverse as "turtles, termites, and traffic jams,"[61] the number of attempts to apply it to existing systemic theories of international politics is remarkably small. Even Axelrod, whose work is foundational in the study of international institutions, rarely addresses realism (institutionalism's *bête noire*) directly. Those works in the EBM or ABM tradition that do specifically address mainstream arguments are a remarkably small subset of their respective literatures.[62]

As a result of this intellectual segregation, mainstream theorizing about the international *system*, though it is open to influences from sociology and history, remains little influenced by *actual systems theory*, or even by international relations research that is informed by it. This is an unfortunate fact, because, as I argue in the next section, dynamic systems theory is the key to resolving the agent–structure dilemma.

---

defines how states stand relative to one another, and not others, should be privileged, is never made clear.

[58] Deutsch and Singer (1964); Deutsch (1966, 1978).

[59] Singer, Bremer, and Stuckey (1972); Bremer (1977); Bremer and Mihalka (1977). Bremer and Mihalka, for example, conclude that "if political entities act according to the dictates of 'realism,' the consequence for the vast majority is extinction, not survival" (326).

[60] Wendt (1999) and Mearsheimer (2001), respectively.   [61] Resnick (1994).

[62] Such works include Cusack and Stoll (1990), Wolfson, Puri, and Martelli (1992), and Cederman (1997).

Nested politics

Despite our interest in high politics, we lack a good understanding of how these elements of the international security environment come about in the first place – how the massive tectonic shifts that determine the configuration and character of the international system actually occur. The task would be easier if we could blame our circumstances on the vanity of the gods or the caprice of fate (or, in terms more familiar to political scientists, leave the structure of the system exogenous – that is, unexplained by our theories), but we cannot – at least, not if we are to overcome the agent–structure problem and arrive at a truly systemic theory. Rather, we must seek the sources of our situation in our interactions with one another.

The structure of the international system consists of nothing more than characteristics of the organized political entities that belong to it – the states. These states, in turn, are made up of nothing more than groups of people – their citizens. These groups of people make their own flags and stamps and passports and so on, but that does not make them anything more than groups of people. There is no way to avoid the simple fact that the circumstances within which people must make history are circumstances that people themselves, however aggregated, create.

The fact that we *create* those circumstances does not, however, mean that any one of us, or even all of us together, can *choose* them. In fact, as Marx correctly noted, they are often entirely beyond our control. This paradox arises because of the peculiar nature of politics in the international realm. The interactions of sovereign citizens with a wide range of needs and desires take place within a hierarchical domestic political arena that is established by the state. The political interactions of states, in turn, take place within the complex environment of the international system – an "anarchical society," to quote the English international relations scholar Hedley Bull, that lacks the formal political institutions of the state but is far removed from the bloody war of all against all envisioned by philosophers like Thomas Hobbes. These different levels of politics are nested within one another, like the wooden dolls in a Russian *matryoshka,* and understanding the whole system requires understanding the parts and the relationship of those parts to one another. Because the people in this system are unavoidably situated in a complex, multilevel system of politics, their desires are inevitably frustrated to some degree, and the outcomes of their interactions are typically unintended and very often undesired.[63]

This, in a nutshell, is the way that I synthesize structural and agent-based explanations of politics: the nested nature of international politics – sovereignty nested within hierarchy nested within anarchy – is the engine of change in international security politics. How exactly it operates is summarized in the next section and taken up in detail in Chapter 2.

---

[63] The idea of nested politics takes inspiration both from Robert Putnam's (1988) idea of a "two-level game" and George Tsebelis' (1990) discussion of "nested games." My intellectual debt to both should be obvious, although as the following discussion demonstrates, the dynamic and systemic nature of this endeavor imbues it with some subtleties that would, for example, make calling it a "three-level game" only superficially accurate.

The argument, in brief

The explanation starts with the premises that the nature of the international system depends on the qualities (or characteristics) of the states that comprise it, and the qualities of those states depend both on their internal political structure and on the desires of their subjects. These are the insights behind the nested politics model.

The heart of the explanation is a very simple one and can be summed up in four points:

1. How citizens understand the world determines what they want and do not want out of it in the realm of security politics – power, territory, ideological or religious unity, nutmeg, or what have you. The less they have of whatever they want at a given point in time, the more they desire a change in the status quo.
2. The political machinery of the state determines how their desires are collected, aggregated, and conveyed to leaders. Leaders, who wish to remain in office, attempt to do so by carrying out the mandates of their constituencies.
3. Leaders are limited in their ability to carry out their constituencies' mandates by the capabilities of their states.
4. The interactions of many different states with different capabilities and diverse national interests determine the most important qualities of the system: how hard the Great Powers play the game of politics and, as a result, the structure – the distribution of spoils that ensues.

The distribution of the spoils – be they material, ideational, political, or what have you – that results from point 4 influences citizens' demands for action in 1, so at this point the process begins anew. Because this process unfolds over time, the model is *dynamic* rather than static: the sequence of events from 1 to 2 to 3 to 4 to 1 to 2 to 3 and so on results in frequent changes in levels of state activity and a constant reevaluation of the distribution of the spoils.

The terms in which the explanation is described are somewhat vague. That is intentional and necessary. They must be specific enough to constitute a useful explanation but flexible enough to be applied to different states and different systems throughout history. At a certain point theory must stop dictating the content of an explanation and allow history to fill in the appropriate gaps.

These few assumptions about how the world works may seem straightforward, and it might seem as though we could learn little from them beyond what they already say, but in fact they are capable of telling us quite a bit about high politics. For example, if we imagine the world in the 19th century as it is often depicted by balance-of-power theorists – say, five Great Powers with roughly equal latent capabilities and citizens who think of security as the maximization of realized power[64] – the nested politics model implies that a balance of power will *always* occur eventually, *regardless* of the initial distribution of power, and will even reestablish itself if it is disrupted.

---

[64] The distinction between *latent* power, the raw material such as manpower and natural resources that can be converted into warfighting capabilities, and *realized* power, the warfighting capabilities themselves in the form of soldiers, weapons, and so forth, is made on page 42.

Conclusions like these, even though they might seem counterintuitive, follow because the international system is a system, and as decades of research have demonstrated, systems in general have many unexpected and unanticipated qualities. One of these is that outcomes, like the balance of power, arise even though they may not be sought by any of the actors.

Advantages

This particular inference leads to a more general question. What does the nested politics approach to understanding Great Power politics give us that others do not? What does it tell us about the world that we did not already know?

Its advantages, I would argue, are threefold. First, the book grounds systemic theory in a coherent and detailed set of microfoundations drawn primarily from public choice theory and models of partial adjustment under conditions of uncertainty. Second, those microfoundations provide very explicit predictions about state behavior and changes in the structure of the international system, and those predictions are borne out by rigorous empirical testing across three separate international systems. Finally, the book expands the theoretical scope of systemic theory, long the near uncontested terrain of neorealism and constructivism, to include the balance of ideology (more specifically, the balance of political regime type) as a key component of the structure of the international system. Moreover, the results in Chapter 3 demonstrate that the findings cannot be reduced to a realist power-only model in which the balance of ideology is omitted.

The signal insight to be gained from the book is an understanding of the process by which states simultaneously shape and are driven by the structure of the international system. In contrast to existing "top-down" (structural) or "bottom-up" (agentic) explanations, such as the ones discussed in the previous section,[65] this one connects parsimonious models of the citizen, the state, and international structure to produce a coherent, dynamic, fully systemic model – one that, unlike the structural theories of decades past, possesses a coherent set of microfoundations at the individual and state level.

One substantial hurdle to theorizing at the systemic level in the past has been the fact that systemic theories' predictions about specific state activities, such as war and peace, alliance vs. armament, and so on, are typically indeterminate. Systemic theorists have been fairly open about this fact. Early efforts (e.g., Gulick 1955, Kaplan 1957) developed explanations of the nature of the international system without attempting to derive or test hypotheses about state behavior; later systemic theorizing embraces the idea of prediction but typically only with the use of ancillary, *ad hoc* theories that are not derived from the premises of the original systemic theory. Mearsheimer (2001, 11), for example, distinguishes between high-level theories such as his own offensive realism and more fine-grained theories like deterrence theory, arguing that only the latter predict war; Organski and Kugler (1980) predict conflict at the point of power parity, but only based on a dyadic argument, similar to deterrence theory,

---

[65] See especially *circa* Footnote 54.

that the challenger will be deterred by imbalances short of parity; Waltz's (1979, 173–174) claims about the military advantages of bipolarity rest on assumptions about the relationship of uncertainty to war which that, in turn, presume a model of war that is only hinted at (Waltz refers to bargaining models in passing). In each case, the systemic component of the argument makes no determinate prediction absent the ancillary assumptions. Little wonder, then, that a group of scholars dubbed "neo-classical realists" by Guideon Rose (1998) have sought to augment structural theory with nonstructural amendments, or that William Wohlforth (2009, 28) concludes that "[m]ainstream theories of war long ago abandoned the notion of any simple relationship between polarity and war."

Yet the conclusion that, because systemic theory cannot explain specific forms of state activity, it cannot explain anything at all at the state level, does not follow. Just as economic theories of supply and demand explain how much of a good consumers will consume but not how they will go about obtaining it, systemic theory can explain how actively a state will seek to increase its security but not the means by which it will choose to do so. The nested politics model demonstrates that systemic theories, without any ancillary *ad hoc* theory from different levels of analysis, can make useful predictions about state behavior at a higher level of generality – foreign policy activity, ranging from essentially isolationist, at one end of the spectrum, to hyperactive or aggressive, on the other. Though underappreciated in the systemic theory literature, this understanding of state behavior has a long history in studies of foreign policy behavior[66] and attitudes[67] and parallels the logic of studies utilizing events data in the quantitative international relations literature.[68]

The argument that systemic theory should be good at predicting something general (levels of state security-related activity) rather than something specific (peace or war, disputes; alliances) is one of the book's most innovative arguments; given that it allows us to make concrete progress in understanding the relationship between structure and state activity, it is one of its most useful ones as well. Although understanding whether states will pursue a more or less active foreign policy is interesting in its own right, however, some scholars may still have more ambitious goals for systemic theory. Those interested in understanding more specific forms of state behavior need not despair: the nested politics model can also serve as the first stage of a more comprehensive, multilevel explanation of specific forms of state behavior. For example, I demonstrate in Braumoeller (2008) that the predicted values for state activity from the statistical model in Chapter 3 can be used as the independent variables in a second-stage, dyadic model of conflict onset based on deterrence theory; the same set of predicted values could easily be used in other studies to generate systemic explanations of other phenomena based on other ancillary theories. The main

---

[66] See, for example, Klingberg (1952, 1983); Langer and Gleason (1952); Jonas (1966); Holmes (1985); Schlesinger (1986); Nordlinger (1995); Gholz, Press, and Sapolsky (1997); Pollins and Schweller (1999); Legro (2000).

[67] Holsti (1979); Wittkopf (1986, 1990); Murray (1996).

[68] For a conceptual introduction see Schrodt (1994); for a prominent application in the security literature see Goldstein and Freeman (1990).

advantage of doing so explicitly is that it forces the logic at each stage to be explicit and clear.

Moreover, although existing systemic theories are often difficult to disprove, because they offer predictions that exclude few outcomes or set few limits on the time within which the theory suggests that they must occur, the nested politics model offers a formal model of a fully systemic theory and a statistical test derived directly from the model that permits its predictions to be evaluated precisely. The results demonstrate that the systemic model is on the whole quite successful with the data from the 19th and 20th centuries. Two instances in which it is not, however, are noteworthy mostly because they prove that the model actually *could* fail, unlike most difficult-to-falsify systemic theories to date – and in the overwhelming majority of cases it does not.

The nested politics model can also inform the contemporary debate among different theoretical paradigms in international politics.[69] The spare logic of the model does not compel a focus on the *a priori* primacy of one determinant of security over all others.[70] The nested politics model can, however, serve as the framework for evaluating arguments about the security motivations and behaviors of states, in the same way that a general utility-maximization model can be used to evaluate arguments about the motivations of individuals once the sources of their utility have been specified. Accordingly, in the third chapter I turn to an examination of the European Great Powers of the 19th and 20th centuries. The findings there and in the following chapter demonstrate that, during that time period, the balance of power consistently drove the Great Powers' security policies, *and* that those policies, in turn, were designed, in substantial part, to shape the balance of power. This examination also demonstrates that the balance of ideologies (or, more precisely, of political regime types) was another important driver of Great Power security policy and was shaped by it as well during these periods. Finally, the realist counterargument that the model can be collapsed to one in which only power explains outcomes is tested and conclusively fails. (For the sake of completeness, a similar test is conducted to determine whether only ideology could explain the model's outcomes. That argument, too, fails the test.) These findings will be of interest to international relations theorists, because systemic theory has generally been dominated by structural realism for many years. Moreover, the fact that realist arguments are evaluated in the context of a systemic model is critical: although some statistical studies of international relations theories have included a variable or two (like the balance of power) in their equations, the overwhelming majority are fundamentally dyadic in nature – a fact that permits structural realists to dismiss their findings as irrelevant.

These advantages are substantial (and, I hope, compelling). They are not, however, exhaustive. The logic of the theory itself implies some conclusions that run contrary to the conventional wisdom, and the integrated nature of the structural theory allows it to speak to the implications of changes in one "level of analysis" for phenomena at

---

[69] See especially Waltz (1959), Singer (1961), Waltz (1979), Moravcsik (1997), and Wendt (1999).
[70] Realists have argued that anarchy compels a focus on power, but as historian Paul Schroeder (1994a) has pointed out, the historical record contains a far more diverse array of state behaviors than anyone could plausibly attribute to a desire for power.

another level.[71] The logic of the model suggests, for example, that structural realism's insights about the formation of balances of power do not follow from its premises, though they can be made to follow with some additional premises; that the argument that Great Powers will choose a more restrained policy as their relative power declines (e.g., Wohlforth 1993) does not follow at all; that purely domestic theories of foreign policy, such as those that explain American isolationism between the two world wars, may have to be revised; and that the logic of socialization, occasionally discussed in the constructivist literature, might actually be linked to balances of power. These points, which depend on a more detailed explanation of the logic of the model, are taken up at the end of Chapter 2.

Plan of the book

All of the nested politics model's advantages would amount to nothing, however, if it could not provide an account of Great Power politics that accords with the facts. Therefore, I devote the bulk of the book to a detailed empirical study of international security politics in the 19th and 20th centuries. My goal is to gauge the validity of the basic premises of the model as well as to flesh it out and determine the extent to which it accurately describes the political processes at work.

Chapter 2 describes the theory in more detail. It discusses the modeling philosophy that underlies the translation of the theory into a formal mathematical model, making the argument that a partial adjustment model is the most appropriate foundation for formalization. It then derives such a model, the specifics of which are recounted in Appendix A, suitable both for simulations and for estimation, and describes the hypotheses that follow from it. Finally, it discusses the ancillary implications of the model for other theories of international relations. The first goal is to to explain the similarities and differences between the nested politics model and each of the other theories and show how the latter can be understood as special cases of the former. The second goal is to use the deductive structure of the nested politics model to illustrate, where possible, the logical implications of those theories that can be understood as special cases. In some cases, the model's implications support the original author's argument or shed light on the other theory's causal logic; in others, the model helps to highlight the exact reasons for which the original theory's conclusions do not follow from its premises, or suggest additional assumptions that would ensure that the conclusions do follow.

Chapter 3 contains a comprehensive statistical test of the nested politics model. It first describes how the model can be applied to the three international systems – the Vienna system, the Versailles system, and the Cold War system – that existed between the end of the French Revolutionary Wars and the end of the Cold War. It then describes the data requirements of a large-N test and outlines how those requirements were met – in large part, using behavioral indicators drawn from existing projects, but where such indicators were not available, using data derived from an expert survey

---

[71] Waltz (1959); Singer (1961).

of professional historians. It then examines the data to assess the extent to which the nested politics model is a reasonable description of reality.

Chapter 4 trades off breadth for depth and examines three historical cases – British liberalization and systemic polarization in the early Vienna period, the American reaction to the rise of Nazi Germany, and the transformation of the Soviet Union that led to, and in part constituted, the end of the Cold War – with the twin goals of evaluating whether the process described by the model is a reasonable one and asking whether any additional, exogenous effects played a substantial role in producing the outcome in question. In each case, I demonstrate how these events can be understood through the lens of nested politics: the model provides the theoretical "skeleton" that gives shape to the history and makes it more comprehensible.

In the concluding chapter I prognosticate about the model's implications for the future – not without some hesitation. A realistic assessment of the ability of social science models to predict is a humbling experience, but an exercise such as this one compels some speculation, however tentative.

2 | *System, state, and citizen*

Introduction

This chapter contains a description of the theory of nested politics that will serve as a framework for the analysis of Great Power security policy throughout the remaining chapters. The heart of the chapter is a description of how the actors (states and, through them, citizens) shape the international system and how the system in turn influences the behavior of the actors. The core *explananda*, or dependent variables, of the theory are the distributions that constitute the structure of the international system – balances of power, ideology, and so forth – on the one hand, and the overall level of the state's security-related activity – ranging from isolationist to normal (for a Great Power) to hyperactive or aggressive – on the other. By explaining their reciprocal relationship to one another, the fundamental dilemma regarding the ontological priority of agents vs. structures can be mitigated.

The theory is based on a formal mathematical model, the nested politics model, first described in Braumoeller (2008). Given that much of the political science discipline, and in particular much of it that is interested in systemic theory, does not consist of scholars with training in formal modeling, however, I have relegated the technical details to Appendix A and described the workings of the model, to the extent that it is possible to do so, in ordinary English.

The nested politics model is a model of the systemic mechanism that produces outcomes, rather than an argument that their actions will be prompted by particular motives.[1] To paraphrase Wendt, international security is what states make of it, and what they make of it is, irreducibly, an empirical rather than a theoretical question.[2] That is not to say that the nested politics model cannot be used to help resolve questions about actors' motives or about paradigms in international relations. Far from it, in fact. The penultimate section of this chapter demonstrates that the theory's implications call into question some of the main conclusions of various other theories in the realm of international affairs, including realism, constructivism, and theories

---

[1] Waltzean neorealism, by contrast, argues both that the most compelling level of analysis for students of international politics is the structural level, which is an argument about the mechanism, *and* that the actors are driven by concerns based on relative power, which is an argument about motive.

[2] It would be ideal, if possible, to derive actors' motives from the nature of the mechanism, which Waltz clearly seeks to do; my position is that whether or not such a feat is possible is an empirical question, and the empirical results in the next chapter suggest quite strongly that it is not.

of foreign policy. And in the next chapter, in which I test the theory, I explore the history of the Great Powers in the 19th and 20th centuries to assess their motives empirically. After finding that states reacted to and shaped balances of power and of political ideology (understood as distributions of political regime type), I then assess the counterclaim that the model could be reduced to one of the "special cases" that constitute it – that a model based only on the balance of power, or only on the balance of ideology, would do just as well with the data. The answer, quite conclusively in all periods, is that it would not. The important implication of this fact is that, for example, the realist claim that states' apparent pursuit of regime change is reducible to the pursuit of power cannot be supported by the evidence.

Before describing the theory, however, I must first address a few issues related to theorizing, which will explain the general nature of the theory and the model that captures its logic as well as provide some of the conceptual language necessary to understand them.

Systems: general principles

As early as 1874, Léon Walras had conceived of a notion that would evolve into what is now known as general equilibrium theory.[3] The motivation for general equilibrium theory corresponds quite closely to the motivation for systemic international relations (IR) theory, namely, that the behavior of one of the key actors has an impact on the behavior of the rest. The goal of capturing the complex implications of general equilibrium theory, in turn, gave rise to the field of macroeconometric modeling. When the economist Jan Tinbergen was director of the Central Planning Bureau of the Government of the Netherlands from 1945–1955, he undertook the impressive task of deriving and testing a macroeconometric model of the Dutch economy. The results were promising enough that before long macroeconometric models of national economies had been established across the globe, from the United States and United Kingdom to Japan to India to Latin America, and initiatives like Project LINK were generating comprehensive models of international economic systems.[4]

Macroeconometric modeling of general equilibrium theories involves, in essence, an attempt to describe the behavior of a system by describing the interrelationships among its parts utilizing a system of equations. The parts can be groups, firms, organizations, sectors, and so forth; the method is (mostly) ontologically innocent, in that nothing inherent in the method limits its empirical scope save the requirements of estimation.[5] Once the model of the economy has been constructed and the necessary data obtained, the system of equations is estimated. In contrast to standard practice in microeconomics and political science, the statistical significance of the estimated coefficients are thought to be of little use in empirical evaluation of the model; rather, the coefficients are used to generate a simulation of the economy as a whole, and the

---

[3] I am indebted to David Lake (personal communication) for the suggestion that I explore general equilibrium theory as a body of work relevant to my own thinking about the international system.

[4] See Bodkin, Klein, and Marwah (1991) for a review.

[5] To be clear, innocence here connotes the absence of expectations, not the absence of guilt.

extent to which the simulation maps to the actual performance of the economy is assumed to be the yardstick by which the quality of the model is judged.

Macroeconometric modeling possesses a wide range of characteristics that make it very intriguing from the point of view of systemic theories of international relations. First, as already mentioned, the focus is on general rather than partial equilibrium: all of the major actors in the system are incorporated into the model and contribute to the outcomes of interest. Moreover, within the time-series framework of a general equilibrium model reciprocal, causal relationships can be captured in a straightforward way. Because systemic theory implies reciprocal causal relationships, and because such relationships cannot be understood at a single point in time, a systemic theory *must* be dynamic.[6] General equilibrium models easily encompass such relationships.

The quantification involved in generating macroeconometric models has implications that have been repeated *ad nauseam* in the ongoing squabble between qualitative and quantitative methodologists and need not be recounted in detail here. On the positive side of the ledger, the act of generating a mathematical model forces the theorist to be explicit about the causal linkages among variables in the theory, and the act of testing it compels both uniformity and clarity of measurement, which may or may not be present otherwise. On the negative side, the much touted clarity of mathematical models does not guarantee comprehension, especially in the case of complex models, which even the most mathematically adept might find tedious to verify, and the need for data tends to draw scholars toward metrics that are available and convenient and toward theories that utilize them.

Perhaps the most impressive feature of this category of models, however, is that they can serve both as a formal modeling enterprise that allows the researcher to see which conclusions follow from theoretical premises and how, and as an econometric test that assesses how well or poorly the outputs of the hypothesized process map to those of the real world. Indeed, these characteristics are inseparable: the dynamic time-series equations that comprise the model also serve as systems of difference or differential equations that can be used both to check the model's implications and to evaluate its fit to the real world when it is run using estimated coefficients.[7]

All of this is not to say, of course, that the method is without its detractors. In the field of macroeconomics, macroeconometric modeling has come under fire for

---

[6] Carlsnaes (1992) makes this point in detail. To summarize, the issue involves solving the problem of "how to make analytically operational the core assumption that both agents and social structures interact reciprocally in determining the foreign policy behavior of sovereign states" (p. 250).

[7] It is worth noting that Pepinsky's (2005) critique of agent-based models in international relations – that agents, environments, and relations among them are taken to be ontologically prior to emergent properties, and that international relations theory does not admit of sufficient consensus to warrant such strong prior assumptions – applies to macroeconometric models as well. Indeed, the estimation portion of the exercise might seem even more problematic (because it is more efficient) than the agent-based modeler's ability to tinker with the parameters of the model until something approximating reality emerges. Two responses are in order. First, the critique applies to all deductive theorizing in IR, not just model building. Second, the force of the critique can be blunted if the model is built in such a way that existing theories can be expressed as special cases of a more general model, as is the case with the nested politics model outlined later.

its predictive lapses, especially in the case of underpredictions of large changes (the current recession as well as those of the 1970s and 1990s, for example, and the boom of the 1980s). Empirically, it has been argued that the stochastic element of economic behavior swamps the systematic component, so that the enterprise stands little chance of success even under the best conditions.[8] Three responses seem reasonable: one, that the ratio of stochastic to systematic variation is phenomenon-specific, and some phenomena are more predictable than others; two, that contemporary research can never actually ascertain this ratio, because the possibility of explaining additional variance always remains; and three, that even if the critique holds, macroeconometric modeling still captures the systematic part of behavior, and nothing save dumb luck would capture the rest. (To put it another way: if the problem is a large stochastic component, what alternative method would represent an improvement?) The econometrics of macroeconometric models has also been challenged: Sims (1980) argues that vector autoregression (VAR) techniques would be preferable, but more recent experience has shown that their atheoretical nature and the inefficiency of their estimates have made VARs unsatisfactory both as explanatory and as predictive models. As one prominent review of the literature concludes, "structural macroeconometric modelling still remains the most promising approach to understanding macroeconomic behaviour generally."[9]

Rational expectations

In addition to these empirical and statistical criticisms of macroeconometric models of general equilibrium theories, there is a theoretical one that merits discussion. The core of the critique is that standard macroeconometric models are problematic because the agents are assumed not to utilize information available to them to make forecasts and act on those forecasts. In the context of general equilibrium models, the argument would be that actors possess the foresight to look ahead, understand how the world would look in equilibrium, and jump directly to that equilibrium rather than engaging in the kind of graduated equilibrating behavior posited by partial-adjustment models.[10]

There are three arguments in favor of partial-adjustment models in the context of systemic theories of international relations. The first was expounded by one of the pioneers of rational expectations: Sargent (1978) pointed out that the existence of costs of adjustment implies that adjustment will be partial rather than immediate – or, perhaps more accurately, that partial rather than immediate adjustment is rational. In many economic applications adjustment is costless, though its consequences may not be: the U.S. Federal Reserve, for example, can simply change interest rates by fiat, is typically composed of experts who can be expected to make forecasts and act on them, and is in many ways intentionally insulated from the political costs of doing so. Under such circumstances, rational-expectations models should work quite

---

[8] Evans (1997).   [9] S. Hall (1995, 975, 983).
[10] For an introduction to this literature see Attfield, Demery, and Duck (1991).

well. In the realm of international security, however, none of these conditions holds. The balance of power or the distribution of political ideologies typically cannot be changed by fiat, except perhaps as part of a comprehensive peace settlement after a general war, and even then the costs of doing so are typically immense.

The second argument for partial-adjustment models was raised by Brainard (1967), who argued that model uncertainty – that is, uncertainty about the data-generating process or its parameters – implies partial rather than immediate adjustment, with the immediacy of adjustment increasing with certainty.[11] Again, in the study of domestic economic policy the nature of the model and the values of its parameters are known to within reasonable approximations, but in the realm of foreign policy such information is both less available and far more contested. Consider that in the 1980s the United States, despite massive expenditures in the realm of intelligence-gathering, produced very controversial estimates of Soviet military power and worldviews: according to a prize-winning study of the subject, for example, "[e]xcept for William Zimmerman's pathbreaking study of the Khrushchev period, we know little about how Soviet foreign policy intellectuals view the structure and tendencies of contemporary world politics."[12] In light of considerable uncertainty even on the part of specialists, the assumption that contemporaneous policy makers in the United States knew the value of these parameters with certainty is likely to lead to flawed inferences.

The final argument for partial adjustment is perhaps the most fundamental, in that it is empirical rather than theoretical: history strongly suggests that immediate adjustment simply does not occur as the rational expectations perspective argues that it should. Such a sweeping statement cannot be defended in depth here – indeed, to do so would require a separate monograph,[13] if not a series of them – but an example of a case in which conditions were ripe for the operation of rational expectations can be briefly described. Winston Churchill's negotiating behavior during his visit to Moscow in October 1944 is a best-case scenario for rational expectations, in that Churchill is widely thought to have been a rather prescient politician and the impending end of a major war made adjustment as costless as it would ever be. In fact, Churchill made an attempt at precisely the kind of immediate adjustment predicted by the rational-expectations school, proposing a division of influence in Eastern Europe that Stalin

---

[11] For this reason, collective action dilemmas in their purest form – i and j want the same thing, they both know it, and each wishes the other to expend the resources necessary to obtain it – are unlikely events. In reality, i never knows with much certainty that j wants the same thing that it wants, so it cannot count on j to do its work for it. At the same time, it is possible to obtain a collective good sequentially, a little bit at a time, until it has been realized in its entirety. Finally, i does know that j, like i, will engage in incremental adjustment, so it is typically likely that regardless of how much j does to obtain the good at a given period in time, i could still improve its utility by doing a little bit more. Collective action dilemmas are therefore resolved with the aid of a combination of incrementalism and uncertainty.

[12] Lynch (1987, 1). On the contestation of military estimates see inter alia Gervasi (1986).

[13] Bartels (2010) is a good example of such a monograph in the American politics literature: the author concludes that voters' behavior is myopic and retrospective rather than prospective. Given that voters' behavior constrains politicians, even the most forward-looking politicians would engage in less than perfect adjustment.

approved with a tick of his blue pencil.[14] Even so, the proposal's divisions – 50/50 splits of Western and Soviet influence in Yugoslavia and Hungary, for example, or a 75/25 split favoring the Soviets in Bulgaria – proved to be quite wide of the mark once the continent polarized and each bloc strove to eliminate the influence of the other in its own sphere.[15]

That said, one argument against a pure partial-adjustment model is compelling enough to be worth both noting and, in the next chapter, testing. The argument, simply put, is that partial adjustment, although a reasonable assumption overall given all of these theoretical and empirical concerns, does not permit for the possibility that states will observe contemporaneous changes in the world whose implications are so obvious that they will choose not to wait for the repercussions of those changes to be felt. Moreover, knowing that other states will also react accordingly, they would also take one another's reactions into account, creating a situation in which the rational-expectations perspective comes into play – but only within the present period, as a reaction to contemporaneous "shocks."[16]

Complexity vs. parsimony

There is one additional issue to be raised regarding how we should go about under-standing international systems – the issue of the tradeoff between complexity and parsimony. It is perhaps most eloquently expressed in Jorge Luis Borges's "Of Exacti-tude in Science." The piece, quoted in its entirety, reads as follows:

> ... In that Empire, the Art of Cartography attained such Perfection that the map of a single Province occupied the entirety of a City, and the map of the Empire, the entirety of a Province. In time, those Unconscionable Maps no longer satisfied, and the Cartographers Guilds struck a Map of the Empire whose size was that of the Empire, and which coincided point for point with it. The following Generations, who were not so fond of the Study of Cartography as their Forebears had been, saw that that vast Map was Useless, and not without some Pitilessness was it, that they delivered it up to the Inclemencies of Sun and Winters. In the Deserts of the West, still today, there are Tattered Ruins of that Map, inhabited by Animals and Beggars; in all the Land there is no other Relic of the Disciplines of Geography. (Borges 1998, 325)

The lesson, of course, is that beyond a certain point the complexity of a model makes it uninteresting as a description of reality: as it approaches the complexity of reality itself, its value disappears. Macroeconomists' quest for accurate models of the national economy has driven them to posit ever larger systems of equations, with hundreds

---

[14] See Churchill (1959, 885–886).

[15] Churchill's predictions were not entirely without merit, of course: Romania, offered almost entirely (90/10) to the Soviets, proved to be a far more reliable client than Yugoslavia. Yet overall it seems fair to say that Churchill's estimate of the extent of Western influence in Eastern Europe was, for the next 45 years anyway, immensely optimistic.

[16] See, for example, Williams and McGinnis (1988).

or even thousands of equations.[17] Political scientists, driven more by the desire to understand the international system than by a desire to capture every last hiccup in every time series, would do well not to emulate such theoretical fecundity, lest they meet the fate of Borges's geographers. Clarke and Primo (2005, 10, 13) make essentially the same point, with the same metaphor:

> Maps, to borrow an example from Giere (1999), are models. Maps are not reality, nor are they isomorphic to reality. Maps are representations of reality. Furthermore, maps are physical objects, not linguistic entities. . . . Maps are partial; they represent some features of the world and not others, and they are of limited accuracy.

Along these lines, Bankes (1993) suggests a philosophy of modeling suitable to the subject matter at hand: given that forecasting in social systems is an uncertain business at best, we should focus less on the use of large, comprehensive models for prediction and more on the use of small, exploratory models for improving our insights about the subject matter. This, it seems to me, is precisely the right approach: to generate models that are small enough that they can be readily comprehended by most specialists, yet complex enough that their workings illuminate something about the subject matter that would not have been readily grasped with unaided intuition. The purpose of such a model is to serve as an aid to the analyst's understanding of a given situation, a means of understanding the likely implications of changes in the world, and a testbed for fine-tuning that understanding.

This more proscribed, less ambitious, but ultimately more satisfying modeling exercise is perfectly suited to the dynamics of the international system, in which the complexity of the interactions among states rapidly outruns unaided intuition. Moreover, it focuses our attention on the actions of a small number of states – the Great Powers – whose activity has the most influence on outcomes in the international system, rather than on every one of the scores of states, principalities, and nonstate actors present at any given time. As we will see, even with a few Great Powers the complexity of the model is sufficient unto the day: although its technical details are most likely of interest mainly to specialists and have therefore been spelled out in Appendix A, the theory that motivates it also benefits from its general spirit of economy.

Components of the theory

Before describing the manner in which the theory works, it is necessary to describe each of the elements of it and explain how they relate both to one another and to similar concepts in the international relations literature. The theory is built around three core elements, at three different levels of analysis: the citizen, the state, and the international system. Each represents an intentionally general theoretical process in the spirit of a broader theoretical paradigm; the section that follows draws them all

---

[17] Hickman (1991) traces the development of the multinational Project LINK from its early days, when it comprised 1,500 equations, to 1985, when it was made up of about 20,000!

together to forge a single systemic theory from the insights drawn from each of its constituent parts.

Citizen

The first element of the theory is the individual citizen. Such citizens, I argue, possess worldviews,[18] variously described as their "belief system," the "prism" through which they views the international system, their "paradigm," "security paradigm," or "foreign policy paradigm."[19] Worldviews can also be thought of as the clusters of *issues* that matter to citizens, or as the *spheres* of international politics that are relevant to them.[20]

The concept, as this list suggests, has appeared in the world politics literature in many forms, though each has slightly different connotations. Most definitions involve constituent elements (generally norms, ideas, perceptions), their relationship to one another (as in beliefs about causal mechanisms), and their relationship to decision makers (as the means by which goals are defined, problems are pinpointed, and the proper means for solving problems and achieving goals are delimited).[21] The school most prominently associated with worldviews, perhaps, is social constructivism, which emphasizes the intersubjective nature of reality and therefore relies heavily on an understanding of the worldviews of individuals and states.[22] A considerable and diverse array of scholars interested in the power of ideas have also evinced considerable interest in the causal role of worldviews, without necessarily overtly aligning themselves with the constructivist camp.[23] Finally, to the extent that

---

[18] Fans of the term *"realpolitik"* may prefer the pleasant symmetry of *"weltanschauung,"* à la Bialer (1986, 264) – not to be confused with the *weltanschauung* of the well-known Sapir-Whorf hypothesis, which is heavily imbued with language.

[19] Holsti (1962); Perkins (1993, 15), Ulam (1974, 347); Zubok and Pleshakov (1996, 4); Nation (1992, xiii); and Checkel (1997), respectively.

[20] I use the terms "issue" and "sphere" almost interchangeably; both refer to characteristics of the constituent units of a system that are deemed relevant to one another by virtue of their fundamental nature. The military sphere, for example, involves the military capabilities (characteristics) of the states (units) within the international system, which are relevant to one another by virtue of their nature (as vehicles for the projection of, or defense against, physical force outside of the boundaries of the state).

[21] My formulation draws on all of the above sources, but most directly on Checkel (1997), who defines a foreign policy paradigm as "an interpretive framework of ideas and norms that specifies the nature of the problems decision makers face, the goals of policy, and the sorts of instruments that should be used to attain them" (p. 103).

[22] Here see, inter alia, the essays in Chafetz, Spirtas, and Frankel (1999b), Katzenstein (1996), and Ruggie (1998), as well as Doty (1993), Erikson (1968), Hopf (2002), Johnston (1995), Laitin (1998), Richter (1996), and Wendt (1999); for a review see Checkel (1998).

[23] One might quite reasonably categorize Axelrod (1976) as a tacit constructivist, especially given the evolution of cognitive mapping evinced in Johnston, previous footnote. Students of belief systems, such as Chittick, Billingsley, and Travis (1995), Converse (1964), Holmes (1985), Holsti (1979), Huntington (1993), Jervis (1970), McCloskey (1967), Murray (1996), Schneider (1983), Wittkopf (1990), and Zimmerman (1969), also qualify. If the category can be stretched to include anyone who demonstrates a generic commitment to the power of ideas, adherents become legion.

worldviews influence policy preferences (as I argue they do), they could be claimed as a subset of liberalism[24] or perhaps of corporatism.[25]

My conceptualization of a worldview encompasses only some of these elements. By a "worldview" I intend to connote the set of structured ideas that determine the dimensions of the structure of the international system that are deemed relevant to a state's security policy.[26] Citizens' need to restrict the dimensions along which they view the system exists because of the wealth of information that is potentially available about other countries: population, wealth, military strength, ideology, ethnic makeup, official language(s), religion, geographic area, average temperature and rainfall, collective tastes in arts and literature, fashion, etiquette. Very few of these dimensions are generally thought to be relevant to security policy, and citizens of different states may come to different conclusions about which are and which are not.

Regardless of one's position on which issues predominate, however, all general explanations of international relations must assume that *some* issues matter and some do not; no theory could be tractable otherwise. Which issues actually *do* matter and how much they matter are factual questions, however, and I will deal with them as such rather than join one theoretical camp or another.

Whichever dimensions are emphasized, a worldview provides citizens with a means of simplifying and interpreting international relations by giving them a lens through which to view other states and identify the salient divisions among them. International relations will then be understandable primarily as relations among states differentiated by such attributes as military capabilities, control of the means of production, democracy, religion, ethnicity, or, more broadly, culture.[27] These "issue dimensions" play a large role in interpreting actions: bombing one group of people might be more justified than bombing another to the same citizenry, largely because the targets of the first bombing were perceived as a threat, were doing something odious, or were simply living their lives in a manner that was de facto unacceptable. Hence, the Irish Republican Army felt justified in bombing the British, though not (say) the French.

Citizens rarely develop an interest in an issue dimension without deciding, in the process, that the world would be a better place if it could be nudged toward a particular

---

[24] Here see Moravcsik (1997); for a relevant application, Kimura and Welch (1998); and for an argument that liberalism and constructivism are indistinct, Sterling-Folker (2000).

[25] Olson (1965); Katzenstein (1985).

[26] Goldstein and Keohane (1993) break beliefs down into three types: worldviews, principled beliefs, and causal beliefs. Worldviews are the broad ideas that make up the fabric of a society, whereas principled beliefs are normative ideas and causal beliefs are, quite simply, beliefs about causation. My definition of a worldview, in contrast to theirs, encompasses the latter two types. For example, a classical *realpolitik* worldview also contains principled beliefs (military security of the state is the primary value to be upheld) and causal beliefs (imbalances of power increase the probability of war, which in turn threatens the security of the state).

[27] Scholarly research often mirrors these ideological predilections, suggesting that, even if scholars themselves do not view the world in these ways, they believe that a substantial proportion of humanity does; see Lenin (1939), Russett (1993), Hero (1973), Said (1977), and Huntington (1996), respectively, for examples. Broader models based on attribute distance have been viewed, perhaps justifiably, with considerable skepticism since Wright (1942), but more recent applications (Altfield 1984; Axelrod and Bennett 1993) have shown more sophistication and promise.

point along that dimension. Few citizens who focused on the Cold War clash between democracy and communism, for example, were indifferent between the two: most could tell you what the structure of the system would look like if they had their way. The most preferred state of the world along a given issue dimension for any citizen is called that citizen's *ideal point*. Moreover, all issues are not equally important to all citizens of all states: on some issues, a wide range of outcomes would be acceptable (that is, the citizenry is relatively indifferent regarding outcomes), whereas on others, only a narrow range of outcomes would be tolerated. This difference constitutes variation in the *salience* of the issue dimension to the citizen in question.

The collection of such ideal points, weighted by salience, correspond to what we would typically call the state's *preferences*.[28] To a state driven by an offensive-realist worldview,[29] increasing the state's military capabilities relative to those of the other states in the system is in its interest; an ideologically driven communist state's interests consist of changing the correlation of forces in favor of world socialism.[30]

State

The manner by which the ideational predispositions of the citizenry of a state coalesce into something that might be called the state's collective preference is a matter of considerable debate. Rarely since the disappearance of the Greek *agora* have demands been expressed directly by the citizenry, and the process of preference aggregation – one of the most fundamental functions of any political system – must be understood as well. This is the traditional redoubt of the liberal paradigm in international relations theory,[31] and of public choice theory in the formal political theory literature.

The conclusions reached by public choice theory are famously grim. The Marquis de Condorcet (1785) was among the first to point out that three voters (or groups)

---

[28] The assertion that preferences follow from interests is widely but not universally accepted. Kratochwil (1982, 5–6), for example, argues that "we can think of cases in which it makes sense to distinguish carefully something wanted or desired – like sitting down in a snowstorm due to exhaustion – from the interest involved – not doing so because of the danger of freezing to death." It seems to me that there are actually two interests here (rest and survival) and two preferences that stem from them (sitting and not dying), and that the latter simply outweighs the former. See Keeney and Raiffa (1993) for a discussion of multiple preferences that would accommodate such an example.

[29] The distinction between offensive and defensive realists is discussed in detail later.

[30] It is worth noting that this conceptualization of interests accords with that of theorists but clashes with that of many policy makers. To the latter group, "the national interest" is often used to refer to a minimalist set of goals more or less consistent with defensive realism – i.e., defense of the homeland in the short term, prevention of developments abroad that might present a threat to the homeland in the longer term, and minimization of loss of life. The contrast can be highlighted by considering the general case of humanitarian interventions, which would be based on the nation's interests according to academics if the impetus to engage in them stemmed from the worldview that motivates the state's security activity, but which would not be in the national interest according to policy makers because humanitarian crises pose no threat to the nation and intervention risks lives.

[31] For a detailed review and canonical statement of the modern liberal paradigm see Moravcsik (1997).

facing policy options A, B, and C and possessing preference orderings A > B > C, B > C > A, and C > A > B could not be said to have a single collective preference: any option forwarded can be defeated by another option that is preferred by two of the three voters. Kenneth Arrow (1951) generalized this point by demonstrating that, under a fairly innocuous set of assumptions,[32] *no* system of preference aggregation other than dictatorship – in which one person's preferences determine society's – can avoid this conundrum.[33] Worse, as Charles Plott (1967) suggested and Richard McKelvey (1976) demonstrated, in a majority-rule contest in the absence of an "undominated point" (a policy that cannot be defeated by any other), any policy at all can be reached by constructing a sequence of proposals, each of which is preferred to its predecessor by a majority of the voters. When politics involves more than a single issue dimension, politicians can garner support from shortsighted voters by finding an "issue niche" – a narrow range of policies that a majority of voters will find (barely) preferable to the alternative that has been proposed.

The unfortunate implication of McKelvey's insight for students of politics is that predicting the relationship of preferences to policy from first principles becomes a very tricky business. Duncan Black's (1958) claim that the preference of the state along a given issue dimension reduces to the preference of the median voter no longer holds when multiple dimensions come into play.

This conclusion, however, is premised on a very brittle set of assumptions about the behavior of voters (or, more accurately, about the perceptions of leaders regarding the behavior of voters). Constituents are assumed to know precisely where each candidate stands on each issue and how much utility they would receive if that stance were translated into policy; moreover, they are assumed to support the candidate whose stance provides a marginally greater expected utility with probability 1. The candidates are assumed to know that they will do so.

It is more realistic to argue that uncertainty exists, both on the part of the constituency about the benefits of the candidates' platforms and on the part of the candidates about the behavior of their constituents. Constituents may be ill informed; candidates might not be able to count on their support even if they were well informed

---

[32] Roughly, they are as follows: 1) The number of alternatives must be at least three; 2) any set of individual orderings should be possible, and the system of preference aggregation should be able to specify a social ordering for any set of individual orderings [collective rationality]; 3) if all individuals prefer A to B, then the resulting social preference ordering should include a preference for A over B [the weak Pareto criterion]; and 4) if A is universally preferred to B, then changing the order of any additional alternatives should have no effect on the collective preference for A over B [the irrelevance of independent alternatives].

[33] It is worth emphasizing that the implications of Arrow's insight are not as horrific as they might at first seem. Arrow did not argue that democratic government was inherently dysfunctional or that dictatorship is desirable; rather, the proof demonstrates that in every form of government other than pure dictatorship the *possibility* of deadlock is unavoidable. To offer a trivial counterexample, if three groups' preferences must be aggregated and all have preference orderings A > B > C, aggregation in a democratic system is easy. In fact, out of all of the permutations possible in the context of the three-voter, three-issue example offered by Condorcet, only 5.6% lack a majority winner (assuming strong preferences; see Jones (1995)).

because they may be incorporating idiosyncratic factors into their decision calculus. The assumptions adopted in the nested politics model reflect this uncertainty.
Constituents are assumed to support a candidate with a probability that increases as
the candidate's platform's utility to them increases and decreases as the candidate's
opponent's platform's utility to them increases. In short, this means that, as the attrac-
tiveness of Smith's policies increase, the probability that I will vote for Smith increases
as well. I may not be likely to support Smith over Jones even if Smith's policies would
be better for me – perhaps I am not perfectly informed about their policies; perhaps
I have watched the debates and Smith just strikes me as a fool – but as the difference
between Smith's policies and Jones's increases from my point of view, so too will the
probability that I will vote for Smith.[34]

It is important to bear in mind that, by virtue of the fact that leaders must constantly
gauge its temper and adjust their policy in order to maximize support, a constituency
can place "demands" on the leadership without ever uttering a word. Just as the
course of a lightning bolt is determined entirely by tiny differences in resistance
among the countless air molecules that surround it, a constituency that makes no
actual policy demands whatsoever but merely reacts to policies as they are enacted
(or debated) guides politics along the path of least resistance. Although this form
of passive compellance is most apparent in democracies in the modern age of near-
instantaneous public opinion polls, it is an inherent feature of government, however
large or small the constituency.[35] The worldviews of constituencies shape the policies
of elites, not by any direct form of coercion, but passively – by virtue of the fact that
satisfying one's constituency also happens to be the best way to get into office and stay
there.

Making allowances for differences in domestic institutional structure, a process
very similar to this one takes place in all political systems. The particulars of this
process may of course vary from one state to another, and not all citizens are capable

---

[34] This is a very "vanilla" probabilistic voting model, meant to apply to a wide range of states. Quite
a few additional nuances, such as interest groups, ideology of voters, etc., have been added to
explain the features of different electoral systems (see Persson and Tabellini [2002] for examples),
but the basic model seems most well suited to describing features common to political systems in
general.

[35] John Zaller (1992) has developed a model of opinion formation in which elites are drawn from
subpopulations with different ideological predispositions, specialize in policy formulation, and
send "messages" in the form of policy statements back to the public via the media. These messages,
when received, resonate most strongly in citizens with sympathetic predispositions. Voter opinion
is therefore seen as a function of attentiveness, predispositions, and the strength of the message
(as well as of any events in the international arena that happen to make one issue or another
particularly salient). To win elections, candidates must adopt clusters of policies that resonate as
strongly as possible with the subpopulation that constitutes their base of support. These themes
are elaborated throughout the book and are neatly captured in Zaller's "Parable of Purple Land"
(311–312). The model is essentially a simple version of a spatial theory of voting in which the
population's preferences in issue-space are bimodal and candidates are drawn to the modes. A
vast literature exists on this subject; for a review and an excellent example see Enelow and Hinich
(1984).

of influencing leaders: a *constituency* is merely the segment of the citizenry that is capable, by virtue of the structure of the state's institutions, of exerting selection pressure on the leadership (Finer 1997, 38–58).[36] One of the functions of the state is to determine how the constituency is defined; variation in the domestic structure of the state can enfranchise different groups of citizens to different degrees.

Though area specialists may argue over precisely which segments of society have how much power to affect policy, examples of leaders without constituencies are exceedingly hard to find. The existence of a de facto constituency in nondemocratic states may not be obvious at first, but enough leaders have been overthrown (or killed) in even the harshest totalitarian states that it cannot be discounted.[37] At a minimum, leaders heavily protected from the public must rely on the fealty of their protectors. In any event, this process points to an important source of policy change: changes in the preference-aggregation mechanism of the state itself, as (for example) might occur when the franchise, representational mechanisms, or institutional decision rules change, produce changes in policy.[38]

Under some circumstances, leaders may be capable of having some influence over the preferences of their constituencies as well. The magnitude of this influence, however, is highly variable, both across and within political systems. Its extent is most likely greater in authoritarian systems, where a "circular flow of power" (Roeder 1993, 27–29) ensures a degree of codependency between leaders and constituencies, than it is in representative ones. Even so, two points mitigate in favor of the standard, bottom-up public choice model of constituent influence: one, the flow of power does come full circle, in that leadership pressures on constituents rarely totally negate the impact of constituents on leaders (to, for example, Khrushchev's dismay); and two, the strength of leaders' influence over constituents varies substantially even within a given political system. Taken together, these points suggest that the backward flow of authority from leader to constituent is neither strong enough nor regular enough to be "hard-wired" into the theory, but that it may merit our attention in individual cases. (Indeed, I argue in Chapter 4 that this ability played a prominent role in allowing Mikhail Gorbachev to modify his constituency and escape the straitjacket of Soviet orthodoxy when attempting to improve relations with the United States.)

System

Finally, once a state's collective preferences have coalesced and the constituency has issued a demand for action on the part of the leadership, leaders must choose a level

---

[36] Finer, having surveyed thousands of years of different forms of human governance, is comfortable using the term in democratic and nondemocratic states alike, and I follow his usage. The international relations subfield is perhaps more familiar with the neologism "selectorate" (Bueno de Mesquita, Smith, Siverson, and Morrow 2003).

[37] Even Hitler narrowly escaped an attempt at extreme selection pressure on July 20, 1944, when Colonel Claus von Stauffenberg's briefcase bomb narrowly missed its target.

[38] For an excellent review of the different dimensions of the foreign policy implications of such changes see Rogowski (1999).

of security activity for the state. Although positions on domestic economic matters often boil down to taking a stand on the question of how much should be given to (or taken from) whom, in the case of foreign affairs leaders must choose how active the state will be in pursuing the constituents' *desiderata* – how hard to work to maintain the balance of power, perhaps, or how much effort to expend in fomenting revolution abroad. Inactivity on the part of leaders in the face of demands for action will be penalized because it will be viewed as neglectful of the national interest. Activity in excess of that demanded by the constituency will be penalized because it will be viewed as a diversion of resources away from more important tasks.[39] The leadership is assumed to be free to take whatever level of action it chooses, though the extent to which leaders' actions are effective is limited both by the potential capabilities of the state and by the actions taken by the leaders of other states. This is the essence of the realist paradigm in international politics: states utilize their power to get what they want, to the extent that they can.

A situation of this sort – one in which a continuum of possible strategies exists and leaders must choose a level of activity that will result in a division of the system that maximizes their payoffs subject to the constraints imposed by the behavior of other leaders – is referred to generically as a "bargaining problem," in deference to its roots in economics, though the moniker is certainly appropriate to the kinds of secret negotiations in smoke filled rooms that the word *realpolitik* conjures up. The idea is that multiple actors know one another's preferences and capabilities, and with or without actual collusion, they have to arrive at a state of the world in which no one has an incentive to change his or her behavior. A classic example is that of a duopoly in which two firms must choose a level of production of a particular good without producing too much and eliminating demand. One very straightforward way to solve a problem of this sort is to find a Cournot-Nash equilibrium that will describe both equilibrium levels of activity and distribution of (realized) capabilities.[40]

The problem with such a general equilibrium model as a description of the behavior of the system in this case is that it describes equilibria but not how those equilibria are achieved, starting from initial conditions. If the system were to reach a general equilibrium immediately and that equilibrium were to adjust itself instantaneously to any perturbation, the Cournot-Nash bargaining solution would be a perfectly serviceable tool for understanding the outcomes of such bargaining situations at the international level. Unfortunately, adjustment to changes, either in worldviews (and hence preferences) or in capabilities, might take years to accomplish, and in that time other changes occur elsewhere in the system that often require further adjustments, and while those adjustments are taking place, still more changes occur, and so on, and so on. If changes in the determinants of equilibria are frequent and adjustment takes time, states can spend most of their time equilibrating – out of equilibrium but moving toward it. Because bargaining solutions like the Cournot-Nash model tell us where states are going but not how they get there, and because much of history

---

[39] Examples in the American context abound; for an example see Gholz, Press, and Sapolsky (1997).
[40] See Rasmusen (1989, 76–78) for a clear discussion of the Cournot-Nash equilibrium concept.

consists of getting there, we need a model of the process by which they arrive at an equilibrium, not just a description of the equilibrium itself.[41]

Security-related activity

The activity, or effort, that states engage in to increase their security requires a bit of discussion. Security-related activity denotes the expenditure of resources in an attempt to change the status quo and thereby to increase the national security of the state. Resources may be real or promised, the latter merely being a conditional version of the former (a defensive alliance, for example, is an expenditure of military resources conditional on an attack on one of the member countries). Examples include increases in expenditures, the formation of alliances, and the issuances of threats.

Although forces operating at the level of the international system prompt the state to pursue a more or less active foreign policy, they typically do not compel any particular *form* of activity – the taking up of arms rather than the formation of alliances, for example.[42] The system provides the impetus to act; other considerations at different levels of analysis (typically, theorists have argued, the relative costs and benefits of each form of activity[43]) determine the form that that action will take.

This is the very narrow sense in which I agree with Kenneth Waltz's famous argument that systemic theories are not theories of foreign policy.[44] Waltz's reasoning on this point is neither entirely consistent nor entirely compelling: for example, the argument (1979, 119) that systemic balances can be predicted with great certainty but the individual state behavior that produces them is entirely indeterminate is logically tenuous. Nevertheless, when Waltz (1996, 54) writes that a theory of foreign policy, unlike a systemic theory, "would explain why states similarly placed in a system behave in different ways," he captures the essence of a crucial distinction: while systemic theories *must* be able to predict that states will act, if only because they must do so in response to structural incentives, systemic theories cannot predict the exact *form* that that action will take. The first part of Wolfers' (1962, 13–14) "burning house" analogy captures this intuition well: individuals caught in a burning house will be compelled to exit. Yet importantly, the existence of the fire tells us nothing about *which* exit they will choose. Accordingly, as Wohlforth (2009, 28) points out, mainstream theories of conflict have long since abandoned the idea that there is a direct relationship between structural configurations and such specific actions as the initiation of conflict.

---

[41] Advocates of the Nash bargaining solution will nevertheless be pleased to know that the variant of the model that permits no joint gains produces equilibrium results, in the long run, that are equivalent to the results of an asymmetric Nash bargaining model, which – as Binmore (1998, 126–128) shows – is also the solution to the Rubinstein bargaining model (Rubinstein 1982) as the response time grows vanishingly small.

[42] It could be argued that bipolarity compels a greater degree of armament than alliance, for example, but even so alliances can play a prominent role, as NATO and the Warsaw Treaty Organization demonstrated during the Cold War.

[43] See, for example, Conybeare (1994), Morrow (1993), and Sorokin (1994); for an arms-alliances argument that does build on a very different systemic logic than the one elaborated here see Saperstein (1992).

[44] See, e.g., Waltz (1979, 121; 1996).

Explaining which specific form of activity will be chosen by a state can, however, be accomplished if systemic theories are augmented with additional, typically non-systemic, theory. Elsewhere I demonstrate that the systemic model developed herein can be successfully married to a dyadic theory – deterrence theory – to create a comprehensive multistage explanation of the onset of conflict.[45] This is but one example of the manner in which the logic of the theory can be augmented with auxiliary theory from different levels of analysis to predict more specific behaviors on the parts of states and dyads. Alliance vs. armament, the initiation and termination of arms races and enduring rivalries, conflict and cooperation, all are plausible extensions – but each has its own logic and merits careful explication. In addition to being of substantive interest in its own right, therefore, the systemic theory can serve as a first stage of a more diverse array of more comprehensive explanations of specific foreign policy phenomena.

As this discussion suggests, the end result of security-related activity may be many things. It might be an alliance, or the dissolution of an alliance, or the onset or termination of a crisis. It might, if the activity is purely unilateral, be an increase in realized capabilities – in which case the relationship of activity to capabilities should resemble the relationship of acceleration to speed. It might, however, be a *decrease* in realized capabilities, if the activity is aimed at increasing cooperation or building confidence. It would be a mistake to associate the concept of activity too closely with any one form of it.

The relative abstraction of the notion of state foreign policy activity, when compared to specific forms of effort or activity such as arming and forming alliances, may have obscured this point to international relations theorists. However, the study of security-related activity in general, in the form of "events" data, has a long pedigree in quantitative international relations scholarship,[46] where it is studied alongside phenomena like alliances and arms races without any sense of contradiction. Events data are a systematic attempt to categorize the (typically) security-related activities of states on a unidimensional scale. Events data scales typically range from most conflictual to null to most cooperative. Because the system compels action rather than cooperation or conflict per se, the more useful conceptualization here is a spectrum ranging from most inactive (essentially, isolationist) to normal (for a Great Power) to hyperactive or, in the case of conflictual activity, aggressive.

The distribution of the effects of a state's security activity should mirror the blend of issues that constitutes its worldview. Ideological states will act to promote their favored ideology abroad; *realpolitik* states will work to disrupt strong (and therefore potentially dangerous) coalitions; and so forth. The actions of a mostly ideological state might nevertheless have some *realpolitik* impact: its primary goal might be to reproduce its ideology abroad, but if its worldview is at least somewhat informed by

---

[45] Braumoeller (2008). See also Fearon (1998) for a thought-provoking essay on theoretical bridges between the systemic level of analysis and other levels, though most systemic theorists would most likely focus only on the second of Fearon's two definitions of systemic theory, and only if it specifically implicated the structure of the international system as a motivating force.

[46] See, e.g., Azar (1982), Goldstein and Freeman (1990), Merritt, Muncaster, and Zinnes (1994), and Pevehouse and Goldstein (1999).

power-politics concerns it will tend to a lesser degree to enact policies that enhance its military security.

Despite the fact that leaders have a strong incentive to act as their constituencies demand, and despite the fact that many of them are in control of sufficient resources to bring about whatever changes their constituency desires, states rarely achieve their goals: few ever reach their constituency's ideal point, whether that be hegemony, religious or ideological unification, or whatever. Most are doomed to some degree of frustration by virtue of the fact that other states with other worldviews also exist and are also attempting to exert their own influence over the international system. The results can range from minor and occasional conflicts of interest to sustained competition to war.

Interactive vs. regulatory politics

The activity of Great Powers in the modern era takes place, broadly speaking, on two levels. The first has to do with everyday *interactive* politics – commercial and legal interactions, territorial disputes, imperial rivalries, and so on. The second level is *regulatory:* it is a (usually explicit) attempt to create an international system that will prevent the frictions generated at the first level from escalating to major war. Similar forms of regulation take place in human societies when, as is almost always the case, people realize that their interests will clash from time to time and agree to set up some form of mechanism (judicial, executive, legislative) at the meta-interaction level to defuse the resulting conflicts. This sort of self-interested regulation is not uncommon and varies widely in degree of complexity, from the evolution of cooperative norms[47] to what international relations specialists call "regimes,"[48] all the way to formal political institutions.[49] Activity designed to alter the structure of the international system is often, even usually, regulatory political activity, though it need not be (as in the case of a pure balance-of-power system with no attempt at regulation or coordination).[50]

There tends to be considerably more change in the qualitative nature of regulatory politics after each systemic war or conflict than there is at any time during the subsequent peace. This fact has led theorists like Ikenberry (2000) to focus on the nature of the world order between wars as a phenomenon of interest. This work follows in that tradition. Like Ikenberry, it focuses on periods between wars as discrete periods with their own logic; a substantial difference between the two is that this work relies on a more general understanding of the mechanisms of regulatory politics, comprising not just formal political institutions but also political regimes in a more general sense.[51]

---

[47] Axelrod (1984), Oye (1986).   [48] Keohane (1983), Krasner (1983).
[49] Axelrod and Keohane (1984, 1986), Ikenberry (2000).
[50] More poetically, Wolfers (1962, 73–74) refers to these as "possession" and "milieu" goals – goals relevant to "the enhancement or the preservation of one or more of the things to which it attaches value" and to the enhancement of the international environment within which interactions take place, respectively.
[51] More specifically, Ikenberry (2000, 13–16) contrasts his liberal institutional perspective with two others: a neoliberal, or "unsticky," perspective and a constructivist one in which institutions are "diffuse and socially constructed worldviews that bound and shape the strategic behavior of

The theory

This stylized picture of the international system contains a set of key elements:

- some number (one, two, or more) of Great Powers;
- issue dimensions or spheres of interest, which delineate the general categories of outcomes within the international system (power, ideology, etc.) with which the state must concern itself to protect itself, survive, and thrive;
- citizens within each Great Power who both
  - ○ find each issue dimension to be salient to some degree and
  - ○ have preferences over outcomes in the form of ideal points along that issue dimension;
- leaders who maximize support by seeking to obtain their constituents' preferred outcomes under conditions of uncertainty;
- levels of state activity aimed at increasing the state's share of the system's resources within a given issue dimension; and
- state capabilities or power, which increase the ease with which a greater share of resources can be obtained.

It only remains to connect these elements in a coherent manner to explain what they imply for the behavior of the actors, as well as for changes in outcomes over time within the system.

The theory, which is based as much as possible on durable insights from the political science literature, is summarized here and described in more technical detail in Appendix A. First, I argue that each state's constituency – those citizens capable, by virtue of the state's institutional structure, of exerting selection pressure on the leadership, whether that state is democratic or autocratic – has a worldview that determines its interests in the security arena. Some constituencies are power maximizers who seek empire; others seek security through trade or the spread of a sympathetic ideology; still others are free traders who seek to lower trade barriers. In any case, those interests will determine both the state's preferences over outcomes and the intensity of those preferences.

Preferences determine how the state's constituency will react to the condition of the international system at a given time. Imperialists without empire will demand action; by contrast, ideologues whose belief system has taken over the world or free traders in a world devoid of trade barriers will demand little or none. In short, worldviews constitute interests, interests are the foundation of preferences, and the combination of preferences and the state of the system determines the magnitude of the demands for action that are placed on the leadership by its constituency.

The further the present structure of the system is from the state's ideal point and the greater the salience of the issue, the greater the constituents' level of dissatisfaction, and the greater their desire for action to redress the present situation. Note the use of

individuals and states" (15). The perspective on offer here may be closest to the latter, constructivist one. Moreover, although Ikenberry's focus is on the reasons for the stability of world order (or lack of it), those concerns are not especially central here.

the word "present": the constituency is not entirely certain about the impact that the state's behavior will have on the future structure of the system. Moreover, because the constituency is radically less certain about the worldviews and capabilities of other states than it is about its own, it cannot anticipate either the impact of the structure of the system on the level of activity of other states or the subsequent impact of those states' activity on the system's structure. The constituency is also secure in the knowledge that other states will engage in incremental policies, for the same reasons that it knows that its own state will do so; moreover, given its much greater level of uncertainty about other states' worldviews, intended actions, effects of those actions on the status quo, etc., the constituency typically does not make any substantial demand that leaders attempt to counter the imagined future actions of other states, preferring instead to wait until those actions have had an impact and to counter them then, if necessary. For all of these reasons, constituents opt for the strategy of "partial adjustment" described earlier.

There is a crucial dynamic element to this relationship over time: to the extent that the leaders of the state succeed in getting what their constituents want, demand for further action is reduced. Those states wishing only to "make the world safe for democracy" could, absent the threat of backsliding, largely pack up and go home once they had accomplished their goal. Few states are afforded this luxury, however, because the system typically contains at least one more sufficiently capable actor whose goals conflict with those of the state in question.

In any case, the implications arising from this perspective are straightforward: changes in constituents' worldviews, reflected either in the salience that they assign to the dimensions of the world that they deem most relevant to security or in their ideal points along those dimensions, produce policy change.

Next, the demands of the constituency are aggregated by the state's political system. This should be an uncontroversial statement: the aggregation of preferences is a large part of what states are designed to do. The process of aggregation often results in a process of distortion as well, so that the preferences of the few (or the one) can come to outweigh the preferences of the many, but this need not be the case. The details of this process of aggregation vary from one state to the next; nevertheless, it can be shown that under a relatively unrestrictive set of assumptions[52] policy will be driven toward the ideal point of the average voter. Because the leadership wishes to maximize its support, it implements a policy designed to produce the greatest good for the greatest number, which implies a policy close to the mean along every issue dimension.

---

[52] To be specific, the uncertainty surrounding constituents' behavior smooths out the relationship between candidates' positions on the issues and the support that they receive, making it impossible for leaders to find "issue niches" that afford a temporary advantage. Instead, a single optimal position emerges. As it happens, this position is the one that is optimal for the entire community – at least by the standards of Jeremy Bentham, who wrote in chapter 1 of *Principles of Morals and Legislation* (1823) that "[t]he interest of the community then is ... the sum of the interests of the several members who compose it." Under the relatively general assumptions described earlier, this position is the one that maximizes the mean of the constituents' utilities (D. Mueller 1989, 199–202).

Next, political leaders receive their constituencies' demands and act on them. Because leaders usually hope to retain office for themselves or for their parties, they typically stray little from the path laid out by their constituencies (although they do try to influence the direction of that path). Their ability to implement the policies favored by their constituencies depends on two things: the raw resources that the state's leaders can bring to bear and the actions of the leaders of other states.

The net result of the actions of the leaders of all states is a change in the structure of the system. Once that change has occurred, the cycle of activity begins anew: the constituency observes the structure of the system in the next period through the prism of its worldview, it makes demands of its leaders, those demands are aggregated, leaders act on them, those actions collectively have an impact on the structure of the system, and so on. Constituents do not consciously equilibrate; that is, they make no detailed calculations about the results of their states' actions in combination with the actions of other states. They merely respond in a very straightforward way to the stimuli provided by the system by demanding action in proportion to their dissatisfaction. This model of how states act tells us how they get to equilibrium and how they should be expected to act when they are not there.

How much impact the state's activity will have on the structure of the international system depends in a straightforward manner on the resources that it can bring to bear in an attempt to change the status quo. Here, an important distinction needs to be made: because the capabilities that states use to attack and defend against one another in wartime and the raw materials that they use to generate those capabilities are both often used as indicators of state power, we must distinguish between *latent* and *realized* capabilities (or power) if the rest of the theory is to be conceptually coherent. Self-defense, in the final analysis, depends on the state's ability to protect itself, which depends critically on its realized capabilities – weaponry, transportation capabilities, intelligence resources, and so on. That ability, in turn, depends on its latent capabilities – the human, material, and technological resources that can be devoted to the task. Latent and realized capabilities must be distinguished from one another both to avoid tautology and because they play different roles in the theory: at least since the early 20th century, realized capabilities determine the state's place in the international power hierarchy and are most relevant to the maintenance of international stability, whereas latent capabilities, which capture the state's long-run or potential strength, are what permit states to alter the balance of realized capabilities, as well as to achieve lasting changes in other structural dimensions.[53]

---

[53] Note that I argue on p. 75 that the relationship between these two forms of capability was transformed after World War I, because the pace of warfare was such that the distribution of realized, rather than latent, capabilities became more critical to war outcomes and was therefore on balance more central to decisionmakers' planning. Compare, for example, Organski and Kugler (1980), in which the authors define historical international hierarchies in terms of latent capabilities, operationalized as GDP, to analyses of more modern balances of power that focus on realized capabilities such as tanks and missiles. Clearly, assuming that only one form of capabilities has an impact on the other is an oversimplification, but, given the far more daunting problems inherent in relaxing that assumption, it is a necessary one.

Finally, the actions of the various states change the condition of the international system: in the previous examples, they might produce a shift in the distribution of power or the spread of an ideology, or a reduction in trade barriers. Because the result of the states' actions may make the constituents of some states more satisfied and those of other states less satisfied than they had been previously, a change in the condition of the international system has an impact on the desires of each state's constituency – and the cycle begins anew.

This, in a nutshell, is the theory.[54] Despite its apparent generality, when elaborated it does imply some very specific hypotheses about the behavior of actors and the workings of the international system. Those hypotheses follow.

Hypotheses

The theory just described and more specifically the model derived from it in Appendix A suggest some focused statements about the working of the system. Individually, the actor-level and structural-level arguments offer insights into the short-term effects of changes in the key theoretical variables that, when combined, provide a comprehensive understanding of the workings of the system. In addition, although the model is agnostic regarding which dimensions of the structure of the international system will be deemed relevant by the actors, a review of the historical literature in the next chapter supports the argument that the balance of power is a consistent focus of states' attention, though the exact form that the balance takes varies somewhat from one period to the next. Given the persistence of power and its inclusion with other independent variables, the literature on political realism offers a third hypothesis worth testing, one that suggests that power, exclusively, should be capable of explaining outcomes.

Actor-level hypothesis

H_{A1}: International structure prompts state security activity in proportion to the product of salience and dissatisfaction with the status quo.

If, for example, the state is completely disinterested in the balance of power, the salience of the balance of power will be zero, and no balance or imbalance of power could possibly prompt state action. In contrast, if the state is perfectly satisfied with the status

---

54 All of the basic elements of the model are taken to be variables whose values are measured rather than assumed. Frieden (1999) makes the case for deducing preferences from theory. Kimura and Welch (1998) argue that preferences, at least the ones that they examine, are idiosyncratic – they cannot be deduced from theory. They should therefore be measured, and "international relations theory should seek patterns and generalizations not among the inputs of state behavior, but in the ways in which states process those inputs" (214). I take something of a middle ground: preferences should be deduced from theory when possible, but the extent to which it is possible to do so cannot be determined without either invoking a Friedmanesque "as-if" clause and measuring whether behavior is consistent with posited preferences (Friedman 1953) or actually coming up with measures of the preferences themselves – at least in the early stages of a research program, so the fit of assumption to reality can be assessed. I am more comfortable with the latter.

quo, no action is necessary. If neither of those conditions holds, the hypothesis argues that the level of state activity prompted by the balance of power will be proportional to the product of the salience of the balance of power and the state's dissatisfaction with the balance of power – and that the same holds true for all other structural dimensions of the international system. Because level of satisfaction can only be gauged relative to the condition of the structure of the system, structure plays the role of an independent variable in this part of the theory.

In terms of comparative statics, this hypothesis implies (assuming that neither quantity is zero) that if a state's ideal point shifts away from the systemic status quo along any dimension, its level of activity will increase, and if a state's ideal point shifts toward the systemic status quo along any dimension, its level of activity will decrease. If the status quo of a given systemic distribution shifts away from or toward the state's ideal point, the effects would be the same. Finally, if a state's worldview changes to increase its emphasis on a given dimension of the system, all else being equal, the state's level of activity will increase, because whatever dissatisfaction it had been experiencing along that dimension would matter more; and a decrease in emphasis would result in decreased activity.

Intuitively, as the extent to which a state cares about the distribution of some good in the international system increases, discrepancies between the status quo point and the state's ideal point will prompt increasingly strong demands for action, and the converse is true.[55]

Structural hypothesis

H_{St1}: State security activity alters international structure in proportion to the product of state security activity, capabilities, salience, and dissatisfaction with the status quo.

Here, the question is, with many Great Powers pushing and pulling at (for example) the balance of power, how much of an impact will each one have? The answer is proportional to activity, salience, power, and dissatisfaction.[56] Inactive states, obviously, will change nothing. Powerless states will have no impact on outcomes; as their power grows, so too will their influence – a result in line with asymmetric Nash bargaining models.[57] States that see no need to alter the balance, either because it is not salient to them or they are completely satisfied, will not do so. If none of these conditions holds, the state's influence in shaping the balance – and in shaping other structural dimensions – will be proportional to the product of its capabilities, its dissatisfaction,

---

[55] Most simply, this follows from (A.1): in terms of the model in Appendix A, α is strictly increasing in ω.

[56] Which form of capabilities, latent or realized, will alter the structure of the international system depends, I argue, on the historical period in question. In the 19th century, states primarily used realized capabilities to alter the balance of latent power, whereas in the 20th century the relationship was reversed: their focus was largely on the balance of realized power, which was derived from latent power. See p. 75 for details.

[57] Binmore (1998, 126–128).

and the salience of that sphere. Note that, in this part of the theory, state activity is an independent variable and structure is the dependent variable.

Realist structural hypothesis

Although the logic of the model itself does not imply it, the history of the three periods under study suggests an additional hypothesis that merits exploration. The model is agnostic regarding which dimensions of the structure of the system will be emphasized by the states, but in each period, both balances of power and balances of ideology are said to figure prominently in systemic politics (see Chapter 3 for details). A fairly well-rehearsed argument in the realist literature is that, although states may appear from time to time to pursue ideological goals, the appearance is more illusion than reality: they only do so when the pressures of the ideological sphere and the pressures of the *realpolitik* sphere are aligned (as, for instance, when regime change will produce a valuable ally). As Morgenthau (1948, 86) wrote,

> It is a characteristic aspect of all politics, domestic as well as international, that frequently its basic manifestations do not appear as what they actually are – manifestations of a struggle for power. Rather, the element of power as the immediate goal of the policy pursued is explained and justified in ethical, legal, or biological terms. That is to say: the true nature of the policy is concealed by ideological justifications and rationalizations.

Similarly, Nicholas Spykman (1942, 18) writes that

> [t]he statesman who conducts foreign policy can concern himself with values of justice, fairness, and tolerance only to the extent that they contribute to or do not interfere with the power objective. They can be used instrumentally as moral justification for the power quest, but they must be discarded the moment their application brings weakness.

These and similar quotes, which could fill a substantial appendix on their own, suggest not that ideological or moral motivations for policies are nonexistent, but rather that, when they do exist, they will invariably align well with the power-politics motives of the state. Either the two do not diverge or, when they do, ideology will not drive policy because the resulting policy would not be in the interest of the state. This logic suggests

H_{R1}: The balance of ideology will have no impact on state behavior, independent of the impact that it has when its prescriptions correlate with those of the balance of power.

Systemic hypotheses

Systemic hypotheses are, by their nature, more convoluted and therefore more difficult to discuss. It should be noted that the value of these hypotheses lies mainly in capturing the more "butterfly-wing" implications of systemic behavior, rather than in laying out hypotheses that could realistically be tested under most real-world circumstances. In practice, it may not often be the case, especially with a large number of Great Powers

and the values of many variables changing all at once, that a clean historical test of these hypotheses will be feasible, especially given the indeterminate time horizons involved. Nevertheless, they are nothing more than the logical implications of the (more readily tested) actor-level and structural-level hypotheses taken together. Therefore, if tests of the latter are borne out by the evidence, those results can be taken to be supportive of the related systemic hypotheses.

In what follows I distinguish, for the sake of convenience, between *sympathetic* and *antagonistic* states. In a sphere in which joint gains are possible, a "sympathetic state" is a state whose ideal point lies on the same side of the status quo as one's own; therefore, in the area bounded by the sympathetic state's ideal point and the status quo point, joint gains are possible. An "antagonistic state" is a state whose ideal point lies on the other side of the status quo from one's own. In a sphere in which joint gains are not possible, all states are antagonistic states.[58] It should be emphasized that these terms do not correspond directly to the level of amity or hostility that characterizes the relationship between the states, which is a function of the distance between their ideal points.

H_{Sys1}: A decrease in a state's latent capabilities will result in a worsening of its position in all spheres that interest it and a corresponding increase in its level of activity.

The first part of this conclusion follows from H_{St1} and the second follows from H_{A1}. Simply put, a decrease in ability without a decrease in desire produces an increase in effort. This point is explored in more depth later.

H_{Sys2}: A decrease in a state's latent capabilities will result in a "joint loss" on the part of sympathetic states and a net gain on the part of antagonistic states. Sympathetic states will therefore increase their levels of activity; antagonistic states will decrease then.

This conclusion follows from teasing out the implications of H_{Sys1} for second, third, or nth states, given that H_{A1} applies to their behavior as well. The logic is straightforward: if state i's latent capabilities decrease, it will experience losses across the board in all the dimensions of the international system that interest it. Sympathetic states – those whose ideal points are on the same side of the status quo point as i's – will experience losses as well; antagonistic states, whose ideal points are on the opposite side of the status quo point, will experience gains, as long as they remain antagonistic.[59]

H_{Sys3}: A shift in a state's ideal point away from (toward) the status quo point along a given dimension will produce an increase (a decrease) in that state's activity, which will produce a shift in the status quo toward (away from) the state's ideal point, which in turn will produce an increase (decrease) in the levels of activity of antagonistic states and a decrease (increase) in the levels of activity of sympathetic states.

---

[58] I make this distinction formally on p. 218.

[59] It is possible for an antagonistic state j to become a sympathetic state if i's latent capabilities decrease enough that the status quo point moves past j's ideal point.

This hypothesis – alternative version indicated by parentheses – follows the logic of H_{St1} and H_{A1} forward as they propagate through the system, with a focus on the result of a change in the state's ideal point. First, we see that the change in ideal point has an impact on the state's level of activity. That change in activity has an impact on the structure of the system. Subsequently, the change in the structure of the system has an impact on the level of activity of all other actors who are at least minimally interested in outcomes in that dimension of the system, and those changes in activity have another impact on the structure of the system. All of these changes will most likely have some impact (albeit a much-diminished one) on the behavior of the original state . . . and back and forth, until a new equilibrium is reached.

It is also worth emphasizing that, because a change in the actor's preferences in one dimension of the system has an impact on its *overall* level of activity, there will be gains or losses in *every* dimension of the system, and this "ripple effect" will play out across all dimensions of the system simultaneously.

H_{Sys4}: Increased emphasis (deemphasis) of a given dimension by one state will produce an increase (a decrease) in that state's activity, which will produce a shift in the status quo toward (away from) the state's ideal point, which in turn will produce an increase (decrease) in the levels of activity of antagonistic states and a decrease (increase) in the levels of activity of sympathetic states.

The logic here is precisely the same as that of H_{Sys3}, except that the circumstance that triggers the chain of events is a change in the degree of emphasis placed on one dimension of the system, rather than a change in the state's ideal point along that dimension.

These implications may seem overwhelming at first glance – but this degree of complexity is inherent to even a relatively straightforward system such as this one. Although the most direct implications of the argument are that the structure of the system has an impact on states' behavior and vice versa, the interconnectedness of states and structure implies that, eventually, a change in any part of the system will have an impact on every other endogenous part of the system.

Implications for other theories

These hypotheses, and the model in Appendix A upon which they are based, have a variety of additional, more tangential implications. Although testing all of them directly is beyond the scope of the present study, because most describe scenarios that are either entirely hypothetical or quite rare, they are nevertheless of interest because they speak to existing conclusions from established international relations theory. To illuminate them I explore the manner in which different assumptions about the values of the inputs to that model produce different behaviors and systemic outcomes. Some of these predictions accord with the claims of existing theories of state or systemic behavior; many do not. To the extent that the hypotheses just presented receive empirical support in subsequent chapters, the following implications should be considered relevant to the literatures that they address.

Offensive and defensive realism

The first, and most obvious, point of contact with the existing literature on systemic theory is the relationship between the nested politics model and realism – either in its offensive (Mearsheimer 2001) or defensive (Waltz 1979) form. As I will demonstrate later, both variants of realism can be understood as special cases of the nested politics model, with the values of certain variables (ideal points and salience) set by assumption.[60]

Offensive realists argue that states seek hegemony at every opportunity; their ideal state of the world is one in which they achieve hegemony, a condition in which no other single state can seriously mount a military challenge against them. In short, states seek to maximize security by maximizing power. In contrast, defensive realists recognize the danger of security spirals and therefore argue that states seek to maximize security by achieving an optimal level of power, one that ensures their safety without threatening their neighbors.

What is at stake in this argument? If we were able to "re-run" the world under both offensive and defensive realist assumptions, how would the differences in states' aspirations alter outcomes within the system? Is hegemony more or less likely in one kind of system than in another? What level of realized capabilities must a state achieve to maintain a hegemonic position over time in each system?

We can determine the answers to all of these questions by establishing an artificial system of Great Powers – three, for the sake of illustration, but as long as there are more than two the number does not matter – that are roughly equal in latent capabilities and have similar domestic politics and *realpolitik* worldviews. We can then determine, via simulation, how they would behave under offensive-realist assumptions and compare those results to those of a different simulation in which they behave according to defensive-realist assumptions.[61] By altering the states' ideal points in terms of military capabilities, we can determine what difference the power-maximizer vs. power-satisficer debate really makes.

We can get some very interesting results out of what seem like a fairly spare set of assumptions. If we start with the kind of system described by offensive realists, we find that the initial distribution of realized capabilities does not matter in the least to

---

[60] The wisdom of making such assumptions rather than measuring the quantities of interest depends entirely on the veracity of the assumptions. Assumptions quite literally take the place of data; if they do so well, then we can benefit both from not having to take measurements and from the additional theoretical knowledge gained from understanding that fact. I am therefore agnostic in principle about assumptions. In practice, however, as Chapter 4 suggests, the values of the variables in question here do vary, sometimes quite substantially.

[61] I also assume that, when seeking to enhance their own security, states seek to undermine the security of other states in direct proportion to those states' current share of realized capabilities. This is not an overt assumption of either variant of realism, but it is consistent with both: powerful states, *ceteris paribus*, constitute more of a threat, so one should seek to undermine them to a greater degree. I should emphasize that this assumption is *not* critical to the results; in fact, dropping it makes no difference at all. It merely adds some strategic sophistication to the *realpolitik* variant of the theory in an attempt to be fair to its proponents.

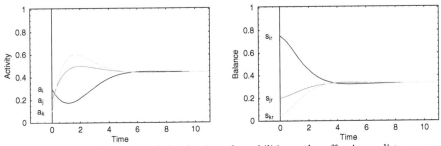

Figure 2.1. Levels of activity and distribution of capabilities under offensive-realist assumptions.

the outcome: in equilibrium, the realized capabilities of all actors will be the same. *No* initial level of realized capabilities will ever suffice to ensure hegemony. In the terms in which I have defined it here, a balance of power will result, regardless of how unequal the actors' capabilities might be to begin with. This explains the curious paradox of offensive realism: although all states seek hegemony, few if any ever achieve it (Mearsheimer 2001, 40–41).

In fact, it is precisely *because* all states seek hegemony that none manages to achieve it. An example of how this outcome occurs is provided in Figure 2.1 The illustration involves three actors, called i, j, and k, though the result holds for any number of actors. The symbols a_i–a_k (left) refer to the level of activity of each of these actors, whereas s_{ir}–s_{kr} (right) refer to the share of realized capabilities in the possession of each actor as a fraction of all of the resources in the system.

At the beginning of the simulation, all of the actors are fairly inactive: each is exerting about one-fifth of the maximum effort that it could devote to increasing its realized capabilities (i.e., its long-term security). As far as the distribution of realized capabilities is concerned, i has the lion's share (70%), while j and k are in relatively bad shape (25% and 5%, respectively). Because their shares of latent power are equal, it would be reasonable to say that i's reach exceeds its grasp: its share of realized capabilities is substantially greater than its share of latent capabilities. Over time, all of these things change. The constituents of j and k, which are most severely disadvantaged by the distribution of power, increase their demands for activity dramatically, and their leaders comply. Actor i also increases its level of activity – even though it clearly has a major advantage over the other states, it is still not satisfied with its position, because it has not maximized its power. Because i is *more* satisfied than j and k, however, its level of activity does not increase as quickly as does theirs, and they focus most of their attention on working to undermine i's position.

These facts prove to be i's undoing. Because j and k push harder to increase their share of realized capabilities than i does, their shares increase, mostly at i's expense: i's share of realized capabilities plummets quite abruptly, j's picks up a bit, and k's jumps up almost as abruptly as i's drops.

The end result of all of this jockeying is an *equilibrium condition* (that is, a condition in which no variable changes from one time period to the next, or a flat line on the

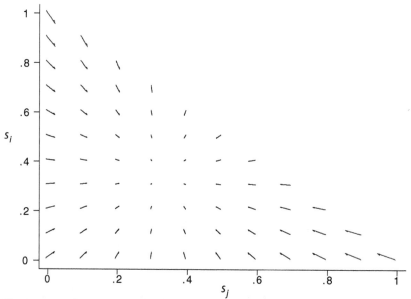

Figure 2.2. A phase portrait of s_i and s_j, demonstrating that a balance of power will eventually be reached regardless of the initial levels of realized capabilities.

graph) that can be characterized as a perfect balance of power: the states' realized capabilities are perfectly equal. None of the states manages to achieve hegemony over the rest, not even i – though it had by far the best running start. This result occurs because the demands of the constituency for security were significantly greater in j and k than they were in i. As a result, even though i worked hard to maintain its position, j and k worked even harder to undermine it. For a brief period, k's massive security effort propelled it above i and j, but their rearguard efforts quickly brought it back down to their own level. In the end, the constituents' demands for security evened out only when a balance of power was achieved.

Moreover, the situation depicted in Figure 2.1 is no fluke: a balance of power will occur regardless of the initial distribution of realized capabilities. The phase portrait in Figure 2.2, like the vector fields in Chapter 4, indicates how both variables will change from a given starting point; it demonstrates that, regardless of the starting point, the system converges to a balance of power. In this case, as in Figure 2.1, each state retains one-third of the system's resources in equilibrium.[62]

---

[62] The difference between the two is that this one is derived analytically from the model given a set of starting assumptions, rather than empirically from the historical data. The field is triangular because, by assumption, $0 \leq (s_i + s_j) \leq 1$. To create a graph like this, one must make assumptions about the values of the other variables. Here, all variables are assumed to be at their equilibrium values except s_i and s_j. Assuming different values does not alter the equilibrium values, which are unique, at least on the $(0,1)$ interval; it merely makes the illustration more difficult to interpret.

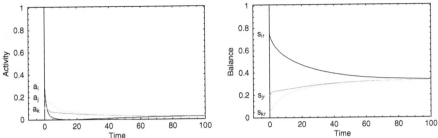

Figure 2.3. Levels of activity and distribution of capabilities under defensive-realist assumptions.

In other words, as Herbert Butterfield eloquently put it,

> the whole order in Europe was a kind of terrestrial counterpart of the Newtonian system of astronomy. All the various bodies, the greater and lesser powers, were poised against one another, each exerting a kind of gravitational pull on all the rest – and the pull of each would be proportionate to its mass.... When one of these bodies increased in mass, therefore – when, for some reason, France for example had an undue accession of strength – the rest could recover an equilibrium only by regrouping themselves, like sets of ballet dancers, making a necessary rectification in the distances, and producing new combinations. (Butterfield 1966, 132)

The existence of a balance of power does not mean, however, that the states settled down into a benign state of indifference toward one another – far from it. Their levels of activity are quite high, indicating that the constituency in each state is greatly dissatisfied with the status quo and is pressing the leadership very hard to do something about it, and the leadership is constantly seeking to alter the structure of the system to its advantage. This is likely to be a world in which alliances are made regularly, crises are initiated, wars are launched, and so on, all in the hopes of altering the balance of power. Those hopes, ultimately, will be in vain, because any perturbation in the balance will be remedied by the actions of the states most disadvantaged by it.

What happens if we create a defensive-realist world instead? The result is far less cutthroat security competition – in equilibrium, states are far less active than they are under offensive-realist assumptions – but one in which a balance of power still comes about regardless of the initial distribution of realized capabilities.

Figure 2.3 illustrates this process. Here, I have changed only the assumption that describes how much power each state's constituency wants. Under offensive-realist assumptions, more is always better. Here, each state would be happiest with half of the power in the system: less would compromise security, and more would constitute an unacceptable threat to the other states. As we can see, the activity levels of the states are quite different than they are in Figure 2.1 – state i comes very close to complete inaction for some time. Before too long the activity levels of both j and k wane as well. In the end, all three states settle on a very low level of activity, resulting from the fact that their constituents are only very modestly dissatisfied with the status quo.

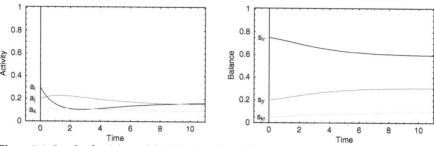

Figure 2.4. Levels of activity and distribution of capabilities with same realized capabilities and different ideal points.

Wars may still occur, of course, but this world should not be the bloodthirsty "war of all against all" that the offensive realists envision.

Interestingly, however, the two worlds are the same in one critical respect: a balance of power results, and it results in almost precisely the same way. It takes a little longer to come about, which reflects the decreased intensity of the constituents' demands, but it comes about all the same. This result, like the previous one, occurs regardless of the initial distribution of capabilities (a proof of this assertion for both offensive-realist and defensive-realist worlds is contained in Appendix A). In short, in a realist world, whether offensive or defensive, "balances of power recurrently form" (Waltz 1979, 124).

Balance of power: two additional assumptions

The results that related realist theories to a balance of power all incorporated two premises: that the degree of "offensiveness" or "defensiveness" is the same for all states and that the latent capabilities of the Great Powers in the system are more or less equal. Absent these two assumptions, it becomes clear that the balance-of-power result, which has been strikingly robust so far, disintegrates.

We can see how this takes place in Figure 2.4. This graph depicts a situation precisely the same as that depicted in Figure 2.1, the only exception being that the states' ideal points have been allowed to vary: i is an offensive-realist state that seeks universal domination, k is a defensive-realist state that seeks only a fraction of the power in the system, and j is somewhere between the two.[63] As one might anticipate, their shares of the system in equilibrium reflect their desires: offensive-realist states end up with bigger slices of the pie.

What this means is that Waltz's assumption that states can seek anything from self-preservation to world domination does *not* ensure that a balance of power will result from their interaction. It must also be the case that the states in question at any given point in time *seek the same thing*. All may seek self-preservation, and a balance

---

[63] To be precise, i desires the entire system, j would be happiest with 70% of it, and k would be happiest with 40%.

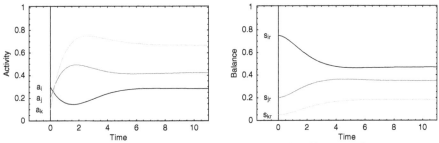

Figure 2.5. Levels of activity and distribution of capabilities under offensive-realist assumptions, with variation in realized capabilities.

will result; all may seek world domination, and a balance will result; but if some seek one and some seek the other, all bets are off.[64]

Similarly, Figure 2.5 reflects a situation that is precisely the same as the offensive-realist world depicted in Figure 2.1, save that the latent capabilities of the actors have been allowed to vary. To be specific, unlike the previous three-way split, i has 60% of the latent power resources in the system, j has 30%, and k has 10%. The result in equilibrium is far from a balance of power. As the graph suggests, i is able to garner enough power to secure for itself a place as systemic hegemon: j and k together cannot match its realized capabilities. Their predilection for sapping i's resources when possible rather than one another's ensures that i's realized capabilities do not quite match its latent capabilities, but nevertheless latent power plays a critical role in determining realized power.

What this means is that it is difficult to understand how, in an offensive-realist world, states with very large amounts of latent power could fail to possess correspondingly large amounts of realized power. Latent power should be translated into realized power, period – but as realists themselves admit, it often is not. To take a single example, Mearsheimer (2001, 71) calculates that the United Kingdom possessed 70% of the total latent power resources of Europe in 1850. A purely realist version of this model would predict that the British share of Europe's military might should have exceeded 70% as well, but as Mearsheimer himself admits, it clearly came nowhere near doing so.[65]

---

[64] Technically, one class of situations constitutes an exception to this generalization: if weaker states are highly ambitious (that is, are more offensive-realist in their outlooks) and stronger states are less ambitious, the two factors could cancel one another out exactly and produce a balance of power.

[65] Mearsheimer's realist explanation for Britain's unexpectedly low levels of military might throughout the mid-1800s is based on two factors: diminishing marginal returns to military expenditures and the "stopping power of water" – the efficacy of the sea as a barrier to combat. The former explanation is hardly consistent with the assertion (p. 34) that "[e]ven when a great power achieves a distinct military advantage over its rivals, it continues looking for chances to gain more power. The pursuit of power stops only when hegemony is achieved." The latter is logically precarious in two ways. First, if a state seeks the ability to dominate others and needs to project power to do

Relative power and levels of activity

In general, the effects of a change in one of a state's characteristics on its level of activity are for the most part hard to predict. A shift toward a more ideological worldview could result in an increase or decrease in a state's level of activity, depending on the worldviews of the rest of the states in the system. This interdependence is one of the most basic lessons of systems theory: simply put, everything depends on everything else.

Surprisingly enough, that lesson does *not* apply to the one characteristic emphasized most often by realists: power. Holding all other characteristics constant, increases in a state's latent power will lead to decreases in its level of activity, and decreases in a state's latent power will lead to increases in its level of activity. This result follows from the fact that decreases in latent capabilities lead to decreases in the ability to capture the kinds of resources demanded by one's constituency, which *inevitably* lead to a higher level of demand for those resources by the constituency and a higher level of activity on the part of leaders. A state with less power must work harder to achieve the same outcome. This result does not depend on the distribution of capabilities in the system, the net capabilities of all of the other states in the system, the worldviews of the actors, or anything else.

The implication of this point is that some outcomes – increases in activity as a result of increases in power, or decreases in activity as a result of decreases in power – are logically denied to realists. In the realist variant of the theory, such outcomes make no sense. If they are to be claimed as successes for realism, something must be added to the microfoundations of this theory that explains them; relative capabilities alone cannot.

This result makes arguments like William Wohlforth's (1993) regarding the end of the Cold War difficult to support, assuming that the nested politics model is supported by the data in the next two chapters. Wohlforth argues that the Cold War ended, in part, because the Soviets' perceptions of their relative capabilities declined sharply; states "may have a multitude of reasons to compete, but one necessary condition is their perception that they have the capabilities to do so" (252). As the Soviets' perceived power declined, they opted not to compete. The realist variant of the nested politics model, in contrast, would suggest that states that fall behind *must* fight harder to keep up. Wohlforth also argues (e.g., 268–272) that, in my terms, a change in fundamental worldviews played a major role in ending the Cold War,[66] and an outcome of that nature *could* follow logically from the basic assumptions of the model, but that does not alter the fact that, all else equal, a decrease in capabilities should lead to an increase, not a decrease, in competitive security activity.

---

so – witness, e.g., the Crimean War – why would not a sea barrier create an incentive to build even *greater* military forces needed to overcome it? Second, it is not even clear that the sea serves as an effective barrier: as the modern shipping industry has demonstrated, large bodies of water can function as exceptionally cost-effective conveyer belts. Why they would hinder rather than help a state's war efforts is unclear. Certainly, to take but a single example, General MacArthur took tremendous advantage of the mobility afforded to him by the sea in the famous Inchon invasion of September 1950.

[66] A view with which I am quite sympathetic, as Chapter 5 demonstrates.

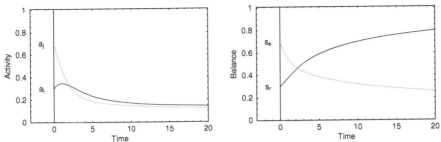

Figure 2.6. A two-state, two-sphere world: one *realpolitik* state and one trading state.

Trading states and balances of power

One of the more interesting results to come out of the model is the fact that balances of power should occur in a world of Great Powers[67] whenever two conditions are met: all states' constituencies are at least slightly interested in relative capabilities, no matter how slight that interest may be; and the extent to which states' constituencies emphasize relative capabilities is equal across states. (The latter assumption is met when a system is, in Aron's terms, "homogeneous," though this is a special case: the assumption is met whenever emphasis on relative capabilities is equal across states, regardless of those states' other values.) These points, taken together, imply that a balance of power can occur even in a world in which all of the states in the system are *almost entirely disinterested* in maintaining it.

Few could be as disinterested in the balance of power as 19th-century British Radical statesman and free trade advocate Richard Cobden, who called it "an undescribed, indescribable, incomprehensible nothing; mere words, conveying to the mind not ideas, but sounds like those equally barren syllables which our ancestors put together for the purpose of puzzling themselves about words, in the shape of *Prester John*, or the *philosopher's stone!*" (1867, 258). Cobden's critique was of the balance of power as a justification for state action; as an unintended structural consequence of state action, even in states that very nearly resemble Cobden's free-trading ideal, the balance of power is far from chimerical.

To illustrate this point, I have simulated two different worlds and illustrated the outcome of each in Figures 2.6 and 2.7. They are the same in many regards: each contains (for the sake of simplicity) two major states; those states are roughly equal in terms of latent capabilities; the constituencies of those states have worldviews that emphasize two spheres – the *realpolitik* sphere of relative military capabilities (call it s_r) and an economic sphere of wealth and trade (s_e); and the constituencies' ideal points are diametrically opposed along both of those dimensions (both, say, want military hegemony and exclusive access to third-party markets). The only difference between the two is the weight that the constituents of the two countries give to each sphere.

In Figure 2.6, i is a classic *realpolitik* state that nevertheless devotes 20% of its activity to economic matters, and j is what Richard Rosecrance (1986) calls a "trading state," one that almost exclusively emphasizeseconomics rather than

---

[67] Assuming, again, rough equality of latent capabilities.

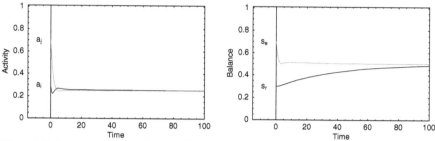

Figure 2.7. A two-state, two-sphere world: two trading states.

realpolitik concerns in its foreign policy (in this case, *j* devotes only 10% of its activity to matters of defense). As one might expect, the *realpolitik* sphere shifts dramatically in *i*'s favor and the economic sphere shifts in *j*'s favor at the onset; in equilibrium, each state dominates the sphere that it considers to be most important.

In Figure 2.7, by contrast, both *i* and *j* are trading states; they spend the vast majority of their time competing over markets, and each devotes only 10% of its time and energy to matters relating to defense. As we can see, the economic sphere polarizes rather quickly, and the result is an even division of available markets. The more unexpected result is that the *realpolitik* sphere, too, polarizes, though it does so more slowly because the states are expending less effort in altering it. In equilibrium, the *realpolitik* sphere, too, is evenly split. In the end, two trading states have achieved a balance of power despite having had virtually no interest in doing so, simply because the amount of attention that they devote to accruing realized capabilities is the same.[68]

This illustration demonstrates a subtle but important point: even if conditions warrant the argument that realism implies a balance of power, the converse – that a balance of power implies realism – does not follow. At first blush this statement may seem to be obviously true: pointing out that realism implies a balance of power, observing a balance of power, and concluding that realism provides an accurate description of politics is a classic example of the fallacy of affirming the consequent. This fallacy takes the form, "If A then B; B; therefore A." Any number of simple examples illustrate the problem: if a 747 is a bird (A) then it will fly (B); it flies (B); therefore it is a bird (A). The conclusion in an argument of this form simply does not follow from the premises and the evidence.

Still, this particular fallacy is problematic only to the extent that other causes could bring about the effect in question. If, for example, birds were the only things in the universe that could fly, then flight would be an accurate indicator of birdhood. It is therefore incumbent on the critic to demonstrate that the effect in question could be produced by other causes – that is, that the balance of power is plausibly the result of the interactions of states that do not behave according to realist assumptions. In a world of trading states, it is quite possible for a balance of power to emerge despite

---

[68] Granted, there may very well be a qualitative difference between a balance of power achieved via intense competition and a balance of power arrived at through indifference. But given that the latter outcome is not much discussed, its implications have yet to be fleshed out.

the fact that states are largely uninterested in it, precisely because they are *equally* uninterested in it.

The logic of hegemony

Organski and Kugler (1980) and Gilpin (1981) are perhaps the two most prominent examples of a tradition that argues against balance-of-power realism. The claim in both is not that systemic balances of power are irrelevant, but rather that *im*balances of power are the norm and that Great Power conflict is most likely when a hegemon and a challenger are roughly equal in terms of capabilities.

First, both of these works endogenize changes in relative capabilities in a way that the nested politics model does not. They point out that state development follows a sigmoid growth curve, though it is often difficult to determine a priori exactly when a challenger will "take off" or whether or not it will succeed in approaching the hegemon in terms of power. For those reasons, although their insights are quite accurate and relevant, they remain difficult to incorporate into the nested politics model. Even contemporaneous evaluations of the speed and likelihood of power transitions have proven to be very difficult to carry out with any degree of accuracy (see e.g., Kennedy 1987, ch. 8).

Second, they are both theories of hegemonic war, whereas the nested politics model does not directly speak to that question. It does speak to the question of a state's foreign policy activity, however, and as I argue in Braumoeller (2008), the probability of war between two states is substantially higher when, as deterrence theory would suggest, one state's level of activity is high and another's is low – but spirals (in which war happens when both states' levels of activity are high) also occur. If joint levels of activity are found to be systematically related to the points at which wars break out during power transitions, it is quite possible to imagine that power transition theory could turn out to be a special case of a more general theory of war.

Nevertheless, as noted in Appendix A Gilpin (1981, 18–23) assumes a relationship between power and preferences – namely, that states' "appetites grow with the eating" – about which the nested politics model is agnostic. This brings up the question of whether the behavior of Gilpin's hegemons is consistent with the argument that they maximize utility. It seems difficult to argue that it is, if maximization of utility is understood in terms of maximization of the state's share of systemic power. This is not, technically, Gilpin's (or Organski and Kugler's) position: hegemons benefit from what Gilpin calls "prestige," the intangible echo of power that permits hegemonic states to produce order by setting the rules of the international system. Prestige comes not just from political and economic power but also from victory in war (32) – implying both that hegemonic war itself has positive value that may outweigh its cost (*contra* Fearon 1995) and must be added to the utility of relative power.

Constructivism and socialization

In some very basic ways, the nested politics model might seem, if not antithetical, at least orthogonal to a constructivist interpretation of systemic politics. A closer

examination of the two, however, reveals that there are at least a few points of contact. On an ontological level, for example, ideas are important in a way that they rarely are in purely materialist formulations: the nested politics model relies critically on worldviews, and as the following chapters will demonstrate, speaks to the distribution not just of power but also of ideology.

That said, the nested politics model takes worldviews to be exogenous rather than endogenous (or even constitutive), and crucially, it does not problematize meaning in the way that constructivist accounts do. The process by which political elites arrive at a common understanding of the balance of power, for example, or of ideology is left unexplored – not because it is uninteresting or irrelevant to the causal processes described herein, but because I have yet to find a constructivist account (or a historical one, for that matter) that suggests that the origins of such understandings can be accounted for in the same way across many states and at different times, except in the broadest terms. That is, I remain unconvinced that the origins of ideas and meanings are systematic enough that they can be usefully "hard-wired" into a causal model. Indeed, if they were, they could be predicted, and the model of their origins would thereby be falsified.

There is one exception to this generalization, and that has to do with the international socialization effects posited by constructivist scholars of international relations. Wendt (1999, 170), for example, points to socialization as the process by which identities and interests are formed; Klotz (1995), who highlights the role of international norms in the definition of American interests in South Africa, notes that "[c]onstructivist theory... claims that agents and structures reconstitute each other in an iterative process" (478).[69] What the simplest possible variant of this argument implies, in terms of the nested politics model, is that the worldviews of states converge over time. The dynamic model described herein provides the perfect opportunity to flesh out the implications of such a process, though the process is a crude one and the conclusions should be considered quite speculative, mostly offered by way of food for thought.

The constructivist claim about socialization leads to two claims about what I have called a state's worldview. The first claim is that, over time, state interaction leads states to emphasize the same dimensions of the international system to the same degree.[70] The second claim is that ideal points along those dimensions will converge over time. If both of these processes actually occur, as long as any single Great Power cares at all about military competition at the onset of the process, the result should be an equal distribution of realized capabilities.

I have illustrated this process in Figure 2.8. The world depicted in this graph is precisely the same as the one in Figure 2.6, with one exception: at time 12, a process of socialization begins in which the emphases that the two states place on the different

---

[69] See also the essays in Checkel (2007), which are notable for their willingness to cross rationalist-constructivist boundaries.

[70] Wendt (1999, 324–335). In fact, such a process is posited by Waltz as well, but not as a result of mere socialization: "Competition produces a tendency toward the sameness of the competitors" (1979, 127).

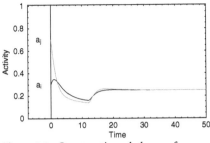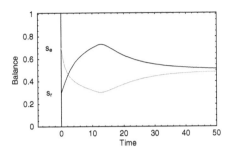

Figure 2.8. Constructing a balance of power.

dimensions of the system start to change. Over time, each state's worldview becomes more like the other's.[71]

As the states' worldviews change, their constituencies come to emphasize the same *desiderata* in the demands that they place on the leadership. The leadership, in turn, complies by increasing its level of activity and changing the thrust of its policies to capture more of its constituency's newly relevant resources. In the end, worldviews are constant across states and – as the previous section demonstrates – the result is an equal distribution of resources across spheres.

This conclusion does not imply that the process of socialization implies a balance of power, strictly speaking. It does, however, suggest that socialization can facilitate such a balance. As the previous sections have demonstrated, the realist balance of power rests on two assumptions not typically mentioned by realists – homogeneity of worldviews and similarity in levels of latent capabilities. This argument demonstrates that socialization can help to produce more homogeneous worldviews across states, thereby fulfilling one of the two prerequisites.

Finally, it is worth addressing the question of whether anything important has been left out of the theory – that is, whether any relationships that have not been theorized up to this point should be included in the model as well. I now turn to this issue.

Second-order effects

It would be impossible to include in the model every relationship between variables that has ever been hypothesized, simply because, at one time or another, theorists have asserted that every part of the nested politics model described earlier causes

---

[71] For the sake of illustration it is assumed that their ideal points along those dimensions are already the same. A process by which this outcome might plausibly occur is described in Appendix A and illustrated in Figure A.1. The process of socialization seems quite abrupt – the distributions of power and markets shift dramatically once socialization has begun. By time 17, *i*'s and *j*'s worldviews have converged, and by time 25 they have achieved perfect balance in both the economic and *realpolitik* spheres. The results were produced by a model that assumes fairly intense socialization processes. The degree of intensity could be modified, but this is merely an illustration, and the time units are arbitrary in any event.

every other part of the model. The abundance of potential second-order effects,[72] the often contradictory claims that they imply, and the fact that each is supported by at least some evidence suggests the absence of a consistent causal impact across time and across countries.[73]

This is the primary reason that these second-order effects have not been hard-wired into the model. One reason for this decision is that existing scholarship on these effects, for the most part, suggests that they are not consistent enough across states and across time to warrant inclusion in the model. The foundations of the model – ideal points and issue salience, the state as preference aggregation mechanism, the conjunction of preference and power that drives action, and the way in which action produces results – are intended to be general, and timeless, enough that most scholars would agree that something like this occurs in the real world, whether or not they agree that the model as written down here precisely captures it. As the following discussions should demonstrate abundantly, this cannot be said of the vast majority of proposed second-order effects. Another reason is that the complexity of any theoretical model must be limited if it is to produce useful and interesting insights about the world.[74] It is difficult to find a variable in social science that someone does not think is caused by *something*, but that fact alone does not justify an endless backward quest for the First Cause of the Universe. A third reason is purely technical – a model in which everything is endogenous would contain an insufficient amount of exogenous variation to permit testing of any kind.

It may nevertheless be worthwhile to spend a little time exploring second-order relationships before proceeding further. They give us some ideas about the kinds of causal forces that might have some impact on the basic elements of the model themselves – the sources of changes in worldviews, perhaps, or sources of change within states' political systems, or even changes *of* political systems. In this capacity, the guidance that they offer us is often fickle: the relationships that they collectively posit are occasionally contradictory, often contingent, and almost always far from certain. But they might, in some particular cases, prove to be very important, and especially in the historical section of this book it would be wise to keep them in mind.

What are some of the possible second-order effects – that is, what according to political scientists, are some of the potential sources of the variables taken to be exogenous here?

For structural realists, worldviews are believed to be shaped by the anarchic nature of the interstate system and the subsequent need to safeguard their citizenry against attack. Anarchy generates the need for self-help on the part of the state, which in turn

---

[72] A *second-order relationship* is one in which the cause (call it X) of a particular effect (call it Y) is itself caused by some prior factor (call it W). W, typically, is thought to be an important prior cause of Y to the extent that the relationship between W and X is a regular one.

[73] Both are implied by the fact that quite a few causes are thought to explain the same effect in different cases, an example of substitutability.

[74] I once had the pleasure of attending a talk by a professor of economics who was asked whether some variable of interest was endogenous to his model. He replied, "No, but it's endogenous to other people's models." A clearer statement of the collective nature of social research could hardly be imagined.

promotes balancing behavior, coalition formation, and all of the different interactions that come under the heading of power politics. Other states are evaluated in terms of the danger that they pose to the physical security and autonomy of one's own state. The relationship is such a strong one – deviant states are either socialized or eliminated – that worldviews to neorealists are thought to be largely epiphenomenal, meaning simply that, although they exist and play the role that I have assigned to them, they are completely determined by the necessities of competition within the international system.

That said, there is significant disagreement within the more general realist camp regarding what exactly an anarchic, power-centric worldview implies for state preferences. Waltz (1979, 118) waffles eloquently and succinctly when he writes that states, "at a minimum, seek their own preservation and, at a maximum, drive for universal domination." Such a statement has the advantage that it can hardly be wrong, but absent more details it tells us little. Two questions must be answered: what, specifically, is the focus of the state's attention in a *realpolitik* world, and what are the implications of the answer to this question for its desire for power?

There are two answers to the first question: power and security. For some, following Hans Morgenthau (1948, ch. 3), whatever a state's long-term goals are, they must be obtained with power, so regardless of the state's worldview it will seek power. Others, like Waltz (1988), argue that "the ultimate concern of states is not for power but for security." The distinction is far from irrelevant; as John Herz (1951) and later Robert Jervis (1978), pointed out, too much power can detract from security by posing a threat to one's neighbors and needlessly provoking opposition.

Regarding the second question, Arnold Wolfers (1962, ch. 6) set the tone for the "revisionist" vs. "status quo" debate that has followed, in one guise or another, for five decades. Realists who focus primarily on security, most notably Waltz (1979), Jack Snyder (1985), and Stephen Van Evera (1985), argue that states seek to maximize security by optimizing rather than maximizing power. They have therefore been dubbed "defensive realists." Offensive realists, by contrast, equate power maximization with security maximization: as John Mearsheimer (2001, 21) puts it, "the international system forces great powers to maximize their relative power because that is the optimal way to maximize their security."[75]

Regardless of whether it is offensive or defensive, realism assumes that a single issue, relative capabilities, dominates the state's decision calculus: "statesmen think and act in terms of interests defined as power" (Morgenthau 1948, 5). Most other approaches posit, implicitly or explicitly, a hierarchy of issues that motivate state behavior and in which no issue necessarily dominates.[76] Mearsheimer (2001, 46) admits that states pursue other goals but insists that they do so only to the extent that such goals further the state's security – an inversion of Morgenthau, who asserts that power and security are sought in order to further the state's other goals.

Domestic politics and the structure of the state are also thought to play either an active or a permissive role in influencing the worldview of the constituency. One of the

[75] Grieco (1997, 186–191) provides a concise summary of this debate.
[76] See, for example, Keohane and Nye (1989, 11–19).

clearest examples of active influence is the remarkable ability of communist governments, once in power, to propagate an official worldview consistent with communist
ideology. It is certainly true that adherence to such worldviews at the mass level is
typically aided by the specter of prison or death or both; nevertheless, a substantial
number seem to swallow Stanislaw Witkiewicz's fictional "pill of Murti-Bing," the
metaphorical medication that permits them to exchange their doubts and worries
for the serenity of ideological conviction (Milosz 1953; Witkiewicz 1977). As to the
permissive role of state structure, Jeffrey Checkel (1993, 1997) and Thomas Risse-
Kappen (1994) argue that new ideas about the fundamental nature of international
security that eventually supplanted communism in the Soviet Union were present in
transnational networks of potential policy entrepreneurs, but that differences in the
structure of domestic political systems influenced both the probability that those ideas
would reach the leadership level and their degree of influence should they manage
to do so. Snyder (1991) argues that extremely late industrialization leads to domestic
political instabilities that require "mythmaking" on the part of the leadership. The latter eventually precipitates a change in the state's worldview, as the "myths of empire"
are adopted and states' demand for power increases accordingly. And so on.

Yet another oft-cited source of state worldviews is identity, which is emphasized
most heavily by scholars writing in the constructivist tradition. To constructivists,
worldviews are shaped not by anarchy or by the exigencies of domestic politics but
rather by state identities: worldviews are the too often invisible link between identities
and interests.[77] Moreover, although states might construct a *realpolitik* worldview
(Johnston 1995), they need not do so: Alexander Wendt (1999) outlines three "cultures
of anarchy" that are differentiated in part by the degree to which the states within
them seek to eliminate one another.[78]

Finally, it is possible that the sources of state worldviews may be brought about by
factors entirely outside of the general explanatory framework devised here – they are
simply given. Students of nationalism disagree over the question of whether national
identities and their associated worldviews are *instrumental* for the achievement of
some other end (say, statehood – see e.g., Tilly 1975) or *primordial* (Geertz 1973) –
that is, exogenous. Though the latter view has fallen into disfavor, especially among
constructivists,[79] it is clear that a purely instrumental view of nationalism implies a
far greater degree of malleability of national identity than is supported by the available

---

[77] Some works do make this connection explicit; for an exemplar see Hopf (2002).

[78] In light of the previous discussion of revisionist vs. status quo powers it is worth noting that Wendt
explicitly denies (p. 262) that, for example, states in a Hobbesian anarchy will have revisionist
interests: "a state might actually have status quo interests, but the threat of the enemy forces it to
behave 'as if' it were a deep revisionist, on the principle of 'kill or be killed.'" This claim is difficult
to square with his earlier assertion (p. 105) that "states with status quo interests constitute one
kind of anarchy. Compare this to an anarchy constituted by states with revisionist interests. In
this world states will try to conquer each other, territorial property rights will not be recognized,
and weak states will have a high death rate" – a clear description of the Hobbesian anarchy that
he later describes but divorces from revisionism. (All emphases in original.)

[79] Chafetz, Spirtas, and Frankel (1999a, xviii, fn. 35). The malleable nature of identity as it is portrayed
by constructivists contrasts with the more fixed primordial view; it should therefore be no surprise
that the former have disavowed the latter. At the same time, the instrumental view implies a

evidence. For that reason, some scholars embrace a hybrid point of view that sees nationalism as malleable within limits and argues that, although while its malleability is evidence in favor of the instrumentalists, the limits are evidence in favor of the primordialists.[80] If these scholars are correct, an important element of nationalists' worldviews is exogenous.

At the level of domestic politics, too, political scientists have suggested a variety of second-order effects that are worth keeping in mind. The nature of the domestic political process is also subject to change as a result of causal factors across all levels of analysis, at least in theory. Arguments that posit systemic causes of changes in domestic regime type or in the alignment of domestic coalitions go, since Peter Gourevitch's (1978) seminal article, under the heading of "second-image reversed" theories. One of the clearest examples of such an argument is Otto Hintze's (1975) claim that the openness of a state's political institutions is a function of its geographical situation: in short, land powers require armies, those with quite a bit of shoreline require navies, and armies are more tempting instruments of despotism. More nuanced variations on the same theme have led some scholars to question the direction of the causal relationship(s) underlying the observation that democratic states tend overwhelmingly not to go to war with one another; peace, they argue, may cause democracy, not vice versa.[81]

Domestic politics can also play a substantial role in shaping domestic politics, a fact often lost in static theories of political behavior. The most obvious example is that of social revolutions.[82] In these situations, the state plays a dual role in its own demise. First, the method of preference aggregation employed by the state's political institutions leads to outcomes so unfavorable that a substantial percentage of its citizens try to discard those institutions in favor of new ones. Second, the state itself becomes unable to defend the existing order against its own citizenry. These two phenomena in combination prove overwhelming, the state succumbs to revolution, and a new domestic political system is born.[83]

Worldviews, too, can shape domestic politics. For example, most state have a relatively small number of people in the governing elite, and those leaders' right to govern must be legitimated somehow. The main reason is a utilitarian one: if a legitimating ideology is disseminated and at least somewhat believed, it is vastly more effective than force in the maintenance of the regime.[84] If people believe that, for whatever reasons, they *should* be ruled by a democratically elected government, or by the Son of Heaven, or by the vanguard of the proletariat, or by the first warrior to return to the

---

rationalist origin for nationalism that many would be loathe to embrace. Instrumentalism, it would seem, is the lesser of the two evils.

[80] For prominent examples see Erikson (1968), Smith (1991, esp. 24–26), and Laitin (1998).

[81] Thompson (1996); Wolfson, James, and Solberg (1998).

[82] Skocpol (1979).

[83] The example is not quite as clean as I have made it sound here. Skocpol also emphasizes the role of external strains, typically military competition, in the increasing debility of the state. This relationship is far from deterministic, however, as the cases of Prussia and Japan demonstrate (99–109).

[84] Schelling (1966, 8).

village with the egg of a sooty tern,[85] then they will readily submit to such leadership. More to the point, if worldviews are *not* consistent with domestic political systems, the leadership must constantly expend resources suppressing rebellion, sometimes at considerable cost to itself, and it is ultimately more likely to fail. Therefore, for the few to lead the many, leaders must often adapt to their constituencies' worldviews. In his massive study of the history of government, S. E. Finer (1997, 28–29) goes so far as to assert that

> it seems to me beyond a doubt that rulers cannot maintain their authority unless they are legitimated, and that they are legitimated by belief-systems. . . . Where the claim of a ruler is out of kilter with the prevalent belief-systems of the society, he must either 'change his plea', that is, make himself acceptable in terms of that belief-system, or else de-legitimize himself and fall.

This relationship is quite probably a reciprocal one: domestic institutions continually reinforce the worldviews that support them. Such belief-systems instill or reemphasize in the constituency a set of normative principles regarding human interactions. Those principles also apply to international relations and provide another way of understanding the system. Monarchies based on divine rights emphasize religious values. Communist systems proscribe capitalist exploitation. Representative governments, which are based on individuals' right to self-government, tend to emphasize the rights of the individual in other contexts as well (i.e., liberalism)[86] and *laissez-faire* capitalism. Beliefs, inspired by or consistent with the legitimating ideology, about the proper allocation of public goods will in turn focus the attention of the state on such allocations internationally and define its preferences regarding each.[87]

The sources of domestic politics could also be largely exogenous. The domestic political systems most readily cited in support of this argument are those that are extreme or incomprehensible in some way. Few theories, surely, would claim to predict the Easter Islanders' remarkable ornoocracy. We certainly hope that Hitler's Third Reich falls into this category: although some fairly radical response to Weimar Germany's dire economic straits could perhaps be anticipated, the particular form that the response took is more readily understood as the result of one man's psychosis than as the product of more systematic factors.[88] Nevertheless, the history of government is replete with innovation, and quite a bit of what we now take for granted as part and parcel of government has its roots in the idiosyncratic inspiration of some ancient ruler.[89]

---

[85] This system survived for some time among the Easter Islanders; see Keegan (1993, 24–28). As a rather minimalist form of selection among potential rulers, it represented a desperately creative waystation on the Easter Islanders' descent from the relative stability of traditional one-person rule into societal disintegration.

[86] By which I mean classical Western, rather than American, liberalism – the belief in positive freedoms (freedom to speak, to associate, etc.), negative freedoms (freedom from arbitrary authority, from oppression, etc.), and representative political institutions.

[87] This is Moravcsik's "ideational liberalism" (1997, 525).

[88] cf. Goldhagen (1996).   [89] On this topic, Finer's text is indispensable.

Even power, which is often treated as if it were independent of other parts of a theory, may or may not be the result of second-order effects. A few pages ago we noted that realists have attempted to undercut constructivists by arguing that ideas are merely a direct function or reflection of power; it should come as no surprise that constructivists have returned the favor. In fact, arguments that power is a function of ideas range across a fairly broad spectrum. At one end, William Wohlforth (1993) argues for joint causation between perceptions and power: he asserts that perceptions of power rather than power itself drive outcomes, but he also notes that "differences in perceptions of power . . . are related to the mix of resources available to a given state's leadership" (303). Wendt makes an argument different more in degree than in kind when he argues that the extent to which nuclear weapons constitute a threat depends in large part on who owns them; material factors still play some role in determining a state's power, but he makes a case for the primacy of ideas (1999, 96–113). At the far end of the spectrum are the postmodernists, such as David Campbell (1998), who argues for example that the ability of America to get exercised over the invasion of Kuwait in 1990 is evidence that power and threat need possess no material basis at all.

The form of domestic politics, too, can have an impact on power. Harold and Margaret Sprout (1951) provide an early post-war tally sheet of the relative advantages and disadvantages of democracy and totalitarianism in terms of their effects on state power: democracies, they assert, are disadvantaged by their inability to maintain a standing army for long periods, their inability to engage in power politics, their inability to rally behind a single goal, their need to engage in public discussions of policy in which private information cannot be revealed, and their relative vulnerability to ideological infiltration. In contrast to these points, a "democratic efficacy" school has arisen in recent years to argue that democracies have substantial advantages in war-fighting due to their tendency to devote greater resources to security (Lake 1992).[90] Fareed Zakaria (1998) argues that America's increasing willingness to convert capabilities to power in the late 1800s and early 1900s and its consequent rise to global power were a result of the impact of industrialization on the balance of power between the executive and legislative branches.

Power also has a way of being its own cause, though both positive and negative feedback are possible. Certainly, the offensive realists cited earlier express concerns that very powerful states will seek to increase their capabilities further via conquest, a process that ensures that power will "snowball." Robert Gilpin (1981), in contrast, argues that a host of factors, from diseconomies of scale to internal fragmentation, will ensure that increasingly powerful states face diminishing marginal returns over time; for that reason, patterns of growth tend to taper off over time.

Related to this argument is the idea that action causes power, or changes in realized capabilities. Indeed, one form of action that is occasionally observed is the arms buildup. It hardly seems desirable to include this as a constant relationship, however,

---

[90] The evidence in favor of this claim – democracies' apparent advantage in war fighting – may instead be due to the pressures of democratic political structures, which encourage leaders to pick fights that they can win; see Gelpi and Griesdorf (2001) and Reiter and Stam (2002). Bueno de Mesquita, Morrow, Siverson, and Smith (1999) hypothesize both processes.

because the effects of action on power are so multifaceted. One form of action might be signing an alliance – a behavior that, by inducing a form of moral hazard, could well allow a state to decrease its own levels of armaments. Sometimes states act in order to secure multilateral arms reductions or arms limitations. States may also seek to influence an ongoing contest among other participants by aiding one of the parties, which might have the perverse effect of decreasing the aid-granting state's relative capabilities. And much normal activity consists of utilizing the realized capabilities that one already possesses rather than augmenting it.[91]

By far the most common way of dealing with power, however, regardless of whether the study is primarily empirical or theoretical, is to treat it as though it were entirely exogenous. The distinction between latent and realized capabilities is typically ignored rather than explained[92]: measures like the Correlates of War project's aggregate indicator of capabilities are adopted uncritically, despite the fact that some of its elements (iron/steel production, energy consumption, urban population, urban agglomeration, and total population) are indicators of latent capabilities whereas others (military personnel and military expenditures) are indicators of realized capabilities.

It is impossible, of course, to compose a comprehensive list of every possible second-order connection among the different elements of the model. Many curious readers will probably have started to formulate an objection along the lines of "Why isn't there a connection in the model between . . . ?" – and I hope that this section has provided a response, if not to the specific objection then at least one that will apply to it. The short answer is that, in many individual cases, there may well be such a connection. However, at the level of more general theory the goal is to select only the elements that recur regularly across systems and across time, rather than the ones that have had an impact (however substantial) in a few cases.

Conclusion

This chapter has described a theory of international politics that consists of three nested levels of interaction. First, it has argued that a state's constituency has a worldview, a set of structured ideas that determine the dimensions of the international system that are deemed relevant to the state's security policy, and therefore to their ideal

---

[91] I was nevertheless curious enough about this link to run some preliminary analyses of the relationship between levels of activity of all of the Great Powers in one time period and changes in the relative capabilities of each in the next. Under the assumption that each state acts primarily to increase its own capabilities, one would expect positive relationships between one's own activities and one's own level of relative capabilities and negative relationships between the activities of others and one's own relative capabilities. The signs of the relationships were right in barely more than half (13 of 25) cases, and levels of both substantive and statistical significance were without exception so miniscule that they inspired no confidence whatsoever. The results looked remarkably like those that would have been produced by random data, save that in the case of random data one would have expected at least one of the coefficients to be significant at the 0.05 level just as a result of chance.

[92] Though see Olson and Zeckhauser (1966), Palmer (1990), Morrow (1993), Sorokin (1994), and Mearsheimer (2001).

points along those dimensions and to the salience of each. Second, it has argued that states function by aggregating the preferences of their constituencies and passing those aggregate preferences along to leaders. Finally, it has claimed that leaders of states, compelled by the preferences of their constituencies, compete in the international arena over fixed resources, and the extent to which they succeed is influenced both by the latent capabilities of their states and by the intensity with which other states are competing for the same resources.

The theory represents a synthesis of disparate elements from a variety of distinct (albeit occasionally somewhat overlapping) theoretical paradigms. There are two major advantages to such a synthesis. First, it permits a much wider range of insights from a wider range of scholars to be brought to bear on a given question than would otherwise be the case. Second, in combination with the empirical sections to follow, it allows us to determine which of those insights are most useful in understanding the sources of change in Great Power politics.

In the following two chapters, I turn to the historical record to evaluate the theory that I have just described. In the first, I take a broad look at data from three international systems spanning nearly two centuries, to assess whether the relationships to be found in the data are consistent with the theory. In the second, I take a deeper look at three individual cases, one from each period, in which most of the variables in the model remain more or less constant but one changes substantially.[93] Each of these cases – the polarization of Europe after the Treaty of Vienna, the American retreat from isolationism, and the end of the Cold War – highlights the key causal mechanism posited by the model: state activity creates a change in the structure of the international system, and that change, in turn, prompts a reaction on the part of other states. Moreover, each of these cases has, until now, been viewed as distinct; I hope to demonstrate that they can be understood as special cases of a more general phenomenon, that of systemic politics.

---

[93] Choosing the cases in this manner permits me to make relatively unambiguous predictions based on the theory: the aggregate effect of many small changes in many variables would be virtually impossible to derive qualitatively (this is, in fact, one of the strengths of the statistical model). Examining isolated cases in more depth also allows me to trace the causal process, or mechanism, at work and assess the extent to which it corresponds to the theoretical model.

3 | *System, process, and evidence*

In this chapter I describe the procedures by which I have attempted to evaluate the theory's predictions. I set out to evaluate the theory in the context of the three European systems that existed between 1815 and 1991 – the Vienna system, the interwar system, and the Cold War system. In each case, the geographic scope of the system is confined to the European continent, the relationship of the structure of the system to the actors is causally homogeneous over time,[1] and the actors are understood to be those Great Powers or superpowers whose involvement in the affairs of the continent is a necessary factor in the calculations of the others. Europe is a natural choice of domain in each period, because the histories of these periods tend overwhelmingly to describe events and actors within the region; all of the Great Powers, with the exception of the United States, were European, and as a result they tended overwhelmingly to focus on one another and on the other states within the region when formulating and enacting security policy.[2]

The goal of the first half of the chapter is to explain the logic behind the choice, coding, and when necessary gathering of the data used to test the theory described in the previous chapter. To provide a preview, and to serve as a reference in what follows, those data are summarized in Table 3.1. As the discussion so far has suggested, I conclude that Great Powers in the past 200 years have largely focused on power and ideology when thinking about security; these concepts represent the structural dimensions of interest. Nevertheless, as that discussion demonstrates, there are substantial differences, from one period to the next, in how those concepts were understood, as their historical, financial, social, and technological context evolved with the times, and therefore how they should be operationalized.

---

[1] This criterion demarcates systems: substantial causal heterogeneity indicates that different rules are operative. See page 108 for a test of the claim that the 19th century represents a unified system.

[2] There is an intuitive correspondence between Bull and Watson's "necessary factor in the calculations of the others" criterion (1984, 1) and a directed version of the "politically relevant dyad" criterion often utilized by quantitative researchers (Maoz and Russett 1993) – that is, one in which Great Powers are relevant to distant small powers but not vice versa, because the latter cannot force themselves into the calculations of the former. Either formulation would argue for a largely European scope. It would be possible, especially in the Cold War years, to argue for the inclusion of the entire world in the system. The drawback to doing so, I think, is coherence: Europe was the source of the three huge wars that initiated each period, and within each period the actors were cognizant of the fact that Europe remained the region of primary importance as far as security was concerned.

Table 3.1. *Measures by period*

	19th Century	Interwar Period	Cold War
Balance of power	Standard deviation of latent capabilities of GPs	German percentage of GP realized capabilities	Diff. between US and Soviet realized capabilities
Arms levels	N/A	Total military expenditures	Mil. spending + nuclear warheads
Balance of ideology	Average regional Polity score	Average regional Polity score, rescaled	Average regional Polity score
Latent capabilities	Urban population Iron/steel production	Urban population Iron/steel production Energy consumption EOY gold reserves	Urban population Iron/steel production Energy consumption
Realized capabilities	Military expenditures Military personnel	Military expenditures Military personnel	Military expenditures Military personnel Nuclear warheads
Ideal points and salience (worldviews)	Assessed via survey of diplomatic historians		
State activity	Assessed via survey of diplomatic historians		

The goal of the second half of the chapter is to analyze the data, to determine the extent to which the argument in the previous chapter holds up to empirical scrutiny. Before turning to the data and analyses, however, it is necessary to discuss the historical context that informed the analysis of each period. This discussion will inform the subsequent section, which describes the data that were gathered and utilized to test the model, and the discussion of the data, along with the theoretical material from Chapter 2 and Appendix A, will inform the statistical modeling that follows.

The European system

1815–1914

The distinction between day-to-day interactive politics, on the one hand, and the sort of regulatory politics that is the focus of the nested politics model on the other, comes into sharp focus when we examine European international relations in the period between the Napoleonic Wars and World War I. Indeed, historians have argued that 1815 was a watershed year for regulatory politics in Europe:

> The impressive thing about the behaviour of the Powers in 1815 is that they were prepared, as they had never previously been prepared, to waive their individual

interests in the pursuit of an international system. This fact is not rendered any less impressive by the recognition that they were prepared to waive their individual interests because it was in their individual interests to do so.[3]

Schroeder (1994b) also argues that this change constituted a fundamental "transformation" in European politics. The European regulatory mechanism was crude when compared to, say, domestic political institutions, but it nevertheless performed some of the same functions.

One form of regulatory politics was based on the notion that war could be prevented if countries could be rendered unable to profit from it. Accordingly, regulation was to be accomplished by maintaining the balance of power. It must be emphasized that the distinction between the dog-eat-dog balance-of-power *politics* of the 18th century and the mutually reinforcing territorial settlement and legal superstructure that came to be called, perhaps misleadingly, the balance-of-power *system* in the 19th century is a critical one. Making this point most eloquently, and convincingly, is Schroeder (1994b): though he eschews the use of the phrase "balance of power," the international regime that he describes, in which states forego short-term gains in order to foster cooperation and peace, reasonably approximates a balance-of-power system in this sense.

The balance-of-power system had two main incarnations: the *static* version of balance-of-power theory emphasized equality of capabilities among units, whereas the *dynamic* version of balance-of-power theory emphasized equality of capabilities among coalitions.[4] To the believers in the static version, "balance of power" was a noun: if the capabilities of states could be made equal, the balance would deter aggression. To those desiring a dynamic balance, "balance of power" was a verb: the proper way of dealing with a threat was to balance against it.

Regardless of the form of balance sought, the emphasis was on the distribution of long-term, or latent, material capabilities and strategic assets of the Great Powers – those that could be brought to bear in an extended conflict such as the one just fought. Nevertheless, the ideal distribution of capabilities depended on whether one was a believer in the static or the dynamic version of the balance of power: a static balance required a relatively equal distribution, whereas a dynamic version permitted an unequal one (and even encouraged it, because the state taking the "balancer" role should ideally be considerably more powerful than the rest in order to perform its function).

It is reasonable to wonder, given both the length of the overall period and the fact that authorities like Schroeder (1994b) argue that the death of the Vienna system far predated the formal dissolution of the Concert system,[5] whether the claim that states

---

[3] Hinsley (1963, 197).

[4] The labels are my own. For a lucid dissemination on the general subject of the meaning of the balance of power see Haas (1953). I have no intention of delving further into definitional intricacies, but the interested reader will find food for thought in Morgenthau (1948, 132–133), Rosecrance (1963, ch. 11), Kissinger (1957, 146–147), Waltz (1979, 117–123, 163–170), and Craig and George (1983, ch. 3).

[5] Here I use "Vienna system" to refer to the regime that Schroeder describes, and "Concert system" to refer to the formal institutions that it created. The latter survived at least until the Concert of Berlin in 1878, but the extent to which the norms that prompted the creation of the institution were still operative at that time is debatable.

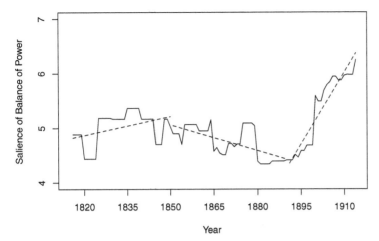

Figure 3.1. Estimates of the salience of the distribution of capabilities, averaged across all five Great Powers. *Source:* historians' survey.

focused on the distribution of material capabilities throughout the entire period – a claim most obviously true in the earliest years – is warranted. Because of the general interest in this period, and in the balance of power within it, this question merits particular attention. There are three reasons to believe that a sustained focus on the balance of power is a plausible assumption.

First, as mentioned earlier, a focus on the distribution of material capabilities is not unique to the Vienna regulatory mechanism: once that mechanism broke down, the one that took its place emphasized the same quantity for different reasons. As the general ideological preference shifted toward states whose borders corresponded with the boundaries of their national units, a static balance became implausible, but it was replaced by a different mechanism, one in which equality among coalitions mattered. This was especially true toward the end of the century, when the system of flexible coalitions maintained by Bismarck broke down and the inexorable formation of opposing camps prompted increased interest in the question of the distribution of their capabilities.

Second, as the following sections make clear, the empirical results do incorporate the salience of each structural dimension: different spheres are salient to different actors to different degrees at different times. So even if the distribution of material capabilities does become less salient at some point as a structural dimension, it will be factored out of actors' decisions and deemphasized as a target of their actions accordingly. In fact, we can examine estimates of the average salience of the balance of power to the Great Powers, based on the data described later (see p. 86), to assess the extent to which the historians surveyed believe the salience of the balance of power, on the whole, to have waxed and waned throughout the period. The overall impression gleaned from this exercise, which is represented in Figure 3.1, is that, while there was indeed a significant decrease in salience of the balance of power in the middle of the period (roughly 1850–1890), it remained a substantial focus of actors' attention throughout (greater than 4 on a 1–7 scale). In fact, according to the historians, the

salience of the balance of power during the later *Weltpolitik* period actually exceeded that of the earlier Vienna period.[6]

Finally, it is possible that, even though changing salience is captured by the model, there was a larger structural change in the relationship between state and structure at one or more of these points: it is not a given, for example, that states will be as reactive to changes to the dynamic balance of power as they would be to changes in the static balance, even if the two are equally salient – admittedly a subtle point. Nevertheless, such a qualitative shift would be captured by a test of structural stability. The results of that test (p. 108) indicate, in short, that no evidence of such a structural change is present in the data.

A second regulatory mechanism revolved around the balance of political ideology rather than the balance of power as a guarantor of peace. Here, political ideology is intended, not in a critical or partisan sense, but in a neutral, positivist vein: political ideologies are sets of related ideas that drive constituents' evaluations of right and wrong and their perceptions of the social status quo and prescribe (and proscribe) action.[7] As a result, governments that claim legitimacy based on a given ideology and act in a manner consistent with its prescriptions can sustain their legitimacy.[8] The sustenance of domestic legitimacy, in turn, reinforces a belief in the universality of the norms and beliefs that underpin it, which, under the right external circumstances, can produce a foreign policy that largely reflects the values that support the regime.

In the case of Vienna, those whose focus was the sphere of ideology generally saw an overwhelming preponderance of shared conservative (or "legitimist") governments as conducive to peace. The principle of legitimacy encompassed both the restoration of monarchs to their thrones and, by some accounts, the recreation of the *status quo ante bellum* in regard to the territorial distribution of states.[9] The logic linking legitimacy to peace was fairly straightforward: the French Revolution, based on liberty and constitutionalism, had snowballed into a general war of immense proportions. Future

---

[6] Interestingly, and encouragingly, the three periods highlighted by the illustration correspond quite closely to the three balance-of-power subsystems identified by Craig and George (1983, ch. 1).

[7] This aggregated definition relies most heavily on those of Seliger (1976, 11), McClosky (1964, 362), and Mullins (1972).

[8] Finer (1997, 29).

[9] See Holmes (1982, 165), for example, for the more restricted version – "the right or title to rule ascribed to hereditary kings" – and Rich (1992) for the more expansive. The latter goal was considerably more difficult to accomplish in 1815 as, e.g., the Holy Roman Empire was clearly beyond salvation, and if it is included in the definition the myriad conflicts with the requirements of an equitable distribution of capabilities become obvious. It is also worth noting that Schroeder (1994b, 530) argues that legitimacy referred to nothing more nor less than the rule of law. Although I am loathe to attempt to adjudicate, it does seem that historical consensus favors the more restricted version of the first definition, as do certain historical details – Metternich's reactions to the entirely legal grant of a Portugese constitution by Dom Pedro, for example, or the plot to overthrow Murat prior to Napoleon's return. On a somewhat more speculative note, it seems to me that Schroeder's understanding of legitimacy and the more orthodox version can be reconciled if we add the caveat that, according to the legitimist powers, only hereditary monarchs are capable of exercising legitimate legal control over the state. Indeed, were it not so, Frederick William's unwillingness to accept the crown of Germany from the Frankfurt Parliament in 1849 – the infamous "crown from the gutter" – would be difficult to explain.

revolutions of the same sort could therefore not be trusted, so the best guarantor of peace was continued conservative rule.

It is worth noting that, whereas the balance of power focused mainly on opportunity, this mechanism focused primarily on willingness.[10] Kissinger (1994, 77) neatly captures the essence of the distinction when he writes that "[t]he balance of power inhibits the *capacity* to overthrow the international order; agreement on shared values inhibits the *desire* to overthrow the international order." Here, the emphasis was not on capabilities but rather on the form of government: liberalism and liberalization were seen as the most serious threats to the peace.

The structure of the international system throughout this period, therefore, consists primarily of two dimensions: the balance of power and the balance of ideology, or the extent to which liberal government had spread throughout the continent.

1919–1939

Regulatory politics were evident in the interwar period as well. Indeed, the institutional infrastructure established in the wake of World War I – most notably, the Treaty of Versailles and the League of Nations, but also the disarmament conferences of Washington, London, and Geneva – was an explicit attempts to create an international environment in which disagreements among nations would be less likely both to occur and to escalate to war. As might be anticipated, the main dimensions of regulatory politics in this period were an extension of the trends evident in the latter part of the 19th century as well as a reaction to the carnage of World War I.

The ideological conflict between legitimist and liberal had been decided rather concretely in favor of the latter: in the immediate post-World War I period, Europe as a whole reached a level of democracy that it would not re-attain until 1989.[11] Nevertheless, despite this apparent unity there were large and growing cracks in the foundations of liberalism in Europe: its shortcomings had manifested themselves in the economic conditions of the last quarter of the 19th century, and many citizens and politicians had begun to yearn for alternative social orders.[12] As a result, the period was characterized by a greater range of rival ideologies than either the post-Napoleonic era or the Cold War. Advocates of these ideologies agreed that this diversity of philosophies posed a danger to the peace, though they differed, predictably, in just how it did so.

Liberals, like Woodrow Wilson, typically saw the existence of autocracy as a threat to the peace. Wilson's view of history involved a steady progression toward a more democratic world, and he believed firmly that the spread of democracy would be beneficial both because of its potential to defuse revolution[13] and because of its

---

[10] See Starr (1978) for a discussion of the breadth of the applicability of these two concepts.

[11] The simple mean of European states' Polity scores, discounting states undergoing transitions, interruptions, and interregna, reached 6.5 in 1918, a score almost exactly equivalent to its score in 1989.

[12] On this period see Dangerfield (1997) for England in particular; Stone (1984) expands Dangerfield's thesis and demonstrates its applicability to the Continent.

[13] On the relationship between revolution and war see Walt (1992).

dampening effects on external aggression. Wilson's vision for a peaceful postwar world, moreover, was centered on an association among free and democratic states that would, when the occasion arose, come together to preserve peace. Democracy was crucial to the plan: "A steadfast concert for peace can never be maintained except by a partnership of nations" because "[n]o autocratic government could be trusted to keep the peace."[14] In a very real sense, Wilson's plan for a system of collective security to replace the old balance-of-power system was not to be an alien system imposed upon the states of the world in direct contradiction to the dictates of their nature, as critics have since argued,[15] but rather the natural international expression of a democratic domestic order.

The liberal vision for postwar peace was far from universal, of course: in Soviet Russia, V. I. Lenin's victorious Bolsheviks had an entirely different view of the march of history. Blinded by theory, the Bolsheviks expected that, in the context of the momentous internal contradictions of capitalist imperialism, the Soviet example would prompt spontaneous and successful communist uprisings throughout Europe. When that hope met with only very limited and transitory success in such places as Hungary and Bavaria, the Bolsheviks proved willing to advance the cause of world revolution by force if necessary, diverting Red Army troops from their struggles in the Russian Civil War to drive Polish troops back to Warsaw. When their military effort stalled and it became clear that neither example nor brute force would succeed, they fell back on promoting communist revolution abroad, but the failure of an attempted uprising by German communists in March, 1921, and rising opposition to the Bolshevik regime at home, prompted a period of internal consolidation. Nevertheless, when the Union of Soviet Socialist Republics was formed, it was the embodiment of an ideology that was, by its nature, devoted to the overthrow of the existing order throughout Europe.[16]

Communism was explicitly a response to the shortcomings of capitalism; fascism, by contrast, was much more a response to the shortcomings of parliamentary democracy. Liberal distrust of executive authority had led the newly democratic states of Europe to rely heavily on political instruments that were subject to popular control – parliaments elected via proportional representation systems – and to vest substantial power in the legislative branch. The results, while democratic, were far from orderly, and for a time politicians sought a more authoritarian solution to the problem of national governance, especially but not exclusively during the period of the Depression. Right-wing governments arose in Italy, Austria, Portugal, Spain, and Romania. At first, authoritarian rule was seen as no threat; indeed, George Kennan proposed "benevolent despotism" for the United States.[17] It was not until the rise to power of the Nazi party in Germany that the dangers of malevolent despotism were made clear. In contrast to Soviet leaders, Hitler did not seek to overthrow existing states by promoting like parties within their borders; it soon became clear, however, that

[14] Ambrosius (1987, chs. 1–2, p. 31); see also Knock (1992, 112–113 and *passim*).
[15] For an eloquent example see Carr (1939, 27–31).
[16] Sontag (1971, ch. 3).   [17] Mazower (1998, ch. 1).

Nazism, if left unchecked, posed a much more direct military threat to their very existence.[18]

In many ways, these developments represented the progression of trends already present in the 19th century – Wilson's desire to forestall revolution with representation, for example, echoes that of Palmerston, and Mussolini's desire to quash republican governments in favor of order bears at least a family resemblance to that of Nicholas I. The ideological breadth of European politics might be reaching an apogee, but in many ways the logic of the conflict that resulted was similar.[19]

Most of the major changes in regulatory politics had to do with the perceived relationship between power and security. The most subtle, yet perhaps most important, of these changes was a reversal of the roles of latent and realized power. When the Vienna statesmen sought to achieve a balance of power, they did so by adjusting the latent power of the major states in a manner designed to discourage aggression by depriving each of the ability to prevail in a large-scale, prolonged, bloody conflict with the others. Two developments in the intervening years changed the way that statesmen thought about the problem of preventing war. First, the spread of the liberal democratic ideal made the option of bartering and absorbing small nations in order to balance latent power resources much less appealing: equality of power would have to be obtained, more or less, within parameters that were established by movements for national independence. Second, World War I demonstrated that it need not take decades to accomplish massive bloodshed: whereas the Napoleonic Wars took somewhere between 2.5 and 3.5 million military lives over the course of sixteen years, World War I managed to deprive 9 million soldiers of their lives in roughly a quarter of the time. Under the circumstances, adjusting latent power was a much less feasible method of preventing war: the contest was likely to be decided far too quickly for latent rather than realized power to be decisive.

Realized power, however, could be manipulated, and it could be used to compensate for imbalances in latent power. It was precisely this goal that the French in particular pursued, proposing limitations on German military power in the hopes of keeping Germany in what Wolfers calls a state of "artificial inferiority" – artificial in the sense that its realized power was not to be permitted to correspond to its latent power.[20] Toward this end, Articles 159–210 of the Treaty of Versailles dealt exhaustively with

---

[18] Lukacs (1998, 162). Lukacs uses the lack of ideological support by Hitler for Nazi parties abroad to demonstrate that Hitler pursued a policy of *realpolitik*, a conclusion that would most likely horrify Bismarck; it seems more accurate to argue that Hitler pursued very ideological ends via traditional power-politics means. Works on Hitler's personal ideology are legion; a well-respected and persuasive example is Jäckel (1972).

[19] It could be argued that international economic activity should constitute a dimension of regulatory politics in this period as well, especially given the importance of reparations payments and the Young Plan for peace at the beginning of the period and the dramatic impact of the Depression toward the end. My reasons for not doing so are that, although management of reparations payments was explicitly regulatory in nature, it does not follow that all economic activity was: most of it was simply interactive – trade for trade's sake – and no obvious subset presents itself as obviously regulatory of security affairs throughout the entire period.

[20] Wolfers (1966, 13).

military affairs: the victorious Allies unambiguously pursued a policy of promoting peace by establishing and maintaining a favorable distribution of existing military forces-in-being. In determining how to order the relationship between latent and realized power, in short, the question that should be asked is "What did states pursue with what?" – and in the interwar period, states pursued a certain balance of realized power, redressing imbalances when necessary by bringing to bear their industrial and financial resources.[21]

Another major change in the relationship between security and power had to do with the distribution of interest. After Vienna, France, devoid for the moment of Bonapartes, had been quickly reintegrated into the European system; Germany, whose aggression was thought to be less a result of form of government than of national character or national interests, was not – at least, not nearly to the same degree. From the onset, the balance of, say, French versus British capabilities was a matter of little concern. Rather, the focus was overwhelmingly on relative German capabilities. The term "balance" came to connote preponderance rather than equality, and in particular, a preponderance that would keep Germany in check.[22]

Finally, citizens and statesmen began to pay serious attention not just to the distribution of power but to *absolute* levels of power as well. The widespread perception that the prewar arms race had played a role in sparking the conflict spurred the belief that the outbreak of another war could be averted if arms levels were kept low. Public sentiment in democratic states ran strongly in favor of disarmament, and statesmen strove to achieve it in the Treaty of Versailles, the League of Nations, and sundry conferences devoted specifically to the subject. Accordingly, absolute aggregate capability levels, at this time, become a third structural dimension, distinct from the balance of capabilities, and a measure of the overall arms levels of nations – total military expenditures – is utilized to capture it.[23]

---

[21] See, e.g., Schweller (1998, 26), Bell (1997, ch. 11). Because it is difficult to argue for the absence of *some* feedback between latent and realized power, I forward this argument with some caution; nevertheless, it seems to me to be the most reasonable one under the circumstances. The structural dimension of interest should be the one upon which decision makers and constituents focus, and it is clear that during this period realized rather than latent military capabilities fit that description (though see Bariéty's [1977] massive work, the relevant section of which is summarized in English in Jacobson [1983, 627–628], for a plausible counterargument). One could, of course, endogenize both, but given the extreme rarity of the use of force in the interwar period it seems implausible to argue that military power was used regularly to redress the balance of latent capabilities, as it clearly was after Vienna (the exception, of course, being the French occupation of the Ruhr).

[22] See, for example, Wolfers (1966, 126), who argues that the French strove to maintain the *équilibre continental*, and that, in his words, "'*Equilibre*' in the French sense of the term called for the unquestioned preponderance of one group of powers, namely, the one which was backing the established order." Although the new Soviet state might not have been counted among the latter, in practice the Germans were a far more pressing concern from a military point of view.

[23] It would be ideal to use a measure of forces-in-being, but qualitative differences in forces as well as differing rates of obsolescence across countries and across time make them difficult to aggregate usefully; as a result, military expenditures are used as a proxy. It is worth noting that, in the context of the present study, this measure raises the issue that military expenditures may also reflect activity as much as forces-in-being, but given that arms levels are aggregated at the level of the system and there are a variety of forms of activity other than arms expenditure, the danger

In addition to these fairly subtle but nevertheless very important changes in the structure of the international system, there were changes in the actors as well. An independent Italy became a marginal, but increasingly prominent, member of the Great Power club, just as Austria, shorn of its multiethnic empire, dropped out. At the same time, the proven military reach and overwhelming postwar financial dominance of the United States made it unambiguously a state that had to be taken into account in the calculations of the Continental powers – a fact that would be obscured, rather than altered, by its (mostly illusory) withdrawals from European politics in the immediate postwar period and the mid-1930s.

1945–1993

World War II and its aftermath produced a system that was in many ways trans-formed. First, technology dramatically altered the meaning and the importance of the balance of power. As Schelling (1966, ch. 1) points out, the combination of aerial transportation, in the form of airplanes and missiles, and staggering firepower, in the form of ever-larger conventional and nuclear explosives, meant that it was no longer necessary to defeat the enemy to threaten the civilian population. Second, the further reduction of the Western European powers by depression and war and the rise of the United States meant that the system was transformed from a multipolar to a bipolar one: only two states, the United States and the Soviet Union, possessed the means to have decisive influence over the shape of the postwar security structure.[24]

The nature of the two states in question also contributed substantially to the structure of the system. The right-authoritarian governments of the interwar years had been swept away, and the main left-authoritarian government, despite staggering human losses in the war, had been dramatically strengthened in the three decades since its birth. In this context, Soviet leaders no longer felt the need to fall back on building communism in one country. As a result, the two states that shouldered the task of building a postwar order soon found that their domestic political ideologies played a powerful role in defining the context of their interaction. As Morgenthau (1948, 147) put it, the United States and the Soviet Union "compete with each other not only as the two political and military superpowers but also as the foremost representatives of two different political philosophies, systems of government, and ways of life."

The Americans of the postwar years were the heirs to the Wilsonian ideal, a form of classical liberalism (that is, liberalism in the European rather than American sense)

---

seems minimal. As a quick check, American and Soviet activity during the Cold War explain less than 10% of the variation in arms levels; although the percentage is considerably higher in the interwar period, it is still lower than the percentage of the variation in the aggregate Polity variable explained.

[24] To argue that the superpowers did not take material capabilities into account in their policies is, for these reasons, patently foolish. Nevertheless, realists of various stripes have disagreed over the question of whether or not they do so exclusively (see Rose 1998 for a review) and have often highlighted the extent to which American foreign policy in particular deviates from the requirements of power politics (Morgenthau 1952, though cf. Mearsheimer 2001, who argues that American national leaders speak the language of liberalism to mollify the masses while acting largely in accordance with *realpolitik* logic).

that emphasizes individual freedom as the ultimate good. The tradition, of course, had its roots in the formation of the American state and its independence from the tyranny of European monarchy.[25] Two elements of liberalism are generally emphasized in discussions of the American foreign policy tradition. The first is political: individual liberties are the highest values to be upheld; free political institutions are the best way to ensure individual liberties; therefore, free institutions are seen as the *sine qua non* of the just state. The second is economic: free trade is the engine of growth and collective prosperity and should therefore be implemented wherever and whenever possible.[26]

The main disagreement among Cold War historians arises from the question of which of these facets was the more important wellspring of American policy. So-called orthodox historians, represented by the work of Arthur Schlesinger, Jr. (see e.g., Schlesinger Jr. (1967)) and Herbert Feis (1970), emphasize the first facet and argue that Soviet ideological messianism posed a grave danger to the interests of the United States; adherents to the revisionist school, represented by the work of William Appleman Williams (1972), D. F. Fleming (1961), Gar Alperovitz (1994), and Walter LaFeber (1985), emphasize the second facet and argue that the free-market compulsion to expand trade ties and secure access to primary goods at the lowest possible cost drove the United States to pursue an "Open Door" policy that could not tolerate a separate communist sphere. A third school, labeled "post-revisionism" (Gaddis 1982, 1983), deemphasized the ideology of both states, rejecting in large part the image of American economic-imperial ambitions while incorporating insights regarding the use of America's economic and military strength to achieve its goals.

Since the end of the Cold War historians have struggled to achieve a larger, more synthetic understanding of the conflict, one that emphasizes not the importance of any one factor as much as the complex interconnections among many of them; Westad (2000) is an excellent exploration of these issues, and Suri (2002) and Leffler (2008) are solid early examples. The main point of contention across the various schools relates to the relative weighting of power and ideology in each state's worldview, with the post–Cold War perspective attempting the most evenhanded combination of the two: although concerns about power pervaded the Cold War, Leffler writes, "[t]he meanings attributed to developments in the international arena were influenced by ideological axioms and historical experience. . . . The Cold War lasted as long as it did because of the ways in which American and Soviet ideas intersected with evolving conditions of the international system" (Leffler 2008, 8, 452).

The Soviet worldview at the end of the war was, to say the least, radically different. One of the most consistent themes in Marxist analyses of inter-class relations is that of the "main contradiction"[27] that drives political evolution. To Lenin (1939), the main

---

[25] On this point see Perkins (1993).

[26] Some scholars emphasize the point that the effects of American liberalism on foreign policy are magnified by its absolutism; hence Hartz's (1955, 286) remark about the American oscillation "between fleeing from the rest of the world and embracing it with too ardent a passion."

[27] In Marxism, a "contradiction" refers broadly to the existence of groups with different preferences within a single system. The main contradiction within capitalism existed because of the fundamentally different preferences of the proletariat and the bourgeoisie. See Valdez (1993, 20–21) for an unusually clear discussion.

contradiction could be found within capitalism. Capitalism's excess production leads to a constant search for new markets (in the form of colonies), which eventually brings conflict. Meanwhile, capital accumulation leads to a falling rate of profit, economic crises, and a general worsening of the living conditions for the working class; as a result of the last factor, revolution soon occurs. The main contradiction, here, was between socialism and capitalism, though the contradiction within capitalism could still be counted on to hasten its demise. Over time, many Soviet scholars have argued, the role of ideology has gradually changed, becoming less of a guide to behavior over time and more of a means of legitimating policy – in other words, becoming one determinant of policy rather than the overriding priority.[28]

The structure of the system reflected these realities. To the extent that Soviet and American political legitimacy depended on the perpetuation of ideologies that were by their nature antithetical to one another, the balance between democratic and communist states remained a matter of utmost importance. Largely due to its role in perpetuating or possibly altering that distribution, the military balance between East and West constituted a security matter of the utmost importance. Finally, because of their ever-increasing lethality and the looming prospect that another world war could exterminate the species, controlling absolute levels of nuclear armaments, like conventional arms control in the previous period, became a key component of maintaining the stability of the system.

Who are the actors?

One could argue that an ideal systemic theory of politics would take into account the worldviews, capabilities, and activities of all of the actors in the system, just as a theory of planetary motion takes into account the sun, the major and minor planets, and their moons. Unfortunately, the requirements of gathering the requisite data on the smaller countries in the European system make such a task quite impossible, and modeling the impact of the behavior of every state in the system itself on the structure of the system, and vice versa, would be technically impossible (given the degrees-of-freedom issues involved). Moreover, from the point of view of theoretical parsimony, modeling the interactions of all of the actors in the system would be entirely undesirable even if it were possible: just as the geographers in Borges' parable had their empire-sized map consigned to the desert, so too would the results of a model of every last state in the system be consigned to a well-deserved obscurity. The most reasonable course of action, given the need for models that are manageable both empirically and theoretically, is to draw a line between the shapers and the shaped, the planets that draw smaller celestial bodies in their wake and those that are, for the most part, drawn.

Such a distinction is bound to be offensive, both to sensibilities and to reason. No resident of a small state wishes to believe that his or her country has no impact on international politics, and indeed, there are many examples of smaller states exerting a

---

[28] Aspaturian (1990, 7–13); Gurley (1976, 54); Zimmerman (1969, 161–162); Lynch (1987); Zubok and Pleshakov (1996, 95).

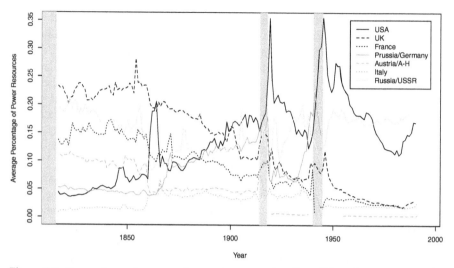

Figure 3.2. Comparison of average of power resources for all candidate Great Powers in the European system, 1815–1990. Gray regions – periods of general war – separate one system from another.

surprisingly impressive amount of leverage over large ones by, for example, setting the agenda for international discussions and acting as norm entrepreneurs (Ingebritsen, Neumann, Gstöhl, and Beyer 2006). It is nevertheless true that the structure of the system is overwhelmingly influenced by the actions of a small number of large states that conventionally go by the title either of Great Powers or, during the Cold War, superpowers.

What distinguishes these states from the others? The usual answer is power: a Great Power should have a fair bit of it, more than 10% of the system's capabilities on average according to some authors (Geller and Singer 1998), as well as interests that extend throughout the system in question and, arguably, recognition as a Great Power by others (see Danilovic 2002, ch. 2 and Appendix B for a survey). A glance at the distribution of resources relevant to capabilities (see Fig. 3.2)[29] demonstrates that in only one period, the Cold War, are the capabilities of the powers so dramatically separated as to permit a line to be drawn with great confidence, though the exclusion of Austria following the World War I seems uncontroversial.

The usual answer, therefore, is convincing, up to a point. To move beyond that point we must ask ourselves what makes it so – what general principle makes the 10% rule of thumb a good first cut? The most reasonable answer, it would seem, is Bull and Watson's definition of a system as a situation in which "the behaviour of each [actor] is a necessary factor in the calculations of the others"[30]: Great Powers were accorded the status of Great Powers precisely because they could not be excluded

---

[29] To be specific, the average percentage of the world total of military personnel, military expenditures, iron and steel production, total population, and urban population – in short, both latent and realized capabilities – over time. Source: Correlates of War data.

[30] Bull and Watson (1984, 1).

from deliberations regarding the fate of the continent. The 10% rule works fairly well because raw material capabilities correlate strongly, but not perfectly, with this status: the strongest states clearly compelled one another's attention, but the states near the 10% boundary are more questionable. To resolve these cases, we need to examine their particulars: factors such as geography and internal cohesion play a substantial role in determining, in this period, whether these powers ended up being necessary factors in the calculations of others.

The main arguments are likely to arise over Italy, the United States, and possibly Prussia prior to German unification, so these cases merit examination. In the years following unification, Italy rivaled Austria-Hungary in terms of its capabilities, but surpassed it in terms of its internal incoherence. In the eleven years that separated the establishment of the United Provinces of Central Italy in late 1859 and the successful siege of Rome in 1870, Italy was focused almost entirely on consolidation and unification of the peninsula. The Italians' success at state consolidation was due in large part to their judicious choice of Great Power allies and often came despite, rather than because of, the outcomes of the battles that they fought.[31] Italy's inability to bring force to bear in a contest with any of the European powers was apparent as late as 1881, when France established a protectorate over Tunis, 100 miles from Sicily and an obvious target for Italian expansion, and Italy was unable to do more than protest. The case for Italy as a Great Power is often based on its subsequent inclusion in the Triple Alliance, but in fact its participation in that alliance reflected the Italians' realization of their own impotence: as one member of Parliament put it succinctly, "Isolation means annihilation."[32]

The United States and Prussia follow remarkably similar trajectories in the 19th century: at the beginning of the period, by the usual 10% criterion neither qualifies as a Great Power, while at the end of the period both do. Nevertheless, geography plays a critical role in distinguishing between the two. When representatives of the members of the Quadruple Alliance arrived in Vienna in the fall of 1814 to prepare for the Congress, no formal distinction between greater and lesser powers existed. Before the Congress formally convened, however, the most powerful states of Europe had arrogated to themselves the authority to decide the most important questions that were to come before the Congress. As Nicolson (1946, 137) put it,

> It must be remembered that at that date the distinction between Great Powers and Small Powers – a distinction which even to this day is invidious and delicate – did not exist. It was born during that hurried fortnight between September 13 and October 1.

---

[31] Hence the question put to Bismarck by a Russian diplomat: "Why on Earth should Italy demand an increase of territory? Has she lost another battle?" (Wiskemann 2007, 52).

[32] The quotations can be found in Langer (1966, 220, 229). See also Sontag (1933, 22–26), who refers to Italy's "[d]ivision of objectives, chaotic internal politics, and limitless ambitions only imperfectly chastened by obvious lack of power." One might argue that Italy's place among the Great Powers of the interwar period is equally questionable, and indeed, it seems the most tenuous of the lot. Out of curiosity, I reran the initial interwar analyses described later without Italy, and I must admit that the results differed very little. For that reason, and because omission of a relevant state would have more serious implications than inclusion of an irrelevant one, I left it in.

The Great Powers – four at first, five once Talleyrand succeeded in insinuating France into the group and Spain had been decisively excluded – included Prussia, the weakest of them all. That was the case in large part because, despite its weakness relative to the remaining powers, its location made it essential from the start in resolving the outstanding territorial issues of the Congress and maintaining the Vienna settlement.[33]

The United States presents precisely the opposite outcome. Despite occasional flourishes of rhetoric like Canning's reference to calling upon the New World "to redress the balance of the Old," the United States did not substantially involve itself in the affairs of the European continent World War I, nor was it remotely essential for the resolution of conflicts. Indeed, the Monroe Doctrine, the development in the New World to which Canning was referring, which established the New World colonies as being within the American sphere of influence, also established the Old World as being outside of it. Only in 1898, with the defeat of the Spanish in the Spanish-American War, do most scholars credit the United States with having achieved Great Power status,[34] but even then its direct involvement in the security politics of the European subsystem remained virtually nonexistent until World War I was actually underway. In short, the United States, unlike Prussia, was never a necessary factor in the calculations of the European Powers from Vienna to World War I.

In the immediate postwar years, the rejection of membership in the League of Nations and America's apparent withdrawal to isolationism seem to argue for its continued exclusion from the ranks of the Great Powers. In fact, however, the League battle can best be seen as a fight between unilateralists and multilateralists, with a small band of "irreconcilables" ensuring that neither could constitute the necessary two-thirds majority. American influence was essential in the signing of the Washington Naval Treaty, the withdrawal of the French after the occupation of the Ruhr in 1923, and the Treaty of Locarno, and direct American involvement in the form of the Dawes and Young plans was the foundation of European recovery. The fact that its involvement was often financial rather than military is a reflection of its strength relative to the shattered European continent: the Americans were able to pressure the French to withdraw from the Ruhr and renounce their right to implement military or territorial sanctions against Germany, and to pressure the Germans to accept the Dawes Plan, using financial muscle alone.[35] In short, for the first time the United States was a prominent participant in the politics of the European continent, and its relative material (and especially financial) capabilities in the wake of the devastation of World War I made it an actor whose behavior had to be taken into account at every step by the European powers.

Data

Having surveyed the history of the periods in question, I now move on to seeking out tangible indicators of the quantities of interest from the theory described in Chapter 2

---

[33] On this point see Peterson (1945).   [34] See Danilovic (2002, 229) for a survey.

[35] Here I rely on my own related research, summarized in Braumoeller (2010a), as well as Cohen (1987, 32–33) and Costigliola (1984, 120–122) for the Ruhr crisis and Kolb (1988, 61) and Jones (1981, 36–37) for the Dawes Plan in Germany.

and formalized in Appendix A. Fortunately, throughout these periods data on both the balance of power and the spread of liberal government are readily available, in the form of data from the Correlates of War project and the Polity IV project. The measures used varied across periods, however, for two reasons. The first, and more mundane, has to do with availability of some data in earlier time periods (see e.g., footnote 37). The second has to do with historical context. To put it simply, the world changed substantially over the nearly 200 years under study here, and different aspects of the world became important to states at different times. The most obvious of these differences is apparent in the measures of the structural dimension of power: whereas the powers at Vienna were, and largely remained, concerned about the equality of the distribution of latent more than realized capabilities, the interwar Great Powers focused overwhelmingly on Germany's share of the system's realized military capabilities, and the Americans and the Soviets during the Cold War worried about a distribution of military capabilities that included nuclear weapons.[36] Confusingly, each of these quantities was referred to at the time as the "balance of power."

What I have done in the coding of the data, therefore, is to retain as much similarity of measures as the history of these three periods permits, but not more. Most of the concepts are common to all three periods, but their incarnations do differ, sometimes radically. In this way I hope to maintain conceptual continuity without sacrificing historical diversity.

Capabilities and arms levels: the correlates of war

In the 1815–1914 period the Correlates of War data were used to construct a rough measure of the balance of latent capabilities in the following manner: both iron and steel production and urban population were divided by total Great Power iron/steel production and urban population, and the resulting fractions were averaged. If a state possessed 24% of the total Great Power iron and steel production and 30% of total Great Power urban population, therefore, it received a score of 27%.[37] The balance of power was then calculated as the standard deviation of the distribution of the Great Powers' scores on this latent power measure. Realized capabilities, by contrast, were calculated as the average of the state's percentages of total Great Power military personnel and military expenditures.

In the interwar period, the metric of realized capabilities remained the same, and the measure of the balance of power became simply Germany's realized capabilities as a percentage of all Great Power realized capabilities. Because overall militarization

---

[36] It seems more than likely that the speed with which outcomes were determined in warfare dictated this change: as military technology improved and increased the odds that wars, once started, would be resolved relatively quickly and decisively, the balance of realized rather than latent power became the quantity of greatest interest for maintaining stability.

[37] This procedure has become standard in quantitative studies of IR, which usually average a wider range of variables; in this case, the distinction between latent and realized power makes a compelling case for analyzing the numbers separately. Unfortunately, energy production could not be used in this measure because Russian energy figures are missing prior to 1859 and no method of backward extrapolation that I tried produced remotely credible numbers.

was the perceived cause of the previous war and the focus of arms control efforts in the interwar period, I simply used the total military expenditures of the Great Powers as a measure of arms levels. I made two changes to the measure of latent capabilities. First, national energy consumption, as a proxy for level of industrialization, was incorporated into the measure in the same manner as iron/steel production and urban population. Second, because of the heightened importance of finance in the security politics of the 1920s in particular (when, for example, the Americans were able to convince the French to withdraw from the Ruhr and undermine German opposition to the Dawes Plan by threatening to restrict access to American financial resources),[38] I also incorporated a measure of the state's financial strength, in the form of end-of-year gold reserves, derived from the League of Nations *Statistical Yearbook, Gold and Foreign Reserves*.[39] Again, each state's percentage of the overall Great Power reserves was calculated and averaged into the latent power measure.

For the Cold War period, I retained the urban population, iron/steel production, and energy consumption dimensions of the measure of latent capabilities. I also incorporated a measure of nuclear firepower, in the form of Western and Eastern stockpiles of nuclear weapons, measured in warheads (Norris and Arkin 1997). The measure served in two capacities. First, because arms control efforts became focused much more intensively on nuclear arms during the Cold War period, I used the total number of nuclear warheads as a measure of overall arms levels. Second, because of their disproportionate impact on the conduct of warfare, I used a weighted measure of conventional and nuclear armaments as a metric of realized power. The balance-of-power variable for this period was simply the difference between Western bloc and Eastern bloc countries' realized power, scaled to lie on the interval between 0 (complete Eastern preponderance) and 1 (complete Western preponderance).[40]

---

[38] On the Ruhr crisis see Cohen (1987, 32–33) and Costigliola (1984, 120–122); on the Dawes Plan see e.g., Sontag (1933, 360–361) and Jones (1981, 36–37).

[39] I am grateful to Beth Simmons for suggesting this measure. I utilized the 1926, 1931, 1939, and 1941 volumes. Estimates varied across yearbooks at times, sometimes substantially, so where possible I used the more recent estimates, which tended to be more stable. The accounts were listed in national currencies, so I converted to dollars prior to normalization, using the exchange rate estimates from December of the relevant year, again from the *Statistical Yearbook*. Also, some data were missing, and some were unrepresentative: I extrapolated backward from 1920 to get the 1918–1919 data and forward from 1936 to get the Soviet data for 1937–1939. I also found a pronounced spike in Soviet gold reserves in 1923 to be less than credible; given the *chervonets* currency reform of that year and the fact that other sources (e.g., Barnett 1994) suggest that steady growth in Soviet reserves should have been evidenced, I simply interpolated between the 1922 and 1924 values. Finally, because the use of financial resources requires a minimal level of government coherence, I concluded that the (already minimal) reserve levels of 1920–1921 for the Soviet Union and those of France in 1940 were unrepresentative of their ready financial resources and coded them as missing instead.

[40] Prior to the formation of NATO and the Warsaw Pact, I used a measure of the individual super-power's capabilities, rather than that of the entire alliance. To be precise, the material capabilities measure consisted of three components – percentage of systemic military expenditures, percentage of military manpower, and percentage of nuclear warheads – weighted equally. Interestingly, this is not an entirely inconsequential decision: when I used a measure of realized capabilities that consisted entirely of nuclear warheads, the results of the statistical model improved noticeably.

One additional note is worth mentioning: the estimated coefficients of the statistical model can essentially resolve any purely multiplicative scaling issue (as when, for example, expenditures in the millions or billions of dollars are used as a measure of arms levels, but preferences regarding arms levels are measured on the unit interval). The basic model does, however, assume that zero means zero – in other words, that the zero point of the dependent variable corresponds to a conceptual zero for the quantity being measured. For most of the variables, this assumption is at least plausible: a standard deviation of zero would correspond to perfect equality among the powers, a Cold War power balance of zero would correspond to complete American superiority, and so forth. Nevertheless, to the extent that the data permit this is an assumption worth relaxing if possible. I did so by rewriting the model to permit the scale of the structural dimensions of the system to be estimated rather than assumed, thus mitigating this potential difficulty.[41] Doing so has the advantage that it eliminates guesswork, but it also has two distinct disadvantages: it dramatically increases the number of coefficients that must be estimated in the actor-level equations (and as a result renders the interwar model inestimable due to lack of information), and it exacerbates multicollinearity issues. Even so, the results are on the whole remarkably similar to those of the unscaled model. For that reason, and to save a substantial amount of space, the results of the simpler model are the ones presented here and in Appendix B.

The balance of ideology: polity

The measure of the spread of liberal government was derived from the Polity IV project. In the 19th century, with a few relatively minor exceptions, a state's position between liberalism and legitimism corresponded reasonably well to its position on the Polity scale between democracy and autocracy. In the interwar period, it became crucial to distinguish between left-authoritarian and right-authoritarian regimes, so I reweighted the scale so that the extremes corresponded to left- and right-authoritarianism and the center corresponded to liberal democracy. To the extent that one extreme found the other more ideologically sympathetic than democracy, the measure will be an imperfect one, but happily there was little love lost between fascists and Nazis, on the one hand, and communists on the other, throughout most of the period. During the Cold War, the continuum from democratic to authoritarian once again captures, in a reasonably accurate fashion, the ideological spectrum between communism and democratic capitalism. In each period, the measure of the

---

My sense is that analysts should be guided by theory but not bound by it, however, and my reading of Cold War history would not support the claim that the balance of conventional forces was entirely immaterial to decision makers.

[41] So, for example, rather than starting with an equation such as $\dot{a}_i = \sum_m \omega_{im}[v_i(c_{im}) - s_m]^2 - a_i$, one would start with $\dot{a}_i = \sum_m \omega_{im}[v_i(c_{im}) - \gamma_{0m} - \gamma_{1m}s_m]^2 - a_i$, which permits s_m to be scaled by γ_{0m} and γ_{1m}. The addition of two parameters might seem straightforward, but given that there are m structural dimensions and that the right-hand side must be multiplied out to produce terms for estimation, rescaling generally creates a large number of additional parameters to be estimated.

balance of ideology is nothing more than the average of the nonmissing Polity scores for all European states in the period, recoded as I have just described them.[42]

Worldviews and levels of activity: the historians' survey

The main hurdle involved in estimating a statistical model was obtaining the remaining data, in particular the extent to which states believe a given dimension of the system to be of importance and their preferred state of the world along that dimension.[43] The latter quantity is analogous to an ideal point, the estimation of which has received considerable attention in recent years.[44] Unfortunately, the data necessary for such an exercise are difficult if not impossible to come by for a cross-national study that spans seven states over parts of nearly two centuries. It might be possible, for example, to utilize a content analysis of party platforms to estimate a party's ideal points, but given the conceptual difficulties of such an enterprise,[45] doing so would rule out nondemocratic states, which comprise a substantial fraction of the Great Powers over that period. For a period, French diplomats were given documents that described the French outlook on world affairs in considerable detail; unfortunately for social science, this practice did not persist, nor did it find its way into the foreign ministries of other states. Also unfortunately, the data problem is most acute prior to World War II, when a multipolar world created the potential for the most interesting tests of the model.

To overcome the problem of obtaining comparable cross-national data over long periods of time, I conducted an expert survey of historians. The sample of historians was drawn from four sources: editorial boards of major history journals; book reviews and the "Other Books Received" section of the *American Historical Review,* dating back to 1993; graduate exam reading lists from an array of top history departments; and the membership rolls of the American Historical Society.[46] For each candidate, a research assistant did a search of past publications to determine whether the historian

---

[42] Non-Great Powers were typically not seen as directly relevant to the balance of power, with some strategically located exceptions. In contrast, the spread of liberalism in those states was seen as a matter of grave concern to the conservative powers, as the first few Congresses attest. Hence the use of all European states in the latter measure but only Great Powers in the former. It is worth noting that I also calculated a weighted measure of liberalism in which the Polity score of each state was weighted by its fraction of the European population. The general trend differed little, and the former measure seemed conceptually more appealing.

[43] These quantities correspond to ω and $v[c]$, respectively, in the model in Appendix A.

[44] See, e.g., Poole and Rosenthal (1997), Martin and Quinn (2002), Lewis and Poole (2004), and Peress (2009).

[45] Foremost, of course, would be the question of whether words are truly representative of worldviews and whether the extent to which this is the case varies across states. One also must wonder how the worldviews of parties translate into state-level worldviews.

[46] The last group proved to be more heterogeneous than anticipated, so the sample was restricted to professional historians (i.e., those who had received a graduate degree and were employed in history departments). Three exceptions were made for graduate students who were at least at the dissertation stage and whose work was so directly relevant to the project that excluding them from the sample seemed pointless.

in question had written on the topic of any Great Power's relations with other Great Powers, belief systems or worldviews of the constituents or elites of a given Great Power, major domestic divisions or the workings of domestic political institutions within a given Great Power, or the general history of a given Great Power or set of Great Powers.[47] An initial draft of the survey was sent to a panel of five historical experts who offered valuable suggestions for revision as well as critical insights into the ontological outlooks of historians.[48]

The survey asked respondents to gauge the quantities of interest and chart any changes in them over time. For example, to gauge the ideal points of leaders and their constituencies (defined as "the people legally empowered to emplace or remove" their leaders), respondents were asked, "If political elites could have had their way, what would the distribution of power in Europe have looked like? What about the preferences of their constituency, if such a group existed?" Answers for both leaders and constituents ranged from 1 ("All major states would have equal capabilities") to 7 ("Even large inequalities of capabilities were fine as long as one state could still balance against threats"), along with "Don't know" and (in the case of constituencies) "Inapplicable."[49] Analogous questions asked about the distribution of political ideology and overall arms levels, when applicable. To measure salience, the respondents were then asked, "As a measure of the general importance of the distribution of power in Europe to the national security of the state, how wide or narrow was the range of outcomes considered acceptable by political elites and (if applicable) by their constituents?" Answers ranged from 1 ("Nearly any distribution of capabilities would have been acceptable from the point of view of national security") to 7 ("Only an extremely narrow range of outcomes would have been acceptable; anything outside of that range would constitute a threat"), along with the same "Don't know" and "Inapplicable" options. Similar questions gauged opinions about the worldviews of leaders and constituencies on the distribution of ideas.

In a more contemporaneous study with more available data, the activity variable might have been operationalized using events data, but coverage of all actors during all periods would be obviously problematic, and the available coverage would raise issues of generalizability.[50] Other indicators of activity were potentially available, such as alliances and militarized interstate disputes (MIDs), but no individual data series or combination of data series produced an indicator with anything like adequate

---

[47] I am most indebted to Jeff Rosenfeld and Yevgeniy Kirpichevsky, without whose tireless research assistance this would have been an even more enormous task.

[48] For example, one historian suggested that the use of the terms "elites" and "constituencies" was both overly vague and reductionist. I was able to work out language that was more precise and useful, but I was unable to do much to assuage the latter concern, because these constructions are central to the theory. Indeed, the discipline of political science in general is probably overly reductionist from an historian's point of view.

[49] I attempted to ensure that the lower end of the scale corresponded to a meaningful zero point in the data, for the reasons mentioned earlier.

[50] On events data see Merritt, Muncaster, and Zinnes (1994) and Schrodt (1994). One alternative would have been a study of the post-World War II period, for which events data might reasonably have been obtained, but the loss of more than half of the data for the sake of a single indicator struck me as unwise if an alternative was available.

surface validity.[51] It seems likely that the reason for this outcome has to do with the fact that the behavioral data are not always consistently related to the underlying concept that they are meant to capture. In a multilateral state, an absence of alliances indicates low levels of activity; in a highly unilateral state, however, an absence of alliances could be associated with any level of activity. A state that relies on strong allies might spend little on its own defense even if it is highly active. A state might be very active for ten years but only experience MIDs in two of those ten years, so the absence of MIDs is an ambiguous indicator.[52] Worse, many of these behaviors may (or may not) be indicative, to some degree, not of an increasingly active foreign policy but rather of an attempt to maintain internal order during an era of uprisings and revolution. In short, the relationship of the behavioral indicators to state activity is highly contextual, depending heavily on the state and period in question.

Expert-generated data are not uncommon in the study of political science.[53] Indeed, expert data have even been shown to be preferable to existing, objective data: Benoit and Laver (2007), for example, compare the results of the Comparative Manifesto Project, a detailed and professional attempt to derive left-right party positions from content analysis of party platforms, to those of an expert survey on the same subject and find the latter to be more accurate. There are good reasons to consider the use of expert-generated data in international relations as well, the main one being the fact that survey data are designed to measure *exactly* the quantity of interest, whereas behavioral data are often very indirectly or imperfectly related to it.

Given that an expert survey had to be conducted to gather data on the worldview questions, therefore, I added an item about the general level of activity of the state, designed to capture much the same concept that events data measure, except without a directional component[54] ("Taking into account all forms of activity designed to increase national security, how active would you say the state's foreign policy was during this period?").[55] Given the unusual amount of leeway granted to respondents,

---

[51] See the appendix of Braumoeller (2008) for details of one such combination, a factor analysis of data from the Correlates of War project – specifically, military personnel, military expenditures, number of allies, number of European opponents in militarized interstate disputes, and the sum of the hostility levels of European MIDs.

[52] It might be possible to use a moving average rather than a yearly measure to mitigate this problem, but doing so would induce massive serial correlation; produce measures that are highly dependent on the number of years used, arbitrarily, for the average; and be inherently unable to pick up transition points – in all, a bad trade.

[53] See, e.g., Budge (2001) on expert data regarding political party positions, and Bueno de Mesquita (1998) on expert data on ideal points.

[54] Events data typically measure the activities that one state takes that are directed *toward* another state. This is a substantial difference between the two indicators; it also suggests that events data run the risk of underrepresenting certain forms of activity, such as extraordinary defense spending, that may not readily be attributable to a reaction against a particular state.

[55] In retrospect, this indicator may be misleading in one specific case: when states engage in rapid transitions from highly internationalist foreign policies to highly isolationist ones – breaking lots of alliance ties, for example – that change could be interpreted as an increase in activity, when its goal is actually to decrease it. That is, incautious respondents might reflexively react to *changes in* levels of activity as if they were *increases in* activity. I am grateful to Lisa Martin for pointing out this possibility. Having looked over the data I am most concerned by this possibility in the immediate post–Cold War period, where America's level of activity drops less abruptly than

the reliability of the measure – the degree to which different observers asked to measure the same quantity would produce the same result – was worth ascertaining and proved to be acceptable.[56]

The main concern regarding survey-generated data of this sort is validity – whether they correspond to known behavioral measures that capture similar concepts. Events data are the closest analog, but of the three periods in question events data are available for only one, the Cold War. A reasonable way to address this concern would be to ascertain whether the survey data are similar enough to existing events data to serve as instruments for them. To do so, I compared the U.S. and Soviet activity series to two plausibly similar events series generated from Edward Azar's Conflict and Peace Databank (COPDAB; Azar 1982). In both cases the degree of similarity was well beyond conventional standards for a sufficiently strong instrument.[57]

The survey permitted respondents to select the state(s) about which they considered themselves to be most knowledgeable. As a result, unfortunately, more data were gathered on 20th century states than on 19th century states, so a second wave of the survey was put into the field and respondents were asked specifically to address questions about states in earlier periods when possible. Finally, two of the respondents suggested that the questions about the Cold War could usefully have been augmented with an additional question about arms control, and in retrospect I agreed; therefore a third "mini-survey" was subsequently put into the field to ask follow-up questions regarding that issue area. In the end, there were 175 responses to the survey, each covering one Great Power over a span of 50 or (in the case of the interwar period) 40 years. Given that there were 18 such country-period combinations, there were an average of nearly ten respondents per data point. The data were then cleaned and averaged[58] to produce a data set containing one quantity per question per country-year.

Now that I have described the data, I move on to the task of interrogating them.

---

intuition suggests it should. At the same time, however, its activity may simply have shifted from conflictual to cooperative, so it is difficult to say with much certainty whether it was overestimated.

[56] Cronbach's alpha measures intercoder reliability, with values below 0.60 considered clearly problematic, those in the 0.60–0.69 range borderline, 0.70–0.79 acceptable, and 0.80 and above very strong. I calculated the average of all of the alpha statistics for all of the country-periods in the survey, weighted by the number of coders in each. The result, an aggregate Cronbach's alpha of 0.72, falls into the unambiguously acceptable range.

[57] Cameron and Trivedi (2005, 96–97, 104–105) discuss instruments and suggest, as a rule of thumb, that the F-statistic for whether coefficients equal zero in a regression of the original activity variable on the instrument should exceed 10. In this case I generated two series – one of all events, rescaled by intensity in accordance with the codebook (p. 37), and one of only negative events, rescaled in the same manner, in light of the potentially ambiguous meaning of positive events (Altfield 1984). Regardless of which is taken to be the actual activity series, the survey instrument serves as an acceptable instrument, with a strong positive correlation ($\rho > 0.6$ in the case of the all-events series) and F-statistics well above the cutoff of 10 (25.64 for the negative-events series, 35.41 for the all-events series).

[58] One result seemed somewhat anomalous: answers to the question about overall levels of activity in Prussia in the early 19th century produced a flat line until the early 1860s. This was a case in which a minimal number of historians had offered responses (to be precise, two) – but despite the fact that the respondents were different individuals answering in different waves of the survey, they both charted the *same* trend, including both the flat line and the upward tick around 1860. In the end, I decided not to second-guess the respondents.

Interrogating the data

If my argument about the systemic nature of international politics is a reasonable one, we should find, first of all, that the measures that I have gathered of the various key concepts across these three international systems are in fact correlated with one another, to a greater extent than one would expect just by chance, as the theory would predict.

To do so, it is necessary to estimate a series of systems of equations, the technical details of which are described in Appendix B. The general outline of the procedure is, first, to arrange the data in a manner consistent with the two key reciprocal relationships implied by the theory:

H_{A1}: International structure prompts state security activity in proportion to the product of salience and dissatisfaction with the status quo.

H_{St1}: State security activity alters international structure in proportion to the product of state security activity, state latent capabilities, salience, and dissatisfaction with the status quo.

The next step is simultaneously to examine the data to determine the extent to which there is a statistically significant correlation between Great Power activity in one time period and system structure in the next, and system structure in one time period and Great Power activity in the next. Doing so allows us to assess whether the relationships hypothesized by the theory are in fact present in the data.

It is not instructive to examine the connections among individual state-level variables and individual systemic variables, for a variety of theoretical and mathematical reasons – foremost among them, the fact that the sheer number of such connections (183) makes it difficult to say anything coherent at all.[59] Nevertheless, if we aggregate the independent variables at each stage – that is, if we examine the impact of Great Power security activity *in the aggregate* on the individual components of the structure of the international system, and then examine the impact of structure *in the aggregate* on the security-related activity of individual Great Powers – we can render the analysis more comprehensible and feasible.

It is also possible to test Morgenthau's argument from Chapter 2 that "the element of power as the immediate goal of the policy pursued ... is concealed by ideological justifications and rationalizations." This amounts to an argument that any claim made that foreign policy serves ideological ends simply masks a deeper end, namely, power.

For this argument to be a reasonable one, the behavior that could be explained by ideological motives must also be explicable by power motives, without exception. To illustrate this point, in Figure 3.3 the circles represent variation in each of three variables – the balance of power, the balance of ideology, and outcomes, whatever they may be (in this study, states' security-related activity), and the overlaps between

---

[59] The results of the various models are reproduced in Table B.7: that spans pages 234–242. Moreover, the degree of multicollinearity among the state-level variables, combined with the small sample sizes, makes individual-level inference particularly challenging.

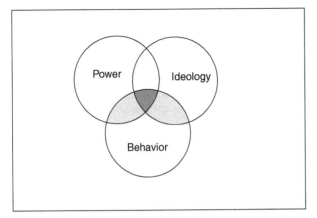

Figure 3.3. Covariation in power, ideology, and outcomes.

and among them represent covariation or correlation. The realist argument about the pursuit of ideological goals in foreign policy boils down to an argument that the rightmost shaded area should be a null set: the only correlation between security-related activity and ideology should also be shared with the balance of power (i.e., the dark gray region in the center).

This logic leads to a straightforward hypothesis:

H_{R1}: The balance of ideology will have no impact on state behavior, independent of the impact that it has when its prescriptions correlate with those of the balance of power.

Estimation

A perfect method for estimating systems of equations has yet to be devised. Ordinary least squares (OLS) coefficients are inconsistent if endogenous right-hand side variables are correlated with the error term; moreover, they suffer from simultaneous-equation bias if error terms are correlated across equations. Three-stage least squares (3SLS), a fully systemic estimator, addresses these issues, but estimates hinge critically on the quality of instruments, which is often mediocre at best. Full-information maximum likelihood (FIML) resolves the latter issue, but as with any systemic estimator, a misspecification in one part of the system can have repercussions throughout the remaining equations; moreover, the technique requires an additional assumption (normality of error terms) that, to the extent it is not met, is another potential source of error. Which method is least flawed is difficult to predict in any particular case.[60]

---

[60] Limited-information techniques are those, like OLS, that estimate coefficients for equations one at a time; full-information techniques, like three-stage least squares and FIML, estimate them simultaneously. The full-information maximum-likelihood technique utilized here is equivalent to the maximum-likelihood version of a three-stage least squares technique, save that the model's

Moreover, the theoretical model itself, although it translates easily into a time-series model, has some features that make it inherently hostile to estimation. Identification issues and the fundamentally interactive nature of the model preclude estimation of coefficients on the individual variables.[61] Estimation of coefficients involved generating aggregate terms, such as the ones derived in Equations (B.3) and (B.4), and estimating a coefficient for each. Bivariate correlations among these aggregate terms were often very high by construction. Multivariate correlations – the correlations between an individual term and the remaining terms in the equation – were of course higher still, ranging in the 19th-century Prussian case from 0.8928 to 0.9969. Multivariate correlations of this magnitude make parameter estimation substantially more uncertain, to say the least. Those seeking to gauge the statistical significance of the estimates should therefore expect rather expansive standard errors.

Research utilizing systems of equations typically evaluates the statistical significance of the results at the level of the equation rather than at the level of the individual coefficient; see Brown (1993) and Goldstein and Freeman (1990, Appendix B) for examples. The reason, simply, is that coefficient-level significance is of little interest when testing a system of equations: the equation as a whole is generally more likely to capture a coherent concept of interest. Following this tradition, I have compiled the equation-level results in Table 3.2.[62] It should be emphasized that these results reflect the joint significance of *only* the variables derived from the model – not the control variables, and not the constant term, because those coefficients are not, strictly speaking, relevant to the question of the model's statistical significance. Nevertheless, the high degree of correlation among these model terms in many cases, combined with their relatively small number in any given equation, makes this a challenging test.

Finally, the argument that power goals are concealed by ideological justification has a surprisingly straightforward statistical interpretation, one that can be tested easily. In statistical terms, it implies that any variation in balance-of-ideology variables that correlates with state activity should also correlate with balance-of-power variables. (To continue the substantive example, the only states that prove to be attractive targets for regime change should also yield demonstrable balance-of-power advantages.) Crucially, in econometric equations of the sort reported later, any variation associated with multiple independent variables as well as the dependent variable (the dark gray region of Figure 3.3) does not influence the results at all. The model coefficients

---

considerable endogeneity required that the instruments be estimated via OLS rather than maximum likelihood. The main advantage over 3SLS is that the maximum-likelihood routine offers robust standard errors. For that reason, and due to the fact that it is a full-information technique, I report the FIML results.

[61] I considered a log-additive model, but Monte Carlo trials suggested strongly that estimation would be unreliable at best.

[62] The first and third period results were calculated using maximum likelihood, with robust standard errors. The interwar model failed to converge using likelihood methods, so the results are based on method-of-moments estimation instead. Accordingly, the numbers in the table represent F-statistics for the interwar period and χ^2 statistics for the other two periods. Full results for all models can be found in Appendix B, Table B.7.

Table 3.2. *Structures and agents: reciprocal impact*

	19th Cen.	Interwar	Cold War
H_{St1}: *Great Power security activity* →			
Balance of Power	32.84***	10.78***	8.98*
Balance of Ideology	13.82	16.89***	34.24***
Arms Levels		24.29***	139.65***
H_{A1}: *Structure* → *security activity of . . .*			
United Kingdom	20.10***	22.99***	
France	18.79***	51.10***	
Austria/A-H	24.65***		
Prussia/Germany	18.56**	21.46***	
Russia/USSR	21.40***	109.56***	32.37***
Italy		19.25***	
United States of America		75.21***	11.62
H_{R1}: *Reject reduction of model to . . . ?*			
Power-only model	132.76***	20.82***	40.70***
Ideology-only model	221.41***	49.03***	319.73***

Note: Numbers represent joint significance of variables derived from model, all equations.
*** $Pr < 0.001$; ** $Pr < 0.05$; * $Pr < 0.10$.

only reflect covariation that is *unique* to the independent variable in question and the dependent variable (the two light gray regions).[63] Therefore, in these results, the coefficients on the balance-of-ideology variables capture only the influence of that portion of the balance of ideology that is *not* correlated with the balance of power.

Therefore, the realist argument that states only react to and shape the balance of ideology to the extent that it serves their balance-of-power purposes suggests a very simple hypothesis. If it is correct, the model described earlier should be reducible to a much simpler model, one in which the coefficients on all of the variables that capture the effects of state activity on the balance of ideology and vice versa are zero.[64]

Results

Given the challenging nature of the test, it comes as something of a surprise that the partial adjustment model performs as well as it does across the board. The results are summarized in Table 3.2.

[63] See Kennedy (1985, 46–47) on this point.
[64] In concrete terms these would be $\beta_4 - \beta_6$ in Equation B.3 and each of the other actor-level equations and all of the coefficients in the balance-of-ideology equation.

The coefficients in the first three rows answer the question of whether the various dimensions of the structure of the system are more responsive to the security policies of the Great Powers than we would expect them to be by chance, and almost without exception the answer is yes. The only exception is the balance of ideology in the 19th century, and it may tell us something interesting about the world. In the 19th-century model, the equation that relates state activity to the balance of ideology is not, on the whole, distinguishable from what we would expect to see by chance despite a lesser multivariate correlation, though it is reasonably close to standard levels of statistical significance. What this fact suggests is that the balance of ideology either did not respond or responded only imperfectly to Great Power manipulation throughout the century. The power projection capabilities of the Great Powers were weakest in this period, and they often had considerable difficulty in suppressing revolution. Moreover, the impetus for revolution quite often came from the smaller states themselves. In short, with regard to the balance of political ideology in the 19th century the results suggest that the system was more independent of Great Power influence than other structural dimensions were at that time or in other periods. (Also, importantly, it demonstrates the fact that the model as a whole *could* be falsified – but in the vast majority of cases is not.)

The next seven rows of coefficients in Table 3.2 answer the converse question: whether the security policies of the Great Powers are more responsive to the structure of the international system than we would expect them to be by chance. Here, again, the answer almost without exception is that they are. The results are quite strong, statistically speaking, and hold across virtually all Great Powers in all time periods. The exception is the United States in the Cold War period, and in this instance seeking a substantive explanation is most likely unwarranted: the multivariate correlation among the model-related independent variables was so strikingly high (0.9998) that statistical significance could hardly be expected.

These inferences hinge critically on strong instruments, and all of the instruments generated by the models were quite strong, as indicated by the F-statistic for whether coefficients equal zero in a regression of the original variable on the instrument.[65] An examination of the error terms uncovers substantial correlation, a fact that justifies the additional effort and assumptions of the 3SLS/FIML approach rather than ordinary OLS. All in all, then, the nested politics model maps quite well to the real world in each of these periods, at least by these metrics.

An additional, reasonable test of the theory, given that the model makes concrete predictions about the signs of the individual coefficients, has to do with the degree to which those signs match the signs of the estimated coefficients. Because the model predicts coefficient sign but not magnitude, and because the standard errors are often strongly influenced by multicollinearity, the inferences that can be drawn from coefficient signs will be somewhat noisy; still, though the predictions are not perfect, they nevertheless do a much better job than we would expect by chance, producing

---

[65] On the issue of weak instruments see e.g., Cameron and Trivedi (2005, 104–110) and Imbens and Rosenbaum (2005, 112–113 and *passim*). Cameron and Trivedi recommend a threshold of 10 for the F-statistic.

more than twice as many correct predictions as incorrect ones in the first two periods and more than *nine* times as many in the Cold War era (the ratio of correct to incorrect predictions is 37 : 18 in the 19th century, 65 : 31 in the interwar period, and 29 : 3 in the Cold War). All are significant at the $Pr < 0.001$ level according to Fisher's sign test, which corresponds to a standard binomial test; the intuition is that the information contained in the signs of the coefficients is like the heads/tails information contained in a coin flip, and by tallying the number of signs that correspond to our expectations, we can assess the overall descriptive, and therefore explanatory, utility of the model.

Reducible to realism?

The last row of Table 3.2 presents the results of the test of the realist reducibility-to-power argument, in the form of a test that the parameters implicated by the argument – that is, those associated with the balance-of-ideology terms, both at the state and the structural level – are jointly equal to zero. To test whether this parameter restriction significantly reduces the model's explanatory power, I utilize F-tests for the interwar period and χ^2 tests for the other two periods.[66] The results indicate that without exception the claim cannot be supported. The joint probability that the coefficients equal zero in each case is trivially small. For the sake of completeness (and out of curiosity) I also test to see whether it would be possible to reduce the model to one in which states are *only* concerned about the balance of ideology and not about the balance of power; the answer, reported in the final row, is that the data do not support such a simplification of the model.

Figure 3.4 displays the results of these tests graphically, for each time period under examination. In each test, a probability density function represents a range of possible outcomes, and an arrow represents the observed behavior of the system. If we were to find that the behavior in the system fell within the center of the density, it would mean that we would be unable to distinguish between a purely realist (or a purely *idealpolitik*) world and the world that we have observed, and we would be unable to reject the hypothesis.

As it stands, however, it is quite straightforward to reject either a purely realist or a purely *idealpolitik* explanation for the workings of the system in each of the three systems. A purely realist explanation is, in each case, less improbable than a purely ideological one, but even in the most likely scenario (the Cold War), which might seem more likely than it is due to the scale in Figure 3.4, the probability that the observed behavior was produced by power considerations alone is still about one in five thousand.

It is worth noting that one version of the realist argument is that ideology can drive policy as long as it does not directly contradict realism; Mearsheimer (2001, 46), for example, writes that "states can pursue [non-security goals] as long as the requisite behavior does not conflict with balance-of-power logic." This argument differs from the classical one in two ways. First, the correlation among realist variables, ideological variables, and behavior is only of concern if the first two are negatively correlated, which the classical realists tend to assume will not be the case; second, correlation

---

[66] Cameron and Trivedi (2005, 278).

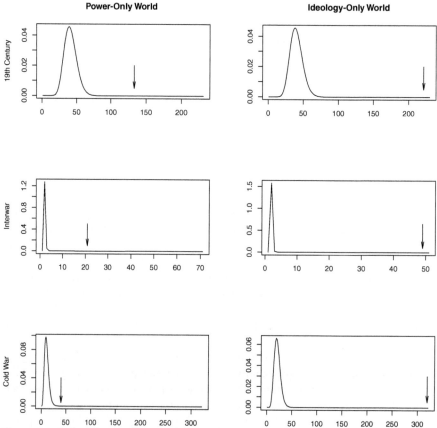

Figure 3.4. Reducible to realism? Probability that observed behavior was generated by either power or ideology alone.

between an ideologically based impetus to act that is *not* correlated with power motivations and behavior is unproblematic. Simply put, unless ideological motives directly contradict power motives, they are not ruled out as a source of behavior. The test just described, admittedly, is not relevant to this variant of the argument; yet the argument not only concedes that nonrealist motives can drive much of state behavior but in fact rules out so few outcomes that a direct test of it is difficult to devise, even in principle.

Rational expectations

Next, it is worth examining the data to see whether they contain any evidence of the sort of coadjustment to within-period innovations that the rational-expectations school would lead us to expect. If they do, we should expect to see large and/or statistically significant correlations among the error terms of the activity equations

Table 3.3. *Correlations among error terms, all systems*

	Activity of UK	Activity of Fr	Activity of Pr/Ge	Activity of Au/A-H	Activity of It	Activity of Ru/USSR
			19th Century System			
aFr	0.1986*					
aPr	0.2226**	0.3077***				
aAu	0.1863*	0.1663	0.3171***			
aRu	0.1423	0.0774	−0.2013**	0.4658***		
			Interwar System			
aFr	0.341					
aGe	0.2245	0.0458				
aIt	0.0523	−0.1878	0.8384***			
aRu	−0.0169	0.0329	0.2922		0.3226	
aUS	0.05	0.057	−0.7387***		−0.5407***	−0.2915
			Cold War System			
aUS						−0.2819*

*** $Pr < 0.001$; ** $Pr < 0.05$; * $Pr < 0.10$.

for the Great Powers in each of the time periods – an indication that, even after all the systemic sources of behavior have been taken into account, they are observing, and simultaneously reacting to, some additional information in the present period.[67] The pure, long-time-horizon rational-expectation argument has become implausible in light of the success of the partial-adjustment model, but it remains to be seen whether states at least engage in within-period adjustment to contemporaneous shocks as well as retrospective adjustment, despite the costs of doing so.

The answer, based on the estimates of the correlations among the error terms in Table 3.3, is "sometimes." In the 19th century, evidence for coadjustment to contemporary shocks is fairly strong, especially between contiguous states (Austria-Russia, Austria-Prussia, Prussia-France), but also between the UK and most of the continental powers. In the interwar period the evidence is considerably less strong, but it must be pointed out in the context of the small sample size that many of the correlations are in fact fairly substantial in magnitude. Stronger evidence of coadjustment can be found among the Germans, the Italians, and the Americans – clearly not evidence of collusion between the United States and the Axis, because the U.S.-Germany and U.S.-Italy correlations are large and negative.

Why are some correlations negative while others are positive? There are theoretical reasons to expect this to be the case: based purely on the model, one might expect negative correlations among reactions to innovations when the states' ideal points are on opposite sides of the status quo and positive correlations when they are not. This

[67] See, for example, Williams and McGinnis (1988, 978).

does not *necessarily* correspond directly to either allied or adversarial status, though adversaries should tend to be on opposite sides of the status quo point more often than not. This would explain the negative correlations just mentioned, but not, for example, the positive correlation between the error terms of the French and German equations in the 19th century.

Visualizing systemic incentives

These results tell us that the partial-adjustment model provides a reasonably accurate description of Great Power behavior and that the structure of the system reacts in proportion to the intensity of the actors' pushing and pulling, as well as to their strength. They also provide the model with the opportunity to make concrete predictions in the aggregate. What these results do not capture, however, is the answer to a more comprehensive question: Given their worldviews, what incentives does the system provide for the actors at any given point in time?[68]

This question cannot easily be answered by looking at the model coefficients, but the model can provide us with a set of predictions – roughly akin to measures of substantive impact in a standard statistical model – that give us a comprehensive illustration of the forces at work in the system. The vector fields it produces capture the sum of the effects of the systemic forces – both unit-level and structural – acting on the states.[69] Take, for example, Figure 3.5, which represents the state of the world in a given year. The X-axis measures the level of activity of one actor, whereas the Y-axis measures the level of activity of another; in a bipolar system this would be a complete depiction of the actors' systemic incentives, whereas in a system with more Great Powers it would represent a cross-section taken from a higher dimensional space. The arrows tell us what incentive, if any, the system gives the actors at different levels of activity – to increase their activity, decrease it, or remain the same.

In this example, if both actors were essentially isolationist, exhibiting very low levels of activity, the systemic incentive would be for both of them to increase their levels of activity – State 1 more than State 2, as indicated by the less-than-45-degree angle of the arrow leading up from the lower-left corner. If State 1 is essentially isolationist but State 2 is extremely active, the conditions present in the system would prompt State 1 to increase its activity and State 2 to decrease its activity, as indicated by the downward-sloping arrow at the upper left. If both states were engaging in intermediate-to-high levels of activity, in contrast, they would be near the equilibrium point, and the system would provide little incentive to change their behavior.

---

[68] It is important to emphasize that these are *systemic* rather than purely *structural* incentives. The actors and the structure together comprise the system, and the impact of the structure of the system is mediated by the worldviews of the actors. A change in either could produce changed incentives; to take a simple example, a change in the balance of power (structural) or a change in a given state's emphasis on the balance of power, even in the absence of a change in that balance (actor-level), could each produce changes in a state's incentives to act.

[69] Technically, we calculate predicted values assuming different levels of activity for the state at year t, and plot the predicted change in activity in year $t + 1$ at each level of activity.

Year

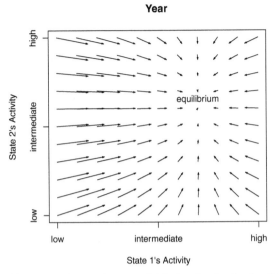

State 2's Activity

high / intermediate / low

low / intermediate / high

State 1's Activity

Figure 3.5. A generic vector field, showing levels of activity for two states on X and Y axes, arrows denoting the direction and magnitude of structural incentives for state behavior, and an equilibrium point.

It is important to emphasize that the prediction of the model is *not* that states will always be at the equilibrium point. Because the partial-adjustment perspective suggests that states will always be feeling their way *toward* equilibrium, and because the estimated coefficients tell us how assertively they will do so, the equilibrium point is not an ironclad prediction as much as a point toward which both states will tend. The overall picture is therefore not intended as a concrete test in the same way as the previous tests were, but rather as an illustration of how, as Waltz puts it, structures "shape and shove" but do not conclusively determine actors' behavior.[70] The large-N statistical results in the previous sections served to evaluate the argument that actors responded to structures (and vice versa). These vector fields cannot help us evaluate that argument with anything like the same precision; they simply serve to illustrate how systemic incentives operate in a way that appeals to intuition far more than the statistical results ever could.[71]

---

[70] Waltz (1986, 343). Waltz attributes the disjuncture between structural incentives and actor behavior to the fact that "unit-level and structural causes interact [and] the shaping and shoving of structures may be successfully resisted."

[71] It is also important to emphasize, though it may seem obvious, that the vector fields only capture the effects of systemic forces on behavior. They could do little else, because there are no other variables in the model. Yet as the case studies in Chapter 4 demonstrate, while the systemic mechanism forms the core of the process driving each of the cases, none of them is entirely complete without the impact of some idiosyncratic exogenous variable. The lesson is that the predictions of the vector fields are somewhat suggestive – as any social science prediction with uncontrolled exogeneity (i.e., any social science prediction) should be.

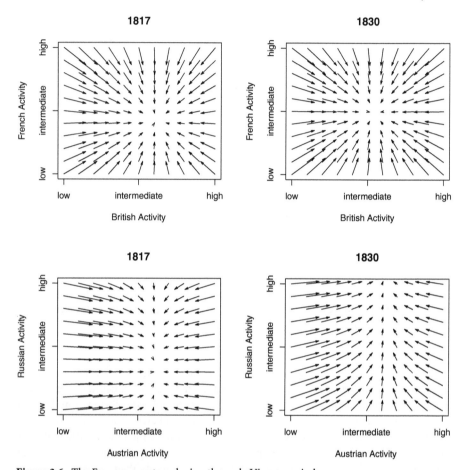

Figure 3.6. The European system during the early Vienna period.

A minute examination of 175 years of interactions among seven Great Powers would take a substantial amount of space, but we can at least examine the predictions that are most relevant to the case studies in Chapter 4. In Figure 3.6, therefore I examine systemic incentives for four of the five actors at two points of interest in the 19th century. In the first, 1817, the Treaty of Vienna, in which the Great Powers reached a wide-ranging accord designed to maintain the peace of Europe, was just two years old. Nevertheless, the legitimist consensus that they attempted to impose did not prove to be universally popular, and the next few years would see Congresses at Aix-la-Chapelle, Troppau, Laibach, and Verona, as well as the French invasion of Spain.[72] The constitutionalist-legitimist split that would soon divide the Great Powers

[72] In terms of the model, it is worth noting that the ongoing unrest in the smaller states of the continent was in part a residual effect of Great Power activity in a previous period – namely, Napoleon's efforts to inspire nationalist risings in order to weaken existing regimes.

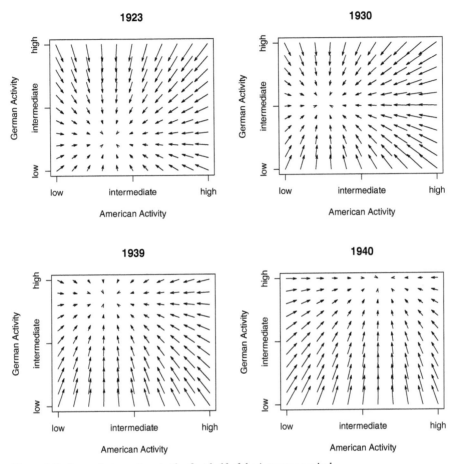

Figure 3.7. Systemic incentives in the first half of the interwar period.

themselves was growing. In short, despite the peace settlement they all had substantial systemic incentives to continue engaging in fairly active foreign policies.

By 1830, in contrast, the July Revolution in France had occurred, Belgium was experiencing a constitutionalist revolution, Poland would erupt in revolt late in the year, and a recognition of Greek independence was not far in the future. British incentives to act are the product of a more liberal worldview in the context of a more liberal system – both more inclined to support constitutionalist causes and, at the same time, more satisfied with the new status quo than it would previously have been. Russia under Nicholas I is a different story entirely: the liberalization of the continent galvanized the Tsar to take action to redress the status quo and shore up the solidarity of the conservative Eastern monarchies.

The second case has to do with America and Germany in the interwar period; Figure 3.7 illustrates this dynamic. In the early interwar period, much of the tension over security in Europe had to do with the system of reparations payments that

had been devised at Versailles. In 1923, the year of the Ruhr Crisis,[73] the Americans had concluded that their reasons for involvement on the Continent did not warrant membership in the League of Nations, and the Germans, appalled at the magnitude of reparations, had nevertheless not yet adopted an openly revisionist stance. Both faced modest systemic incentives to act.

After 1923, a few trends are noticeable in the incentives presented by the system. The first is in Germany, which witnessed gradually increasing incentives to act throughout the 1920s – due not to any substantial changes in the structure of the system itself, but rather to changes in how it was viewed within Germany. In short, there was a gradual erosion in the already modest willingness of the Germans to tolerate the provisions of the Versailles settlement, and as those provisions became more intolerable, the structure of the system itself, although not substantially different, constituted an ever-greater incentive to act throughout the 1920s and 1930s.[74]

At the same time, Germany remained largely powerless actually to do very much to resolve its dissatisfaction. Its substantial reparations burden meant that even if its economy were the strongest in Europe it would be unable to devote a substantial percentage of its resources to altering the status quo, especially prior to Hitler's abrogation of the Versailles treaty's military restrictions. As Chapter 4 shows, only in the late 1930s did Germany reach the point at which it could alter the structure of the system, and only when it did so did the United States respond.

America's focus on the threat posed by Germany underwent a substantial shift in 1940, the year of the abrupt and unexpected fall of France – the point at which the ideological and material balances of the system tilted abruptly and without warning in Germany's favor. This change in the structure of the system provided the incentive for the United States to act to oppose Germany, and indeed, upon closer examination the historical record suggests that the fall of France, rather than the bombing of Pearl Harbor a year and a half later, was in fact the event that precipitated the end of American isolationism.

Finally, the latter years of the Cold War system, with its two superpowers, presents a relatively straightforward illustration of the effects of systemic pressures on Great Power behavior. The transition from 1981, when the abrupt end of détente focused both sides' attention on the arms race and marginally increased the intensity of the struggle between them (Fig. 3.8, left), and 1987, when Mikhail Gorbachev's reforms had institutionalized a "new thinking" that cast the world in de-ideological

---

[73] In early 1921 the Reparations Commission issued its first assessment, in the amount of 150 billion gold marks. A brief German revolt led to the occupation of three German cities and capitulation by both sides. By May 1921 a debt of 132 billion gold marks ($30 billion; Pulzer 1997, 106) was agreed upon, and yearly payments began, but it soon became clear that the combination of Germany's inability to pay and France's insistence upon compensation left no middle ground. Accordingly, on January 11, 1923, French and Belgian troops moved into the Ruhr with the goal of occupying it and using the proceeds as reparations.

[74] See, e.g., Mommsen (1996, chs. 6–7). Italy also demonstrates a substantial shift toward revisionism, even earlier than that of Germany: after Mussolini came to power in 1922, Italy became an increasingly illiberal regime with expansionist aspirations, one that increasingly viewed the status quo as unacceptable.

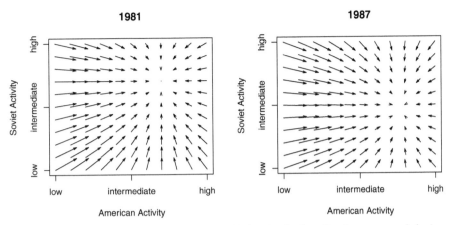

Figure 3.8. The United States and the Soviet Union in the late Brezhnev era and during *perestroika*.

terms and emphasized a more modest defense policy of "reasonable sufficiency" (Fig. 3.8, right), is substantial. It is clear from the relationship between the two graphs that this shift had produced a marked change in Soviet incentives. The graphs also provide a nice illustration of the intuition behind the systemic model: although Soviet incentives had changed, decreased Soviet activity had not yet had a major impact on the structure of the system in either the arms control arena or in the realm of ideology. Structural change in those areas would not be pronounced until late 1989, when the Soviets permitted the Berlin Wall to be breached. As a result, Washington, which was responding not to changes in Soviet declaratory policy but to tangible changes in outcomes, saw no such changes and therefore remained wary of Moscow's overtures. American systemic incentives reflect this outcome, with the Soviet Union being drawn toward intermediate levels of activity while American incentives remain nearly unchanged from the early 1980s.

Diagnostic checks

Before concluding, it is worth engaging in some diagnostic checks on the data to ascertain the extent to which some of the assumptions of the model hold. Two in particular merit scrutiny: the relationship between constituents and elites, and the decision to break the period under study down into three periods for analysis.

Domestic constraint

Recall the discussion of constituents and elites in the previous chapter, in which the constituency placed demands on the leaders, potentially without uttering a word, much as the path of a lightning bolt is determined by tiny differences in resistance among air molecules. This argument implies that the worldviews of leaders and those of their constituencies should be more or less aligned at any given time – more so

in very democratic states, to be sure, but even loosely in nondemocratic states. To the extent that that is the case, elites will be constrained in their actions by their constituencies.

Because the data contained information regarding the positions of both elites and their constituencies in each country, it was possible to establish a rough test of the extent to which the results are consistent with the basic probabilistic-voting model posited earlier, and therefore of the extent to which elites in a given country in a given time period were constrained with regard to a particular issue. The method of gauging this relationship is straightforward: I simply generated a new variable, consisting of the historians' estimates of the constituency's position subtracted from the historians' estimates of the elites' position – the idea being that, if constituency and elite positions do, in fact, line up, this quantity should be equal to zero. I then broke this measure down by time period, country, and issue and graphed the densities, along with the overall (all-country) densities, in Figures 3.9–3.11 for visual inspection.

We can use these diagrams to assess the manner in which states aggregate preferences in two ways. If elites accurately reproduce the worldviews of their constituents on average, the density's center of mass should be near zero. If they do so consistently, the density should not be very spread out. Needle-thin distributions centered on zero would therefore resemble the ideal of consistent accurate representation, whereas wide distributions centered away from zero would deviate from that ideal.

The distributions in these diagrams are mostly quite thin and centered quite closely on zero. This fact strongly suggests that, for most countries at most times, the model is not glaringly inaccurate. It is reasonable to expect that even highly representative political systems will occasionally produce slight deviations between the views of elites and those of their constituencies, but on average the two mostly coincide, as we can tell by examining the overall densities in each figure.[75]

There are some noteworthy deviations. Nineteenth century elites, especially in authoritarian states, are on the whole less enthusiastic than their constituencies about the prospect of the success of continental liberalism, which is perhaps to be expected given that the 19th century was a period of more or less continual liberalization, and the devolution of political power is inevitably more popular among the recipients than among the donors. The distributions suggest that they were relatively free to depart at least modestly from the preferences of their constituencies on this score. It is worth noting that some level of domestic conflict is often associated with marked diversions between elite and constituency opinion on this issue. For example, Russia undergoes such a transition on the liberal question after the revolutions of 1848 and again after the assassination of Alexander II by revolutionaries and the rise of the reactionary Alexander III in 1881, as does France not long after the founding of the Second Empire in 1852. These trends explain the particularly noteworthy divisions within these countries on the question of the success of liberalism.

---

[75] In fact, the diagrams prompt some musings about the normative advantages of democracy. Does democracy produce leadership preferences that correspond, on average, more closely to the preferences of the constituency than do preferences in authoritarian states? Or perhaps less variation around the mean? Or does its value lie primarily in a more inclusive constituency? Or perhaps all three?

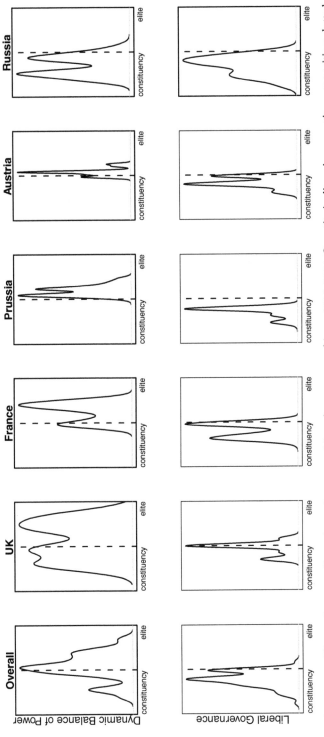

Figure 3.9. Difference between elite and constituency positions, by country and issue, 1815–1914. Quantity is elite minus constituency position; dotted vertical line at zero. For power, positive numbers mean that elites are more inclined than constituents toward a dynamic, rather than a static, balance of power; negative numbers mean the converse. For liberal governance, positive numbers mean that elites are more inclined to support the spread of liberal governments throughout Europe than their constituents, whereas negative numbers indicate that the constituencies are more inclined to do so.

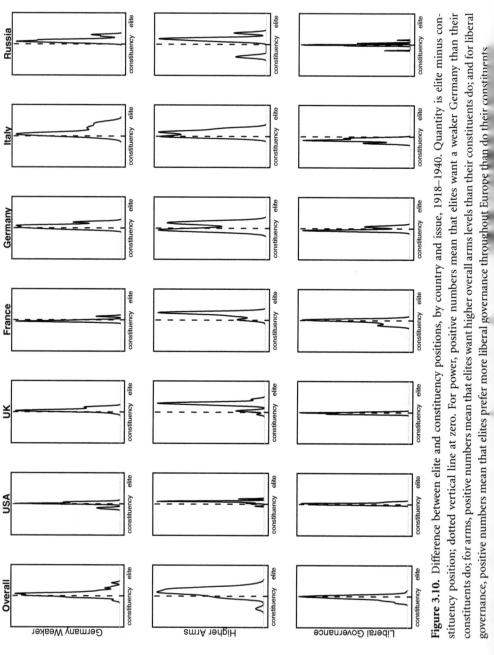

Figure 3.10. Difference between elite and constituency positions, by country and issue, 1918–1940. Quantity is elite minus constituency position; dotted vertical line at zero. For power, positive numbers mean that elites want a weaker Germany than their constituents do; for arms, positive numbers mean that elites want higher overall arms levels than their constituents do; and for liberal governance, positive numbers mean that elites prefer more liberal governance throughout Europe than do their constituents

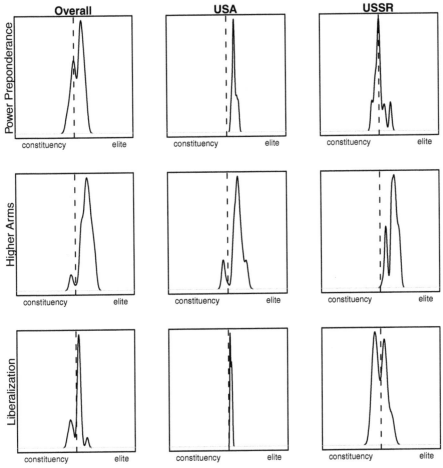

Figure 3.11. Difference between elite and constituency positions, by country and issue, 1945–1993. Quantity is elite minus constituency position; dotted vertical line at zero. For power, positive numbers mean that elites are more inclined than their constituents to seek a preponderance rather than a balance of power; for arms, positive numbers mean that elites want higher overall arms levels than constituents do; and for liberal governance, positive numbers mean that elites prefer more liberal governance throughout Europe than do their constituents.

Similarly, there is a slight tendency for elites to be more focused on the balance both of power and of ideology than their constituents. The tendency is less pronounced than students of public opinion might anticipate, but then again, for most of the states in this period the constituency represented a small fraction of the general public.

In the interwar period, the first thing that seems noteworthy is the extent to which elite and constituent worldviews are not just aligned on average but aligned more consistently: the variance of the densities relative to those of the 19th century has shrunk considerably. Political elites also tend to be more in line ideologically with

their constituencies than they were in the 19th century. Finally, constituencies are, across the board, marginally more in favor of arms control and lower arms levels than are contemporaneous elites, a result consistent with the popular origins of the interwar arms control movement. Only in the United States, where elites became world leaders in the arms control movement, was elite and constituency opinion more in line. On the question of the balance of power, most constituencies were squarely in line with political elites, though in Italy and to a lesser extent in Germany itself constituents leaned slightly more toward a stronger Germany than did elites – a reflection of the unpopularity of the Versailles settlement.

The Cold War period represents the apogee of the success of the preference-aggregation model. On issues of the balance of power and the balance of ideology, constituencies are squarely in line with elites in terms of both ideal points and salience, and the variances of the densities are so narrow that they often appear to be spikes. The only exception is arms control, an issue area in which constituencies are consistently slightly more doveish (and, perhaps explaining the divergence, consistently slightly less interested) than elites.

The overall lessons are fairly straightforward. First, although there are clearly periods in which constituencies and leaders are at odds, at most times in most states the ideal points of the constituency are fairly well aligned with the ideal points of the elites, and the same can be said for their assessments of the salience of the various structural dimensions. Second, when there are systematic differences between the two, they tend to come during times of change (e.g., periods of liberalization in the 19th century and arms control in the 20th). Finally, the extent to which the model accurately describes reality seems to increase over time, in liberal and autocratic states alike.[76]

Are there more than three systems?

One of the concerns of time-series modeling, in addition to the degree of the empirical fit, is the possibility that there will be a structural change in the data – that the relationship between independent and dependent variables will change substantially enough to warrant the estimation of separate regressions. In the context of the present study, although I have taken this issue seriously enough to conclude that there are three systems distinct enough to warrant the estimation of separate statistical models, it is nevertheless possible that those three systems themselves are not causally homogeneous. If that is the case, the period might be better understood as consisting of four or more systems, divided by events less obvious than general wars, and reestimation would be in order.

---

[76] Out of curiosity, as a first cut to see whether the data could speak to the question of whether constituency opinion primarily leads elite opinion or vice versa, I calculated the simple correlation coefficients for constituency ideal points at time t and elite ideal points at time $t + 1$, on the one hand, and elite ideal points at time t and constituency ideal points at time $t + 1$, on the other, by country and period. The differences between the two correlation coefficients were generally trivially small – so small that they could easily be attributed to chance – and the few situations in which they were more substantial displayed no particular pattern.

Such caution may seem unwarranted; after all, international relations scholars typically utilize data from the end of the Napoleonic Wars to the present without concern for structural changes in the data. Nevertheless, the possibility of such a change is far from fanciful, based on a reading of the historical literature. For example, Craig and George (1983, 28) argue that

> [t]hree generations of statesmen struggled with the problem of establishing a viable equilibrium of forces in Europe [in the 19th century], and their efforts found expression in three quite different systems of balance of power, each of which reflected the characteristic tendencies of its time.

I have argued that the distinction between the static and the dynamic balance of power, although of considerable historical interest, is not a threat to inference here because both implied a focus on the balance of power (understood as the variance of the distribution of capabilities), albeit for different reasons. That argument is certainly open to question, however, both because the transition from one system to the next may have produced a qualitative difference in the relationship between the activity of states and the balance of power, and because the actors' emphasis on their own individual capabilities at various points throughout the century may have weakened the structural dynamic to such a degree that it was no longer operative. This is a concern that should be addressed in historical models in general, both because the assumption of a constant causal process across a long time span can be a heroic one and because changes of this nature can be of great substantive interest.

I have therefore run MOSUM (*moving sum* of residuals) tests to evaluate the stability of the OLS series. The intuition behind such a test is straightforward: an *empirical fluctuation process* consisting of a moving sum of model residuals is constructed and charted over the duration of the time series. The balance-of-power line, for example, represents the moving sum of errors in the balance-of-power equation from year to year – variation not explained by the behavior of the actors. A substantial increase or decrease in the value of the process being charted suggests that a structural change may have occurred: to continue the example, if the behavior of the actors suddenly becomes a much poorer predictor of the balance of power and something else becomes a better one, we would expect substantial *non*random fluctuation in the empirical fluctuation process. Confidence intervals built around the process provide a straightforward visual test: if the change is larger than one that would be expected given random variation, we should see the line that represents the empirical fluctuation process cross the confidence intervals.[77]

Such a test is presented in Figure 3.12. Each graph charts the empirical fluctuation process for one variable in the model – either a structural dimension, such as the distribution of capabilities or ideology, or an actor's level of activity. The dotted lines at top and bottom represent the 95% confidence intervals within which the solid line should, if all is well, be contained. Encouragingly, not a single one of the 21 empirical fluctuation processes examined wanders outside of the confidence intervals, and very few come particularly close. Therefore, the available evidence suggests quite strongly that, within each of these systems, the assumption of a single, ongoing regime is justified.

---

[77] See Chu, Hornik, and Kuan (1995) for details of this procedure.

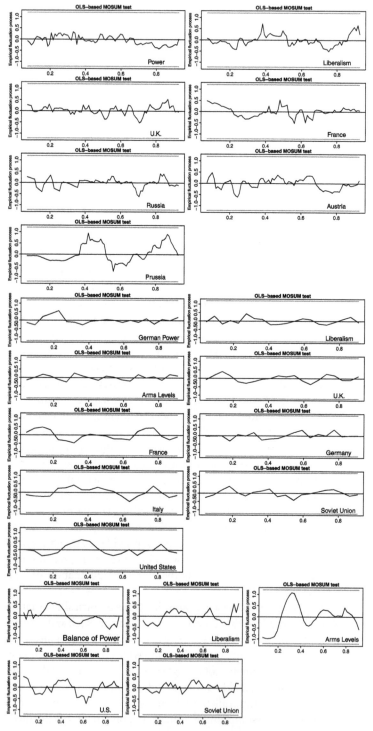

Figure 3.12. Testing for regime change: Moving sum of residuals (MOSUM) tests of structural stability, 1815–1914 (top), 1918–1940 (middle), and 1945–1990 (bottom).

Conclusion

What I hope to have shown here, in a more compelling manner than previous systemic theories have been able to do, is that a model of the international system in which the structure of the international system has an impact on the security policies of states *and* those policies simultaneously shape the structure of the system fits the historical record from the past two centuries. Moreover, the results demonstrate that, in the context of such a model, the balance of power cannot be given pride of place: the balance of political ideology both shapes and is shaped by the security policies of the Great Powers. The predictions of the partial-adjustment model are borne out, on the whole, suggesting that states engage in retroactive adjustment to counter changes to the status quo once they have occurred. Moreover, the predictions of the rational-expectations school are borne out as well, though perhaps less consistently, suggesting that states sometimes engage in prospective adjustment to counteract unexpected within-period innovations. Finally, the model's qualitative predictions of the incentives produced by the system, though not determinate, provide additional indications of the model's plausibility.

The next chapter takes a closer look at a series of historical cases in an attempt to do two things. First, it offers a better sense of the workings of the causal mechanisms posited by the theory: Are the causal processes that comprise the theory in evidence in the cases? To what extent are they augmented, or nullified, by other processes? Second, it demonstrates how the bare-bones model here can be seen to operate in conjunction with other, often more idiosyncratic or ephemeral, factors that nevertheless play a substantial role in a given case.

4 | *Systems in historic perspective*

Investigating the origins of state behavior, like any other social science investigation, should not stop with an estimation of the magnitude of the relationship among theoretically relevant variables; it should also assess the plausibility of the causal mechanism that the theory posits (Gerring 2007, 43–48). This chapter, therefore, contains a different form of historical investigation than the previous chapter. Rather than examining a large number of cases over the entirety of the period between the end of the Napoleonic Wars and the end of the Cold War, it takes a more focused, in-depth look at three events of considerable interest to students of international politics – the polarization of the European continent after the Vienna settlement, the end of American isolationism, and the end of the Cold War.

Each of these cases demonstrates the utility of a systemic perspective. Each case represents a full cycle of systemic politics: in each, a state acts to produce a change in the structure of the international system, and that change in the structure of the system produces a subsequent change in the behavior of the actors. The importance of the structure of the system can be understood counterfactually, by asking whether the actors change their behavior based solely on their understanding of one another's characteristics; in each case, there is a period after the change in the actors' characteristics, but before the change in the structure of the system, that provides a critical test. In each, the systemic model predicts that the actors' main behavioral changes will be occasioned by structural changes rather than changes in one another's characteristics, and in each case the prediction is borne out:

- The European Great Powers divide after the 1830 revolutions in Belgium and France rather than during the British liberalization of the 1820s.
- The Americans rearm dramatically and engage in undeclared warfare on the open seas with Germany after the fall of France but not before, despite being aware of Germany's barbarism.
- The Bush administration responds to Mikhail Gorbachev's announcement of deep unilateral arms cuts and renunciation of the class basis of international politics not with accommodation, but rather with a determination to "test" the Soviets that lasts until structural change, in the form of the fall of socialism in Eastern Europe and a breach in the Berlin Wall, takes place.

In the third example, President G. W. Bush himself summarized his unwillingness to act before seeing concrete change in the balances of ideology and power, in a phrase

that could apply to any of the statesmen in any of the situations just listed: citing Missouri's state slogan, he said of the Soviets, "show me."

The cases also enable an exploration of the causal mechanisms that the model posits. A narrower historical focus permits a more in-depth examination of not just the outcomes described by the theory but also the processes by which those outcomes were brought about. There is typically a tradeoff in studies such as these between breadth and depth, and the statistical study has provided breadth. These case studies, by contrast, provide more depth. In so doing, they permit us to ask whether the processes that take place in Great Power interactions are consistent with the ones posited by the theory. The cases also enable us to ask us whether any additional processes were important in telling the story of this particular case. It is simply implausible to claim that the causal relationships laid out in the model are the only relationships that could ever exist among the variables of interest: second-order effects that temporarily link one variable to another in a manner not anticipated by the theory have almost certainly already occurred to people familiar with the history of this period. Although such relationships are not consistent enough to merit being "hard-wired" into the general theory, they nevertheless can improve our understanding of individual cases.

Finally, the fact that the theory explains each of the cases well implies that all of them can be understood as special cases of the more general phenomenon of systemic politics. There is a caveat, of course, that none of them is totally generic: although each contains idiosyncratic features that have to be understood as well, the core processes of the nested politics model can be seen operating in each of them. Nevertheless, the prospect that a single theory can usefully explain such a diverse set of cases is an exciting one.

The main problem with finding appropriate case studies to test a systemic theory is that cases in reality rarely approximate the ideal. In a perfect world, we would have a situation in which the values of all variables are constant for some period of time, after which one of them, and only one of them, changes while the others remain constant. One could then derive the comparative-static predictions of the model, make predictions, and test them. In a system such as the international system, unfortunately, most of the variables seem to be changing most of the time. When those changes predict similar outcomes, it can be difficult to untangle their effects; when they predict opposite outcomes, their net impact on the system is nearly impossible to predict. The best that one can do, under these circumstances, is to find situations in which the values of most of the variables do not change *much*, but the values of a small number of variables change very substantially. That is what I have attempted to do in this chapter, and that is the primary reason that these cases rather than others were chosen.

Case 1: the polarization of Europe, 1815–1834

The years following the end of the Napoleonic Wars witnessed a remarkable degree of consensus on the future shape of the Continent. This consensus comprised two mechanisms designed to ensure peace: a distribution of material capabilities such that

no one state constituted a threat to the others, and a consensus of shared conservative values such that no revolutionary movements would threaten the peace.

The outcome that one would expect from such a settlement is straightforward: each of the major powers would continue, for the most part, to be content to be checked by its neighbors as long as those neighbors, in turn, were checked by theirs, and before long any revolutionary rumblings would be put down by the combined efforts of the Great Powers. As a result, after some postwar mopping up, the major states would settle into a period of relative inactivity, and the states that make up the Continent would remain in the hands of autocratic rulers. Yet such an outcome did not occur: within twenty years, the Continent had divided itself into two hostile ideological camps, allied against one another. What explains this outcome?

The main change that occurred between 1815 and 1834 that drove this result via its impact on the international system was the liberalization of the British worldview. During the Vienna talks, the British foreign secretary more than once took positions that were more favorable to the cause of legitimacy than those taken by the Russian Tsar.[1] By the mid-1830s, the British had become the champions of constitutional liberty as it was then understood. The transition was a substantial one, and given the influence of British military and financial power on continental events it had a substantial impact on the balance of ideology there. As the gap between the British ideal point and that of the conservative powers widened (Figure 4.1), two things happened: the status quo point moved toward the liberal end of the scale and farther from the ideal point of any one state, and all states therefore became more dissatisfied with it. As a result, rather than sliding into relative inactivity, they took increasingly strong action to attempt to undermine one another and ultimately ended up forming two rival ideological blocs.

Recalling the model's main hypotheses,

H_{A1}: International structure prompts state security activity in proportion to the product of salience and dissatisfaction with the status quo.

H_{St1}: State security activity alters international structure in proportion to the product of state security activity, state latent capabilities, salience, and dissatisfaction with the status quo.

we should expect to see that, as Britain's dissatisfaction with the status quo increases due to its changing worldview, its level of security activity should increase as well (H_{A1}). The impact of its increase in activity should be a shift in the structure of the international system toward its ideal point and away from the ideal points of the conservative Great Powers (H_{St1}). Once that shift has occurred, the conservative powers should experience greater dissatisfaction with the status quo than they had previously and should increase their levels of activity accordingly (H_{A1}).

---

[1] Admittedly, the Tsar in this case, Alexander I, was atypical of the species, a fact that is discussed later.

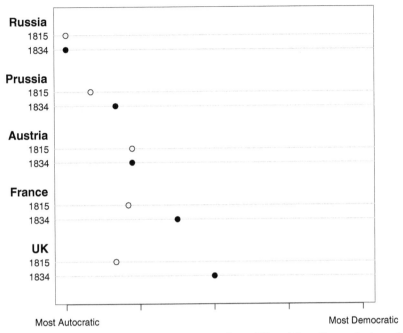

Figure 4.1. The widening rift between conservative and liberal Great Powers in the early Vienna Period. *Source:* historians' survey.

The Vienna settlement

After the Napoleonic Wars, the Great Powers were virtually unanimous in their desire to suppress revolution in order to prevent another war. They were also convinced, as they never had been previously, that the institution of a distribution of capabilities that would prevent any one state from threatening the rest would be in the interests of all of them, and that an international legal superstructure that would sustain both the prevailing conservative order and the territorial distribution would be preferable to the every-state-for-itself politics of the 18th century.

The demands of an equitable distribution of capabilities and of the principle of legitimacy were not always compatible, however. As a result, the Vienna settlement was something of an amalgam of the legitimist political philosophy underpinning monarchical rule and the desire for a territorial distribution that would promote peace on the Continent by making aggression unwise. To consolidate Austrian strength, the former Austrian Netherlands were traded for much of Italy. The Rhineland states were consolidated and handed to Prussia along with most of Saxony, and a German Confederation under Austrian leadership was established, largely as a barrier to French expansion. To hem France in from the northeast and to keep the Scheldt River, considered strategically crucial by the British, out of the hands of any other Great Power, Holland and Belgium were united. Sweden and Norway were united, and

the Ottoman Empire, *sans* Bessarabia, was left intact as insurance against Russian expansion to the south. The most substantial inequity resulted from the Russian ingestion of most of Poland, Bessarabia, and Finland, an outcome that the other Allies tried in vain to prevent. Spain and Portugal were restored to independence, and the Bourbons returned to the throne of France.

The vulnerability of states to the influence of the Great Powers in the aftermath of war and the widely accepted task of reconstructing the continent meant that, in the early Vienna period, state activity was more diplomatic and legal than military in form, and given the diplomacy of the day, that it was often entrusted to a small number of people or even a single person. States had often seen, in the preceding quarter-century, multiple forms of government and a variety of national borders, and the right to go about settling those competing claims had already implicitly been established by virtue of victory in war. The context, for a brief time, was a fairly unusual one, in which diplomacy rewrote the map in the shadow of power.

The specifics of these settlements are important for two reasons. The first, which is discussed in detail later, is that they represent a conservative, balance-of-power[2] base-line to which later deviations can be compared: later territorial and legal reshufflings often reflected the increased importance of liberal and constitutional values. The second is that the British, far from protesting the details of this essentially conservative settlement, were often instrumental in bringing them about. In addition to compelling national unions such as those of the Norwegians with the Swedes and the Belgians with the Dutch, the British often actively sought to repress constitutional government abroad. Britain's main concern with movements for national self-determination and constitutional government in this period was not the danger of liberalism *per se* but the danger of liberalization. If Castlereagh is to be believed, and this seems a common enough argument, he feared foreign constitutions not for their own sake but because of the threat of democratization and war. He made this point quite plainly in his letter to Lord William Bentinck of May 7, 1814, on Italian affairs, in which he wrote, "The danger is that the transition may be too sudden to ripen into anything likely to make the world better or happier," and in his letter of the previous day to Liverpool in which he mentioned "all the new constitutions which now menace the world with fresh convulsions."[3] That said, this fact does not alter the British preference, which was for near-autocracy rather than even moderate constitutionalism: it merely explains it.

In Italy in the immediate postwar period therefore, the British conspired with Metternich to suppress liberal government. At times, they even had to conspire against themselves in order to do it. Bentinck, a British general, had secured the surrender of Genoa by promising its liberty and compelled the king of Sicily to grant his subjects a constitution. The former maneuver was easy enough to undo at the Paris negotiations, where Castlereagh simply gave Genoa to Sardinia. The latter required

---

[2] It is important to emphasize that this was a balance-of-power *system*, rather than a system that was conducive to balance-of-power *politics*; the distinction is discussed in the previous chapter.

[3] Webster (1931, 386). In the case of Italy, Hayes (1975, 194–195) argues that the British were equally if not more concerned with preventing the extension of French influence into Italy via the encouragement of revolutionary propaganda.

more substantial maneuvering, because simply abolishing the Sicilian constitution outright would certainly have attracted the attention of Parliament. Castlereagh pointed out this fact to Metternich, and after considerable discussion, the two agreed to reinstate the constitution that had existed prior to Bentinck's arrival – an essentially worthless document that seemed to bestow certain rights upon the populace but in reality was a vehicle for complete monarchical control. Castlereagh's public instructions to A'Court, the British minister, demanded that the Sicilians be allowed all of the rights that they had enjoyed prior to 1813, and before long the deed had been accomplished.[4]

Moreover, the British government was the most active advocate of the Bourbon restoration in France. Tsar Alexander I, whose combination of a liberal upbringing and tendencies toward both mysticism and congenital eccentricity made him more than a little unpredictable,[5] was in a decidedly liberal mood when he announced in March 1814 that the French should have whatever form of government they desire, even if it were a republic. On March 31, he went further, pledging to respect a French constitution regardless of its contents. The British, in contrast, pushed for the return of the Bourbons to power in the name of stability, even covertly offering cash to the reactionary Comte d'Artois to ensure the Bourbon restoration.[6]

Even the case of Poland reflects exceedingly illiberal behavior on the part of Britain, though in the end it came to naught. Alexander proposed to reconstitute the Kingdom of Poland within the section of Poland that fell within Russian borders. The Poles were granted a constitution guaranteeing freedoms of speech, press, and association, and a bicameral Diet was instituted, the lower house of which was elected. The voting requirements were the most inclusive in Europe. Admittedly, the Tsar's control over the entire apparatus of government remained substantial, and the extent of Polish self-governance deteriorated markedly after 1820, but the Tsar's plan for the future of Poland was a surprisingly liberal one.

In its rhetoric and in its official documents, Britain seemed to pursue an even more liberal course, demanding the complete independence of Poland from Russia. The reality was quite different, however. Castlereagh realized from the beginning that Polish independence could not be forced on the Tsar and would not be granted. He therefore pursued a course of re-implementing the three 18th-century partitions of Poland. A plan more abhorrent to liberal opinion could hardly be devised, and Castlereagh knew it. Following Liverpool's instructions, he made Britain's quixotic

---

[4] Webster and Temperley (1924, 161–162), Taylor (1957, 35); see also Temperley and Penson (1938a, 4).

[5] Alexander's was a colorful family. His father, Paul I, was, depending on the source to which one lends credence, either extremely strange or simply mad (Ragsdale 1988). Nicolson (1946, 106) refers to his brother, the Grand Duke Constantine, simply as "that insane hyena." As Artz (1934, 172) notes, "Metternich once shrewdly remarked that in the character of Alexander there was always some element lacking, but that it was impossible to tell in advance just what the element would be." Lord Byron characterized him succinctly: "Now half dissolving to a liberal thaw, / But hardened back whene'er the morning's raw, / With no objection to true liberty, / Except that it would make the nations free" (Thomson 1978, 159).

[6] Webster (1931, 241–242, 248–249).

public position on Poland clear in the public record; meanwhile, he sought to re-divide Poland among its neighbors in order to ensure a more equitable balance of power among them.[7]

Secret diplomacy nevertheless has its limits. When Castlereagh was asked by the Cabinet to state his views on the revolts in Naples, he replied in a famous State Paper of May 5, 1820, that Great Britain had not made and would not make any pledge to maintain the ideological status quo in Europe. He agreed that liberal revolution was a threat to the stability of all governments, though its impact on the balance of power was likely to be minimal. More importantly, he pointed out that British opinion would never permit intervention to prevent it.[8]

Meanwhile, the Tsar's flirtation with liberalism was coming to an end. In March 1819 a Russian agent, August Kotzebue, was killed in Germany; Alexander suspected that a secret revolutionary group was to blame. In June of that year there was an uprising closer to home, in Chuguev. The uprising itself was not of direct concern to Alexander, but in combination with the stories of a better life abroad brought home by returning soldiers it served to increase liberal agitation elsewhere in the country. From abroad, revolutionary agitations in western and southern Europe gave Alexander reason to rethink the viability of liberal and monarchic cohabitation. At the Congress of Troppau in 1820 Alexander received news of the mutiny of a unit of the elite Semenovski Guard. Though the uprising had less to do with liberalism than with a deep dislike of the unit's commander, Alexander nevertheless interpreted it as a sign that the revolution was knocking on his door. The result was the Troppau Protocol, signed by Russia, Prussia, and Austria, a document that proclaimed those states' right to intervene by force if revolutionary trends in one state appeared to threaten another. Given that revolution was widely thought to be inherently contagious, this amounted to a justification for intervention against the forces of revolution anywhere.[9]

The year 1820 was therefore a crucial nexus. The Troppau Protocol of December converted the Holy Alliance, heretofore a rather vague and meaningless institution, into a unified force for legitimism. The conservative states reached this point as Britain, unable "under the special circumstances of its national institutions" to support more

---

[7] On Castlereagh's deception and Liverpool's instructions see Webster (1931, 385); on his pursuit of a renewed partition see Webster and Temperley (1924, 160).

[8] "There can be no doubt of the general danger which menaces more or less the stability of all existing Governments, from the Principles which are afloat, and from the circumstances that so many States of Europe are now employed in the difficult task of casting anew their Governments upon the Representative Principle; – but the notion of revising, limiting, or regulating the course of such experiments, either by Foreign Council or by Foreign Force, would be as dangerous to avow, as it would be impossible to execute; and the illusion too prevalent on this subject, should not be encouraged in our intercourse with the Allies.... [T]he sooner such doctrine shall be distinctly abjured as forming in any Degree the Basis of our Alliance, the better; in order that States, in calculating the means of their own Security may not suffer Disappointment by expecting from the Allied Powers, a support which, *under the special Circumstances of their National Institutions* they cannot give." Ward and Gooch (1923, Appendix A), emphasis added. Nevertheless, Bartlett (1996, 20) makes note of Castlereagh's "discreet" backing of Austria.

[9] Lobanov-Rostovsky (1954, 11–12); Almendingen (1964, 172–173, 188, 196); Palmer (1974, 363–366).

overt antirevolutionary activity, reached the limits of its own conservatism. Faced with the active and armed hostility of the majority of the Great Powers and only a thin promise of nonintervention from Britain, liberal movements on the continent soon faded. There were some minor exceptions, of course. Poland has already been mentioned. Some of the German states – Bavaria, Baden, Württemberg, and Hesse-Darmstadt – received constitutions as well, though the rights that they conveyed dwindled as time went on. The larger point, however, is the most important limitation on these and other constitutions of the period: the authority upon which they were founded. Each was granted by the sovereign rather than being grounded in the natural rights of the governed. The distinction was crucial, for what the sovereign could grant, the sovereign could retract, and often did. David Harris put it well when he wrote that the years after 1814 were "the period of liberalism by princely grace."[10]

The liberalization of Britain

In the two decades that followed the end of the Napoleonic Wars, British worldviews liberalized substantially, meaning that the British ideal for continental governments moved away from near-autocracy and toward limited but genuine popular sovereignty in the form of constitutional monarchy. They did not, with the exception of the Radicals, advocate anything approximating what Europeans in the 21st century would understand as democracy; having liberal attitudes in this period meant advocating governance by male landholders. Nevertheless, the British attitude toward national independence and constitutional government warmed considerably over the course of these years. The results in British foreign policy were realized gradually, first in the policy of nonintervention announced by Castlereagh and promoted by his successor, George Canning, and later in active intervention on the side of new nations and constitutional government.

One can point to three reasons for the liberalization of the British worldview in this period. The first is the waning of the fear of revolution at the end of the 1810s that permitted the expression of moderately liberal sentiment. The rhetoric of the French Revolution, writings such as Paine's *Rights of Man,* and governmental repression sparked a domestic radical spirit that endured through the period under study and beyond, eventually culminating in Chartism. Though the French descent into violence gave even the most ardent radical pause, the end of the war brought a proliferation of such movements: radicals met and organized clubs and societies, typically seeking some combination of electoral redistricting, broadened or universal suffrage, and reduction in taxes and often advocating the violent overthrow of the existing political order as a means of achieving these goals. Economic hardships in 1816 and 1817 produced riots among the working class and the farmers, which in turn inspired a greater fear of revolution among the middle and upper classes. In August 1819, further unrest culminated in the "Battle of Peterloo," an episode in which government troops fired on a group of protestors in St. Peter's Field, Manchester, killing 11 and wounding hundreds. The apogee of English reactionary sentiment

---

[10] Harris (1955, 502–503).

came in November and December of that year with the passage of the "Six Acts," which rescinded a range of traditional British liberties with the goal of preventing revolution.[11]

At the same time, more moderate opinion liberalized as well. Britons who did not seek the violent overthrow of the government nevertheless sought to influence its politics in more liberal directions. The composition and distribution of the electorate, similar in its essentials to that prescribed by the electoral law of 1429, were a focus of particular attention: although the outright purchase and sale of seats in Parliament had been outlawed (in 1809 – June 12, 1809), many "pocket" or "rotten" boroughs had become small enough that they could effectively be bought by individuals of sufficient means.[12] In the postwar years, opposition to this relatively closed and aristocratic system made itself known: at its peak in 1817, for example, more than 600 petitions for the reform of Parliament were received. The passion for reform comprised two main surges, from the late 1810s to 1823 and from 1829–1832, the latter culminating in the passage of the Reform Act of 1832.[13]

The liberalization of British public opinion provided opportunities for both political parties that they were not slow to recognize. The resulting liberalization of British political elites was the second key to the liberalization of the British worldview. Its development was inextricably intertwined with the third cause: the increase in the extent to which public opinion provided a constraint on the leadership.

The concept of liberty was central to the political identity of the Whigs, long out of power save for a brief moment as part of the Ministry of All the Talents; the radical movement offered them an opportunity both to improve their domestic political strength by harnessing popular opinion to their cause and to shape the reform movement in such a way as to prevent the kind of violent revolutions that threatened Europe in the latter part of the decade.[14] The Tories, too, were able to accommodate

---

[11] Archer (2000, ch. 5); Lasky (1973); Dinwiddy (1990); Halévy (1926, esp. 4, 9–29, 63–70). Parssinen (1972) constitutes an illuminating case study of one of the more influential of these groups, the Spenceans.

[12] Sack (1980, 914) provides a few examples of boroughs and their prices – Old Sarum, bought by the second Earl of Caledon for £60,000; Camelford, bought by the third Earl of Darlington for £58,000; and Gatton, bought by the fifth Lord Monson for £180,000 – as well as the ongoing expenditures that ensured the fealty of these boroughs. The latter include a reduction in rent and a free half-ton of coal at Christmas to loyal voters in Newark and outright cash payments in Shaftesbury and Stockbridge. The author also notes that Gatton was purchased just before the Reform Bill of 1832 abolished the borough entirely and, "perhaps understandably, changed Monson from a whig to a tory overnight."

[13] Hay (2005, 12–13); Caramani (2000); Wasson (1977, 595–597).

[14] The Whigs might seem at first blush to be curious reformers, because they were not of even remotely humble origin; they were, in the memorable words of Peter Mandler, "the people's aristocrats." In fact, they sought not to eliminate aristocratic privilege but to preserve and bolster it against the power of the crown by making it more legitimate, a goal that they sought to attain by strengthening the relationship between electors and elected. Put succinctly, the Whigs sought to replace a system of royal and aristocratic governance in which the aristocracy was unfairly influenced by the sovereign, with a system of royal, aristocratic, and middle-class governance in which the middle class happily allowed itself to be influenced by the aristocracy. See L. G. Mitchell (1999, esp. 351–362); Mandler (1990, 28); Ellis (1979); A. Mitchell (1965). Making the

minor reforms sought by the middle classes once fear of revolution had passed; the early 1820s marked the inauguration of what came to be called "liberal Toryism," a trend that would ultimately separate moderate Tories like Palmerston and Canning from their more conservative, royalist cousins.[15]

More important, in the immediate sense, were the increasing constraints that liberal public opinion in Britain provided for the foreign secretary and the willingness of Castlereagh's successors to inform the public of their policies in order to exploit those constraints. In the immediate postwar years the British government had been, as some of the earlier examples have suggested, largely able to conduct foreign policy without the criticism, or indeed even the knowledge, of the vast majority of the country. Even the Cabinet tended to view foreign policy as the exclusive domain of the foreign secretary, and Castlereagh at least did nothing to discourage that attitude. Webster recounts an incident, the ratification of a secret treaty with Austria and France against Prussia in early 1815, that is highly illustrative:

> Liverpool was still at Bath and most of his colleagues were in the country. But he had no intention of interrupting his cure or summoning a Cabinet. He assumed that Bathurst, who as usual was at his post, would agree, and that the Cabinet would acquiesce. The matter was indeed decided and Castlereagh informed before the Cabinet was shewn the treaty.[16]

Nevertheless, there were limits to what Castlereagh could do without public support. Once postwar governments had been established and postwar boundaries had been set, the sort of activity needed to revise them changed considerably: the foreign secretary could no longer shuffle governments and influence constitutions nearly by fiat. Increasingly, armed opponents opponents with entrenched interests had to be compelled to accept change. More overt actions, such as intervention and aid to constitutionalist factions, could hardly be hidden.

The uprisings of 1819–1820 therefore put Castlereagh in a delicate spot. Now that Naples was in a state of revolt, he was caught between his pledges to Metternich and the sympathies of the British people. His response, the State Paper of May 5, served to reassure the Cabinet and the public that Britain was not pledged to a general policy of intervention to prevent domestic political change. It also served as a signal to the conservative powers that, as he put it to Esterhazy, the Austrian ambassador, "However much we may disapprove and lament so disastrous an innovation [the revolts in Naples], the British government cannot take any part forcibly to counteract or control it."[17]

Toward the end of his life Castlereagh began to show signs that the fear of rapid liberalization, revolution, and war that had weighed so heavily on him in 1814–1815 had begun to abate. He began to differ more substantially with Metternich on the

forceful point that reform movements in the early 1800s were not social movements, in that their instigators were not from the middle and lower classes, is Sked (1979b).

[15] Goodlad (2002).

[16] Webster (1931, 374); see also Hayes (1975, 77–78). On the nature of public opinion as understood by elites see Davis (1999) and Fraser (1961).

[17] Hayes (1975, 195).

question of revolutionary movements abroad, and the instructions that he drew up for the conferences of autumn 1822 demonstrate that, although he was not prepared to aid the Greeks in their war of independence against the Ottoman Empire, he was at least prepared to consider some aid short of intervention. His suicide on August 12 of that year ensured that the extent of his willingness to break with the conservative powers of the Continent and risk destroying the Concert that he had been so instrumental in creating would remain uncertain.[18]

The rise of Canning to the Foreign Ministry produced a dramatic change in the relationship between public opinion and foreign policy. Canning held radical royalists and radical democrats in roughly equal contempt, though as he made clear in a letter to the future Charles X, if given a choice between them, he would have to side with the latter:

> Your Royal Highness will not suspect me (I venture to believe) of being infected with Jacobinical principles.... But I do frankly and sincerely declare to Your Royal Highness ... that if I were called to choose between the principle laid down in the speech of H.M. the King of France, and its antagonist principle, the sovereignty of the people, I should feel myself compelled to acknowledge that the former is the more alien of the two to the British Constitution.[19]

That said, Canning was committed to the idea of permitting states to alter their own political institutions, should they choose to do so, without interference from foreign powers. Here, his policy most closely mirrored the reasoning that he expressed in a letter to the Portuguese ambassador in London on the occasion of a Portuguese request for a British commitment to ensure the Portuguese line of succession, when he reaffirmed Britain's pledge

> to deny, and if need be to resist, the pretension of any foreign Power to subvert the reigning dynasty in the other country ... [but not to interfere] with those internal changes or arrangements, which are the result either of civil contest or of legislative policy, and upon which every independent nation rejects the arbitration of a foreign Power.[20]

As the next sections show, these ideals consistently informed his policies as foreign secretary and in his brief tenure as prime minister. Canning initially sought to stalemate the conservative powers of the Continent by practicing and enforcing non-intervention in the affairs of other states; then, having succeeded in disrupting the system of Congresses that met periodically for precisely this purpose, he drifted slowly into measured intervention in behalf of self-determination. Because the latter principle, in the context of the interventionist efforts of the conservative powers, usually implied support for the more liberal side in a dispute, in practice it translated into moderate support for liberal movements abroad. Canning's desire to prevent the intervention of others, by intervention if necessary, explains his support for

---

[18] Scott (1972); Hayes (1975, 79–80).

[19] Stapleton (1887a, 74). The speech to which Canning refers is discussed on page 125.

[20] Stapleton (1887b, 3).

constitutional movements despite his frequent dislike of actual constitutionalists.[21] Nevertheless, when in a speech in April of 1823 Canning asked, "Can it be either our interest or our duty to ally ourselves with revolution?" and answered that "Our station . . . is essentially neutral: neutral not only between contending nations, but between contending principles,"[22] he had already staked out a policy considerably more liberal than that which had been pursued by his predecessor at Vienna and beyond.

This substantial shift in British foreign policy was made possible and then accelerated by Canning's strategy of appealing to public opinion in support of his desired policy. In situations in which Castlereagh might have sought to downplay the differences between the British and the conservative powers to maintain the modicum of cooperation among them that circumstances now permitted, Canning horrified both foreign dignitaries and the more conservative members of his own government by publishing official communications that were likely to provoke a public reaction against the illiberal policies of the Continental powers. Canning was not, as Metternich claimed in 1823, a Radical who "flatters revolution" – he was, after all, a Tory, albeit a liberal one, and he had little interest in the masses. At the same time, however, he realized that liberal middle-class opinion was fast becoming a force that could not be ignored. He also realized that invoking public opinion meant, for better or worse, a decrease in the government's latitude to collaborate with conservative states for illiberal ends.[23]

There was a brief fluctuation in the British worldview in the years between 1827 and 1830. The 1826 election and the sudden incapacity of Liverpool had elevated Canning to the prime ministership, and the government that he formed was an admixture of liberal Tories and Whigs, the "Ultras" under Wellington and Peel having absented themselves. This coalition continued under Goderich following Canning's death in 1827, but the coalition soon fell apart and Wellington was asked to form a government in 1828. Wellington was thought by many Tories to be too conservative; indeed, his articulate advice to post-Vienna foreign secretaries was clearly shaped by the same outlook that had produced the Vienna settlement – a concern for the material balance of capabilities among states, with no regard for self-determination or self-governance. His government lasted until the death of King George IV necessitated new elections in 1830, which returned a Parliament that ousted the government. The combination of a more moderate monarch in William IV, dissension among the Tories, and popular discontent brought the Whigs under Lord Grey to power in 1830.[24]

The new government placed Lord Palmerston in charge of the Foreign Office; in that capacity, with brief interruptions, he embodied British foreign policy for the better part of three decades. Palmerston, a liberal Tory who had been "slowly drifting

---

[21] In the case of Portugal, he referred to them as "the scum of the earth . . . fierce, rascally, thieving, ignorant ragamuffins, hating England and labouring with all their might and cunning to force or entrap us into war" (Seton-Watson 1937, 90).

[22] Therry (1836), cited in Temperley and Penson (1938b, 87).

[23] Webster and Temperley (1924, 165); Hayes (1975, 85–87).

[24] Mitchell (1967, 250–251).

towards Whiggery"[25] since his break with the Tories in the late 1820s, represented the culmination of the process of liberalization that had begun under Canning.

A great deal of ink has been spilled on the question of the influence of liberalism in Palmerston's foreign policy, much of it premised on the untenable assertion that the policy was either completely dominated or totally unaffected by a desire to spread constitutionalism abroad. In the latter case, Palmerston is typically portrayed as a clear-eyed pursuer of the national interest, a statement that is as true as it is meaningless. A more nuanced and meaningful interpretation is offered by Charles Webster, who writes that "Palmerston ... began to take a keen interest in the Liberal Movement apart from British interests, or rather he began to include in those interests the extension of constitutionalism to parts of Europe with which Britain had not hitherto concerned herself."[26]

Palmerston considered constitutional states to be, in his own words, "the natural allies" of Britain. He therefore saw the spread of moderate constitutional government, with its ability to defuse potential revolutionary crises, as a boon to Britain, and as a result he sought to introduce liberal change even in cases, such as that of the Papal States, in which British public opinion was indifferent. His liberalism was by no means absolute – he tended to believe that the Reform Bill of 1832 represented the limit of acceptable liberal reform – but within those bounds, Palmerston became, in the words of the most prominent chronicler of his foreign policy, "the principal exponent of Liberalism in Europe."[27]

Throughout, it is striking to reflect on how thoroughly divorced the issues that prompt most of the conflicts of the period are from *realpolitik* concerns. Though many of them would subsequently involve issues of obvious relevance to realists, many revolved around issues such as the form of a constitution or the choice of a more or less liberal sovereign. The most obvious exception is the Greek revolt, with its clear implications for the Ottoman Empire and Russia; and in that case, as we see, when ideological and *realpolitik* incentives diverged, the latter took a back seat.

The growing liberal challenge

As a result of this change in the British worldview, British foreign policy underwent a quiet but significant liberalization in the 1820s. Although there were few incidents in this decade in which liberal principles were put to the test, British foreign policy evinced a growing affinity for liberal goals and an increased preference for such outcomes relative to those dictated by concerns based purely on relative power.

The first substantial issue that Canning had to deal with was that of Spain, in which a revolt by two military detachments in 1820 had spread and had forced King Ferdinand

[25] The quote, though not its source, is reprinted in Seton-Watson (1937, 153).

[26] Webster (1951, 179). For an example of an argument that Palmerston championed Britain's national interests, see e.g., Hayes (1975, 99).

[27] Webster (1951, 179). See Temperley and Penson (1938b, 101), Southgate (1966, 56), Bartlett (1993, 122–123), Reinerman (1995, 702), Hayes (1975, 98–100); cf. Rooney (1984). For a recent historiographical review of research on Palmerston see D. Brown (2002).

to reintroduce the Spanish Constitution of 1812 – an exemplary document to liberal minds, not in the least because it was founded on the sovereignty of the people, not the king. The Spanish situation and the Greek revolt, as well as a handful of less pressing matters, prompted the Congress of Verona in 1822, and the latter prompted Canning's first attempt to stalemate the conservative powers. Speaking for Canning at Verona, the Duke of Wellington stated unequivocally that the British would not take part in any expedition to restore the Spanish monarchy. Canning then committed Britain to this course of action by making part of his dispatch to Wellington public. Agreement on Spain proved elusive, and the Congress of Verona broke up. Canning thought the dissolution of the Congress to be a fitting end to an undesirable association: "Things are getting back to a wholesome state again; every nation for itself and God for us all."[28]

Nevertheless, the conservative powers sanctioned French intervention in Spain in early 1823. A speech on January 28 by Louis XVIII to Parliament contained a passage that gave Canning an opening to try to prevent this outcome: the French king argued that Ferdinand should be "free to give to his people the institutions they cannot hold but from him." The passage became widely known in Britain, and its reassertion of the doctrine of legitimacy proved most distasteful. Canning used that reaction to his advantage in a letter on February 3, in which he stated that Britain "could not countenance a pretension on the part of France to make her example a rule for other nations, and still less could it admit a peculiar right in France to force that example specifically upon Spain." Canning's reaction proved to be quite popular. Sixteen days later he took further action by announcing an increase of nearly 20% in the number of men in the British Navy, and two days after that he lifted the British embargo on arms exports to Spain. He thought that these measures would prevent a French invasion, but his conservative colleagues, including the king, succeeded in undermining his message. In the end, Canning found himself unable to do more than enumerate the conditions of British neutrality. The French invaded in early April, the Spanish Constitution was abolished, and savage reprisals followed.[29]

Britain, therefore, failed in its first concrete attempt to prevent a conservative restoration, although given the intervention of the king and the Tories it can reasonably be said that the government as a whole only half tried, if that. The attempt itself is noteworthy, however, and subsequent efforts would meet with considerably greater success.

British policy regarding Portugal was somewhat more active and became increasingly so over time. A revolt in 1820 prompted the return of King John VI from Brazil and established a constitution based on the same Spanish Constitution of 1812, to

---

[28] Harris (1955, 502); Artz (1934, 167–170); Webster and Temperley (1924, 165).

[29] Temperley (1966, 77–83); Hayes (1975, 142). Those conditions were no permanent French occupation of Spain, no French attempt to take any colonies from Spain, and no French invasion of Portugal. It is worth mentioning that British acquiescence in the French occupation also stemmed from the fact that the French Army played a key role in keeping the Absolutists from slaughtering the constitutionalists to an even greater degree, though given the fate of individuals like the revolutionary leader Riego, one wonders what more Ferdinand could have imagined. See Halévy (1926, 245).

which the monarch swore allegiance in October 1822. Subsequent unrest in Brazil forced John's eldest son, Dom Pedro, to declare independence, an act that provided fodder for anticonstitutionalist forces in Portugal, whose number included the queen and her second son, Dom Miguel, both reactionaries of the purest stripe. Forced to repeal the constitution, John nevertheless sought to establish a more moderate constitutional regime based on the English model. When Miguel and his followers began to intrigue against him, engineering revolts in 1823 and 1824, John invoked British aid.[30]

Canning's measured response ensured John's retention of the throne without giving the conservative powers, in particular France, a pretext for involvement. While formally declining John's appeal for support, Canning sent a naval squadron to the mouth of the Tagus River. John fled to the British flagship and sent for Miguel. There, under the shadow of British cannon, he suggested to Miguel that he consider an extended vacation abroad, and Miguel agreed to do so, thereby defusing the crisis.[31]

Its abatement, however, proved to be temporary. The death of John VI in 1826 brought Pedro, now Emperor of Brazil, to the throne. Pedro, faced with the untenable prospect of ruling both countries, abdicated in favor of his infant daughter, Maria, and sought to ensure her continued rule by granting Portugal a constitution of his own devising.[32] Canning again stalemated the conservative powers, this time with logic: in June he pointed out to them that, because the constitution had been granted by a legitimate monarch, intervention would constitute interference in the domestic affairs of a fellow sovereign, an act that no true legitimist could countenance.[33]

Disgruntled Miguelist soldiers nevertheless crossed over into Spain, where they were armed and began to make incursions back into Portugal, a situation that prompted another appeal for British aid. Canning responded more forcefully this time, sending 5,000 British troops to preserve the regime of the Infanta.[34]

Reasonable scholars differ on the question of whether Canning aided the Portugese constitutionalists solely because of British treaty obligations. Nevertheless, after the death of Canning and the rise of the conservative Duke of Wellington, British troops were withdrawn, and within three months Miguel had had himself declared king, abolishing Pedro's constitution in the process. The duke, bound by the same treaties as Canning had been, saw no compelling reason to intervene. Moreover, once the Whigs had come to power, the British promptly renewed their support of Maria, with results to be discussed later.

The Greek revolt provides perhaps the most interesting continuous study of the liberalization of British foreign policy in this period. At first, the British had no interest in aiding the Greek rebels; to do so might have encouraged revolution elsewhere and certainly would have helped to weaken the Ottoman Empire, the doddering but still

---

[30] Artz (1934, 156–157).   [31] Hayes (1975, 138–139); Temperley (1966, 194–201).

[32] Of this constitution, Temperley (1966, 366) writes, "It issued from his head alone, and did not altogether do credit to that organ." Pedro sought in part to buy off his brother Miguel with the offer of a marriage to Maria; see Seton-Watson (1937, 90–91), especially the extended footnote at the bottom of p. 91, for a lurid account of the precedents for internecine Iberian solutions to crises of succession.

[33] Hayes (1975, 139–140).   [34] Halévy (1926, 246); Hayes (1975, 140).

substantial impediment to Russia's southward expansion. Whereas the Castlereagh of July 1821 commiserated with Alexander about the "dreadful events" in Greece,[35] however, the Castlereagh of mid-1822 pondered the possibility of some manner of involvement on the side of the rebels, and by March 1823 Canning had recognized the Greeks as formal belligerents, an act that infuriated Metternich.

The most interesting aspect of the conflict may have been the evolution of the legal status of the Greeks. Steven Schwartzberg has argued, in a detailed and extended case study, that British policy sought to extend the right of self-governance, and ultimately full independence, to the Greeks through such vehicles as the Protocol of St. Petersburg of April 1826; he also points out that in doing so the British established a precedent in international law – namely, that intervention of foreign states on behalf of national liberation movements is justified. This doctrine was, of course, the antithesis of the legitimist creed that justified intervention *against* precisely these movements and in favor of established authority. Metternich was not slow to vent his displeasure in a letter to Count Apponyi: "Is England then ready to regard as a Power equal in rights to that of the King the first Irish Club which declares itself the Insurgent Government of Ireland?"[36]

Moreover, the British proved not to be averse to more substantial means of assistance. When loans were raised in London to help the Greeks – the first, in February 1824, for £350,000, and the second, a year later, for £566,000 – Canning attended the banquet that launched the initiative. Britain's first concrete threat of the use of force seems to have come in October 1825, after Canning learned that Ibrahim Pasha, the Ottoman general who brought an army from Egypt to intervene, planned not just to subdue the Greeks but also to rid the islands of them permanently by removing them to Egypt as slaves and repopulating the area with Muslims. In November 1825, Lord Cochrane, naval hero of the Napoleonic Wars, agreed to take command of the Greek Navy. In July 1827 British negotiations produced the Treaty of London, which strove to assure Greek autonomy and, in a secret article,[37] promised intervention in pursuit of that goal if its terms were not accepted. Finally, in October 1827 the tense situation in Navarino Bay, where a Turkish and Egyptian fleet had been contained by their British and (subsequently) French and Russian counterparts for more than a month, exploded into a lopsided close-quarters battle that crippled the Ottoman Navy.[38]

---

[35] Schwartzberg (1988a, 145).

[36] Schwartzberg (1988a, 1988b); the quote, from a letter of October 17, 1826, can be found in Temperley (1966, 360–361).

[37] The sense in which this article should be considered "secret" is rather unclear. When the treaty was published on page 2 of the London Times of Thursday, July 12, 1827, the secret article was printed along with it, under the heading, "ADDITIONAL AND SECRET ARTICLE" (emphasis in original). The Ottomans could hardly have missed the point.

[38] Brewer (2001, 251, 254, 289–291, ch. 13). The amounts of the loans are not trivial. Utilizing the index developed by Allen (2003), their value in the year 2000 would be in the trillions of pounds. Admittedly, given changes in the value of items, the distribution of wealth, etc., over such great periods, a comparison of this sort must be taken with a hefty grain of salt, but even so it represents a substantial commitment.

From the onset, the Greek struggle contained a constitutional dimension as well: while the Greeks experimented with relatively liberal constitutions from early 1822 through 1827, when the most noteworthy, the Trizini Constitution, was established, the Ottoman Empire was entirely illiberal both in its policies and in its political structure. Moreover, British policy by 1827 represented a very substantial departure from the earlier strategy of maintaining a unified Ottoman Empire to prevent southward Russian incursions. Indeed, such thinking is well reflected in the letter sent by Wellington to Canning in November of 1825, in which the duke urged the foreign secretary to issue a joint declaration with Austria and France "not to submit to any further aggrandisement of the Russian empire" and, should the declaration fail, to "resort to the only effectual measure for saving the Turks."[39] The course of action chosen – supporting Greek independence at the expense of Ottoman territorial integrity – reflects the British shift toward a more liberal worldview.

What is most striking, in light of the theory and the events to come, is what did *not* happen during this period: the conservative powers of the East did not react in a substantial manner to the ongoing liberalization of British foreign policy. Neither the transition from Castlereagh to Canning to Palmerston, nor the Iberian stalemate, nor the increasingly liberal British policy in Greece alerted them to the fact that a closer alignment among them would be wise. It took a substantial change in the ideological structure of the system – in the form of revolutions in the west, sustained by the liberal powers against eastern opposition – to cement that realization.

The early 1830s: revolution and schism

By 1830, worldviews had diverged enough that no general European consensus could be reached on the question of revolution. Therefore, when revolutions did come at that time, they succeeded in the west, where Britain and Orleanist France were able to intervene with greatest effect, but failed farther east. Within a few years, the outcome was a substantial gain for the cause of liberalism as well as a set of standing alliances that divided the continent along ideological lines.

The conflicts that ultimately produced this schism were precipitated by the July Revolution in France and the rise of the Whigs following the elections of 1830.[40] In France, although the revolution produced only a modest change in the composition of the political elite, it nevertheless led to a very substantial change in the foundation of political authority: Louis Philippe took the title "King of the French," rather than "King of France," a distinction made meaningful by the formal subjugation of the monarchy to the law of the land.[41] These events produced great chagrin among conservatives.[42]

---

[39] Schwartzberg (1988a, 161–162).

[40] On relationships between these events see McGee (1977) and Quinault (1994).

[41] Pilbeam (1982, 366) describes the change in the elite and argues that Charles X and the Ultras were "the real revolutionaries" in that they sought, and were prevented from realizing, a far more substantial change than that accomplished by their successors. For a general review and discussion of the foundation of legal authority see Pinkney (1987).

[42] Metternich's reaction is telling: Alan Sked reports that "his doctor, who had to be called in, found him slumped on his desk sobbing that his life's work was at an end" (Sked 1979a, 10). At the same

Although the new French king, aware that substantial support for revolutionary movements abroad would most likely doom his regime, soon succeeded in convincing Austria and Prussia of his peaceful intentions, the Tsar remained implacable, and rumors of a Franco-Russian war persisted in France through the winter of 1830-31.[43]

Under these circumstances the French looked to Britain to prevent their own isolation. The Belgian revolution provided both the first opportunity for the two states to cooperate and the severest test of their ability to do so. The United Kingdom of the Netherlands owed its agglomerated existence to British security needs, which were brought forward in sharp relief by the prospect of French intervention of any sort. The uneasy settlement of 1815 that created the United Kingdom of the Netherlands, along with growing tensions between the Belgian church and the Dutch government, produced an increasingly volatile situation that reached a turning point when the Belgian Provinces demanded autonomy under the Dutch King William. Negotiations ensued for a month but ultimately broke down, and four days of fighting in the streets removed Dutch troops from Brussels by the end of September, 1830. By early November Belgium had been liberated from Dutch control, and a National Assembly had declared its intention to establish an independent monarchy and write its own constitution. The resulting document was substantially more democratic than Britain's, even after the passage of the Reform Bill; it survived, largely unaltered, into the 1970s.[44]

From the point of view of power politics, very little commended the Belgian cause in British eyes. The dissolution of the Netherlands would be a blow to British security in one of the few places on the Continent that it considered to be strategically vital. Moreover, the process by which that dissolution was taking place invited French intervention and raised the serious danger of French territorial aggrandizement. Looking back on the situation in 1833, Wellington stated that if he had remained in power his primary objectives would have been to hold the Netherlands together and to contain France.[45]

The fact that Palmerston came to office committed to the independence of Belgium, therefore, testifies to his valuation of constitutional government.[46] He favored an alternative scheme, the guaranteed neutrality of Belgium, by which the Great Powers would resolve the strategic issue without coercing Belgium into rejoining the Netherlands. When the Dutch invaded Belgium in August 1831, the British

time, "[t]he appointment in November 1830 of a Whig government in England, committed to a measure of parliamentary reform, was regarded by many European conservatives ... as an event not very different in its consequences from the French revolution of July" (Bridge and Bullen 1980, 50).

[43] M. Brown (1978); Pilbeam (1970). Louis Philippe was most likely correct in his assessment: see Webster (1951, 93).

[44] For a clear account of these events see Artz (1934, 273–275).   [45] Bartlett (1979, 154).

[46] It may also, admittedly, have reflected a desire not to drive the Belgians into the arms of the French – see e.g., Rich (1992, 60) – but it seems more reasonable to argue that this desire prompted Palmerston to moderate the terms of the eventual settlement; Ward and Gooch (1923, 147). Moreover, the Duke of Wellington, who had surely not been unaware of this possibility, and whose strategic acumen was beyond question, had nevertheless sought to reunite the two countries.

and the French combined to drive them out, after which Palmerston ensured that the French removed their troops in timely fashion. Despite the desire of the Eastern powers to intervene, Palmerston was adamant that a solution would be worked out at the conference table. Had Britain not served as midwife to the new Belgian state, its viability would have been tenuous indeed.[47]

The revolutions in France and Belgium had been a matter of considerable concern for Nicholas: he found the affront to the legitimist principle that they constituted odious, but he remained somewhat uncertain about how serious a threat they represented to the peace of Europe. His darker fears were realized in November 1830, when a brewery fire in Warsaw signaled the start of a revolution in Poland. The Polish uprising, in tilting the balance of the system abruptly away from legitimism, demonstrated beyond doubt the threat that revolutionary, constitutional movements represented.[48]

In Portugal, Miguel's victory was all but certain by 1830. Only a single garrison remained loyal to Maria. In 1832, Dom Pedro returned and sought to reassert his daughter's claim to the throne by force of arms, but to little effect. The forces remained stalemated. Following the July Revolution, however, the French government had removed its objections to British support for Maria, and British volunteers, many from the military despite the Foreign Enlistment Act,[49] rallied to Pedro's side. By mid-1833, the Miguelists had been driven back and Pedro's forces occupied Lisbon.[50]

Similarly, in Spain another succession crisis loomed. Ferdinand VII died in 1833, leaving a young daughter, Isabella, as his heir. Britain and France recognized the new queen, but Ferdinand's brother, whose own claim to the throne had only recently been erased by Ferdinand's nullification of a 1713 law that would have barred Isabella from the throne, rose in armed opposition to his niece. The queen regent announced a constitution modeled on the French Charter, rendering the similarities between the two Iberian struggles eerily complete. The Eastern states had had no need to intervene in Spain previously, because France had done so for them; now they provided material and financial aid to the supporters of Don Carlos. These events prompted Palmerston to write to his ambassador in Madrid that the object of British policy should be "to form a Western confederacy of free states as a counterpoise to the Eastern League of arbitrary governments. England, France, Spain and Portugal, united as they now must be, will form a political and moral power in Europe which will hold Metternich and Nicholas in check ... and all the smaller planets of Europe will have a natural tendency to gravitate towards our system."[51]

In the midst of these developments, Nicholas met with his Eastern counterparts to resolve their outstanding differences and to attempt to shore up the Eastern bloc. Their first article of cooperation was the *Chiffon de Carlsbad,* a joint resolution to prevent

---

[47] On the desire of the Eastern monarchs to intervene see e.g., Hayes (1975, 178–179) and Ward and Gooch (1923, 145).

[48] See Lincoln (1978, 130–144).

[49] One of the most important victories of the campaign at sea was won by the vice admiral of the loyalist fleet, Carlos Ponza – also known as Post Captain Charles Napier of the Royal Navy.

[50] Rich (1992, 60); Ward and Gooch (1923, 188).

[51] See Bridge and Bullen (1980, 58–59) and Bullen (1977) for details; on Palmerston's reaction see Rich (1992, 65).

French influence from spreading across the continent. Russia and Austria came to a more concrete mutual understanding in the Treaty of Münchengrätz of 1833 and included Prussia in the separate Convention of Berlin of the same year. The new agreement established the right of rulers to call on one another for assistance in the event of a revolt and explicitly denied the right of intervention to any state *not* called upon to help. In the event of unwanted intervention, the agreement emphasized the right of legitimist states to come together in collective self-defense.[52] Obviously, the only states that might desire to intervene absent invitation would be Great Britain and France. In practice, then, the treaty was an attempt to deter antilegitimist intervention by threat of force.

The solidarity of the Eastern monarchs, in turn, facilitated Western cooperation. Britain and France took the occasion of intervention in Spain and Portugal to form another Quadruple Alliance, this time with the two peninsular countries. In the end, revolutions in Poland and Italy, outside of the Western sphere of influence, were quashed, but thanks in large part to British influence the Western revolutions held. The latter constituted the first serious threat to the legitimist consensus established at Troppau. More significantly, in the case of Belgium Britain had established the legitimacy of territorial revisions based on popular uprisings.[53]

The larger significance of the Quadruple Alliance was obvious, and it demonstrated how much the world had changed in just under 15 years. One of the lesser known passages in Castlereagh's May 5 State Paper gave a clear depiction of the author's view of the Continent:

> In considering Continental Europe as divided into two great Masses, the Western, consisting of France and Spain, the Eastern of all the other Continental States still subsisting with some limited exceptions, under the form of their ancient Institutions, the great Question is, what System of general and defensive Policy . . . ought the latter States to adopt with a view of securing themselves against those dangers, which may directly or indirectly assail them from the former.[54]

Palmerston's letter to his brother, William Temple, regarding the Quadruple Alliance shows an entirely different perception both of the struggle and of England's role in it:

> it will settle Portugal, and go some way to settle Spain also. But, what is of more permanent and extensive importance, it establishes a quadruple alliance among the constitutional states of the west, which will serve as a powerful counterpoise to the Holy Alliance of the east.[55]

Summary

The Treaty of Vienna set the stage for stasis in the European theater. The distribution of capabilities among the Great Powers was designed to deter any of them from altering it, or anything else, by force of arms, and propagation of the principle of legitimism

[52] Riasanovsky (1959, 243–244).   [53] Thomson (1978, 170–172).
[54] Ward and Gooch (1923, 630).   [55] Bourne (1970, 224); see also Bulwer (1871, 180–181).

held forth the promise of checking the threat of revolution. In the absence of changes in the basic parameters of the model, once the nationalist uprisings inspired by the Napoleonic Wars had been quelled it would have been very reasonable to expect a long period of inactivity and an absence of competition.

The most substantial challenge to a quiet European order came from the evolution of Britain's domestic political ideology, which was reflected in particular in its policies toward the Iberian states and Greece: the British rarely instigated change on the Continent, but increasingly over time when there were constitutionalist movements, revolts, or revolutions, the British worked not to undermine them but rather to protect them and secure their gains. Nevertheless, the conservative reaction to the liberalization of Britain's worldview was neither contemporaneous nor proactive: rather, as the results were felt in places like Portugal, Belgium, and ultimately another of the Great Powers, France, the conservative Great Powers grew increasingly restive. Ultimately, provoked by the deterioration of the status quo, they moved to form a coalition against the constitutional states of the West, which responded in kind.

This dynamic would be impossible to understand without taking a systemic perspective. The actors established the structure of the international system in a very self-conscious manner in an attempt to avoid further large-scale warfare. Once British liberalization began, its impact was felt at the level of the structure of the system (particularly in the balance of ideology), and only after that balance had shifted abruptly did the conservative powers react to it.

Case 2: the end of American isolation, 1940

American passivity in the face of Nazi aggression in the years leading up to World War II has become legendary. Like the ostrich to which it has subsequently been so often compared, the United States hid its head in the sand while Europe fell, state by state, to Nazi aggression. It was not until the Japanese attack on Pearl Harbor that American isolationism was finally banished. As no less prominent an historian than John Lewis Gaddis writes, "Pearl Harbor was, then, the defining moment for the American empire. . . . Isolationism had thrived right up to this moment; but once it became clear that isolationism could leave the nation open to military attack, it suffered a blow from which it never recovered."[56]

How does the nested politics model explain both the fact and the ending of America's inactivity? Given the American tendency to view the world in terms of its -isms, the rise of fascism in Europe should have occasioned considerable alarm. To some extent the hope expressed later by Harry Truman – that the fascists and the communists would obliterate one another – could be cited as a possible explanation of American inaction, but it can only be taken so far, because it soon became clear that the democratic states of Europe would not be able to escape such a conflict, and the threat to the balances of power and ideology should have prompted an American reaction. It is unsurprising, then, that Randall Schweller (1998, 172) concludes that "[s]tructural-systemic theory

[56] Gaddis (1997, 35–36).

cannot explain why the United States did not play a more active mediator or balancer role in Europe."

Schweller's inference about the prediction of systemic theory, in this case at least, is correct. The nested politics model does suggest that, although the United States should have been relatively unconcerned with the Nazi threat during the 1930s, it should have become much more active once that threat was realized and the structure of the international system tipped substantially in Germany's direction. Translated into the terms of the model's main hypotheses, the argument suggests that, once the Nazi worldview changed and Germany's ideological ideal point shifted, the result should have been an increased level of activity on the part of Germany (H_{A1}), resulting in a change in the structure of the international system (H_{St1}). After that change had occurred, but not before, the result should be an increase in the levels of activity of those states, like the United States, whose ideal points were rendered abruptly more distant from the new structural status quo (H_{A1}).

As I intend to demonstrate in the following case study, however, Schweller's abandonment of systemic theory is nevertheless premature. The model is actually quite correct in making this prediction; it is the popular perception of America as having been inactive in the face of Nazi aggression that is mistaken. America reacted, not to Nazi intentions or characteristics, but to tangible changes in the systemic status quo. Those changes were long in coming because Germany was, at the time of Hitler's rise, unable to do much to alter anything outside its own borders, but it set about to do so with single-minded determination. Once Germany achieved that goal, in the late 1930s and especially in 1940, America took notice and took countermeasures. The most reasonable point at which to date the demise of American isolationism is not December 1941 but nearly a year and a half earlier, in the summer of 1940 – precisely the point at which France fell to Nazi Germany and the threat of fascism became manifest.

The legacy of Versailles

Accounts of the rise of the Third Reich often emphasize the role of the Great Depression in increasing the popularity of Nazism. Its role, however, may well be overstated:

> [T]here are serious reasons to question the widely accepted thesis, according to which the 1930–33 Depression not only contributed to but made it possible for Hitler to acquire power. We know that a most important step – literally a breakthrough – in his fortunes was the September 1930 Reichstag election, when the National Socialists received nearly seven times more votes than they did two years before – from less than 3 to almost 19 percent of all votes cast. Yet historians have devoted relatively little attention to the already rapid increase of National Socialist votes in the summer of 1929 and in early 1930 in the municipal and state elections..., rising at times to 13 or 14 percent. This happened *before* the worldwide Depression and the tide of unemployment in Weimar Germany.[57]

---

[57] Lukacs (1998, 209; emphasis in original).

It did *not* happen, however, before the conclusion of the Young Plan in the spring of 1929. The Young Plan, for the first time, specified the exact amount that Germany would have to pay in reparations: 120 billion marks, or $28 billion. At the end of a decade of privation, Germans learned that they had paid off only 7% of their debt and would be continuing to pay reparations for another six decades.

This debt and the evisceration of the German armed forces[58] were the centerpieces of the Versailles settlement, an attempt to structure the system in a manner best suited to prevent war. Even a cursory glance at the distributions of capabilities in the two systems, however, makes one fact glaringly apparent: the authors of the Versailles treaty, unlike their counterparts at Vienna, were *not* agnostic regarding which Great Power posed the greatest threat of war, and they designed their system accordingly.

The leader of the right-wing German People's Party, Alfred Hugenberg, initiated a petition demanding the repudiation of the Young Plan and everything else associated with the Versailles settlement; in this he was joined by, among others, Adolf Hitler. Four million Germans signed the petition and six million voted for the subsequent referendum. Even though it did not pass, the referendum succeeded in forming a bridge between the German right and the Nazis.[59]

Nazi ideology

Two elements stand out in Hitler's worldview.[60] The first is a broad social theory that corresponds in large part to Darwin's theory of species: the *Lebenskampf,* or "struggle for life." It is especially important to note that, in Hitler's schema, the analog to a species is a people, not a state or a race.[61] The main components of this theory were that the goal of a people is self-preservation and that territory defined the limits of growth. The combination of these two components implied a life-and-death struggle among the peoples.[62]

The second element is a hierarchy of peoples which that lent content to the Darwinistic form. The criteria for ranking the various peoples are rather unclear to this day, as are the relative rankings themselves, but the primary criterion seems to be industriousness, which was analogous to fitness. The Nordic peoples were consistently placed in the highest tier, well above Slavs, Africans, and so forth. The position of the Jews is somewhat controversial: Hitler often referred to their subhumanity, but

---

[58] The army was limited to 100,000 men, the navy to ships of under 10,000 tons displacement, and combat aircraft, tanks, and submarines were banned; further articles eliminated conscription, limited the Germans to no more than 4,000 officers, and so on. See Shuster (2006) for details.

[59] Pulzer (1997, 118).

[60] In this case more than any of the others, with the possible exception of the Soviet Union under Stalin, one person's worldview has become that of a country. Such cases provide the advantage of precision at the cost of accuracy: no society could formulate its views in as much detail as Hitler did in *Mein Kampf* – but it is much easier for Hitler to lie in *Mein Kampf* than it would be for a society to lie in, say, a national survey.

[61] The distinction between a people and a race may seem vanishingly small, but in Hitler's mind a people was characterized by a mixture of racial traits. See Lukacs (1998, 123).

[62] Messerschmidt (1990, 544–545).

at the same time he seems to have considered their racial characteristics to have been among the strongest. This bizarre duality contributed to Hitler's image of Jews as being simultaneously beneath contempt and immensely threatening.[63]

Such theories were not, unfortunately, all that rare; even Theodore Roosevelt had written that it would be in the world's best interest "that the English-speaking race in all its branches should hold as much of the world's surface as possible."[64] The practice of Western colonialism was often tinged with such notions (if not based on them outright); even Americans had enslaved an alien people, and in the coming war they would inter another. Kaiser (1990, 370) places Hitler squarely in the European political tradition by noting that "[h]is most extreme views dealt with precisely the two questions around which European international politics in the late nineteenth and early twentieth centuries had hitherto revolved: imperialism and nationalities questions."

Even though it must be admitted that the core elements of Hitler's worldview were not unique, however, their combination has rarely proven so pernicious. Why this was the case in Germany and not elsewhere (at least not to anything like the same degree) is perhaps not answerable.[65] To some extent, on a purely practical level, it can be explained by Germany's industrial base: Hitler quite simply had resources that other would-be Hitlers did not. To some extent, too, it can be explained by the heavy emphasis in Nazism on social Darwinism: without it, nationalism need not be particularly internationalist. (Indeed, the two are often thought of as opposites.)

Once the conclusion had been reached that international relations is a life-and-death struggle of one people versus another, it was clear from a glance at the map that Germany was playing an exceptionally poor hand in the early 1930s. Alsace-Lorraine was French, as was the Saar; Poland possessed most of Upper Silesia and a corridor separating East Prussia from the rest of the country. German cities had been ceded to Lithuania (Memel) and Poland (Danzig), and Germany and Austria had been separated. All told, Germany had lost (relative to what it had had at the beginning of World War I) 13% of its population, 26% of its coal resources, and 75% of its iron ore.[66]

These conditions, imposed by the Versailles settlement, were meant to weaken Germany so that it could cause no more trouble. They made sense from the point of view of solving the perennial French security dilemma, but to a German who saw the world as a life-and-death struggle of peoples they seemed a grave threat. The transition from the Weimar Republic to Nazi Germany, therefore, was accompanied by a drastic reevaluation of the status quo: the overthrow of the European political order, not just minor adjustments within the existing order, was called for.

The most important task in Hitler's mind was the unification of the German people. Two things would have to be accomplished if this goal were to be achieved: territorial expansion of the German state and the "purification" of the German people. The next

---

[63] On this point see Lukacs (1998, ch. 4) as well as Goldhagen (1996, 411–412).

[64] Quoted in Finkelstein and Birn (1998, 83–84).

[65] I remain unconvinced by theories that posit that some irreducible element of Germanness is to blame; for the most notable exposition of such a thesis see Goldhagen (1996, 77–78, 428, and *passim*); for an occasionally *ad hominem* but ultimately useful reply see Finkelstein and Birn (1998).

[66] Pulzer (1997, 98).

goal would be to ensure the survival of the *Volk* by securing agricultural land to the east and, ultimately, by establishing continental hegemony.[67]

Formulating such a worldview was, in Hitler's mind, the task of the "programmatic thinker"; implementing it was the task of the politician.[68] Hitler saw himself as both. In the former capacity he was clearly an idealogue and a fanatic – by which I mean that his conclusions were often more consistent with his goals than with his premises (a characteristic that has already been noted in his extremely inconsistent depiction of Jews). In the latter, however, he proved more adroit. He realized from the onset that the most serious opposition to German continental hegemony would come from France, and therefore that France would have to be defeated before he could complete his plans for eastward expansion. He also realized that Italy was his only potential continental ally and that, to stay on good terms with it he would have to renounce his claims to the territory occupied by ethnic Germans in the Southern Tirolian Alps.

In other areas Hitler proved a less canny politician. Most notably, he underestimated the ability of the Soviet Union to wage war. His expectations regarding the British reaction to his foreign policy were not only wrong but stupid: he expected that Britain would aid him against France as a means of reestablishing a balance of power on the Continent but also believed, against all reason, that Britain would then quietly acquiesce to a gross imbalance in favor of Germany – this despite Britain's long-standing and well-advertised policy of preventing any single power from achieving continental hegemony – and content itself with overseas expansion.[69]

The German historian Eberhard Jäckel sums up Hitler's foreign policy objectives neatly:

> Hitler's foreign policy was thus divided into three major phases. During the first phase, Germany had to achieve internal consolidation and rearmament and to conclude agreements with Britain and Italy. During the second phase Germany had to defeat France in a preliminary engagement. Then the great war of conquest against Russia could take place during the third and final phase.... It was, of course, not a timetable or even a detailed prospectus, but a definite and structured list of objectives, priorities, and conditions.[70]

It is important to note, as Jäckel does, that these foreign policy priorities, derived directly from Hitler's worldview, had been formulated well before he took power.

The combination of the extremist, ideological core beliefs of a "programmatic thinker" and the pragmatic tenets of a politician formed a foreign policy of rational means and irrational ends. Hitler's tactics, taken one at a time, might seem perfectly reasonable to the most calculating *realpolitician*, but taken as a whole they spelled

---

[67] Jäckel (1972). The extent to which Hitler's ambitions extended beyond European hegemony is unclear. He rarely advocated world domination explicitly – but he may not have done so only because he thought it impractical. See Weinberg (1970, 2–7), Stoakes (1986, 220, 234–236), and Jäckel (1984, 24).

[68] Dredging *Mein Kampf* for references to the distinctions between the two would be quite time consuming; they are neatly collected in Jäckel (1972, 13–14).

[69] Jäckel (1972).   [70] Jäckel (1984, 25–26).

disaster: Hitler took immense risks and spurred a powerful countercoalition in an attempt to achieve goals far beyond those implied by the cold calculus of power.

German foreign policy

A debate has arisen among historians of Nazi Germany as to the fundamental source of policy activity throughout most of the Nazi period. "Intentionalists" find a strong continuity between Hitler's goals and German actions. "Functionalists" describe a polycratic Nazi state consisting of coalitions (party, state, military, etc.) jostling for control over a wide range of policy issue areas. To the former school, Hitler guided German policy entirely; to the latter, he still controlled policy but was constrained by the practical necessity of coalition-building and maintenance.[71]

The debate is relevant to the manner in which worldviews are translated into actions. On this point, however, the differences between the two schools are actually quite minor. Broszat (1981, 352–353), speaking for the functionalists, concedes the point that the effects of Nazi "polycracy" were more tactical than strategic – that they were more important in determining the means to the end than in determining the end itself. He maintains that tactical decisions were often critical, a point with which I largely concur, but here we are concerned with the end, not the means. The only way in which a functionalist account would be relevant in this case would be if the politics of the Nazi state altered its long-term goals or paralyzed it, preventing it from attempting to achieve those goals. My reading is that the functionalist literature makes neither claim.

In fact, after about 1934, Hitler's constituency was redundant, in that his position was ensured only by those whose positions he ensured.[72] Although he was beholden to a variety of groups for his position, he was fully capable of eliminating or subverting them if they became a threat. The most obvious example is that of the Nazi storm troopers, the *Sturm-Abteilungen* (SA), thugs organized by Ernst Röhm whose nominal job was to protect Nazi speakers but who specialized in picking fights with (and beating up) the Nazis' political opponents and victims. By 1934 the SA were half a million strong, and Röhm's political ambitions were becoming apparent. Accordingly, on the night of July 29–30, 1934, Röhm and 95 other leaders of the SA were surprised in their homes and executed. After the "Night of the Long Knives," as it came to be called, the SA ceased to represent a political threat.[73]

German weakness

Absent hindsight, the conclusion that Germany's military was not to be feared, especially on the high seas, was a reasonable one at the time. Admittedly, the pace of rearmament was startling. In 1933, the Germans instituted a plan that would bring them up to 21 fully functional standing divisions (expandable to 33 in wartime) by

---

[71] See, e.g., Jäckel (1984), Broszat (1981).
[72] Previewing an argument made in the next case study, Roeder (1993, 27–29) argues that this characteristic of reciprocal accountability is a regular feature of autocratic states.
[73] Pulzer (1997, 134–135).

1938; they achived their goal in 1935, by which time they were already planning for a total of 36 (54 in wartime). Twenty-nine divisions were in existence by the end of 1935, and in the following year the pace was picked up and the goal set to 41 standing and 102 wartime divisions. By the eve of the Nazi invasion of Poland in 1939, 103 divisions had been mobilized. Expenditures on the navy increased more than fold between 1932 and 1939, though here the net effect was much smaller, given its initially miniscule budget. The growth of the *Luftwaffe* was most astounding: Germany went from 3 "aerial advertising squadrons" in 1933 to 302 combat-ready squadrons, with a total of 4,093 front-line aircraft, in 1939.[74]

Nevertheless, such numbers could be very misleading. Impressive German aircraft production figures mask the fact that the majority of the aircraft produced through mid-1937 were trainers, and most of the bombers and fighters were obsolete.[75] Germany was deficient in nearly every category of strategic raw materials except coal: its shortages in such obviously crucial materials as iron ore and petroleum, as well as in nickel, manganese, and molybdenum (all important for the production of steel), were critical. A shortage of hard currency ruled out the option of trading for sufficient quantities of these commodities to make up the shortfall. In the period between September 1937 and February 1939, no more than 58.6% of German armament orders could be met by industry due to shortages of material and capacity.[76] Truman Smith, American military attaché in Germany, reported on February 20, 1939, that German military action in the West "is recognized as an absurdity by all Germans, whether military or of the party"; the U.S. Embassy in Germany, relying on an informed and confidential source, reported that German plans involved not invasion but rather the formation of a customs union with the states to its southeast and east.[77]

Germany's economy, moreover, was operating very nearly at full steam even during peacetime. The *Wehrmacht*, therefore, had to achieve victory very quickly, before war could become a competition in mobilization (as it eventually did), and the overtaxed German economy seemed unlikely to be able to sustain the strain to which it had been put for very long.[78] The strains on the German economy produced numerous reports that coups, either popular or military, were likely.[79] A recent appraisal of Roosevelt's assessment of German strength in the late 1930s is illustrative: "While he recognized that the Nazis were clearly acquiring the power to do some damage beyond

---

[74] Deist (1990).

[75] Overy (1984), reviews the state of the *Luftwaffe* and concludes, "During the period 1933–8 offensive operations against a major power could not be seriously contemplated."

[76] Ellis (1993, 273–274); Murray (1984, 16).

[77] Foreign Relations of the United States (*FRUS*) 1939, i, 24, 11.

[78] For a detailed review see Harrison (1988); table 4 demonstrates the inelasticity of Germany's economy.

[79] On September 25, American Ambassador Joseph Kennedy reported that Lord Halifax anticipated an increase in popular unrest and a military coup; *FRUS* 1939, i, 453–454. When Sumner Wells toured Europe in early 1940, he met with Hjalmar Schacht, former president of the Reichsbank, who told him of an impending military coup (*FRUS* 1940, i, 57).

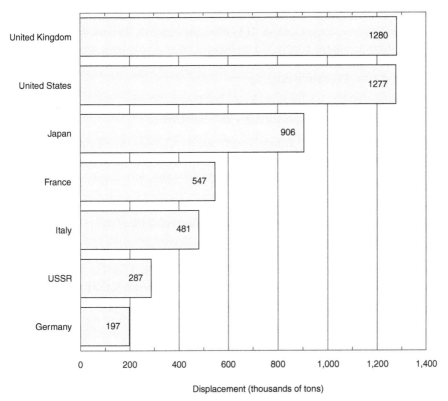

Figure 4.2. Naval strength of major powers, 1939.

their borders, he detected numerous signs below the surface that Hitler's rearmament program was engendering political and economic difficulties."[80]

Moreover, however debatable the German threat on land and in the air, its surface navy was in abysmal shape. As Figure 4.2 demonstrates, the ability of Germany to project power over water as late as 1939 was virtually nil. The entire fleet consisted of a total of 102 vessels, 57 of which were U-boats. Only two battleships were in service (although the massive *Bismarck* would soon be launched – and sunk). The navy possessed no aircraft carriers. The German experiment with superheated steam engines for larger vessels had produced little success, and mechanical difficulties were commonplace. These factors limited the range of the larger ships to about 1,000 nautical miles; even if Germany had had aircraft carriers, therefore, it would not have been able to bring air power to within striking distance of the American mainland. Although Nazi U-boats were capable of disrupting a considerable amount of sea traffic, they were useless for transporting equipment or troops in any significant number. Admiral Raeder remarked of his country's surface fleet that "even at full strength, they can do no more than show that they know how to die

[80] Casey (2001, 8).

gallantly."[81] Given that the United States had, in the previous year, decided to increase its fleet by 20% to include a total of 21 battleships, 7 aircraft carriers, 40 cruisers, and 252 destroyers, Germany simply had no hope of being able to wage any sort of war in the Atlantic in the foreseeable future. Even if the United States stood still, Germany would need 12 to 15 years to catch up.[82]

Initial American indifference

Threat is a combination of malign intent and capabilities. In Europe in the early 1930s, neither was apparent. The absence of American activity in this early period, therefore, tells us little about American internationalism or isolationism. The first of these prerequisites was only met as the nature of the Nazi regime became clear. The second was met after the fall of France in 1940.

The initial reactions of American officials to the rise of the Nazi Party in Germany demonstrated only relatively minor concern about the possibility of a dictatorship and virtually none about the rise of an ideology fundamentally incompatible with liberalism. In fact, the American chargé d'affaires in Berlin, reporting on the substantial Nazi gains in the September 1930 elections, specifically noted the party's apparent lack of any ideological coherence; their promises seemed to depend most on what the listeners wanted to hear. Quoting a Nazi pamphlet, the diplomat reported that the group was formed "without a definite goal, without a program and only the one desire of emerging somehow or other from the muddle of the times."[83] Once Hitler came to power, his goals became clearer, but not transparent: foremost among them, it seemed, was the reestablishment of Germany as a Great Power, perhaps even the dominant power in Europe.[84]

For some time after his ascent to power, therefore, Hitler seemed to many Americans to possess goals no more or less morally repugnant than those of his neighbors. To some extent this was by design: Hitler's speeches regarding peace and noninterference in his neighbors' affairs were designed to nullify American opposition.[85] The absence of any moral issue other than imperialism meant, to an America in a progressive state of mind, that there was no overlap of interests between the United States and the Western democracies: "America might favor their form of government but, it was argued, had no valid reason for aiding them in the preservation of their imperial domains."[86] Because experience had proven that taking sides in a war among empires did nothing to slow the spread of imperialism, European conflicts seemed irrelevant to American interests.

---

[81] Langer and Gleason (1952, 246). The remark referred to an Anglo-German conflict, but the numbers suggest that German prospects in a naval war with the United States were little better.

[82] Stegemann (1991). If the Germans had managed to capture the British fleet, of course, the story would be entirely different, but to do so they would have had to fight their way through the fleet and probably would have destroyed the bulk of it in the process. If their experience with the French fleet was indicative, moreover, conquering Britain would do little to aid their navy. See Langer and Gleason (1952, ch. 16).

[83] *FRUS* 1930, iii, 85.   [84] Lukacs (1998, 131).

[85] See Adler (1965, 169).   [86] Jonas (1966, 112).

As the Neutrality Laws were being passed and implemented, Americans started to revise their image of Europe. It was clear from the onset that Hitler's ideology was nondemocratic, and his soothing words aside it was not too difficult to discern that it was even anti-democratic. The extent of the Nazi regime's illiberalism, however, came as a considerable surprise.[87] Refugees' stories became increasingly horrific. In late July of 1935, the New York *Times* ran a story arguing that the Nazis were "in the midst of a violent campaign to eliminate Jews from Germany's cultural and political life."[88] By 1936, John Gunther was able to amass enough information to write *Inside Europe*, a book that detailed Hitler's early atrocities; the book became a bestseller in the United States.[89] The worst was still far off – available evidence points to some time in 1941 as the point at which Hitler made the decision to implement the Final Solution[90] – but as the 1930s progressed Americans became increasingly aware that Nazism was anathema. By early 1939, when Hitler was named "Man of the Year" by *Time* magazine, the nature of Nazism was hardly in doubt: breaking with its tradition of depicting the Man of the Year in a somber and respectful light, the magazine chose as a cover a painting by a Catholic emigré of the Führer as a mad organist in a desecrated cathedral, his victims dangling from a Saint Catherine's wheel.[91]

Still, it is striking, and noteworthy from the point of view of the systemic argument being evaluated here, that despite increasing recognition of the nature of Hitler's regime, America did little if anything to oppose it. Military spending increased, but it did so in response to the situation in the Pacific, and it failed to keep pace with the Japanese buildup. The American reaction to the *Anschluss* was virtually nonexistent. As the crisis in Czechoslovakia worsened, Roosevelt wrote to his European counterparts that the United States "has no interest in Europe and will assume no obligations in the present negotiations."[92] At the same time, Americans thought Hitler a vicious barbarian. Had the Americans been responding directly to changes within Germany, American foreign policy should have followed changes in the characteristics of the German state much more directly. As it was, America evinced strikingly little concern until there was actually a substantial change in the structure of the international system, in the form of the fall of France.

This peculiar mix of disgust and inaction is the hallmark of American foreign policy in the late 1930s. Its source is not difficult to discern: although Americans realized that Hitler was evil, they believed that American intervention was unnecessary because the democratic states of Europe were in no immediate danger. The same issue of *Time* noted that British control of the seas was incontrovertible and that "[m]ost military men regard the French Army as incomparable." Extensive eastward expansion seemed

---

[87] On the willingness of the West to accommodate a "normal" state and Germany's failure to meet the criterion see Pulzer (1997, 140–141).

[88] Abzug (1999, 47).   [89] Adler (1965, 198).

[90] Goldhagen (1996, 147) claims that the decision was made in late 1940 or early 1941; Gerlach (1998), argues that the decision was not made until December 1941.

[91] *Time*, January 2, 1939. A Saint Catherine's wheel consists of four large wheels, each turning in a different direction and each armed with serrated blades, knives, etc. It was among the most ghastly of the instruments of martyrdom, which says quite a bit.

[92] Duroselle (1963, 255).

possible but unlikely. The widely cited statistic that 95% of Americans thought that America should keep out of the war[93] reflects the belief that the democracies were in little danger even without formal American participation.[94]

Structural change: Germany's rise

The recognition of Hitler's odious program fulfilled the first prerequisite for American internationalism: politics on the European continent became relevant to American ideals. Only later, when the structural balance tipped heavily and abruptly in favor of Germany, was the second prerequisite fulfilled: the threat to those ideals became a serious one.

The *Anschluss* had done little to ease Germany's chronic shortages; nor did the Munich agreement, though it left Czechoslovakia defenseless. The seizure of Prague on March 15, 1939, was a different matter. Czech industries had stockpiled raw materials, Czech armament factories were well supplied and were not difficult to utilize, existing Czech munitions were quite substantial, and plunder from the Czech national bank combined with profits from the sale of some Czech arms alleviated Germany's hard-currency problems. Germany's capabilities had also been amplified by doctrinal innovation in the use of air power and, as Poland soon discovered, mechanized land power.[95]

The invasion of Poland in September brought a declaration of war by the Allies and a blockade designed to deprive Germany of the supplies it would need to wage further warfare. The blockade, though imperfect, nevertheless cut Germany off from vital strategic supplies. Germany immediately lost access to 43% of its imported iron ore, and in the nine-month *sitzkrieg* following the invasion of Poland, Germany's petroleum reserve fell by a third. Combat operations for any substantial period of time, given these conditions, were increasingly inconceivable.[96]

Accordingly, as the weeks passed in early 1940 it seemed increasingly likely that Germany was reaching a critical juncture, if it had not passed it already: the point at which its dwindling strategic reserves and strained economy would render it impotent. Indeed, a review of American diplomatic communications during this time mostly reveals discussions of a European settlement, the form that such a settlement should take, and the problems to be dealt with in the postwar period.[97] Although some may have anticipated that Hitler would lash out in a desperate westward gamble, therefore, few anticipated the speed or the extent of its success.[98]

The events of May and June 1940, especially the surrender of France on June 22, produced a drastic change in the European balance. By the end of June the number

---

[93] The figure remains constant across a variety of surveys from February 1937 to October 1939; see Cantril (1948).

[94] On this point see Reynolds (1982).

[95] Murray (1984). Murray (292) puts the Czech munitions totals at "1,231 aircraft (with material for the construction of another 240), 1,966 antitank guns, 2,254 pieces of field artillery, 810 tanks, 57,000 machine guns, and 630,000 rifles. . . . The equipment was sufficient to equip nearly thirty divisions."

[96] Murray (1984, 328–330).   [97] *FRUS* 1940, i, 1–135.

[98] See May (2000) for an excellent analysis of just how surprising the German victory over France was.

of Americans who thought France and Britain could prevail barely exceeded 30%.[99] The fall of France fulfilled the second prerequisite for American internationalism: the threat to American ideals became a serious one.

End of isolation

Even before the summer of 1940, the United States was already cooperating to some extent with the European democracies. On January 23, 1939, an investigation into the crash of a new American bomber, the Douglas DB-7, during a test flight revealed that one of the passengers, Captain Paul Chemidlin, was an official of the French Air Ministry. The crash brought to light Franco-American collaboration in the production of military aircraft: France, concerned by the growth of the *Luftwaffe*, both ordered as many aircraft as the United States could produce by the end of 1939 and invested $10 million in the United States in order to double American production of aircraft engines. Despite the Neutrality Laws, American airplanes were being transported to Great Britain via Canada, and American ships laden with supplies ran the German blockade.[100] It is therefore inaccurate to portray the United States as having been entirely isolationist during that period, though its participation on behalf of the Allies remained covert and modest.

A dramatic turning point in American public opinion occurred in mid-1940 – nearly a year and a half before Pearl Harbor. In the public at large, noninterventionist sentiment melted away. In February 1939, 30% of respondents in a national survey had been willing to help England and France in the war. When the question was phrased differently and respondents were asked specifically whether they would be willing to go to war for England and France, between March and August 1939 the percentage responding in the affirmative never exceeded 20%. Another question, asking whether we should go to war *if* England and France were to lose, produced 29% in favor of doing so in both August and November 1939. Finally, a fourth question, which was to be put into the field repeatedly throughout the rest of 1940 and into 1941, asked respondents whether helping England and France was more important than avoiding war with Germany; in late May of 1940, with the German invasion underway, the question netted a still-meager 33.6% in favor of aiding England and France.[101]

---

[99] Cantril (1948). The percentage subsequently rebounded, though the later estimates may have reflected the greater likelihood of American assistance.

[100] Haight (1970); Langer and Gleason (1952, 48, 222). One case of the smuggling of aircraft across the Canadian border – ironically, in the home state of isolationist Senator Gerald Nye – is documented by Shoptaugh (1993).

[101] Given the quality of public opinion polling in this era, it is reasonable to wonder about the quality of these numbers. Professor Adam Berinsky of the Massachusetts Institute of Technology has engaged in a long-term project involving reweighting public opinion data from this period, including the last of the four questions described earlier, and his conclusions with regard to these data were, first, that underrepresentation of women and people with low education (who are less hawkish) is canceled out by underrepresentation of Southern states (which are more hawkish), and, second, that correction for nonrandom respondent selection has little if any impact (personal communication). In the end, the trajectory of his corrected series matches that of the reported series to within a few percentage points. Professor Berinsky has kindly offered his

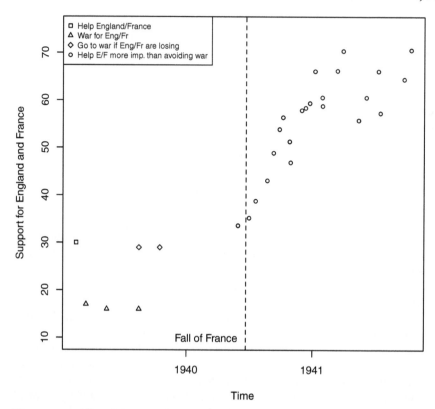

Figure 4.3. Public opinion on aiding England and France.

That percentage trended abruptly upward following the French surrender: by August the percentage that preferred aid to Britain over noninvolvement had risen to 43%, opinion was divided almost 50/50 in September and October, and after October it never dropped below 50% again. By 1941 almost two-thirds of the respondents (66.1%) chose aid to England over staying out of war; twice – in March and October 1941 – the number passed the 70% mark. In short, more than a year before Pearl Harbor occurred, a majority of Americans were willing to prevent German victory by armed force if necessary, and that majority seems to have solidified and stabilized some time in early 1941. Figure 4.3 illustrates this trend. The increased perception of American vulnerability trended upward at the same time: the percentage of Americans who believed that they would be personally affected by the war, which had been at 48% in March 1940, jumped to 67% in July and remained there (71% in January 1941),[102] and although 75% of those who favored aid to Britain even if it meant risking war also responded that they thought that Germany and Italy would attack us

data, for which I am grateful. The earlier series are uncorrected, but given Professor Berinsky's results, an error of sufficient magnitude to warrant revision of these conclusions is exceptionally unlikely.

[102] Casey (2001, 24).

within 10 years if they defeated the British, only 33% of those who did not favor aid to Britain said they feared such an attack.[103]

Americans still thought that the war could probably be won without their participation. One trend illustrates this fact: the percentage of people responding that the United States should enter the war immediately never passed 30% – it remained below 10% prior to the invasion of France, hovered in the high teens through September 1940, and with few exceptions remained in the 20–30% range thereafter. Nevertheless, the percentage of respondents who replied that we should enter the war *if there were no other way to defeat Germany* was much higher: 72% in late September 1940, 68% in early April 1941, and 70% in November 1941.[104] The unwillingness of Americans to enter the war immediately is therefore a rather misleading indicator. By November 1941, 72% of Americans agreed with the statement that the country's most important task was "to help defeat the Nazi government."[105] "Keep out of war," by contrast, netted a meager 2%.

Official reaction to the invasion of France was abrupt. At the beginning of the year President Roosevelt had asked for just under $2 billion for national defense, up only slightly from the previous year. After the invasion of the Low Countries, the President asked for an additional billion; Congress gave him $1.5 billion. At the end of May, Roosevelt asked for and received another billion. On July 10, following France's surrender, he asked for and got an additional $5 billion. In all, appropriations for national defense reached $10.5 billion in 1940,[106] an impressive figure compared to previous years – $500–$700 million in the early Depression years of 1931–1935, $1.12 billion for 1939, and an initial $1.77 billion for 1940.[107] The destroyers-for-bases deal, in which the United States transferred 50 warships to Great Britain, followed in September; 70% of the public was in favor.[108] The Selective Training and Service Act of 1940, the first peacetime draft in the nation's history, passed in mid-September by votes of 232–124 in the House and 47–25 in the Senate. Lend-lease was proposed by the president in December and passed both houses with broad popular support within three months. Top-secret military collaboration began as well: by September 1940 a group of American scientists had begun to work with their British counterparts in a secret laboratory at MIT on the development of high-frequency radar, an asset that greatly aided the Allies during the war.[109]

The domestic political landscape, too, was transformed. The Republican Convention, meeting two days after the French surrender, bypassed its strongest presidential contenders – Senators Robert A. Taft of Ohio and Arthur H. Vandenberg of Michigan and New York's Governor Thomas Dewey, all isolationists to varying degrees – and instead nominated a political novice and former Democrat, Wendell Willkie, who

---

[103] Bruner (1944, 24).
[104] These are the only three occasions on which the question was asked. See Cantril (1951, 966–973) for these and preceding figures.
[105] The question asks respondents whether or not they agree that the defeat of the Nazis is the country's most important task, rather than simply asking what the country's biggest task is; the percentage, therefore, should be taken with a grain of salt, as the question was rather loaded. See Cantril (1951, 503).
[106] Divine (1979, 86).   [107] Shepardson and Scroggs (1941, 330).
[108] Divine (1979, 91).   [109] Conant (2002).

had the advantage of being a staunch internationalist.[110] Isolationism was a dead issue in the presidential election. A sea change occurred in congressional elections as well; to take a single example, Cooley reports that the Maine delegation to the House of Representatives was transformed by the 1940 elections. Only one isolationist remained, Rep. James C. Oliver, and "[b]y 1941 [his] isolationist stand ... was an albatross around the congressman's neck."[111] The people and the government made the commitment to win the war even at the cost of fighting it.[112]

Whether measured in terms of public sentiment, political alignment, or governmental preparation for conflict, therefore, American involvement had moved rapidly from benevolent neutrality to armed and active belligerency. On March 15, 1941, as the Battle of the Atlantic intensified, the Atlantic Fleet was ordered to return to port, don camouflage paint, and prepare for active duty. On April 10, FDR outlined plans for four task forces to patrol the Atlantic; if U-boats were found they were to be tracked and their locations broadcast for the benefit of the British. In mid-1941, American ports began the regular repair of British ships, first military, then merchant; during the last nine months of the year the tonnage of British ships repaired in American shipyards averaged 430,000 per month.[113] On May 21, the *Robin Moor,* an American freighter, was torpedoed and sunk by a German submarine in the south Atlantic. In June, American ships helped search for the German cruiser *Prinz Eugen* after it escaped the battle in which the massive battleship *Bismarck* was sunk. On July 1 the United States agreed to defend Iceland and sent troops outside the Western Hemisphere for the first time since World War I. In August, Churchill and Roosevelt proclaimed via the Atlantic Charter their mutual goal of the destruction of the Nazis. Finally, on September 4 the inevitable occurred, and a German U-boat, U-652, fired on the American destroyer *USS Greer.* By the middle of the month FDR had given the authorization for the American Navy to fire on sight at any German or Italian warships encountered anywhere in the west Atlantic – *casus belli* if ever there were one.[114] On October 17, the American destroyer *Kearny,* responding to a distress call from a convoy under attack, was torpedoed by a German submarine. This was not, as Bailey and Ryan point out, a chance encounter, but rather "deadly and prolonged combat between German submarines and American warships."[115] The sinking of the destroyer *Reuben James* thirteen days later served only to confirm America's status as a silent belligerent.

It should be emphasized that American involvement was neither secret nor unpopular: a Gallup poll taken after the president announced the "shoot on sight" order found 62% of the public in favor and only 28% against.[116] The fig leaf of noninvolvement was held in place only by Hitler's determination not to bring the United States formally into the war.[117]

---

[110] On the relationship between Willkie and the Republican isolationists see Johnson (1960).

[111] Cooley (1998, 217).   [112] Duroselle (1963, 266); Adler (1965, 243).

[113] The monstrous *Bismarck* displaced 41,700 tons, whereas aircraft carriers and battleships often displaced 20,000–30,000 tons or a bit more, and destroyers under 5,000 tons. This therefore amounted to a substantial quantity of assistance.

[114] See Heinrichs (1988, 31, 47–48, 80–81, 109, 110, 166–168).

[115] Bailey and Ryan (1979, 197).   [116] Heinrichs (1988, 168).   [117] See Jäckel (1984, 74).

Summary

There are two surprising insights to come out of this history. The first is that American isolationism, as the theory predicts (but as the conventional wisdom, and many students of the period, tend not to notice), did not survive until Pearl Harbor. Far from it – Americans, both at the elite and mass level, reacted quite strongly to the fall of France and were waging undeclared war against Nazi Germany in the Atlantic by 1941.

The second, related insight is that the end of American isolationism is an instance of a systemic phenomenon rather than a purely domestic one. More generally, the model suggests that a knowledge of the interests and capabilities of *all* of the relevant actors within a system, not just those of a single actor, is crucial to any explanation of any single state's level of involvement in the system. Despite the straightforward nature of the story, this idea runs contrary to a wide range of scholarship that seeks the sources of isolationist (or internationalist) behavior largely if not entirely within the confines of the state itself.[118]

A systemic perspective does not contradict those so much as point out that they cannot tell the whole story. Germany acted to shape the structure of the international system by changing the balances of power and ideology; only after it had succeeded did the United States react – but react it did. American foreign policy was a reasoned, prudent reaction to the structure of the international system, and when that structure experienced an abrupt shock, the United States reacted appropriately. Changes in levels of American internationalism cannot, therefore, be understood without looking beyond America's shores. In short, it is impossible to understand the extent to which America will choose to engage the rest of the world without understanding both America and the rest of the world.

Case 3: the end of the Cold War, 1985–1990

Introduction

The final case of the three that helps both to test and to illustrate the workings of the model is the case of the end of the Cold War, from 1985 to 1989. To understand this case it is important to understand the Cold War both in its own, historical terms and in terms of the model; fortunately, each usefully informs the other. And to understand why the Cold War ended, we need to know when it ended, and therefore what it was, both historically and in the context of the model.

Whereas the Vienna system was constructed for stasis and peace and was undermined by a desire for liberty, and the Versailles system was constructed to keep the

---

[118] Such diverse scholars as Lenin (1939), Williams (1972), Cohen (1987), and Snyder (1991) assert that internationalism is a result of what Doyle (1986) refers to as "metropolitan" forces – internal coalitions that push for greater international involvement, generally to protect their own interests (in the American and British cases, usually investments or potential investments). In a similar vein, Roeder (1984) and Volgy and Schwartz (1994) point to domestic institutional factors that blunt a state's responsiveness to events in the international system. Nincic (1996) relates isolationism to domestic conditions, such as unemployment and inflation. Wittkopf (1990), Holsti (1979), Hero (1973), Klingberg (1983), McCloskey (1967), and Zaller (1992) suggest that isolationism is plausibly a function of a disparate range of attitudinal dispositions and sociodemographic characteristics.

peace by keeping Germany down, the Cold War system arose organically from the interactions of the two main participants. It was qualitatively different from its predecessors, both in the destructiveness of the weapons wielded by the actors and in the mode of security that it employed – deterrence rather than defense, a practice that preserved peace by constantly risking war.[119] It was perpetuated until one of those actors, appalled by its *in*security and drawn to a vision of an alternative system that enhanced security by reconstituting it in fundamentally different terms, sought to transcend the Cold War system entirely.

Understood in terms of the model, the Cold War system was one in which security, as viewed by the main actors, was defined as having both ideological and traditional *realpolitik* components. Increasingly, as the destructiveness of nuclear weapons became known, a third dimension, that of absolute material capabilities, became relevant, as both sides sought to create security via arms control. Because the two main actors after World War II had strong preferences that were largely, and at times diametrically, opposed along the major dimensions that comprised the structure of the international system, their attempts to influence the distributions of ideology and capabilities would inevitably bring them into conflict with one another. Their roughly matched capabilities in the context of the European theater ensured a stalemate and, the existence of that stalemate ensured that each would persist in high levels of security-related activity aimed, at worst, at maintaining that stalemate, and at best, at gaining an advantage. That joint, sustained security activity on the part of the main actors constituted the Cold War.

By that understanding, the end of the Cold War occurred when the levels of security-related activity of the two main powers in the system dropped below a threshold that informed observers would expect of adversaries, and the reasons for that change provided all actors involved with reasonable certainty that it would persist.[120] Expert

---

[119] See Schelling (1966, 78–86) for a clear discussion.

[120] In the context of the Cold War case this formulation immediately highlights a key semantic distinction in the meaning of "security-related activity" that the conceptual framework of the model can help to resolve. Was Gorbachev, for example, engaging in more, or less, security-related activity when he sought nuclear arms reductions in Europe and withdrew Soviet forces from Afghanistan and Eastern Europe? He did so because he believed that his actions would improve global security and therefore the security of his country. His vigorous statesmanship, especially compared to the inertia of his sclerotic predecessors, makes a good case that he was quite active. Yet an American president who engaged in parallel behavior – unilaterally cutting nuclear forces, withdrawing troops from Europe and allowing the Warsaw Pact to expand to the west – would surely have been accused not of activism but of profound isolationism. That would have been the case even if those actions had been taken in an attempt to improve American security by reducing international tensions and limiting unnecessary American commitments. One has the disturbing sense that the difference between the two cases lies not in an objective assessment of the nature of the activity itself but in a subjective judgment of the guilt of the participants: Gorbachev's activity is seen as contributing positively to international security because previous Soviet activity was seen as detracting from it, whereas American activity was not.

Such a view, I would argue, cannot be sustained. One purpose of a model of this sort is to help resolve terminological ambiguity of this sort. Here, more activity in the *realpolitik* sphere refers to more guns, more airplanes, more missiles; more activity in the sphere of ideology means more attempts to spread one's own domestic political ideology abroad. When people's understandings

opinion may vary on precisely when the two superpowers actually reached that point, but it seems reasonable to conclude, based on lingering American wariness, that they had not reached it until the Malta summit in December 1989.

The story of the end of the Cold War is one that has been told before, perhaps exhaustively, from a multiplicity of perspectives. Examining the role of material capabilities, Wohlforth (1993) makes the canonical case for the importance of declining power in influencing Soviet behavior, whereas Kydd (2005) explains the gradual American reaction to costly Soviet signals as a case of the development of trust between rational actors in a world of uncertainty. English (2000) and Checkel (1997), conversely, make the case for the importance of an alternative and more benign conceptualization of the international system, the roots of which can be traced back to the 1960s, that gained currency under Gorbachev. Many of Gorbachev's biographers and aides make the case for the importance of the man himself in the process of bringing the Cold War to an end (see, e.g., A. Brown 1996, Chernyaev 2000, Grachev 2008, and Stein 1994), whereas Roeder (1993) focuses most directly on the institutional features of the Soviet system.

Time-honored political science tradition would involve positioning one's explanation within a given theoretical paradigm and arguing for the primacy of that one over the rest.[121] As historians have come to realize, however, a better approach is to synthesize them into a larger, more comprehensive explanation. As described in the previous chapter, the orthodox, or traditional, school of Cold War history emphasized the active and ideologically motivated role of the Soviet Union in the origins of the Cold War, whereas the revisionist school focuses on America's promotion of capitalism as the engine that drove the conflict and the post-revisionists shift the emphasis away from ideology and toward national interests. As Leffler (2000, 43, 53) argues, however,

> If we are to capture the Cold War in all its complexity, we . . . must find a way to see the interconnectedness of many factors. The conflicting interpretive approaches lead us in interesting but sometimes misguided directions because they tend to focus on a specific set of variables and hypotheses rather than allow us to see the interrelatedness of the whole. . . . Parsimonious theory and single-minded interpretations cannot do justice to the complexity of the historical process.

Lundestad (2000, 75) is more blunt in his recommendations: "[M]ove away from analyzing one side or the other and instead emphasize the interactions between the

---

of security change, those changes are reflected in changed ideal points along those dimensions: fewer guns, perhaps, or less aggressive ideological proselytizing, might be optimal for security. It is crucial to distinguish between a *change* in levels of activity, which could be in the direction of more or less activity (but which is generally evidenced by much diplomacy either way), and an *increase* in levels of activity, which *must* be aimed at seeking more of whatever good (here, capabilities or ideology) is at issue.

These conceptual distinctions help to clarify the end of the Cold War as it relates to the model: Gorbachev sought, very vigorously, to *change* Soviet levels of activity, in both the ideological and *realpolitik* spheres – but *not* to increase them. Rather, he sought to decrease them, precisely because he believed that decreased levels of activity were optimal for security.

[121] For a lively discussion of this practice see Wohlforth (2000).

two sides.... [And] stop believing in one-factor explanations for the behavior of the Soviet Union or, for that matter, the United States, and instead analyze how many different factors blended together."

In the following study, I argue that there were four key precursors to the end of the Cold War: the reformist ideas harbored in various institutes and intellectual circles throughout government and the intelligentsia from the 1960s onward, the ongoing stagnation within the country and its broader implications for the Soviet socialist experiment, the reciprocal flow of power between the general secretary and his constituency, and the rise of the open-minded reformer Mikhail Gorbachev.[122] Each of the first three was present for some time before Gorbachev rose to the position of general secretary; his attainment of that office was the catalyst that rendered the others operative.

At that point, we can begin to derive concrete predictions from the model. Given Gorbachev's perception of the need for reform, the availability of a coherent alternative set of reformist ideas that presented the international system in more cooperative terms, and his ability to alter his own constituency, it was likely from the onset that a decrease in international tensions – a second détente, perhaps – was likely. But it was not until Gorbachev himself had been decisively influenced by what would come to be called "new thinking," and in particular by a conceptualization of the international system that was based fundamentally on universalist, humanitarian principles rather than on class interests (an event that occurred, most likely, early in 1986), that an end to the Cold War became a likely outcome.[123] At that point, although he still possessed substantial remnants of "old thinking," he had made a conceptual breakthrough that, when followed to its logical conclusions, would imply radically different foreign policy preferences for the Soviet Union, including a dramatic deemphasis on the importance of ideology in international affairs and a preference for much lower levels of conventional and nuclear arms, even if the price of arms reduction was a gross imbalance in favor of the United States.

The general secretary could not, however, dictate Soviet policy. He had to carry the Politburo with him, and ultimately he was responsible to (and could be removed by) the Central Committee of the Communist Party; in the mid-1980s both bodies were dominated by orthodox Communists who would find such views heretical. Because of the reciprocal flow of power that characterized the Soviet state, however, Gorbachev possessed the ability to influence the composition of his constituency. As general

---

[122] For a parallel argument see Hopf (2006, 694–700). These precursors are, of course, exogenous, meaning that the model explains none of them, any more than it could explain the Armenian earthquake of 1988; it is simply not designed to explain them. But I explore them here because, although they are not sufficiently generalizable to warrant inclusion in the model in more generic form, they are critical to understanding its operation in this particular case.

[123] One might argue that, in choosing the advisors that he did, Gorbachev made such a reconceptualization inevitable, and that therefore the end of the Cold War might have been predicted from an earlier date. Such an argument is not entirely implausible, but one wonders where such an increasingly tenuous chain of causation might end: did coming to office make choosing those advisors inevitable? Did securing the #2 position in the Kremlin under Chernenko make coming to office inevitable? Did Andropov manage to secure the #2 position in the Kremlin for Gorbachev? And so on.

secretaries before him had done, therefore – only more quickly – he assembled a constituency that supported his views, even as those views continued to evolve.

The change in official Soviet worldviews, therefore, was predictable,[124] as was its result: a series of asymmetric arms agreements and initiatives, on the one hand, and an abandonment of the Brezhnev Doctrine of support to socialist states threatened by revolution or substantial reform, on the other.

The model also helps us to understand the likely implications of those developments given the interactions between the powers. The United States, facing what theorists would call a substantial amount of "model uncertainty," or uncertainty about the changes that they might be witnessing in the parameters of the model in which they themselves were embedded (i.e., not being at all certain about the true implications of Gorbachev's "new thinking" for the foreign policy preferences of the Soviet state), should prefer to wait to witness the concrete results of those changes – i.e., the shifts in the ideological and military spheres that should occur if Gorbachev had in fact undergone a fundamental reimagining of the system. That evidence took nearly a year to arrive – Gorbachev's foreign policy aide, Anatoly Chernyaev (2000, 201), described 1989 as the "Lost Year," referring to the Bush administration's puzzling hesitation. However, but the necessary evidence arrived most conclusively in the fall of 1989 when the Soviets acceded to the revolutions in Eastern Europe and, most startlingly, to the breach of the Berlin Wall, an outcome that even the most cynical American observers had difficulty dismissing as a diabolically clever tactical move.[125]

Once the evidence was in, the model would argue that the American side should decrease its levels of activity in proportion to the magnitude of the change witnessed in the system – that is, quite dramatically. In concrete terms, the United States should have been fairly quick to decrease the levels of security-related activity that, along with Soviet activity, had constituted the Cold War for nearly a half-century. By most accounts this is precisely what happened, as the two superpowers cemented the end of the conflict just days later at a summit off the coast of Malta. Moreover, as Chernyaev points out, the events of the following year suggest quite strongly that the security-related activity of the two states had undergone a qualitative as well as a quantitative change, from fundamentally conflictual to fundamentally cooperative, with the goal not of striving to overcome a rival's vision of world order but rather of working together to achieve a new one:

> [T]he Cold War ended in Malta, it ended in 1989 rather than in 1991 when George Bush visited the Soviet Union or when the Soviet Union collapsed. If we don't

---

[124] It was predictable, that is, given the assumption that Gorbachev would not overstep his bounds, move too quickly, and be removed from office – and, of course, that nothing else fundamental about the situation changed (he wasn't run over by a bus, for example).

[125] This account accords, for the most part, with that of John Mueller (2005); in both retellings the Cold War was about the Soviet threat to the United States, a threat that was primarily ideological in nature. The primary difference is that, whereas Mueller sees that threat as having ended at the beginning of 1989 when the nature of Soviet policy itself had fundamentally changed, I argue that, from a systemic perspective, the Cold War had not come to an end until *both* of the superpowers had undergone such a transformation – if for no other reason than that continued American obduracy would eventually have undercut Soviet reform.

accept that the Cold War virtually ended in 1989, then we will not be able to explain German unification, not be able to explain collaboration of the Soviet Union and the United States during the Gulf crisis.[126]

In short, then, the change in the Soviet worldview and Soviet understanding of their interests produced a change in Soviet levels of activity (H_{A1}), which in turn produced a change in the structure of the international system (H_{St1}) along both military and ideological dimensions. Only after the change in the structure of the system had occurred, moving the status quo along both dimensions toward the American ideal points, did the United States decrease its level of activity (H_{A1}) and pursue a more accommodationist policy, a shift that marked the end of the Cold War.

Background

Having described the expectations of the model and sketched the historical evolution of the end of the Cold War, I now turn to a discussion of the end of that conflict in more depth. I first describe each of the four precursors to reform and then explain how they interacted via the mechanism of institutional constituency change once the last of them, Gorbachev, arrived to serve as a catalyst. The implication of that change in constituency was a change in worldview, and in the next section I trace out the qualitative changes in the Soviet worldview that transpired as Gorbachev's domestic reforms took hold. I then examine the model's predictions regarding systemic change – shifts in structural dimensions as well as the levels of activity of the other key actor – that flow from the change in the Soviet worldview. A concluding section discusses the implications for existing international relations theory and history.

Previous cycles of reform

As Robert English (2000) demonstrates, earlier cycles of liberalization and reform in the Soviet Union had by the 1980s produced the nearly invisible, authoritarian equivalent of a shadow government: a network of reform-minded individuals who both exchanged ideas with one another and remained adept at survival during periods of conservative rule, in the hopes that a Politburo more sympathetic to their ideas might someday come about.

The 20th Party Congress in 1956 marked the watershed, the point at which Khrushchev declared that war was no longer inevitable and that, although class struggle remained fundamental to international politics, states were entering a period in which that struggle would take a different form. That form, known as "peaceful coexistence," marked a decrease in tension between the two social systems. Nevertheless, peaceful coexistence "did not touch the bedrock principle of a world divided into antagonistic camps. The rivals could no longer go to war, but the international class struggle would continue, and even *intensify*, as they competed and confronted each other diplomatically, economically, and even militarily, in old venues and new ones."[127]

---

[126] Wohlforth (2003, 22).   [127] English (2000, 50, emphasis in original).

The more lasting ideological legacy of Khrushchev's rejection of Stalinism was actually institutional in form: the Khrushchev period witnessed the creation or revival of many of the major journals, policy institutes, and Central Committee consultant groups that became centers of reformist thought in subsequent decades, including the Institute of World Economy and International Relations (IMEMO), the Institute of the USA (later to become the Institute of the USA and Canada, or ISKAN), the journal *Problemy Mira i Sotsializma* in Prague, and the Novosibirsk Institute. Once reform-minded intellectuals had been put into place as directors of many of the more important centers, they institutionalized their gains by creating a variety of "closed" sections and departments within those centers. Each was tasked with analyzing international affairs in non-ideological terms and producing working papers, or *zapiski*, for internal consumption and limited circulation. These could be passed up to the senior party leadership, though they generally fell on deaf ears unless the general secretary favored reform: Georgi Arbatov, the first director of what would become ISKAN, described Andropov's insistence that no subject be sacred behind the closed door of his office, and after he rose to membership in the Politburo in 1979 Gorbachev became an avid consumer of such material, often inviting its authors to his office to brief him.[128]

When the ideas they espoused came into favor, the reformers were ushered into Central Committee consultant groups, where they could most directly serve as idea vectors to political elites. When they were out, during more conservative periods, they spent time in research institutes or, occasionally, in more remote locations – as in case of Aleksandr Yakovlev, who, having published a prominent criticism of anti-Western Russian nationalism in *Literaturnaya Gazeta* in late 1972, was removed from the Propaganda Department and installed as ambassador to Canada, where he remained in political exile until rescued by Gorbachev and Andropov and placed at the head of IMEMO a decade later.

Within various departments of the Central Committee, as well as within research institutes like ISKAN and IMEMO, the reform-minded individuals who were gathered together lived in a condition of dynamic tension with conservatives. They formulated policy positions that occasionally deviated from the party line; occasionally they faced censure. Mostly, they were careful to respect the limits of criticism of official policy, but not always.[129] It should come as no surprise that Yurii Orlov and his colleagues at the Institute of Theoretical-Experimental Physics, who were so carried away by Khrushchev's denunciation of Stalin that they called for full democratization

---

[128] Arbatov (1992, 85–86); English (2000, 70–73); Grachev (2008, 28–30). Also starting under Khrushchev, the reformist ideas that were introduced were reinforced by contact with citizens of other states over time as well. This process took place both because direct contact with Westerners debunked many of the official portrayals of the miseries of life in the West that had achieved a sort of taken-for-granted status even among top-level political elites (English 2000, 75) and because epistemic communities formed with professional colleagues outside of the Soviet Union constituted environments within which reformist ideas could be developed openly and, later, conveyed to the political leadership at crucial moments (Evangelista 2002).

[129] An interesting longitudinal case study that illuminates the changing limits of the regime's toleration of reformist ideas over time is Spechler (1982).

of the Soviet system, soon found themselves fired and expelled from the party. In more reactionary times, subtler offenses were censured as well: Tatiana Zaslavskaia's Novosibirsk Report earned her a reprimand from her regional party committee – but, later, a position as Gorbachev's advisor; and conservatives, goaded by reformist reactions to the collapse of détente and events in Eastern Europe, engaged in the beginnings of a new purge of the academic institutes in the late Brezhnev era, arguing that the institutes had become agents of ideological confusion that benefited the enemies of the state. Only the death of Brezhnev and the rise of Andropov brought the process to a halt.[130]

Despite the commonality of their background and their opposition to conservative forces, it would be a mistake to assume that all reform-minded political elites were homogeneous in their own preferences. Very few were classical Western democrats in outlook. Others retained a belief in an ideal socialism but were largely disillusioned with the ability of the Soviet state as presently constituted even to approximate that ideal. Still others were convinced of the necessity of a modernized, reformed Soviet state but not that such a state would be insufficient once reformed.[131] Because there was still a substantial commitment to some variant of socialism (however liberalized and idealized) within the reform community, and because Gorbachev's own ideas on the subject wandered somewhat erratically from the reformed-socialist to the social-democratic camp, his ability to draw on the reform wing of the party for support dwindled over time.

Stagnation

The story of Soviet economic stagnation requires, at this point, little elaboration: economic torpor during the Brezhnev era, exacerbated by an increasing defense burden and the remarkable inefficiencies of a large and increasingly backlogged planned economy, gradually eroded the Soviet Union's standing relative to the West – not in terms of forces-in-being or realized capabilities (for increasingly, more and more were being sacrificed to maintain exactly those capabilities), but rather in terms of the latent capabilities that would, in the long run, permit the Soviets to maintain them.[132] Although in retrospect this trend was arguably clear even from the early 1970s, détente, a global recession, and unfounded American concerns about that state's relative decline combined to make it easier to miss or to ignore. In the aftermath of the recession, however, with Western economies rebounding, Soviet economic

---

[130] Brown (2007, 183); English (2000, 68, 169–176). For Zaslavskaia's report and commentary see Zaslavskaia (1989).

[131] Grachev (2008, 35–36).

[132] Nothing is explicitly assumed, in the statistical model, regarding the contribution of latent capabilities to realized capabilities, largely because my sense is, historically, that the relationship between the two is not consistent enough to warrant attempting to link them empirically, except to say that latent capabilities provide an upper bound for realized capabilities. Few states, even Great Powers, really push their realized capabilities to that upper bound in peacetime, and how close they come probably depends on a variety of factors that merit a book all their own. This, however, is a relatively rare case of a Great Power pushing its realized capabilities to, and perhaps beyond, the limits of what its latent capabilities could support.

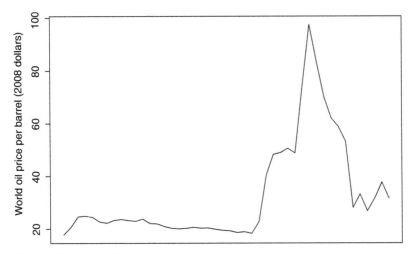

Figure 4.4. Postwar oil prices.

performance still making marginal gains at best, and an abrupt increase in international tension following the invasion of Afghanistan, Soviet vulnerabilities became all too apparent. After 1980, there was widespread consensus among elites regarding the deterioration of the Soviet Union's international position, if not regarding what exactly should be done about it.[133]

It is worth noting in passing, though it is not a central theme here – its exclusion is due to the fact that it represents one of many peripheral causal connections that, although important in a given case, do not recur with sufficient regularity to merit inclusion in the general theory – that the need for internal reform and the appeal of new foreign policy ideas, although both exogenous to the model, were not unrelated to one another. A new vision of foreign policy was appealing in part because it implied much lower military costs for the Soviet Union, which were a prerequisite for domestic economic reform; domestic political and economic reform were inextricably intertwined; and domestic political reform was needed if substantial change in foreign policy were to be achieved. Each, therefore, supported the other. Gorbachev proved to be adept at finding ways to leverage foreign policy liberalization to accelerate domestic reform and vice versa, as in the case of his reaction to the military's opposition to the inspection regime included in the Intermediate-Range Nuclear Forces (INF) treaty: when military leaders objected that inspections would reveal the ramshackle condition of the Soviet military, Gorbachev promptly suggested a more rigorous regime in the hopes that international scrutiny would improve the state of the Soviet military (Grachev 2008, 99, 161 and *passim*).

The inefficiency of the Soviet economy was, it must be said, masked to some degree by skyrocketing oil prices in the 1970s. As Figure 4.4 demonstrates, the world price of oil more than doubled, and for a time tripled, during this period. That

---

[133] Wohlforth (1993, chs. 7–8); see also Sestanovich (1988).

surplus alone made it possible to ignore the fact that inefficiency, measured by state investment necessary to produce growth in the economy, was steadily growing. A CIA report delivered to Congress in November 1982 went so far as to conclude that the Soviets might be able to compete in the arms race without sacrificing their standard of living.[134] But the larger point is that the oil windfall should have permitted the oil-rich Soviets to dominate the Cold War, rather than merely giving them a second wind; and once the Soviets started to look beyond traditional measures of power, such as industrial output, and focus more on such metrics as productivity, finance, and agricultural output, the more aghast they became.[135]

The reformist leadership seems to have thought about the country's sclerotic condition in very holistic terms. There was certainly some concern over the implications of the economic situation for the country's international standing, but the problem was seen as much larger than that, and generally as one that had resonance because of its implications for the Soviet people themselves. Some of Gorbachev's conversations prior to his ascent to the position of general secretary reflect this sense of an all-encompassing crisis: "Everything's rotten. It has to be changed," Shevardnadze said to Gorbachev in December 1984 when the two were in the Crimea, and when Gorbachev was about to succeed Chernenko he said to his wife, "*Tak dalshe zhit nelzya*" – "We can't go on living like this."[136]

More generally there was, as Gorbachev's last official spokesman, Andrei Grachev, put it, "a growing feeling within Soviet society that the *civilization project* initiated at the time of the 1917 October Revolution had reached a stage of general exhaustion, if not fiasco."[137] Economic stagnation was the most prominent, and most readily measured, indicator of this exhaustion, but for citizens daily life brought constant reminders that the state both pervaded society and was unbelievably incompetent. Clothing available only in a single size (not intended to fit all) was not uncommon, nor were lengthy waits for mediocre services. *Blat,* a system of informal connections based on influence and reciprocal favors, permeated society and provided a means for citizens to achieve alternative, better, or faster results than those they could achieve through the state. In all, far from being the dynamic challenger to capitalism that its founders had envisioned, the Soviet state by the early 1980s was thoroughly pervaded by a desultory dysfunction that had achieved a taken-for-granted quality.[138]

To be clear, however, stagnation did not imply actual decline: although the economy was undoubtedly stagnating, it was still growing. The Soviet economic crisis of the 1980s and early 1990s *followed* reform rather than preceding it. As Myron Rush (1993, 19) argued, "[t]he Soviet Union, while manifestly in trouble as many observed, was not poised for a collapse, nor was it even in acute crisis. The Soviet Union was viable and probably could have lasted another decade or two, with fortune a good

---

[134] Walker (1995, 280–282).   [135] Wohlforth (1993, 242–243).
[136] Shevardnadze (1991, 37); Brown (1996, 81).   [137] Grachev (2008, 10, emphasis in original).
[138] On the specifics of *blat* see Ledeneva (1998). For excellent portraits of the dysfunction of life in the Soviet Union in the later Brezhnev years see Smith (1976), which offers a journalistic perspective, or Yurchak (2006) for a more academic analysis.

bit longer."[139] Nor were the reformers' sense of crisis and the citizenry's frustration with the inefficiencies of the Soviet system reflected in any urgency for reform or sense of political crisis in society at large. In short, although the status quo was deeply objectionable to Gorbachev and his team and clearly constituted an impetus to act, that impetus was more subjective in nature than based on compelling social or material circumstances.[140]

Institutional influence

There was, in the Soviet system, a very substantial, though not unlimited, capacity for what Kathleen Thelen (2004) calls "institutional conversion" – the co-opting of existing institutions for purposes that differ, sometimes dramatically, from their original ones. The general secretary could produce this outcome, in large part, because of the structure of *reciprocal accountability* present in the Soviet system, which ensured that the constituency relied on the leader for support. The structure of the Communist Party of the Soviet Union entailed exactly this sort of mutual accountability. The general secretary was by far the most influential voice in appointments and the determination of personnel policy, but he still had to carry the Politburo, and in extremis he could be removed by the Central Committee. His ability to influence the composition of the Central Committee and the Politburo made it possible for the general secretary to co-opt Soviet political institutions.[141]

Specifically, the general secretary could produce institutional conversion in one of three ways, each more effective (and, accordingly, more difficult) than the previous one:

- *Overhaul of the constituency* – either replacing those party members whose support ensured the general secretary's ability to remain in office with others who would

---

[139] Belanovsky (1998) consists of interviews with top Soviet military personnel and provides worthwhile context: even among those who were aware of the staggering magnitude of the military burden there is considerable disagreement regarding its long-run sustainability. For a counterargument that makes the case for the Soviet Union's inability to maintain its international position due to its economic weakness see Brooks and Wohlforth (2007).

[140] See Shlapentokh (1998) for a compelling succinct account, and Duch (1993) for a description of the dearth of popular support for free-market reform in the Soviet Union. The image of stagnation without crisis that emerges from this and similar accounts makes historian John Lewis Gaddis' now-famous assessment of the Soviet Union prior to Gorbachev's ascent somewhat questionable: "[I]magine a troubled triceratops. From the outside, as rivals contemplated its sheer size, tough skin, bristling armament, and aggressive posturing, the beast looked sufficiently formidable that none dared tangle with it. Appearances deceived, though, for within its digestive, circulatory, and respiratory systems were slowly clogging up, and then shutting down. There were few external signs of this until the day the creature was found with all four feet in the air, still awesome but now bloated, stiff, and quite dead" (Gaddis 1997, 284). We may have been fooled by its demise into thinking that the triceratops' illnesses were more serious than they actually were. By many accounts, a rigorous exercise and diet regime would have done wonders, but the animal panicked and committed suicide for fear of death.

[141] Hough (1987) documents this "circular flow of power" theory, whereas Roeder (1993, 27–29), whose terminology I borrow, argues that it, or something very much like it, is a characteristic of most authoritarian systems.

be more likely to provide that support, or convincing the existing constituency to provide it (often through the threat of replacement)
- *Alteration of political institutions* – alteration of the formal rules or practices that govern the functioning of political institutions, or the balance among them, in such a way that they more fully support the general secretary's preferred policies
- *Constitutional transformation* – wholesale replacement of the domestic political institutions of the state

Of these, the first was common practice for general secretaries, who accomplished it via different means. Stalin relied on his absolute authority to have his opponents arrested, convicted on bogus charges, and shot; Khrushchev chose to replace them at Party Congresses, in a manner described later. Gorbachev, too, used the Party Congress as a means of overhauling his constituency, but remarkably, he also managed to talk many of his opponents into retiring, voluntarily, when circumstances required it and no Party Congress was near at hand to provide a convenient means of exit. The second, alteration of political institutions or the balance among them, was not impossible: Khrushchev had, for example, altered the state's economic institutions in such a way that his major competitors within the state administration were cut loose, and had divided the lower levels of the party into separate industrial and agricultural hierarchies – not for the purpose of efficiency, but rather to increase the number of positions available for him to fill with supporters.[142]

The Central Committee was a body comprising a few hundred top party and government officials from the center and from around the country. Its composition changed no less often than every five years, at Party Congresses; it also met at biannual plenary sessions to evaluate Politburo decisions, including changes in the composition of the Politburo itself. In normal periods, the Leninist stricture against factionalism was sufficient to ensure that the Central Committee remained united behind the Politburo, serving essentially to ratify the decisions of the higher body: although there was discussion, and even occasional criticism, votes were overwhelmingly unanimous. That unanimity tended to convey the impression that the Central Committee was a rubber-stamp organ that served to do nothing more than provide a veneer of legitimacy to the Politburo's policy; in reality, however, as the ouster of the "antiparty group" that tried to unseat Khrushchev in 1957 demonstrated, unanimous or not, it remained the body to which the Politburo was ultimately accountable.[143]

The general secretary generally had to persuade the Politburo and, in the long run, the Central Committee to support his desired policies; for their part, they tended to defer to his authority, though not by any means absolutely. The principle that factionalism was inadmissible justified the practice of selecting Central Committee candidates to stand for election, a process that was carried out by delegates selected by

---

[142] Roeder (1993, 168–171); Brown (1996, 187). As this account suggests, in addition to his influence over the Central Committee itself, the general secretary also controlled the Central Committee Secretariat, which in turn ran the Central Committee *apparat*, the bureaucracy responsible for the implementation of policy.

[143] Hough and Fainsod (1979, 217–219).

regional party secretaries. Those secretaries answered to the head of the Central Committee Department of Party Organizational Work, the body responsible for supervising them; the head of that department, in turn, answered to the Politburo member in charge of personnel. (For that very reason, the secretary in charge of personnel was generally a close ally of the general secretary and was often well positioned when it came to succession.) In this manner, the reciprocal relationship between leaders and constituency came full circle: the general secretary wielded enormous influence over the selection of representatives to the body to which he was accountable – often before he even ascended to the post.[144]

It should be emphasized that, in changing his constituency, Gorbachev was pulling himself up by his own bootstraps: he could only promote the most reformist elements of the existing party elite, which could then work to do the same at lower levels. Drawing on a substantial reformist constituency from outside of the party was not an option nor, realistically, was converting the mass of the party to the cause of the radical reform. Moreover, while he was engaged in the process of institutional conversion, the extent to which he could reveal his own reformist predilections was limited by the constituency that he sought to transform. Critical to the process of transformation, therefore, was leeway to stake out a policy position outside of what would have been that of the median Soviet "voter" – and indeed, the deference to the general secretary and the principle of democratic centralism, grounded in Lenin's injunction against factions, was such that his voice carried far more weight in the Politburo than any other, and within limits, their collective position *became* the median voter's position by fiat.[145]

In this manner, given the nature of the Soviet political system, the worldview of the leader would, over time, shape the worldview of his constituency. In the long run this process should be fairly conclusive, because the general secretary would eventually have the opportunity to remove most opposition. That said, the speed with which any general secretary could accomplish this task is indeterminate, though even so, the speed with which Gorbachev did so was fairly remarkable – at least by the standards set by his predecessors. One illustration of Gorbachev's impressive ability in this regard was the case of Alexander Yakovlev, who, as Archie Brown notes, by virtue of his exclusion from the Central Committee was, at the end of 1985, not among the top

---

[144] Brown (1996, 49–50, 66, 97); Hough and Fainsod (1979, 144); Hough (1990, 157–166).

[145] It is worth noting that the extent to which Gorbachev was able to reform the domestic political system did vary substantially, depending on the number, size, and complexity of the bureaucracies involved in a given issue area (Brown 1996, 131–132). Foreign policy, for example, was an area that fell under the purview of a single ministry, the Ministry of Foreign Affairs; in principle it should prove to be amenable to attempts at transformation, as in fact it proved to be. At the other end of the spectrum was the sprawling and entrenched economic bureaucracy, divided across at least five departments (Heavy Industry, Light and Food Industry, Planning and Financial Organs, Trade and Consumers' Services, Transportation-Communications) of the Central Committee, each one comprising a handful of individual ministries (Trade, Gosplan, Gosbank, etc.), each with its associated *apparat*, the support staff collectively responsible for implementation of policy. Compared to the foreign-affairs bureaucracy, economic institutions were a hydra, and they proved accordingly difficult to overcome (Hough and Fainsod 1979, 412–417; Brown 1996, 135–137).

470 members of the CPSU; yet within eighteen months Gorbachev had elevated him to one of the top three positions in the party hierarchy.[146]

The rise of Gorbachev

The reciprocal relationship between the top leader and his constituency was a constant feature of Soviet politics, one that ensured that Soviet leaders' individual preferences could, in the long run, come to exert decisive influence over the collective preferences of the state. The economic and ideational preconditions for reform were present in the country for many years, and under three different leaders, before Mikhail Gorbachev came to power, but except briefly under Andropov, they remained preconditions. Gorbachev, or someone like him, was the catalyst needed to activate them.

Gorbachev was, for the reasons mentioned earlier, a reformer, and the reforms he envisioned were substantial ones. His general orientation, therefore, was to seek out the support of those elements of the elite who were similarly inclined. Moreover, the new general secretary was relatively young, and by temperament quite engaged, so he had a tendency to seek out not just the support of reformist members of the elite but their advice as well. Largely because his portfolio had mostly included responsibilities in domestic policy, this was particularly the case in the area of foreign affairs. Though his views were largely unformed, it is noteworthy that he was deeply committed to a foreign policy that stopped short of the use of force – a position consistent in kind, if perhaps not in degree, with his emphasis on universal human values.[147]

Gorbachev's rhetorical talents were a key element in his ability to achieve political success. He often spoke at great length, and at times his speeches contained contra- dictory elements and obfuscations. He was aided by the institutionalization of what Westerners came to call "doublespeak," or the use of words to mean something other than (possibly including the opposite of) that which their standard definitions would imply, in Soviet political dialogue – a practice that allowed him to send important signals to supporters without immediately mobilizing opposition. For example, he talked about democratization (in the sense of a broadening of societal inputs that fell well short of Western parliamentary democracy) as early as 1984, but he was able to do so because "socialist democracy" had a specific meaning (in opposition to bourgeois democracy), and he could rely on that interpretation to cloud his meaning in the minds of his political opponents. Indeed, even taboo concepts could be discussed openly as long as he added the word "socialist" to them (e.g., "socialist pluralism"), and that after their meaning had been debated and the concepts taken up by reformers

---

[146] Brown (1996, 106). Of course, domestic structure was not irrelevant to the ability of ideas to spread – see Checkel (1993) and Risse-Kappen (1994). Of more interest here, however, is the general secretary's substantial ability to influence the composition of his constituency given that structure so that the ideas that he wants to receive reach him.

[147] Stein (1994) speaks to his penchant for "learning by doing," whereas Brown (1996) remains one of the more compelling portraits of Gorbachev. Zubok (2003) discusses his atypical degree of pacifism and its relationship to new thinking, pointing out that most systems of ideas, liberalism included, sanction the use of force in extreme circumstances to defend that which they most value; many dissidents, Zubok notes, believed that Gorbachev's *unconditional* emphasis on nonviolence was therefore problematic, if not immoral.

he could drop the "socialist" modifier.[148] As a result, conservatives could take comfort in some parts, while he could later point to tacit consent to others as justification for policies of reform.

There was, initially, some doubt and concern on the part of conservatives regarding how far Gorbachev sought to take reforms, but the combination of the ritualization of doublespeak in Soviet political dialogue and the deference traditionally accorded the top leader gave him substantial room to maneuver. By the time his political opponents worked their way through his befuddling avalanche of rhetoric and realized to their horror that his most extreme language pertaining to reform and, later, systemic transformation was entirely sincere, he had managed to succeed to a substantial enough degree that they had already been marginalized. Domestic and international events in 1988 and 1989 were increasingly alarming to conservatives in the party, but the formation of the Congress of People's Deputies in 1989 (and the communists' dismal showing in the elections to it) soon provided Gorbachev with a locus of power that was independent of the party.

Changing constituencies

Before tracing the process by which the change in Soviet worldviews led to the Cold War's end, it is necessary to describe an ancillary process that is critical to an understanding of this case but not central to the general model – namely, the process by which Gorbachev was able to co-opt his constituency, changing their worldview piecemeal from that of relatively conventional Soviet communism, driven by an admixture of Marxist-Leninist ideology and *realpolitik,* to one that was sympathetic to the rejection of the class-based foundations of international politics.

The change in Gorbachev's constituency was, necessarily, gradual: he needed to improve his support little by little in order to garner increased support for further changes. But its gradual nature hides the fact that, over time, Gorbachev himself revised his understanding of the extent to which a change in constituency was necessary. At first, he was convinced that within-system reform was possible, with the Communist Party playing a leading role (if, in the case of many party members, a somewhat reluctant one). As his ambitions for reform became more substantial and opposition within the party grew, however, the prospects for within-system reform dimmed, until finally, in the summer of 1988, Gorbachev announced plans for an entirely new set of political institutions that would make him accountable to a broader and more representative constituency altogether.

---

[148] For an argument that heresthetics, or the use of language to manipulate the political agenda, was key to Gorbachev's success see Evangelista (2001). Gorbachev's predecessor, General Secretary Leonid Brezhnev, spoke of the need for *glasnost,* or openness, throughout the Soviet system in 1974, without intending anything as radical as Gorbachev had in mind when he used the term ten years later. *Perestroika* was another such term: as long as Gorbachev did not define it clearly, it could mean anything from a modest administrative reshuffling to a complete overhaul of the institutions of governance. See Brown (1996, 124–129). For a description of the difficulties that Vadim Medvedev encountered when tasked with integrating Gorbachev's positions into a broader, coherent CPSU ideology see Harris (1992).

Loosely, Gorbachev's transformation of the Soviet constituency can be grouped into three periods. In the first, which began prior to his ascent to the office of general secretary and lasted through his first year in office, he worked from within the Politburo to neutralize his future political opposition and, when possible, consolidate power. In the second, while continuing to consolidate power and overhaul his constituency, Gorbachev embarked on a reform of the existing political system, a course that he pursued until he realized that resistance would be too great. In the third and (for our purposes) final phase, he retained control of the party while at the same time constructing a political institution, the Congress of People's Deputies, designed to supplant it as the state's locus of political authority.

Neutralizing opposition, enhancing support (1982–1986)

The rise of Andropov to the post of general secretary in late 1982 was the trigger for the beginning of Gorbachev's own ascent. Andropov, too, sought reform, though he intended primarily to rectify the inefficiencies and corruption that plagued especially the latter half of the Brezhnev years. Toward this end, Andropov handed the personnel portfolio to Gorbachev, a vigorous reformer who had carefully kept the full scope of his ambitions from his Politburo colleagues, and the two of them chose Yegor Ligachev, another energetic reformer with a reputation for uncorruptibility, as the head of the Central Committee Department of Party Organizational Work.[149]

The material from which the three had to draw when making promotions was mixed, in that Konstantin Chernenko, a Brezhnev crony who was among the least interested of all Politburo members in reform, had held the position of secretary in charge of personnel since 1977. His predecessor, Andrei Kirilenko, had held the post since 1966, however, and Chernenko had had only one Party Congress (the 26th, in 1981) in which to consolidate a base of support – and there was no love lost between supporters of the two. Andropov, Gorbachev, and Ligachev were therefore able to draw from the reservoir of Kirilenko appointees when transforming their basis of support. Andropov himself, however, did not remain in office for much more than a year, and his attempt to replace Chernenko with Gorbachev in the #2 position prior to his death was thwarted;[150] nevertheless, Gorbachev retained his personnel portfolio under Chernenko, though with considerably restricted freedom of action.[151]

Upon his ascent, Gorbachev quickly convinced one of the most respected members of the old guard, Andrei Gromyko, to retire from the position that he had held at the head of the Foreign Ministry for nearly three decades, by offering him the position of Chairman of the Presidium of the Supreme Soviet instead – technically a promotion, but one that rendered Gromyko far less capable of hindering reform, especially in Soviet foreign policy. At about the same time he engineered the promotion of key

---

[149] Brown (1996, 53–57).

[150] Hough (1987) describes Gorbachev's constituency-transforming activities under Andropov; Brown (1996, 67–68) relates the story of the Central Committee plenary session at which Andropov's written statement, conveniently lacking the paragraph that would have made it clear that Gorbachev was his chosen successor, was distributed, and of Andropov's "incandescent" fury at the news of the omission.

[151] Hough (1990, 163–164).

allies (Ligachev, Ryzhkov, and Chebrikov) to full, rather than candidate, Politburo member status and ensured that additional allies were either brought into the Politburo (Gromyko's surprise replacement, Eduard Shevardnadze) or positioned in such a way to be brought in soon (Aleksandr Yakovlev was positioned at the head of the Central Committee's Ideology Department in late 1985 and elected to the Politburo in 1987). In all, he managed to remove three of ten voting members of the Politburo (Nikolai Tikhonov, Viktor Grishin, and Grigorii Romanov) and neutralize a fourth, Gromyko – his most substantial opponents, while at the same time promoting five allies to voting member status in that same body.[152] This was an important accomplishment because, although his support in office ultimately derived from the Central Committee, the Politburo was responsible for guidance on such matters as the limits of policy during negotiations with foreign leaders.[153]

At the same time, Gorbachev was able to use his ability to alter the balance among institutions to improve the prospects for reform. As Grachev (2008, 10–11) explains, the dual pursuit of ideological and *realpolitik* goals at the heart of Soviet foreign policy had actually been incorporated into the institutions of the state:

> Soviet foreign policy never abandoned the "double track," constantly oscillating between support for "revolutionary forces" (thus challenging the existing world order) and a quest for stability that required traditional great power behaviour and the application of *realpolitik*.
>
> [T]his policy ... found its reflection in the parallel handling of the different aspects of foreign policy by its two "arms" – mutually complementary and at the same time rival structures – the Ministry of Foreign Affairs (MID) and the International Department of the Central Committee (ID).... While the MID was charged with looking after "stability" and assuring the Soviet state's presence and position in the world "concert of powers," the ID was supposed to encourage and introduce the "change" needed to provide evidence of the advance of the world "revolutionary process" and of the continuous shift of the world balance of power to the advantage of the USSR. These two dimensions of Soviet foreign policy, the "realist" and the "ideological," not only often were in competition with one another but also regularly changed places in the hierarchy of the Soviet leadership's political priorities depending on internal policy concerns.

Gorbachev could, accordingly, rely on either institution for research, guidance, ideas, and support, depending on his predilections. The replacement of Ponomarev with Dobrynin as head of the International Department constituted a shift toward a more reformist chief, to be sure, but given Ponomarev's dogmatic views it was a low bar: Dobrynin was a moderate reformer, and despite the fact that Gorbachev selected a few key aides (such as Chernyaev) from within the International Department the bulk

---

[152] Hazan (1987, 163–209) covers the period in remarkable detail.

[153] The key positions in the realm of foreign policy were foreign minister, defense minister, heads of the International Department of the Central Committee, and foreign policy aide. Gorbachev was able to make changes in most of those positions relatively early, with Anatoly Chernyaev coming in as his foreign policy aide, Shevardnadze replacing Gromyko at the Ministry of Foreign Affairs, and Anatoly Dobrynin heading the International Department, all by 1986, though changes in the Defense Ministry would have to wait until the next year.

of that institution remained unreformed. It was more straightforward to Gorbachev to use his ability to choose among institutions to emphasize the Ministry of Foreign Affairs and to fill its ranks with reformers, which he did; the International Department, accordingly, was increasingly marginalized.[154]

The most reasonable point at which to date the end of this period was the 27th Party Congress of February-March 1986, which marked the juncture at which Gorbachev had achieved a substantial enough change in his constituency, both within the Politburo and in the Central Committee, to have a much freer hand in implementing fundamental policy changes than he would have had just a year earlier. At the level of his broader constituency, Gorbachev had managed very substantial changes: whereas the previous two Party Congresses had returned more than 90% of the membership of the Central Committee, the 27th returned only 62%.[155] Such placements were crucial, because deference was not absolute: Khrushchev's experience had shown that party leaders are vulnerable to sanction, and a sufficiently large conservative coalition would be able to block the path of reform.

Continued reform, increasing resistance (1986–1988)

As perestroika proceeded and Gorbachev encountered increasing resistance within the party, he continued to believe for a time that the party could be the vehicle for reform, but only if it were suitably reformed itself. During this period the general secretary displayed a remarkable, though not absolute, ability to engage in institutional conversion within the parameters of the system. By its end, he had concluded that reform within the existing system was impossible. He did, however, maintain enough control over the institutions of the state to transform them to a more pluralistic set of institutions that would make him accountable to a broader constituency – one that was far more amenable to reform than the Communist Party. He began that process of transformation at the end of 1988.

Gorbachev started laying the groundwork for the process of political decentralization within the party immediately after his consolidation of authority at the 27th Party Congress. When he met with top Central Committee officials in the summer of 1986, he astounded them by ruminating about the limitations of the single-party system and arguing that their main concern should be revamping their outdated personnel policy to improve its methods of selection and nomination. "Without a 'minor revolution' in the Party we will not get anywhere, because real power is in the hands of Party organs," he argued. "We always have to remember about the limitations of the single-party system."[156]

Gorbachev initially did little to restructure the military, in part because his very early goals mostly involved economic restructuring (a goal with which military leaders were mostly in accord) and in part because, when he did turn to the subject of unilateral military cuts, he had not yet consolidated enough power either to remove them or to overcome their opposition. The situation changed in May 1987, however, when Mathias Rust landed his Cessna in Red Square and gave Gorbachev a rare opportunity

---

[154] Hough (1990, 220–225), Brown (2007, 167–172); though, curiously, *cf.* Brown (2007, 84–85).
[155] Hough (1990, 170–171).   [156] Chernyaev (2000, 68).

to create vacancies in the upper echelon of the military – an opportunity that he did not forego. Marshal Sokolov, the defense minister and a forceful advocate of military preparedness who had already expressed opposition to those aspects of reform that involved cuts to the military budget, was berated by Gorbachev so thoroughly that he had no choice but to offer his resignation; he was replaced with the far more pliable Dmitri Yazov and was followed into retirement by about 100 top military officials who were also opponents of Gorbachev's reforms. From that point on Shevardnadze and Gorbachev found that opposition to reform from the military wing of their domestic constituency had decreased considerably.[157]

Political reform continued until an event in March of 1988 signaled that Gorbachev was reaching the limits of institutional elasticity and occasioned a momentary pause. No matter how persuasive he was in convincing old-guard communists to retire or promote his allies, there simply were not enough potential allies *within the Communist Party* to support a radical revision of the ideology underlying the state's domestic and foreign policies; no matter how he couched his language, its meaning was becoming increasingly clear.

In early February, the right-wing newspaper *Sovietskaya Rossiya* had received a letter from an unknown lecturer from a chemical institute in Leningrad named Nina Andreyeva. The author's purpose in writing was to voice her support for the paper's scathing review of Mikhail Shatrov's play *Onward Onward Onward,* a bold new play in which the tyrant was portrayed as a murderer who had betrayed the principles of the October Revolution. Andreyeva used Shatrov's play as a springboard for a criticism of liberals, Westernizers, and those who would sully the heroic past of the Soviet people. Accounts understandably vary regarding what happened next.

Yegor Ligachev asserts to this day that he had no hand in promoting or modifying the letter. According to Vladimir Denisov, an editor at *Sovietskaya Rossiya* who was handed the letter by the paper's main editor, Valentin Chikin, however, Ligachev had not only advised Chikin to publish the letter but had also returned an annotated copy with suggestions regarding which sections to emphasize. Chikin sent Denisov to Leningrad to meet with Andreyeva and to play up those parts of the letter that would make it a comprehensive anti-perestroika dissertation, a plan that met with the ready approval of Andreyeva, a self-professed Stalinist. The result was a full-page letter entitled "I Cannot Forsake Principles" that ran on page 3 of the Sunday, March 13 edition.

It should be emphasized that the Soviet media at this time were controlled entirely by the state, and no content – including letters to the editor – that were inconsistent with official state ideology were permitted. *Sovietskaya Rossiya* was a major press organ, with circulation in the millions. Given its prominent placement, its tone, and the Soviet tradition of state control of the media, it was understood to be an official pronouncement that reform had come to an end. It was reprinted widely, and Soviet reformers, sensitive to the direction of the political winds, fell abruptly silent, awaiting further developments.

---

[157] Mendelson (1998, 104–105); Dobrynin (1995, 625–626).

Gorbachev was preparing to depart for a trip to Yugoslavia and Yakovlev was in Mongolia, so neither was in a position to counteract the piece's immediate influence. It took the two nearly a month to develop and implement an effective response to the conservative broadside. When Gorbachev returned to Moscow and found some of his Politburo colleagues to be quite enthusiastic about the letter, he made it clear that he did not share their enthusiasm; support for the Andreyeva letter dwindled, though divisions within the Politburo remained. Gorbachev and Yakovlev nevertheless managed to use the party tradition of unity to ensure unanimous support for a full-page rebuttal of the Andreyeva letter, which ran on page 3 of the April 5 edition of *Pravda*. The result was a rout for conservatives, who had to endure an avalanche of pro-reform sentiment in newspapers and magazines that never would have been possible before the publication of the Andreyeva letter.[158]

In August of that year, a response from his most prominent critic underscored the fact that Gorbachev's reforms would be doomed were he to continue to pursue them with the party as his chosen vehicle. Ligachev, undeterred by the outcome of the Andreyeva affair, gave a speech in Gorky in the late summer of 1988 in which he directly challenged the reformers' renunciation of the ideological character of international politics and Gorbachev's emphasis, as recently as the 19th Party Conference, on universal human values, by reaffirming "the strictly class character of international relations." Gorbachev, who had carefully maintained the appearance of Politburo unity during the Andreyeva affair and had avoided singling out Ligachev for punishment despite having known that he was behind it, now decided that Ligachev's talents could best be applied to the area of agriculture. Accordingly, he relieved him of any obligations in the area of ideology, leaving that portfolio to Ligachev's rival, Yakovlev.[159]

These developments prompted Gorbachev to push for deeper reforms and ultimately for a fundamental transformation of the political system. Following the Nina Andreyeva affair and Ligachev's Gorky speech in 1988, and in light of the ability of the *apparat* to block economic reform, Gorbachev set about to reorganize the Central Committee *apparat* itself and loosen its hold on important policy functions. In this attempt he was only partly successful, and the resulting *apparat,* now deeply divided between hardened (and forewarned) veterans and reformers, fought a second reform two years later with greater tenacity.[160] Most importantly, however, it was during the leadup to the 19th Party Conference in late June and early July 1988 that Gorbachev made the decision to use the occasion of that gathering to change the locus of political authority in the state from the Communist Party to a new legislature that would be composed of delegates selected in contested elections.[161] There simply was not a sufficiently reformist constituency to be had within the Communist Party, nor would conservatives willingly comply with an agenda as radical as Gorbachev's; he therefore had no choice but to transform the basis of his support entirely.

---

[158] Remnick (1994, 72–85); Chernyaev (2000, 153–157).

[159] Chernyaev (at 172) notes that the newspaper accounts softened the speech somewhat by omitting the word "strictly." Chernyaev (2000, 170–173).

[160] Hahn (1997).   [161] Brown (1996, 166).

Transformation (1988–1990)

As his goals became more ambitious and as resistance within the CPSU became more entrenched Gorbachev reached the limits of institutional conversion and had to jettison the state structure in favor of a new one, the Congress of People's Deputies. The clearest point at which to date the onset of this transformation would be Gorbachev's speech to the 19th Party Conference in the summer of 1988, when his major speech outlined an attempt to make "a peaceful, smooth transition from one political system to another."[162]

Gorbachev chose to situate his power in the office of president, which would be one that was chosen by the Congress of People's Deputies rather than by the electorate as a whole – a fact with a few important implications. The Congress consisted of 2,250 seats, divided equally among territorial units by political division (750 seats), territorial units by population density (750 seats), and public organizations such as the Academy of Sciences, the Communist Party, and the Komsomol (750 seats). Discounting noncompetitive seats allocated to territorial units and all seats allocated to public organizations, direct competition only characterized about half of the seats for the Congress.[163] Because the unopposed candidates and the representatives of the public organizations tended to be more conservative than the rest, the overall composition of the Congress itself was more moderate either than that of the increasingly reformist population as a whole or of the Communist Party – a position that suited Gorbachev well.

It was important for Gorbachev to maintain control over the Communist Party as well during this process – not for the sake of using it for its intended purpose, governance, but rather to ensure that it was *not* used by conservative elements to block the creation of the new Congress. Gorbachev put it most succinctly to Chernyaev when he said, "You mustn't let go of the reins of a mangy, mad dog." Once the transfer was complete, however, Gorbachev felt free to loosen his hold on the reins considerably, and as a result top political organs met far more rarely than they had (once a month rather than once a week in the case of the Politburo and, after the fall of 1988, the Secretariat adjourned for what turned out to be about a year).[164]

In March 1989, the first (and, as fate would have it, only) elections to the new Congress of People's Deputies took place. The results were difficult to interpret in the usual way given the absence of coherent party affiliations (other than an increasingly meaningless Communist Party membership), but it was apparent that, despite the fact that most deputies were still drawn from the ranks of the party, Gorbachev's goals had been achieved: the most conservative party members had been turned out at the polls, and reformers had done disproportionately well. Indeed, a bloc of deputies calling itself the Inter-Regional Group of People's Deputies soon formed, including such popular reformers as Andrei Sakharov, Boris Yeltsin, and Yurii Afanasiev; before long

---

[162] Brown (2007, 202).

[163] Admittedly, this figure underrepresents the Congress's representativeness, because voters could – and did – reject unopposed candidates by crossing out their names on more than 50% of the ballots. For an account of the elections and their results see Brovkin (1990).

[164] Brown (1996, 196–200).

it became apparent that Gorbachev's constituency now contained even more radical reformers than he. Obtaining a mandate for reform and support for new thinking would no longer be a problem; instead, Gorbachev had to defend his evolutionary approach against those who preferred more radical, revolutionary means.[165]

Equally important from the point of view of policy was the creation of two bodies that, together, supplanted the Politburo: the Federation Council, which consisted of the presidents or chairmen of the Supreme Soviets of the various republics of the Union, and the Presidential Council, comprising Gorbachev's advisors and key members of his inner circle. The mechanisms of government available to Gorbachev at the Cold War's end, in addition to being more streamlined and more directly under his control, were also more sympathetic to the direction of his reforms.

The trigger: changing Soviet worldviews

I now turn to a discussion of the main elements of the model, starting with the change in Soviet worldviews that accompanied Gorbachev's rise and tenure in office. When Gorbachev came to power, cooperation with the West was still seen as a tactical matter in the long-run class struggle, though the ideological dimension of foreign policy was increasingly hortatory rather than a matter of practical policy. Still, the ideas that the fundamental nature of international relations was dictated by the class struggle, and that peaceful coexistence with the West was merely a means to ensuring Soviet survival until that struggle could be resolved in its favor at a later date, ran deep.[166] Gorbachev's rise did not signal an immediate change in this perspective, as even the new general secretary himself had not fully developed his ideas about foreign policy upon taking office. Nevertheless, his rise accelerated his existing conceptual evolution, a process that would deal a serious blow to the class-based foundations of international politics among the very top leadership within a year's time and obviate them entirely at the level of state ideology in just over three and a half.

Gorbachev himself had traveled widely, and his conversations with foreign leaders and experiences in foreign societies had forced him to realize, even before he became general secretary, how substantial the disjuncture between the reality of the outside world and the Soviet portrayal of it really was – a fact mentioned spontaneously, and independently, by many of his aides. In particular, he gradually lost faith in the superiority of Soviet communism over Western capitalist systems as he observed their standards of living and the functioning of their political institutions first hand; he also concluded that the imperialist world, far from representing a hostile monolith, comprised a diverse community of states that seemed not to be planning to attack the Soviet Union.[167]

Gorbachev had also consulted widely with members of the liberal intelligentsia before becoming general secretary, both to enlist their support against reactionary elements in the party and to solicit their ideas for domestic reform. Over time, he found that these contacts led him to question the foundations of his understanding

---

[165] McFaul (2001, 69–74).   [166] Grachev (2008, 11–12).
[167] Brown (2007, 230, 232); Grachev (2008, 46).

of international politics as well. The beginnings of this change go back at least to early 1982, when Gorbachev began to make contact with reform-minded sociologists and economists in the agricultural sphere. Contacts continued and their scope broadened as his portfolio expanded under Andropov, and their pace accelerated when, as general secretary, he drew from his now-extensive list of contacts to fill out his team – Anatoly Chernyaev, from the Central Committee's International Department, became his foreign policy aide, whereas Arbatov of IMEMO, the previously reprimanded Zaslavskaya, and Primakov all became advisors.[168]

All of these influences began to bear fruit as early as 1986, when Gorbachev asked Yakovlev to prepare the foreign policy section of the Political Report for the upcoming 27th Party Congress.[169] Yakovlev's mandate was to answer the question, "What is 'new thinking'?" Yakovlev, along with Nikolai Kosolapov and Valentin Falin, used the opportunity to produce a coherent, and radical, statement of principles that, among other things, rejected the traditional class-based understanding of international politics in favor of "competition and struggle between the two systems with a growing tendency for independence among the states forming the world community" and abandoned what had become a ritual statement about the inevitability of the final victory of communism.[170]

Gorbachev, Yakovlev and Shevardnadze subsequently retired to a government *dacha* to hammer out the details of the foreign policy section prior to the Congress and soon found themselves questioning the very foundations of Soviet foreign policy. In the end, after vigorous and passionate debate (punctuated by at least one prolonged period during which the three literally were not speaking to one another), they ended up concluding that they had no choice but to reject the premise of a class-based, divided world that had informed Soviet policy since the inception of the state.[171]

Gorbachev's discussion of the basic trends and contradictions of the contemporary world, with which he opened his report, contained some traditional Soviet formulations about world socialism and the aggressive nature of imperialism – due in part, to be sure, to the need to reassure the largely unreformed constituency to which the speech was addressed, but also because, at this point, Gorbachev had not entirely shed these beliefs himself: Chernyaev writes that Gorbachev's idea of new thinking at this stage was "still contaminated by ideological and class mythology" and cites conversations with foreign leaders at the time of the Congress to illustrate the fragments of class-based thinking that remained.[172] At the same time, however, Gorbachev introduced some stunning innovations into the Soviet theoretical dialogue: rather than emphasize, as previous leaders always had, a world strictly divided between socialism and imperialism, he introduced the concept of a single world, with problems "on a

---

[168] Brown (1996, 60–61; 111–112).
[169] Party Congresses in the Soviet Union served a function not unlike that of elections in the American system: they served not only to renew the membership of the Central Committee but also to focus the attention of the leadership on the Soviet equivalent of the party's "platform," or the statement of general principles underlying foreign and domestic policy.
[170] Grachev (2008, 71–73).   [171] English (2000, 209–10).
[172] Chernyaev (2000, 51–52). English (2000, 205) also argues that Gorbachev was slow to shake off the traditional Marxist understanding of a fundamentally class-based international system.

global scale" like pollution, nuclear war, and depletion of natural resources creating a compelling degree of interdependence among states.[173]

At the Congress he spoke at length about the nature of the international system and the contradictions within it. He stressed, in order, the contradictions

- between the states of the two systems (capitalism and socialism);
- within the capitalist world, especially
  - between labor and capital,
  - between transnational corporations and the nation-state, and
  - among the three main centers of imperialism (the United States, Western Europe, and Japan);
- between imperialism and the developing countries; and
- on a global scale, including such issues as the environment, resources, and the possibility of nuclear holocaust.[174]

The last point reflects the first new element to be introduced into the Soviet security dialogue.

At the same time, Gorbachev discussed the forms of security and military doctrine that were consistent with this understanding of international politics. Security, he argued, had to take the form of "mutual security": states in the modern, nuclear era could not be safe unless their adversaries were as well. Accordingly, to provide security for oneself and one's adversary, the state should seek "reasonable sufficiency" rather than attempting to match every weapon and every system deployed by one's opponent.[175]

Reasonable sufficiency was a concept that Gorbachev had hinted at previously, on a visit to France in late 1985, but had not developed fully prior to that point. The term "sufficiency" had been used by Brezhnev to repudiate the goal of Soviet strategic superiority; in this sense it meant that Soviet nuclear forces should be sufficient for deterrence but no more, and in the event the Brezhnev Politburo's perceived requirements for deterrence proved to be rather expansive. Gorbachev applied this term to conventional as well as nuclear forces, and given the ambiguity of the term it was not immediately clear to conservatives, and in particular to the military, that it implied very substantial force reductions.[176] The approval of this early, amalgamated version of "new thinking" by the Congress provided Gorbachev with the foreign policy mandate that he needed to move forward.[177]

Gorbachev had laid out, in essence, the central tenets of the official worldview: it remained for some of the liberal intelligentsia to rearrange them. Yevgenii Primakov, who followed Yakovlev as director of IMEMO, promptly stepped forward to fill the breach. In May and June 1986 he wrote articles in the Institute's official publication, *Memo,* and in the Communist Party's central organ, *Kommunist,* suggesting (as had his more distant predecessor, Varga) that capitalism may be capable of long-term stability despite its contradictions.[178]

---

[173] Garthoff (1994, 253–258).   [174] Livermore (1990, 13–16).   [175] Brown (1996, 221).
[176] Allison (1992, 239–240); English (2000, 218).   [177] Grachev (2008, 77).
[178] Checkel (1997, 94).

Primakov fared better than Varga. In March of 1987, IMEMO sponsored a conference on the topic of the "Contemporary Features of the General Crisis of Capitalism." At that conference, Primakov directly challenged key parts of Lenin's analysis of capitalism: because of its unanticipated vitality, capitalism's external behavior would pose no threat.[179] This analysis, a complete and explicit break from orthodoxy, provided one of the most crucial components of "new thinking": the decoupling of capitalism and militarism. That such a theoretical innovation could be forwarded in the shadow of a tremendous American arms buildup is testimony to the conviction of its authors. Primakov would take it to the pages of *Kommunist* in September.

During the summer, Primakov and Lev Semeiko of ISKAN combined the themes of the demilitarization of capitalism and the importance of global-level concerns to advocate a defense policy of "reasonable sufficiency" in *Pravda* and *Izvestia*, respectively.[180] Because of the danger that any conflict represented, and because capitalism in the long run was likely to realize that reciprocating was in its best interests, logic dictated a military build-down. Any forces beyond those required for self-defense would aggravate security dilemmas and increase tension without providing any additional benefit.

Meanwhile, Gorbachev continued to weave elements of the new thinking into his discussions of international affairs. A firsthand account by a member of the Central Committee who attended a speech that Gorbachev gave in May 1986 at the Ministry of Foreign Affairs nicely captures both the manner in which he did so and the uncertainty created by Gorbachev's exploitation of the ambiguity of official Soviet language:

> The speech contained – and, of course, could not but contain – trivial propagandist clichés and the usual calls to turn imperialist contradictions to our advantage, "to prevent our potential adversaries from uniting." It also included a statement that positive movement toward disarmament was unlikely from the Reagan administration. Even so, the dominant theme of the speech, its main tenor, was different. . . . He announced that peace was the highest value and took priority over the interests of the workers' movement, while a world war would be an absolute evil; that we could no longer live according to the principle of "might makes right," because civilization required new approaches; that we could not force happiness on other nations that were not ready for it or did not want it; and that improving our situation abroad meant creating conditions that would reduce military spending, and diplomacy must do all it could to limit the arms race. . . .
>
> His speech met with a mixed response from the audience. . . . My neighbor, then still a minister of the Russian Soviet Federated Socialist Republic (RSFSR), said something like: "As a propaganda device, it's not bad. But look at it another way, and you should give it a lot of thought before accepting it."[181]

Meanwhile, reform-minded intellectuals busied themselves with the task of undermining the role of contradictions between capitalism and socialism in international affairs. In a *Pravda* article, Primakov forwarded a startling proposal that amounted

---

[179] Checkel (1997, 95–96). [180] Livermore (1990, 27–29); Tarasulo (1989, 248–253).
[181] Brutents (2006, 76–77).

to nothing less than a complete deemphasis on the ideological foundations of foreign policy – one that could be justified in orthodox Leninist terms, no less. The passage is worth quoting at length:

> Of course, one of the main questions that cannot be ignored is the extent to which [the Soviet Union's new foreign policy] philosophy takes into account the social changes that are objectively occurring in the world and what the relationship is between ideology and foreign policy. The social renewal of the world is an objective requirement of mankind. But the mechanism of this renewal – both revolutionary and evolutionary – is put in motion by the internal contradictions in each country. Back at the dawn of Soviet power, V. I. Lenin spoke out resolutely against the transformation of the first state of victorious socialism into an exporter of revolution to other countries, limiting its international influence to the framework of setting an example.

To borrow a line from John Winthrop, the Soviet Union was to become the "city upon the hill" that would provide the beacon for others to follow! Primakov continues:

> Excluding the export of revolution is an imperative of the nuclear age.
> At the same time, the stabilization of the international situation not only should not but also cannot take place through the artificial maintenance of the social status quo, or, in other words, through the export of counterrevolution.
> Interstate relations in general cannot be the sphere in which the fate of the confrontation between world socialism and world capitalism is decided.[182]

The IMEMO and ISKAN scholars had elaborated a detailed critique of the Soviet worldview along three major dimensions: the nature of capitalism, the relative priority of class and non-class interests, and the fundamental character of international relations.[183] These dimensions set the terms of debate regarding foreign policy: it was left to Gorbachev, and to his evolving constituency, to settle on a position along each.

The doctrine of reasonable sufficiency, meanwhile, was elaborated in a document titled "On the Military Doctrine of the Warsaw Treaty States," adopted in Berlin on May 9, 1987, which stated that "the military doctrine of the Warsaw Treaty states is strictly defensive" and that, accordingly, the Soviets would seek arms levels that "strictly comply with the limits of sufficiency for defense." What the limits of sufficiency for defense were, however, remained a contested issue. The Soviet military initially interpreted it to mean a "level and character of military activity that secures the solution of military tasks and the prevention of war by lowest possible forces and means" – and given that these goals required that Soviet forces be, in Yazov's words, "commensurate with the threat of aggression," Soviet force levels would need to be maintained at a level that would preclude Western superiority. In short, "reasonable sufficiency" was interpreted by the military to imply parity.[184]

---

[182] Livermore (1990, 28).

[183] This characterization is derived especially from Parrott (1988), Nation (1992), and Lynch (1987); emphases and some nuances differ from account to account.

[184] Kokoshin (1998, 187); Allison (1992, 251–252).

That was not the general secretary's intent, however, and his interpretation, backed by reformist elements, soon won out. Colonel Lev Semeyko, writing in *Izvestiya* in August of 1987, described reasonable sufficiency in detail:

> The sufficiency of military potential ... must convincingly show the absence of aggressive intentions. In this context the Warsaw Pact countries' doctrinal purpose is of fundamental significance: to implement the reduction of armed forces and conventional armaments in Europe to a level at which neither of the sides, while ensuring its defense, has the means to suddenly attack the other side or to unleash offensive operations. This purpose is indeed revolutionary, because it proposes for the first time that both sides reject such a military option as an attack, which is traditionally considered to be fundamental.
>
> The second criterion is that military might and combat readiness must be sufficient to permit them not to be taken unawares (let us recall the sad experience of 1941) and, if a hostile attack occurs, to deal the aggressor a crushing rebuff. While the first criterion is aimed at ensuring that the other side has no unwarranted fears, the point of the second is that we and our allies equally want to be spared the sense of an imminent threat looming over us.[185]

It is worth emphasizing the fact that the proponents of reasonable sufficiency believed that it would be optimal even if the West did not pursue it, at least in the short to medium term. As Semeyko wrote, "We cannot fail to take into consideration the fact that the U.S. armed forces' structure is now based not on the concept of reasonable sufficiency but on the concept of military supremacy.... But in any case the limits of our armed forces' sufficiency must be reasonable and not exceed actual defensive requirements" (1989, 252).

Gorbachev's speech on the 70th anniversary of the October Revolution in November of 1987, which he wrote with Yakovlev, drew all of these themes together. He forcefully emphasized the increased role of global interdependence in international relations, going so far as to redefine the concept of "peaceful coexistence": whereas previously the term had applied to a phase of the class struggle in which the Soviet Union was at a relative disadvantage (and therefore had to make a virtue of necessity), the new "peaceful coexistence" referred to a genuine nonconflictual cohabitation of socialism and capitalism in light of the need to ensure the survival of the human race. He therefore advocated a defense posture of reasonable sufficiency. Regarding capitalism, he acknowledged its potential for fundamental stability and the possibility that it could be separated from militarism, but he left unanswered the question of whether its fundamentally aggressive nature could be influenced.[186]

The Andreyeva affair prompted a rearguard action in the spring of 1988, but the development of new thinking continued through the summer. Gorbachev touched only briefly on international affairs at the 19th Party Conference in late June and early

---

[185] Semeyko (1989, 251).

[186] As Lynch (1987, xxvii) notes, however, "[s]imply to raise such ideologically charged questions, not to mention answering [some of them] in the affirmative, implicitly challenges central Leninist tenets on the nature of imperialism and the wellsprings of conflict in world politics."

July,[187] but in late July at a conference at the Ministry of Foreign Affairs Shevard-nadze expanded on his remarks and pushed new thinking forward, reaffirming the decoupling of peaceful coexistence from the class struggle and stating quite flatly that the struggle between socialism and capitalism is no longer the axis that defines world politics.[188] In Gorbachev's United Nations speech in December of the same year, he quite explicitly stated,

> The new phase also requires de-ideologizing relations among states. We are not abandoning our convictions, our philosophy or traditions, nor do we urge anyone to abandon theirs.
>
> But neither do we have any intention to be hemmed in by our values. That would result in intellectual impoverishment, for it would mean rejecting a power-ful source of development – the exchange of everything original that each nation has independently created.
>
> In the course of such exchange, let everyone show the advantages of their social system, way of life or values – and not just by words or propaganda, but by real deeds.
>
> That would be a fair rivalry of ideologies. But it should not be extended to relations among states. . . .
>
> [W]e have concluded that it is on those lines that we should jointly seek the way leading to the supremacy of the universal human idea over the endless multitude of centrifugal forces, the way to preserve the vitality of this civilization, possibly the only one in the entire universe.[189]

This speech constitutes a reasonable capstone to the development of new thinking, both because it represents a clean break from the old – Chernyaev (2000, 201–202) notes that "an ideologically conscious retreat from orthodox class theory and methodology in analyzing international affairs, and so in formulating our foreign policy . . . did occur at precisely" this time – and because Gorbachev himself explicitly intended it to be a summary of the main tenets of new thinking, his "anti-Fulton" speech. In April 1989 these fundamentals were codified and passed as a Politburo resolution, making its formal incorporation into state policy a matter of record.[190]

The upshot of Gorbachev's liberalization is captured well by Archie Brown (2007, 257, 259):

> A conventional view of Soviet state interests, which had prevailed up until the point when Gorbachev became General Secretary, was that the more territory the Soviet Union controlled in Eastern Europe and beyond (politically, militarily, and ideologically), the better, and the more weapons it accumulated, the more it would be respected. . . . In place of the Soviet Union's previous utopian goal of building communism worldwide . . . , Gorbachev saw a world which was interdependent, in which interests and values common to the whole of humanity had acquired priority over all others.

---

[187] And, to the extent that it was, it was discussed in largely conventional terms; see Aspaturian (1990, 9–10).

[188] Livermore (1990, 23).   [189] *New York Times*, December 8, 1988, page A-16.

[190] Wohlforth (2003, 35).

Interpretation

In terms of ideology, new thinking constituted a substantial shift away from what had become traditional Soviet communism as an ideal point for ideological dimension, toward European-style social democracy. Its more important implication, however, was a graduated – and, before long, essentially complete – deemphasis on the importance of ideology in general in international affairs, so much so that the location of the Soviet ideal point in the ideological sphere became very nearly moot. It is true, as Lévesque (2004, 109) puts it, that new thinking "sought an entirely new form of socialism for the USSR and the future world order, a new 'synthesis' of socialism and democracy based on 'universal values.'" The most remarkable change, in terms of the elements of the model, was *not*, however, the shift away from a preference for socialism and toward a social-democratic ideal somewhere between it and Western democratic capitalism. This change would have been remarkable, even astounding, by historical standards had it not been mooted by an even more momentous one that took place at about the same time: the range of outcomes in the realm of ideology that were considered acceptable in other states in the system by Soviet elites became, for practical purposes, limitless. In terms familiar to formal theorists, their indifference curve, having widened enough to accommodate Solidarity in the early 1980s, became essentially a flat line, making the location of their ideal point irrelevant.

The implication of the change in the military dimension of the Soviet worldview was that key elements of the Soviet leadership were increasingly of the opinion that fewer weapons, both in absolute terms and relative to the number amassed by the West, would not only be tolerable but would in fact be *optimal* from the point of view of security. Fewer Warsaw Pact arms would improve Western security and in so doing would increase the chances that the East would have far less to fear from the hostility generated by competing arms spirals.[191] Moreover, because of the deemphasis on ideological rivalry as the primary engine of international affairs and the corresponding softening of the Soviet image of capitalism, little was to be feared, and much was to be gained, from asymmetric arms reductions: attack from the West was not a serious concern, but if the West could be induced to reciprocate deep Soviet reductions in armaments, the result would be a much safer world. Another implication, therefore, was that the leadership was quite willing to envision, in the short to medium term, an imbalance, even a profound one, in the distribution of material capabilities between the two blocs.

This ideational transition occurred in early 1986 at the very latest, and in some cases and to some degree much earlier, among Gorbachev and his closest advisors, though it took more time to permeate the top leadership deeply enough to constitute a substantial change in *Soviet* worldviews. This was a gradual process. Gorbachev's message to the COMECON leaders at the Kremlin in late 1986, followed closely by his publication of his views in *Perestroika* the next year, supports the argument that he had gained the upper hand by that point, but the conservative backlash in the summer of 1988 demonstrates that the opposition had not yet yielded. The process

---

[191] The logic of this argument bears obvious similarities to a standard spiral-model argument; see Jervis (1976, ch. 3) for the seminal cite.

was completed, arguably, either when Gorbachev codified new thinking in his UN speech in December 1988 or when it was accepted by the Politburo four months later.

Reaction: red tide's ebb

The main implications of the changes in the Soviet worldview documented earlier should have been decreased attempts by the Soviets to maintain favorable military and ideological balances and a resulting shift in those balances to favor the United States, and this was precisely what occurred.

Afghanistan

Gorbachev laid the groundwork for a withdrawal from Afghanistan early on and in doing so showed a hint of the deemphasis of ideology in foreign policy that was to come (although, by nearly all accounts, it had not yet fully arrived in his own thinking at this point). It was not long after Gorbachev took power that he advised Afghan leader Babrak Karmal to seek a broader base of support, in essence abandoning the ideological nature of his revolutionary movement, and told him that Soviet aid for their Afghan comrades would not long be supported. His Foreign Policy Aide, Anatoly Chernyaev, recalls the events of a Politburo meeting on October 17, 1985, in which Gorbachev recounted the details of the meeting with Kamal. In it, the new head of the Soviet Communist Party describes to the highest organ of that party in matter-of-fact terms the manner in which he advised a client state to abandon the cause of socialism:

> He said Karmal was dumbfounded. . . . Gorbachev had to make himself perfectly clear; by the summer of 1986 you'll have to have figured out how to defend your cause on your own. We'll help you, but with arms only, not troops. And if you want to survive you'll have to broaden the base of the regime, *forget socialism*, make a deal with the truly influential forces, . . . , revive Islam, respect traditions, and try to show the people some tangible benefits.[192]

At the 27th Party Congress in 1986, Gorbachev pointedly avoided the standard Soviet formulation "national liberation movements" when referring to Afghanistan, preferring instead "regional conflicts" – a rhetorical shift that sapped the ideological underpinnings of support for the conflict. Given that the Americans had no interest whatsoever in continuing to supply the Afghans with arms if the Soviets ceased to do so,[193] the absence of an ideological justification for the war made a continuation of Soviet losses nonsensical: as Gorbachev would put it to the Politburo in November, "We don't seek socialism there. . . . If there are no US airfields or military camps, anything else they can decide on their own." Karmal proved to be unreceptive to Gorbachev's suggestions that he abandon socialism and share power, however, so in March 1986 a decision was taken in principle to replace him as head of the party and the Afghan state with Dr. Najibullah, and in November 1986 that decision was carried

---

[192] Chernyaev (2000, 42, emphasis added). See also Mendelson (1998) and Brown (2007, 242).
[193] Matlock (2004, 285–286).

out. Najibullah promptly traveled to Moscow and upon his return disavowed both Marxism-Leninism and any attempt to build socialism in Afghanistan.[194]

Both public opinion, which was slow to adjust to the new line on Afghanistan, and American policy, which was not entirely accommodating, hindered an immediate exit strategy; nevertheless, another year's work culminated in a February 9, 1988, speech devoted entirely to the war in Afghanistan, in which Gorbachev announced that Soviet troop withdrawals would begin in May 1988 and would be completed by February 1989.[195] The Geneva Accords between Afghanistan and Pakistan, with the United States and the Soviet Union serving as guarantors, covered an array of issues surrounding the settlement of the war and included a timetable for Soviet withdrawal; they were signed in April 1988, and Soviet troops left ahead of the proposed deadline, by February 1989.

Armaments

After the death of Andropov, the Soviet leadership under Chernenko had fallen back on a view of the world that more closely resembled Stalin's portrayal of a "hostile capitalist encirclement" than anything had in the years since the tyrant's death, and military policy had been consistent with that shift: the preparations for the 1986–1990 Five-Year Plan included a staggering 45% increase in military expenditures. Gorbachev's policies after he took office in March 1985 could hardly have been more different. On March 22, he proposed a freeze on the development of strategic nuclear weapons and on the development of intermediate-range missiles in Europe; almost immediately thereafter he declared a moratorium on the deployment of Soviet SS-20s and offered to reduce the Soviet strategic nuclear arsenal by 25% if the United States were to abandon the Strategic Defense Initiative. In August he initiated a unilateral moratorium on nuclear testing. All of these steps could reasonably have been interpreted as ways of scoring relatively inexpensive propaganda victories against the United States in traditional Soviet fashion, and indeed given how recently he had come into office it would have been difficult for him to forward initiatives that did not at least appear insincere to conservatives at home. At the same time, however, he began to lay the groundwork for real change. At the April Plenum in 1985, for example, he floated the idea that military forces should be limited to the criterion of "sufficiency" and, accordingly, made more defensive.[196]

One of the next steps was the announcement, on January 15, 1986, of a plan for a graduated abolition of all nuclear weapons. This was, to all appearances, another apparently cynical Soviet gesture designed to force the West to demur and therefore produce a propaganda victory. It had, in fact, been prepared by the leadership of the Soviet military in precisely that spirit: it was intended to be so alarming to the Americans that they would never accept it, and the Soviets could portray themselves as peace-loving. It goes without saying that the idea was no less odious to the Soviet military. Gorbachev, however, realized that it could be a vehicle for genuine arms reductions and used it as such. He seized on the offer to demonstrate to conservative

---

[194] Grachev (2008, 104–106).   [195] Mendelson (1998, 116).
[196] English (2000, 190, 193, 200); Grachev (2008, 56–57).

critics that the military itself was willing to reduce its nuclear armaments by half in the first stage, apparently without detriment to national security. The military leadership, having formulated the plan, could scarcely admit either that it had merely been seeking a cheap propaganda victory or that it had forwarded a plan that would be damaging to Soviet security if implemented. When the Western response raised the issue of conventional weapons, which Gorbachev also wanted to reduce, he readily agreed to include those in the discussion as well. Again, although no immediate results with the West resulted, the exercise served to set the stage for future progress.[197]

The Reykjavik Summit of October 1986 gave an early and more tangible indication of Gorbachev's intentions in the military realm, though it too failed to result in an agreement. The main Soviet goals were to remove the American Pershing II medium-range ballistic missiles from Europe and to stall development of the Strategic Defense Initiative. To achieve those goals, they were willing to offer a package of concessions far out of proportion either to the gains they would achieve or to previous Soviet concessions: a 50% cut in land-based ballistic missiles, full acceptance of the "double zero" option for intermediate-range nuclear forces (an asymmetric proposal that the United States had forwarded years earlier, also without any realistic intention of seeing it implemented), a withdrawal of the usual Soviet demand that British and French nuclear weapons be included in the calculation of the balance of forces, and, if necessary, the elimination of medium-range nuclear missiles in Asia and nuclear artillery.[198]

Most importantly, however, while at Reykjavik Gorbachev and Reagan agreed in principle to the elimination of intermediate-range nuclear forces in Europe. Over the course of 1987 the details were worked out, and when the negotiations slowed Gorbachev dropped the range of included missiles to 500 km and further disadvantaging the Soviets, a fact that made rejecting the treaty even more difficult for the United States to justify. When the INF treaty was signed in December 1987, the entire category of weapons was eliminated – a dramatically asymmetric reduction that the Soviet General Staff accepted only very reluctantly, given that the Soviets possessed more than twice as many warheads of that type.[199]

The most dramatic change in the Soviet Union's efforts to maintain the military balance, however, was completely unilateral and was announced a year later, when Gorbachev addressed the United Nations. The general secretary promised Soviet troop reductions of a half-million men out of a total not much more than ten times that size. Such a number was consistent both with the Soviet need to integrate such a large number of people into its faltering economy slowly and with a force reduction aimed at increased efficiency rather than genuine disarmament, so Western observers were free to draw either conclusion. More startling, and far less ambiguous, was his pledge to withdraw and disband no fewer than *half* of the 10,000 Soviet tank forces in the three Warsaw Pact states bordering the West, along with river-crossing forces and other equipment designed most obviously to support offensive operations. In all, the announced reductions, when implemented, would render the Soviet Union

---

[197] Grachev (2008, 68–70).   [198] Grachev (2008, 83).

[199] The Soviets possessed 1,846, to the Americans' 846. Garthoff (1994, ch. 7; figures in fn. 64).

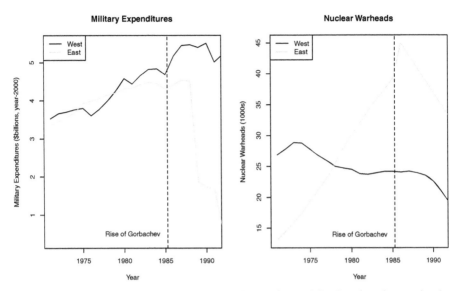

Figure 4.5. Levels of military expenditures (in billions of 2000 dollars) and nuclear warheads. *Sources:* Correlates of War data and Norris and Arkin (1997).

incapable of offering "fraternal assistance" to socialist regimes in distress in Eastern Europe, much less of launching a sudden invasion of the West.[200]

As Figure 4.5 demonstrates, the effects of these reforms in the military sphere were not subtle. Both conventional military spending and the number of nuclear warheads, which had been trending upward for the Warsaw Pact countries, reached a peak in 1987–1988 and then plunged dramatically: nuclear warhead stockpiles fell by more than 20% in the four-year period following 1987, while overall military spending fell by nearly 30% in just half that time. Because the West's military expenditures continued to rise while those of the East plunged precipitously, and its number of nuclear warheads decreased less dramatically, this reversal represented a substantial shift in the overall military balance in a relatively short period of time.

The announcement of troop withdrawals from Eastern Europe in Gorbachev's UN speech of December 1988 had two effects. In addition to being the most detailed statement to date of the Soviet doctrine of noninterference in the form of government of sovereign states, it also contained the deep, unilateral cuts in Soviet military forces – in particular, a half-million men overall, and 10,000 tanks from Eastern

---

[200] Evangelista (2004, 94–95); Gordon (1988); Grachev (2008, 250). Evangelista argues that this moment, rather than the Malta Summit a year later, marks the end of the Cold War, because it marks the point at which one side announced plans to render itself incapable of participating in it. That interpretation is a reasonable one; nevertheless, I prefer the Malta Summit because it seems difficult to declare the Cold War to be entirely over as long as one side remained committed to waging it, which proved to be the case. For a more diverse array of interpretations regarding the meaning of the Cold War and therefore the timing of its end see Herrmann and Lebow (2004, ch. 1).

Europe alone – that made that statement both credible and very public.[201] Moreover, the time that had passed between Gorbachev's initial statements and the summer of 1989 ensured that those statements reflected more than just the preferences of a reformist minority. As we have already seen, Gorbachev's power of appointment and ability to transform the Soviet political establishment had by that point ensured that opposition to his hands-off policy in Eastern Europe, though far from nonexistent, would prove ineffectual.

Eastern Europe

In the early 1980s, the Brezhnev Doctrine was at least as infirm as the country's senior leadership. The Solidarity movement in Poland had exposed the potential costs of supporting communism in Eastern Europe. Hardliners and reformers alike had learned the lessons not just of Poland but of Afghanistan and Czechoslovakia as well: whereas new thinkers were morally opposed to the use of force, few remained enthusiastic about its efficacy. The result was a surprising degree of unanimity on the subject of military intervention, albeit for different reasons. This fact explains Gorbachev's statement that "the Brezhnev Doctrine, or the doctrine of limited sovereignty, was ended even before Chernenko was buried."[202]

Gorbachev may not have chosen Chernenko's funeral as his point of reference arbitrarily: he took the opportunity of the gathering of the Eastern European leadership on that occasion in March 1985 to make it clear to them that Soviet military intervention on their behalf would not be forthcoming. It needs to be emphasized that, at this point, Gorbachev still labored under the misapprehension that these leaders were capable of earning the support of their people, so it is difficult to say whether or how he might have tempered his remarks had he understood the full force of public sentiment.[203] Nevertheless, this was among the first of a series of statements that constituted, in the context of earlier Soviet policy, a substantial degree of disinterest in the ideology of client states.

Another signal came a few months later, when an anonymous article in *Pravda* criticized reformist tendencies in Eastern Europe and called for greater discipline and

---

[201] The fact that little of note happened in Eastern Europe for nearly three years after Gorbachev first repudiated the Brezhnev Doctrine makes it seem as though the Soviet lack of interest in the form of Eastern European governments was late in developing; we tend intuitively to think that cause and effect have to be proximate in time. But in this case, despite the lack of Soviet support for client regimes and a widespread desire for change, the people went about doing what they had been doing. Much like a coyote in a Saturday morning cartoon, they kept running because they were unaware that the earth under their feet had disappeared. The status quo persisted mainly because, until 1989, an insufficient number of people who had an interest in political liberalization were aware (or really believed) that such change would be entirely unopposed by Moscow. For a discussion of the sorts of "informational cascades" that brought these facts to light see Lohmann (1994).

[202] Bennett (2005); Ouimet (2003, 234–235, 255 and *passim*). That said, the freedom of choice that they envisioned for Poland, though considerable at the time, paled in comparison to what would come: none imagined a transition to capitalism or a withdrawal from the Warsaw Pact.

[203] Brown (2007, 242–243).

unity under conservative principles. Traditionally, an article of this sort would have been taken as a clear signal from the Soviet leadership, but in this case no such signal was intended, a fact that Gorbachev conveyed via a personal message to each of the leaders – and by ensuring that the author of the article retired from his position in the Central Committee department responsible for relationships with other socialist countries. For the first year or so, however, Gorbachev limited himself to negative statements – indications that the new Soviet policy would not resemble the old one in its reliance on the use of force – without making any positive statements regarding the new principles upon which relations were to be based. At first, this truculence could well have been based on his still moderate views: Andrei Grachev writes that the early Gorbachev "certainly did not envisage the possibility of some autonomous political evolution independent of the elder brother."[204]

The 27th Party Congress, unlike previous Congresses, emphasized ensuring the progress of the *country*, not of the international socialist *movement*, as the vehicle for ensuring the Soviet people's peace and security and therefore as the Soviet Union's main international duty. Given that it contained both that statement and an explicit rejection of the legitimacy of the use of force in international relations, the general secretary's report at the Congress provided the ideological foundations for the repudiation of the Brezhnev Doctrine – though, given the substantial opposition to reform at the time, the report also contained enough contradictions and traditional formulations to placate, or at least confuse, Gorbachev's ideological opponents.[205]

In November or December 1986, Gorbachev called a private meeting in the Kremlin of the top leaders of COMECON member countries, informing them not only that the Soviet Union would not intervene militarily to bolster their governments but also that he expected that they would have to transform themselves into national parties that were, in fact, accountable to their own populations in order to retain power. Reactions ranged from cautious optimism (on the part of reformers) to barely concealed skepticism.[206]

Having given the leaders of Soviet client states advance warning, Gorbachev proceeded to make his views public. "Universal security in our time rests upon the recognition of the right of every nation to choose its own path of social development," he wrote bluntly in his book, *Perestroika*.[207] At the 19th Party Conference in mid-1988, he was more explicit still: "[T]he imposition of a social system, way of life, or policies from outside by any means, let alone military, are dangerous trappings of the past period."[208]

---

[204] Grachev (2008, 117–118).   [205] Garthoff (1994, 258).

[206] On the dating of the meeting, accounts differ; see English (2000, 335, fn. 183). On the substance of the meeting itself see Grachev (2008, 118–119) and English (2000, 224).

[207] Gorbachev (1987, 143).

[208] Aspaturian (1990, 9). cf. Lévesque (2004, 113–114), who argues that Gorbachev *was* inclined to encourage reformist governments throughout Eastern Europe, but that he was deterred by the balance of forces in the party leadership.

The emphasis in the new thinking on freedom of choice did not imply that Gorbachev himself had abandoned his commitment to the ideal of socialism; his statement in *Perestroika* about states' freedom of choice was followed by the statement that "[e]conomic, political, and ideological competition between capitalist and socialist countries is inevitable. However, it can and must be kept within a framework of peaceful competition which necessarily envisages cooperation. It is up to history to judge the merits of each particular system." Other statements reveal that he remained confident about history's judgment even at a surprisingly late date: in December 1989, Gorbachev told Romanian leader Nicolae Ceausescu that, because of the democratic nature of the revolutions sweeping the region, "there was no reason to fear the collapse or the end of socialism." When he was subsequently asked about this remarkable statement, Gorbachev confirmed that "we believed that the guarantee of real freedom of choice and of real sovereignty in Central and East Europe would play in favor of socialism."[209]

Regardless of its source, however, official Soviet indifference to the state ideology of its neighbors was essentially absolute, a point that was made clear to the world in 1987 if not before. Gorbachev's speech in December 1988 underscored the fact that the Soviets would not rely on force to keep Eastern Europe in the Soviet sphere: "[T]he use or threat of force no longer can or must be an instrument of foreign policy.... All of us, and primarily the stronger of us, must exercise self-restraint and totally rule out any outward-oriented use of force." Freedom of choice, he said, is a universal principle that "applies both to the capitalist and to the socialist system." In July 1989, when addressing the Council of Europe, he made the point even more unambiguously: "The social and political order in some particular countries did change in the past, and it can change in the future as well. But this is exclusively a matter for the peoples themselves and of their choice. Any interference in internal affairs, any attempts to limit the sovereignty of states – whether of friends and allies or anybody else – are inadmissible."

At the beginning of 1989, concerned about the increasingly unstable situation in Eastern Europe (particularly in Poland and Hungary), Yakovlev commissioned four reports from various agencies and institutes regarding future scenarios and how, if at all, the Soviet Union should act to affect them. The Brezhnev Doctrine was a dead letter, but no one was entirely sure what would replace it. The agencies were asked, in essence, to address this question. Three of the reports – from the Institute of the Economy of the World Socialist System, Ministry of Foreign Affairs, and the

---

[209] Lévesque (2004, 122). That said, the nature of his ideal form of socialism changed substantially throughout his period in high office: from an initial preference for a more efficient and humane version of Soviet communism, Gorbachev developed to the point at which his views bore a strong resemblance to those of traditional Western social democrats. In the end, his understanding of socialism as "a movement towards freedom, the development of democracy, the creation of conditions for a better life for the people [and] the raising of the human personality" placed his version of socialism at a remove from either traditional Soviet communism or American capitalist democracy, of which he remained critical in principle (Brown 1996, 102–117; quote at 116).

International Department of the CPSU's Central Committee – were subsequently obtained and summarized by a Canadian academic.[210] The Institute and Central Committee reports take reformist and conservative positions, respectively, with the Ministry report falling in the middle.

Two interesting points emerge from these reports. First, even the Institute report placed considerable emphasis on the goal of maintaining a socialist orientation among the governments of the region. Second, even the Central Committee report emphasized the freedom of choice over the need to maintain such a government. Some passages qualify this ranking somewhat; for example, it was recommended that the Soviet Union not stake out such a position publicly for fear of encouraging antisocialist elements throughout the region. The Institute report, on the other hand, recommended *support* for such elements as a means of ensuring true pluralism. The main point, however, is this: in all instances the best-case scenario involved reformed socialist governments, freely chosen. The main difference among them revolved around the weights placed on each of these two goals should a tradeoff become necessary, but in the end even the most conservative chose the latter over the former. With regard to Eastern Europe, nonclass interests took precedence over class interests.

Reformers seeking to test the limits of Soviet tolerance soon found that, effectively, there were none: Soviet indifference to the form of government instituted by popular demand in its client states was, as Gorbachev had stated years earlier, absolute. Poland, where the Solidarity movement had become a significant political force, was to provide the first test of Soviet intentions. When the June 4 elections, the first in which Solidarity was permitted to take part, resulted in a stunning display of support for Solidarity, no one knew what the Soviet reaction would be. Eastern Europe held its collective breath until Gorbachev, speaking in early July at a meeting of the Council of Europe in Strasbourg, made his remarks indicating unambiguously that changes in the social order of a sovereign state did not justify intervention by others – an unambiguous (re-)repudiation of the Brezhnev Doctrine.

Nevertheless, there were additional points along the road to revolution at which reformers not only feared Soviet intervention but also contacted the Soviets to ask whether it would be forthcoming. The fact that the Soviets were repeatedly asked, and that they generally declined even to offer *advice* of a non-neutral character, illustrates the extent to which they had ceased to exert any degree of control over the ideology of their client states. For example, in the spring of 1989 Hungarian Foreign Minister Gyula Horn traveled secretly to Bonn to negotiate a deal: a loan of DM1bn in exchange for Hungary opening the border with Austria, which would (and did) undermine the authority of the government of East Germany. At the same time, the Hungarian Foreign Ministry, fearing the possible repercussions of this act, notified Moscow of its intentions and received a response from Eduard Shevardnadze stating, "This is an affair that concerns Hungary, the GDR and the FRG" (Lévesque 1997, 153). Similarly, a 40-minute phone call to Gorbachev on the eve of the Polish Communist Party's decision to share power with Solidarity produced no objection to the proposed

[210] See Lévesque (1997, 93–109).

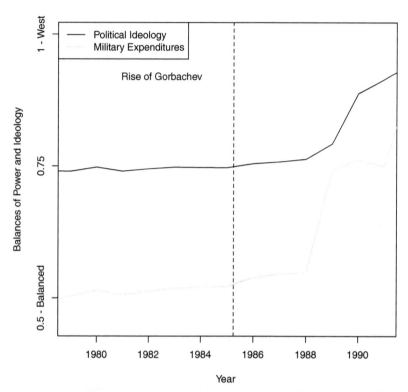

Figure 4.6. Balances of military expenditures (Correlates of War data) and ideology (Polity data).

arrangement. Even more remarkably, given that party leaders in previous years might have been called to the Kremlin in person to explain themselves, Polish First Secretary Rakowski's offer to visit Moscow to discuss the matter further was brushed aside.[211]

Figure 4.6 charts trends in the structural balances of the European system along both the ideological and military dimensions, in relative terms. Beginning at the culmination of two exogenous events in the late 1970s – the Carnation Revolution

---

[211] Lévesque (2004, 119). Soviet noninterference may, it should be noted, have reflected a compromise with conservatives in the party who feared that, should Gorbachev intervene in Eastern Europe, it would be on behalf of reformers – and who never imagined how quickly or completely Eastern Europe would throw off Soviet-style socialism once it became widely understood that the threat of Soviet intervention had evaporated. Even in July 1989, the Soviet leadership, aware that Erich Honecker's time as East German leader was limited, believed that his successor would ensure that the GDR remained a model socialist state. Gorbachev's sympathy for Eastern European reformers became increasingly clear over time, though his encouragement of them remained indirect (Lévesque 2004, 112–113; Grachev 2008, 136–137). The fact that the Soviet preference for freedom of choice in Eastern Europe was realized as thoroughly as it was, therefore, may be due in part to the fact that it represents an amalgam of conservative preferences for the status quo and liberal preferences for change in the context of a gross misreading of the likely implications of noninterference.

in Portugal and the death of Franco in Spain – the balances of both prove to be remarkably stable until Gorbachev's consolidation of power is complete, at which point both trend sharply in the expected direction.

Partial adjustment: American prudence

From Gorbachev's rise to power in 1985 to the end of Ronald Reagan's term in 1988, the two leaders succeeded in finding common ground and reducing tensions between the two states, but they did so largely if not entirely in ways that were advantageous to the United States. As we have seen, for example, the INF treaty culled more Soviet than American warheads, by a ratio of more than two to one, and the Americans stood firm on the issue of Afghanistan until the Soviet Union simply chose to abandon the field. There were, therefore, decreases in levels of security-related American activity during this period, but they were relatively cautious – that is, they were not as marked as those taking place contemporaneously in the Soviet Union.

This caution neatly reflects the partial-adjustment idea embedded in the model, as well as the assumption of model uncertainty upon which it is based. American decision makers were not at all certain about how, or even *whether*, the key parameters of the model relating power and ideology to Soviet foreign policy changed after Gorbachev came to office – indeed, they remained deeply divided on that question for years afterward, despite what seems in retrospect to be a surfeit of evidence. The clearest evidence they could hope for of change in the parameters of the model was change in the structure of the system itself – in the balances of power and ideology that comprised it. In the presence of great uncertainty about changes in model parameters, they hedged their bets, accommodating the new Soviet position while waiting for unambiguous evidence of a genuine transformation in Soviet foreign policy. That evidence did not arrive until late in 1989, in a series of events culminating in the fall of the Berlin Wall. Scholars have forwarded similar arguments, though not explicitly in the context of a partial-adjustment model, to explain American hesitancy: Kydd (2005, ch. 8), for example, explains it as a matter of the rational development of trust in light of new evidence, whereas Chollet and Goldgeier (2003, 143–144) simply point out that "in foreign policy, accepting too easily that an adversary has changed his stripes can have such high costs. Therefore, being slow to accept change in the harsh Hobbesian world of international politics may be an 'adaptive' error of intelligent decision makers" (and therefore not an error at all).

When George H. W. Bush came to office in January 1989, he proved to be acutely sensitive to a constituency that was divided on foreign policy: although the balance of public opinion had come to favor cooperation rather than confrontation with the Soviets since Gorbachev's rise to office (Holsti 1996, 74–76), many prominent conservatives were of the opinion that an accommodationist policy would be a mistake and would leave the country vulnerable because Gorbachev's reforms were tactical rather than transformational in nature. In this opinion they were backed up by the intelligence establishment: a CIA assessment in February 1989 argued that "Gorbachev's broad strategy is in the Leninist tradition: it calls for weakening the main enemy – the United States – by exploiting 'contradictions' between it and other centers of capitalist

power in Western Europe, East Asia, and the developing world" and that Gorbachev's foreign policy was driven by the need "to conserve resources – primarily by reducing military spending, but also by rationalizing economic costs and benefits in the USSR's foreign relations."[212] A National Intelligence Estimate produced two months later, although agreeing that "[f]or the foreseeable future, the USSR will remain the West's principal adversary," captures the policy community's ambivalence about the longer term prospects of Gorbachev's reforms well enough that it merits quotation at length:

> Some analysts see current policy changes as largely tactical, driven by the need for breathing space from the competition. They believe the ideological imperatives of Marxism-Leninism and its hostility toward capitalist countries are enduring. They point to previous failures of reform and the transient nature of past "detentes." They judge that there is a serious risk of Moscow returning to traditionally combative behavior when the hoped for gains in economic performance are achieved.
>
> Other analysts believe Gorbachev's policies reflect a fundamental rethinking of national interests and ideology as well as more tactical considerations. They argue that ideological tenets of Marxism-Leninism such as class conflict and capitalist-socialist enmity are being revised. They consider the withdrawal from Afghanistan and the shift toward tolerance of power sharing in Eastern Europe to be historic shifts in the Soviet definition of national interest. They judge that Gorbachev's changes are likely to have sufficient momentum to produce lasting shifts in Soviet behavior.[213]

The same National Intelligence Estimate concluded that, because of the uncertainty surrounding Soviet intentions, it was necessary to wait for concrete indicators to determine whether a fundamental rethinking of the international situation was in fact in evidence. Such indicators included "Soviet acceptance of real liberalization in Eastern Europe" and "Full implementation of announced force reductions."

This desire to wait for concrete change is noteworthy. It captures perfectly the manner in which agents in the model react not to changes in the nature of other agents but to changes in the structure of the international system. The nature of Gorbachev's thought on international relations was clear to American political elites; the same February 1989 CIA assessment that was cited earlier also described the tenets of new thinking in impressively accurate terms, including such passages as "Global nuclear annihilation is a real and rapidly escalating danger. Preventing its occurrence is the paramount task facing mankind," "Ideological differences should not be transferred to the sphere of interstate relations, nor should foreign policy be subordinated to them," "Security can only be mutual," and "Equal security is guaranteed not by the highest possible but by the lowest possible level of strategic balance." Gorbachev's

---

[212] CIASOV 89-10014X, February 1989.

[213] NIE 11-4-89, April 1989. The tension between the equivocation evident in these statements and the tone of grim certainty about future antagonism that runs through earlier sections of the document is, at times, considerable. One can only infer that, at this point in history, "the foreseeable future" may have been very short. There were no dearth of evaluations in academic and policy journals to support a skeptical position at the time – see e.g., Weinrod (1988) and Weiss (1989).

commitment to change had been made clear in front of a worldwide audience at the UN in December, when he promised dramatic cuts in Soviet troops and armaments that would greatly hinder the maintenance of an Eastern European empire by the time they were completed in late 1991. The late winter and spring of 1989 therefore represented a critical period, one in which everything *but* actual structural change was clearly in evidence. Structural change came only in the fall, when the revolutions in Eastern Europe liberalized the continent and made the irrelevance of Soviet troops clear (and their likely tenure far more brief). The theory would suggest that the United States would move conclusively to decrease its levels of activity in a manner that would constitute the end of the Cold War only in the second period, after a shift in the systemic balance had occurred; in the end this is precisely how events unfolded.

Testing the Soviets

The first step in the Bush administration's assessment of the situation was a request for a National Security Review, designated NSR-3, from the State Department, on America's policy vis-à-vis the Soviet Union, to be completed by mid-March. When it arrived, the review's ambiguity and caution reflected the variety of interpretations that were consistent with the available evidence, and its recommendations, again, included a list of metrics – this time internal, such as a secret ballot, freedom of the press, and the end of the monopoly of the Communist Party – that could be taken as concrete evidence that an optimistic assessment of Gorbachev's reforms was warranted.

As the months passed, the Bush administration faced a frustrating dilemma: although conflictual policies were clearly counterproductive and cooperation absent concrete evidence of change would enrage the anticommunist right, inaction was becoming increasingly unpopular with the general public. In the face of what many believed to be the most monumental changes in modern history, the administration could only spend so long prudently reviewing its options. Accordingly, in May Secretary of State Baker attempted to chart a more active course by stating that the United States would do the only thing that it could, under the circumstances. "We want to test the new thinking across the whole range of our relationship," the Secretary said in an interview with the *New York Times* before departing for Moscow to meet with Gorbachev.[214] "If we find that the Soviet Union is serious about new global behavior, then we will seek diplomatic engagement in an effort to reach mutual beneficial results." The theme of "testing" the Soviets is one to which the administration would return throughout the spring.[215]

An incident during that Moscow visit illustrates the fundamental difficulty that American decision makers faced when dealing with Soviet arms control proposals. Gorbachev presented Baker with a surprise offer of a "third zero" – the elimination of short-range nuclear forces, an SNF agreement to match the 1987 INF agreement. It seemed a difficult offer to turn down: the Soviet SNF launchers numbered in the

---

[214] Thomas Friedman, "Baker Plans Test of 'New Thinking' while in Moscow," Tuesday, May 9, 1989, section A-1. The Kennedy School's Graham Allison had also advocated such a course the previous fall, in exactly these terms; see Allison (1988).

[215] Beschloss and Talbott (1993, chs. 3 and 4).

thousands, whereas those of the West numbered fewer than 100. Yet short-range nuclear forces were a very divisive issue among the Western allies, and Baker, who at that point was more favorably inclined toward cooperating with the Soviets than many in the administration, left the meeting thoroughly irked, concluding that the offer was a "propaganda initiative... an effort to continue to try to drive a wedge between us and our Western European allies.... [F]rankly that set us back a little bit in terms of our being a little bit more forthcoming and a little bit more trustful."[216]

At about the same time, President Bush unveiled his first initiative in response to the changes in the Eastern bloc, and its timidity illustrates the depths of American reluctance to engage the Soviets. Given that the Soviet leader's speech to the United Nations had touched on themes as fundamental as the decreasing relevance of ideology in the nuclear era and had promised substantial reductions in Soviet troops and armaments, President Bush's speech at Texas A&M, in which he revived the Eisenhower-era "Open Skies" proposal for unarmed aerial surveillance flights, constituted a muted response at best – especially given that the president, a former CIA director, was more aware than most of the satellite capabilities that made such overflights far less relevant than they had been when they had originally been proposed in 1955. "For those in the audience at Texas A&M and the millions more around the world who were waiting to see what he was willing to do in response to Gorbachev's initiatives," wrote Beschloss and Talbott, "the president had pulled out of his hat not a live rabbit but a dead mouse." In Moscow, Soviet leaders puzzled over the address, thinking that something must have been lost in translation. The president's subsequent emphasis on his "obligation to temper optimism with prudence" in his Soviet policy may be a reasonable summary of its first four months, if not an overstatement of its dynamism.[217]

By the end of May, the president had decided on a more ambitious initiative, a Conventional Forces in Europe (CFE) initiative that he proposed to the NATO Council in Brussels: a 15% cut in NATO and Warsaw Pact conventional arms and a 20% cut in United States and Soviet military personnel. Although this indication that the United States might be moving beyond its ambivalence about Gorbachev's reforms was greeted warmly by the Soviets, the proposed timetable was not: the Soviets had already pledged substantial reductions and could not absorb career military officers into civilian life in such a short period. Deservedly or not, the American ambassador was chastised for "proposing deadlines for propagandistic effect." Later that summer, the United States again demonstrated an unwillingness to yield that, in some ways, was extraordinary given the positions that it had taken just a few years earlier, at the height of the Cold War. To kick off the START negotiations in June, Bush sent Gorbachev a private list of arms control proposals that put such a lopsided onus on the USSR that the offended Soviet leader sent no direct reply. In July, Bush visited Warsaw, where

---

[216] Wohlforth (2003, 32). Scowcroft had already indicated, in a television interview in January, that he believed that Gorbachev was "interested in making trouble within the Western Alliance. And I think he believes that the best way to do it is through a peace offensive, rather than bluster, the way some of his predecessors have" (Zubok 2003, 156).

[217] Beschloss and Talbott (1993, 71); Garthoff (1994, 380).

he had been not two years earlier to demand liberalization and the incorporation of Solidarity into the political process. In 1989, however, with reform movements on the rise on the continent and Solidarity less than two months away from forming the first noncommunist government in Eastern Europe since the 1940s, Bush praised Poland's President Wojciech Jaruzelski for the stability that he brought to Polish politics and sought to moderate the pace of change. When he heard that Jaruzelski had decided, after his visit, to run for president in the upcoming elections, Bush was relieved. Jaruzelski should, he said, "hang in there and see this thing through."[218]

The world was even treated to the unusual spectacle of an American president lecturing a separatist Soviet Republic *against* self-determination. When President George H. W. Bush spoke to the Ukrainian Supreme Soviet on August 1, 1991, and warned that "freedom is not the same as independence. Americans... will not aid those who promote a suicidal nationalism," *New York Times* columnist William Safire dubbed it the "Chicken Kiev speech" and chastised the president for discouraging Ukrainian freedom.[219] Far from calling for Mr. Gorbachev to "tear down this wall," as his predecessor had famously done, President Bush attempted to shore up the remaining ramparts of the Soviet state.

This moment in the case nicely illustrates the role that the structure of the system plays in the theory. Soviet levels of activity had clearly changed or were in the process of changing, both quantitatively and qualitatively – but constituencies and leaders do not respond to changes in activity. Rather, given the myriad uncertainties in the system, they await tangible changes in the structure of the system. And that was precisely, during this period, what President Bush was doing. His reluctance to engage the Soviets or to take part in bold initiatives was born of the fact that he had yet to see the tangible results of the change in the Soviet worldview. His desire for evidence, in turn, makes sense of the "testing the Soviets" statements.

Passing the test

Between late August and November, the Bush administration finally received the proof it had been looking for, as the Soviet Union's commitment to noninterference in the internal affairs of its satellite states gradually became undeniable. On August 22, the Polish Communist Party, having lost overwhelmingly in the June elections, finally yielded and agreed to join a Solidarity-led government after General Secretary Mieczyslaw Rakowski spent 40 minutes on the telephone with Gorbachev, who apparently convinced him to stand by his government's decision to heed the voice of the electorate. The next day, Hungarian Foreign Minister Gyula Horn informed the government of East Germany that Hungary would no longer restrict Germans

---

[218] Beschloss and Talbott (1993, 80, 88–89, 116).

[219] The president and his national security advisor would later argue that the warning had been intended not specifically for Ukrainians but for nationalist separatists there, in Yugoslavia, Moldavia, and elsewhere; see Bush and Scowcroft (1998, 516). This interpretation seems somewhat strained, given that Bush was clearly not arguing that independence might bring liberty in the absence of nationalism, but was rather arguing for democracy in the context of a revitalized Soviet state: "We will support those who want to build democracy.... And now, democracy has begun to set firm roots in Soviet soil."

from moving through the rift in the Iron Curtain between Hungary and Austria, a decision that was made public on September 10. East Germany stanched the flow of refugees, but not until 13,000 had fled; while pressure for further exodus built, the Hungarian Parliament abandoned communism, adopting a series of measures designed to transform it into a parliamentary democracy. As demonstrations in East Germany swelled and party leaders, unable to restore order, were forced to resign, it became evident that nothing short of an opening of the Berlin Wall would ensure order; accordingly, after another call to Gorbachev, this time by new East German party chief Egon Krenz, the Berlin Wall was opened on November 9.[220]

The Bush administration's public statements about the Soviet Union neatly parallel these changes. On September 15, five days after the Hungarian decision to allow East German egress, the president told a group of media executives that, as far as the Soviets were concerned, "I'm like the guy from Missouri: show me." It would be among the last of the "testing the Soviets" statements to come from an administration official. The meeting between Baker and Shevardnadze at Baker's ranch in Jackson Hole in late September constituted a breakthrough in relations.[221] In early October the secretary of state established a more cooperative line on the Soviets, arguing that Gorbachev's reforms were sincere and that "points of mutual advantage" were worth pursuing. When Vice President Dan Quayle responded to Baker's statements by questioning Gorbachev's sincerity in an interview and asserting that *perestroika* was "a form of Leninism," Baker let it be known that he, not the vice president, had been speaking for the president; and when Deputy National Security Advisor Robert Gates forwarded a speech arguing that Gorbachev's reforms were really a screen for the enhancement of Soviet power to the State Department for vetting, Baker's reaction was so negative that Gates shelved the speech. When the Wall finally came down, Bush, watching from his study, said to his aides, "If the Soviets are going to let the Communists fall in East Germany, they've got to be really serious – more serious than I realized." At that point – but *only* at that point – American political elites were finally on the same page regarding Soviet intentions. As Haas (2007, 171) notes, "the most powerful leaders of the Bush presidency, including Bush, Baker, and Scowcroft, asserted that New Thinkers' acceptance of liberal ideology in combination with the creation of democratic political institutions were critical factors pushing them to believe that the Soviet Union was no longer a significant international threat." A CIA memorandum for top administration officials concerned with the USSR written just a few months later would strike a completely different tone than had its predecessors in February and April by noting, "We can say a few important things with confidence; . . . . Most importantly, the familiar or 'canonical' threat is gone or rapidly going, namely, a hegemonical USSR animated by a hostile universalist ideology, present in the heart of Europe with powerful offensive forces."[222]

Accordingly, the president ordered his staff to assemble a package of economic and security initiatives for the December summit off the coast of Malta that constituted a

---

[220] Oberdorfer (1998, 360–364).
[221] On this meeting see e.g., Zubok (2003, 162–163).
[222] Beschloss and Talbott (1993, ch. 5, 132); Ermarth (1990).

genuine and tangible démarche. An array of economic measures to assist the Soviet transition to a market economy were complemented by a substantial increase in both the proposed scope and pace of arms control agreements covering everything from strategic nuclear weapons to chemical weapons to conventional forces to nuclear testing. When the president finished talking, 70 minutes after he started, Gorbachev responded that, although he had never questioned Bush's support for perestroika, he had not been certain, until that morning, that the president was ready to take concrete steps to improve relations between the two countries (Oberdorfer 1998, 378–379). Chernyaev, too, points to Malta as a crucial turning point, noting that the Soviets had been concerned that "the Heritage Foundation dominated White House thinking" until Bush's extraordinary candor and wide range of concrete concessions convinced them that "[t]he external threat, although it had always been largely an ideological myth, was now no more." Foreign Ministry spokesman Gennadi Gerasimov, whose well-turned phrases often captured the essence of crucial moments such as these, said of the Malta Summit that "We buried the Cold War at the bottom of the Mediterranean Sea."[223]

This judgment accords both with the intuition of the actors at the time[224] and with the understanding of the Cold War constituted by the model: high levels of security-related activity aimed either at maintaining a hostile stalemate or at gaining an advantage. The internal institutional conversion of the Soviet Union that constituted Gorbachev's consolidation of power transformed the Soviet leader's constituency to bring its median member increasingly close to his own worldview (though Gorbachev himself was something of a moving target in that regard), and as that worldview took hold, Soviet activity in the spheres of security and ideology decreased. It was not, however, until the effects of that decrease in activity were felt at the level of the system that the United States reacted and initiated a systematic series of measures designed not just to realize a wary new détente but also to bring to an end the competition that had constituted the main axis of international relations for more than four decades.

Over the course of time, absent a security and ideology "push" from the Soviet Union, the general expectation of the model would be for a shift toward the American ideal points in the realms of both security and ideology and a corresponding decrease in levels of security-related activity on the part of both actors. Although the dissolution of the Soviet Union makes this a difficult prediction to assess (the fairness of evaluating a theory when, strictly speaking, one of the two agents at the heart of it ceases to exist is certainly debatable), the liberalization of the European continent, the gradually slowing spread of NATO in the face of increasing Russian resistance, and the continued decrease in levels of nuclear warheads, with a balance shifting to favor the West, that have characterized the post–Cold War period are all in broad strokes entirely consistent with the logic of the theory, as is the shift from a U.S. defense budget of around 5–6% of GDP in the latter years of the Cold War to 3–4% of GDP from the mid-1990s on.

---

[223] Chernyaev (2000, 233, 235); Beschloss and Talbott (1993, 165).

[224] Note, for example, Robert Blackwill's reaction to the Bush-Gorbachev dialog at Oberdorfer (1998, 379).

That said, America's continued association with the alliance is more anomalous, explicable perhaps as a result of that association's relative costlessness: were it called on to make a substantial sacrifice in the name of NATO, one might expect the costs and benefits of membership to be scrutinized more closely. One might wonder whether the expansion of NATO represents an increase rather than a decrease in security-related activity; two facts mitigate against such an interpretation. First, although NATO is formally a defensive alliance, expansion has been justified as a means of creating a Europe that is, in former President Clinton's words, "free, democratic and undivided" – and one that, not coincidentally, will be good for business by providing Americans with "stable partners for trading purposes" (Broder 1998). Second, the Department of Defense initially estimated the cost of NATO expansion to United States to be $400 million (note the *m*) over ten years. By comparison, the U.S. Navy anticipated spending $6.5 billion over the next five years to upgrade its LPD-17 amphibious transport dock ship – enough to cover the American costs of bringing another 45 countries into NATO. In short, the anticipated American expenditures on NATO expansion were trivial in comparison both to its historical levels of expenditures and to the Defense Department's overall budget, expected to stabilize at around $260 billion per annum in the first years of the new century (Office of Assistant Secretary of Defense, Public Affairs 1998).[225]

Summary

As the amount of space devoted to it suggests, the end of the Cold War is easily the most complicated case of the three presented here. There are a substantial number of background conditions that need to be in place in order to be activated by Gorbachev's rise. Because Gorbachev himself proves to be a politician whose views of foreign policy are only imperfectly formed at the time he reaches the highest office in the country, his worldview is something of a moving target, as are changes in the worldview of his constituency. All in all, the process is a remarkably dynamic one.

As in previous cases, a systemic perspective proves indispensable. Gorbachev's foreign policy was aimed at transforming the structure of the system, or (in the realm of political ideology) allowing it the freedom to transform itself should its component elements so desire. That transformation – and *only* that transformation, not Gorbachev's words or domestic reforms – convinced the United States to reciprocate, to scale back the security competition that constituted the Cold War, and bring that conflict to a close.

It might seem plausible to argue that the Bush administration was uncertain regarding Soviet intentions and was waiting for a credible signal of Soviet "type," but in light of the signals the Soviets had already sent out such an interpretation

---

[225] I have no axe to grind regarding amphibious transport dock ship upgrades. They are merely an example, and not an unusual one: over the same period, the U.S. Army planned to spend $5.5 billion on trucks and support vehicles, the Navy and Air Force planned to spend a total of $7.5 billion on development of tiltrotor aircraft (designated V-22 by the Navy and CV-22 by the Air Force), and so on.

strains credulity. The unilateral reductions in Soviet offensive capabilities announced in December 1988, coupled with the dramatic dilution of the influence of the CPSU in Soviet politics in 1989, are simply too difficult to dismiss as credible signals. Arguably, they even rose to the level of far less ambiguous indices (Jervis 1970), that is, behaviors that are tied to some characteristic (here, capabilities and ideology) that helps predict future behavior. In short, if events of the magnitude of the fall of the Eastern bloc are required for actors to update their beliefs, then beliefs will rarely if ever be updated.

Conclusion

I hope to have shown three main things in this chapter. First, I hope to have shown that the theoretical model laid out in Chapter 2 is a sound one by virtue of having illuminated the causal processes that animate it in three diverse historical cases. Each had idiosyncratic, or exogenous, factors that were important – the general continental drift toward liberalism after Vienna; the exact form of Hitler's pathological worldview (if not the appeal of nationalists in general in the context of a reaction against the Treaty of Versailles); and the various prerequisites to Gorbachev's foreign policy revolution, to name a few. Even so, the fundamental mechanism at the heart of each could be made out clearly and corresponded quite well to that embodied by the model.

The second is that, although each of these three historical events is undeniably unique, they nevertheless all contain a core set of similarities that warrant the conclusion that they can reasonably be understood as special cases of a more general phenomenon, that of systemic politics. That conclusion, itself, is a striking one, because consumers and producers of historical literature tend to emphasize the uniqueness of events, not their commonalities. It is also, as the astute reader will have guessed, only the thin edge of the wedge, for it is not far to go to suggest, particularly in light of the large-N data from the previous chapter, that not just these events but also the ones that came in between, and before, and after can be understood in the same way.

Finally, a third point stemming from the second: the irreducible complexity of these cases makes it difficult if not impossible to imagine any of them being explicable purely in terms of any one theoretical perspective. To ask whether the end of the Cold War, or the early years of the Vienna system, or the end of American isolationism were primarily the result of the characteristics of people, institutions, or the structure of the international system (Waltz 1959) is to miss the point: the interplay among them was essential to each. Just as the statistical results demonstrated in Chapter 3 that neither power nor ideology alone can explain outcomes as well as the two in combination, each of these cases demonstrates the importance of the fundamental and complex interconnections among agents and structures.

5 | *Conclusions and implications*

Prediction is difficult, especially if it's about the future.

– Niels Bohr

The overall theme of the book – that Great Powers are neither wholly free nor entirely driven by circumstance, but rather, are capable, at least in part, of shaping the international environment that will subsequently compel them to act – leads us naturally to wonder how much states are capable of foreseeing the outcomes of their own actions. Put another way, having examined the model and evaluated it empirically, it is worth asking, by way of conclusion, whether the light that it sheds on the past can tell us anything valuable about the present or, more tentatively, about the future.

In this concluding chapter I focus in a somewhat unorthodox manner on the question of what we can and cannot learn about the future based on the model. I start out with a discussion of some of the issues facing the United States and the international system in the 21st century. I discuss the model's implications for likely long-term systemic outcomes, and then I look at the direct impact of changing just a single parameter of the model in a manner that corresponds with some interesting qualitative change in the world. Next, I examine the *indirect* impact of changing one parameter of the model on the rest of the system. What this discussion demonstrates is the fact that, given the interconnectedness of systems, that change reverberates through every other aspect of the system. When we understand both the wide-ranging implications of a change in just one part of the system and the fact that the rest of the system will rarely remain constant for long, we start to comprehend the difficulties facing any systemic forecast.[1]

What this discussion seems to amount to, incongruously, is the use of forecasts to demonstrate that forecasts are nearly useless. The point is actually more subtle. Although the interconnectedness of systems does not render forecasts completely impossible, it does put a premium on understanding the system in the here and now. The best we can reasonably hope for are very short-run forecasts, and even those will necessarily be contingent. Current trends, as the fall of the Berlin Wall and the

---

[1] It should come as no surprise that forecasting is a daunting exercise; after all, the partial-adjustment model developed in Chapter 2 is precisely a concession to the incredible difficulty of anticipating future developments in a complex system.

September 11th attacks demonstrate, can easily be disrupted. Barbara Tuchman's "lantern on the stern," which illuminates where we have been,[2] does cast *some* light past the prow – but never as much as would like. That fact emphatically does not mean that looking forward is a worthless exercise; rather, it puts a premium on making the most of what we can see.

Into the future?

One useful pattern we can point to, going forward, is that the settlement of a large war or conflict has an impact on the shape of the peace that follows, a point made well by Ikenberry (2000). In contrast to Ikenberry, whose focus tended to be more on international institutions consciously created by states, the focus here has been on the tendency of states to engage in regulatory politics, preventive diplomatic activity designed to keep everyday interactive politics from escalating to conflict – whether or not those regulatory politics are pursued through formal political institutions.

Peace settlements or their equivalent provide the occasion for large-scale reordering of the system, an event that creates the context within which politics will play out in the coming decades. The end of the Cold War should almost certainly be considered to be a transitional point of this type, given the magnitude of the change in the structure of the system. Statesmen lacked the excuse of a systemic war to engage in systematic reordering, however, and the post–Cold War world may be somewhat lacking in conceptual coherence as a result – though that judgment can probably only be fully rendered in retrospect.

Still, we can point to a few tentative conclusions at this stage. Though the concerns of statesmen and their constituencies have varied substantially over time, the dimensions along which the structure of the international system is ordered can usefully be gathered under the two general dimensions of opportunity and willingness.[3] As a general rule, in each period states sought to have an impact on the balance of material capabilities as a means to influence the ability (or opportunity) that other states had to initiate conflict, and they sought to influence political ideology, admittedly often as an end in itself, but also as a means to influence the willingness of other states to initiate conflict – under the theory that revolutionary constitutional regimes, or imperialist capitalist states, or nondemocratic states are the ones that start wars.

It is worth noting that, while material capabilities and political ideology, in various forms, have been taken to be primary determinants of opportunity and willingness in the past, their relationship to those concepts in the present may be more tenuous. In addition to the arguably increasing role of "soft power" in international politics,[4] smaller actors, perhaps prompted by the lopsided distribution of capabilities in the international system, have chosen to pursue unconventional military strategies, such as terrorism and nuclear proliferation, that hold forth the promise of magnifying their effective capabilities via alternative (and generally reproachable) means.

---

[2] Tuchman (1985, 379).   [3] Most and Starr (1989).   [4] See Nye (1991, 32 and *passim*).

Sovereignty, terror, proliferation, and deterrence

One trend that is worth emphasizing, and one dimension of conflict that may well rise to structural prominence for the first time in many centuries have to do with the strength of the norm of sovereignty.[5] Deviations from the Westphalian ideal of sovereignty, understood as the ability of the state to exclude external actors from its territory,[6] have taken on a considerable degree of importance in the post-Cold War world. The reason lies in the relationship between sovereignty and deterrence, and in the implications of that relationship for two more widely discussed phenomena: terrorism and nuclear proliferation.

There are, in general, two ways in which to obtain security: defense (ensuring that an attack will be ineffective) and deterrence (ensuring that the undesirable results of an attack would outweigh the desirable ones in the aggregate). Defense succeeds best when defensive forces are inexpensive relative to offensive ones; deterrence succeeds when offensive forces are inexpensive (but not so inexpensive as to render a crippling knockout blow possible).

Critically, however, deterrence relies on a target against which to retaliate. When a nonstate actor launches a strike against a state from territory in a second state that is not well controlled, the missiles or guns are fired, effectively, with no return address.[7] Retaliating against the country in which the originator resides is both normatively unacceptable (especially if, as is usually the case, the territory in question contains a high proportion of noncombatant civilians) and often unwise, because the cooperation of that country's government is generally being sought at the same time to root out the organization in question. The result is a breakdown of deterrence, because the target is left with no one against whom to retaliate.

In the post–Cold War world, many revisionist actors fall into the category of non-state actors operating from poorly controlled or uncontrolled territory: al Qaeda, Hezbollah, insurgents in postwar Iraq, and so forth. Were their hosts able to exert control over the use of force throughout their territory, the probability of attack would be greatly reduced, either because the host government could prevent the attack or because it would choose to do so for fear of retaliation.

Moreover, uncontrolled or poorly controlled territory creates security issues in a variety of other ways. Sometimes, the reason why the state is unable to control its territory can also be a reason for international conflict, as when weak or failed states pose a danger to their neighbors. In other cases, such regions present an opportunity for traditional Westphalian states to act with relative impunity by sponsoring an imperfectly controlled proxy inside the region. Iran, for example, can further its interests by using Hezbollah as its cat's paw, free from any concern that Israel will retaliate against Iran for Hezbollah's activities.

---

[5] Spruyt (1994) is an excellent exposition; see Krasner (1993) for a thoughtful critique of the concept.

[6] Krasner (1999) labels this form of sovereignty, appropriately, "Westphalian" (in contrast to three others: international legal, domestic, and interdependence).

[7] In the bipolar Cold War world order, this problem existed as well but was mitigated by virtue of the fact that one superpower could often be held responsible, rightly or wrongly, for the actions of a nonstate actor.

Furthermore, weak sovereignty provides nonstate actors with considerable opportunity to make trouble for traditional states. Hezbollah's strategy of providing social services – hospitals, schools, and so on – to fill the void in southern Lebanon seems to have been a successful one at this stage, from the point of view of winning the loyalty of the people.[8] At the same time, however, Hezbollah must avoid taking on too many of the tasks of governance: actual secession of southern Lebanon would be a disaster from Hezbollah's point of view, because Israel would then have a target against which to retaliate that would be seen by much of the world community as an entirely legitimate one.

American foreign policy in the post–Cold War world has been aimed, albeit sporadically, at reinforcing the norm of Westphalian sovereignty at key points of weakness. After the attacks of September 11, 2001, President Bush announced that the United States would make no distinction between terrorists and the states that harbor them when it came to combating terrorism – a remarkable claim clearly aimed at states like Afghanistan and Pakistan whose uncontrolled regions were home to terrorist training camps. This doctrine was enshrined in the September 2002 version of a document produced by the National Security Council titled *The National Security Strategy of the United States of America*,[9] which noted in the preface, "The events of September 11, 2001, taught us that weak states, like Afghanistan, can pose as great a danger to our national interests as strong states"; it also and flatly stated, "We make no distinction between terrorists and whose who knowingly harbor or provide aid to them." It went on to elaborate,

> We will disrupt and destroy terrorist organizations by. . . denying further sponsorship, support, and sanctuary to terrorists by convincing or compelling states to accept their sovereign responsibilities.[10]

For a variety of reasons,[11] the initial attempt to shore up the sovereign state met with modest success. The 2006 version of the *National Security Strategy* seems to have deemphasized this strategy, both reducing the prominence of its discussion and qualifying it by placing the wording in the context of rogue states.[12] However, with a substantial increase in American involvement in the form of a quantity of troops that roughly tripled the American commitment at the end of 2008, President Bush's successor showed early signs of pursuing it with more single-mindedness.[13]

---

[8] See e.g., Kifner (2006).   [9] National Security Council (2002).

[10] National Security Council (2002, v, 5, 6).

[11] The war in Iraq was almost certainly one; the fact that radical Islamic activity in the northwest regions of Pakistan is supported by a domestic faction that includes the security services (the ISI) is another; and the well-established difficulty of imposing regime change on Afghanistan from outside may play a role as well.

[12] The paragraph, demoted to page 12 from page 5, reads, "Deny terrorist groups the support and sanctuary of rogue states. The United States and its allies in the War on Terror make no distinction between those who commit acts of terror and those who support and harbor them, because they are equally guilty of murder. Any government that chooses to be an ally of terror, such as Syria or Iran, has chosen to be an enemy of freedom, justice, and peace. The world must hold those regimes to account" (National Security Council 2006, 12).

[13] See Bumiller (2009).

The reasons, perhaps, are understandable: the obstacles to success are daunting. To deny nonstate actors the opportunity to launch attacks, the United States would have to remove all potential bases of operation – and as Krasner (1999) argues, though states pretend otherwise, in reality sovereignty in the Westphalian sense is typically far from complete.[14] The developing world is replete with weak states. It would take a very substantial effort to strengthen all of them sufficiently to enable the weakest of them to keep terrorists off of its soil, if indeed such a goal is even attainable. The real problem, in short, is not denying terrorists access to Afghanistan, although that problem may prove formidable; the problem, rather, is denying them access to every other place that could serve the same function.

The United States may therefore continue to pursue more direct means of countering terrorism and proliferation than via the strengthening of the sovereign state, or at least it may pursue a set of policies that includes other means in addition. That fact would not necessarily remove terrorism and proliferation from the roster of structural concerns, however, if outcomes in those spheres constitute security-related distributions that are deemed sufficiently important by the main actors. For the sake of argument and discussion, we assume for the moment that they qualify, one way or the other.

What might these indicators suggest for likely outcomes, especially those having to do with terrorism and proliferation, in the long run? Although the historians' survey did not include questions that would have produced data for the post–Cold War period,[15] we can at least speculate about what the world might look like under different possible scenarios and how those scenarios might inform foreign policy choices. It makes little sense, of course, to model Hezbollah as a Great Power, given its lack of systemic interests; instead, we can model it as influencing the distribution of outcomes in the dimension of the system to which it is relevant, as if those outcomes varied exogenously, to see how the United States responds. To understand the impact of foreign policy choices, I vary American salience and examine the impact on the output of the model. Doing so makes sense from a policy perspective, because policy disagreements can most readily be interpreted as arguments over how much weight *should* be accorded to outcomes in each dimension of the system. Given that interpretation, policy debates translate into debates about the most desirable level of salience to assign to a particular dimension in the future.

In Figure 5.1, I present the results of a simulated world in which the United States simultaneously reacts to and shapes a range of structural dimensions, which correspond to those mentioned here and later.[16] Figure 5.1 demonstrates the likely impact of American activity on the success of terrorist movements over time, given the assumptions of the model and given different assumptions about the salience of terrorism to the American citizenry.

---

[14] Hence the subtitle of the book, "Organized Hypocrisy."

[15] Even if it had, the period would most likely not be quite long enough to produce any but the most tenuous inferences.

[16] Specifically, these issues are terrorism, nuclear proliferation, democratization, the potential rise of China, and environmental degradation. The details of the simulations are in Appendix A.

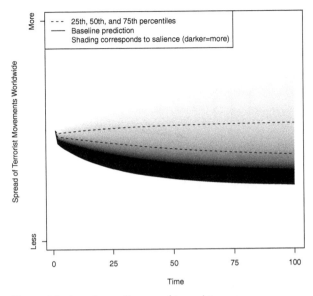

Figure 5.1. American salience and terrorist success.

What is important in this illustration is not the location of the outcome on the Y-axis, the change from the initial position, or the hypothesized baseline prediction, all of which are somewhat speculative (if not arbitrary), but rather the comparative statics. In this case, the results comport comfortably with intuition: as the issue of terrorism becomes more salient to the American public, it will demand that more action be taken, and terrorist movements worldwide will achieve less success (more darkly shaded region) as a result. This is not a particularly counterintuitive outcome; indeed, it comports perfectly with the theoretical intuition guiding the construction of the model.

Figure 5.2 illustrates a similar set of hypothesized outcomes, regarding the proliferation of nuclear weapons. Here, however, I present two different scenarios. The first reflects the assumption from Mueller (2009, ch. 13) that nuclear proliferation among terrorists is exceedingly difficult. Accordingly, for a wide range of feasible values most plausible levels of U.S. salience are sufficient, in combination with the country's strength, to produce downward pressure on proliferation in the long run.

Equally noteworthy, however, is the scenario on the right, in which the potential proliferator is substantially more capable – a small regional power, perhaps, with capabilities equivalent to one-half of one percent of world GDP (not coincidentally, roughly the amount possessed by Iran today). Altering nothing else in the model at all, we can see that the assumption regarding the capabilities of the proliferator can make a very substantial difference in the outcome – so much so that, in the former world, the best-case scenario still involves downward pressure on proliferation, whereas in

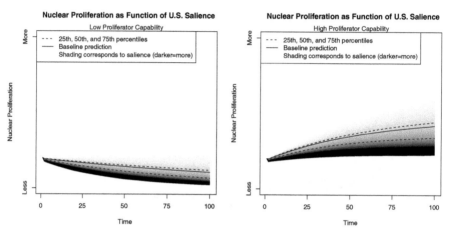

Figure 5.2. American salience and nuclear proliferation.

the latter world even the most vigilant possible United States is unable to do anything about at least a modest degree of proliferation.

Figures such as these are useful introductions to simulated results, because they give a good sense of the trajectories of outcomes over time, the distribution of outcomes, and the development of that distribution over time. Unfortunately, they do a poor job of illustrating how those outcomes vary as a function of salience, which is the question that we would probably most like to understand from a policy (and forecasting) perspective.

I have therefore graphed the outcomes in year 100 of Figure 5.2 against one another in a single graph in Figure 5.3. The dashed line represents the relationship between proliferation and salience in year 100, assuming low proliferator capabilities (left-hand graph of Figure 5.2); the solid line represents the relationship between proliferation and salience in year 100, assuming high proliferator capabilities (right-hand graph of Figure 5.2). Even without any explicit scale – which would only provide the illusion of specificity, given that no data have been collected or coefficients estimated – the simulations can provide some interesting conclusions.

The first is that there are diminishing marginal policy returns to increasing salience (or, from a policy perspective, to increasing the state's focus on a given issue): simply put, focusing more and more on an issue brings fewer and fewer results.[17] This is not an immediately obvious conclusion based on the theoretical assumptions about salience; rather, it comes from a subtle interplay among levels of activity, the degree to which the state's objectives have been satisfied, and the status of the system at a given point in time. As we see, the degree to which marginal policy returns diminish does vary, sometimes substantially, from one situation and one scenario to another, but in general this is a recurring pattern.

---

[17] Because utility is often modeled as a nonlinear function of policy outcomes, it does not automatically follow that there are diminishing marginal *utility* returns to increasing salience, of course.

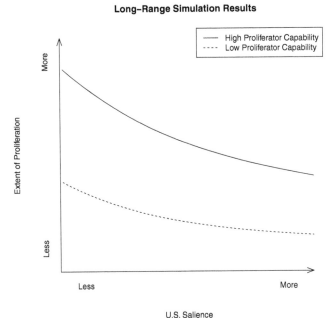

Figure 5.3. American salience and nuclear proliferation.

The second is that the hypothetical change in capabilities of the proliferator produces a substantial vertical shift in the curve without having much of an impact on its slope. That is not to say that the American calculus is unaltered, of course: given that the resulting policy outcomes are, from the point of view of the citizenry, dramatically worse than they were when the proliferator was weaker, citizens and leaders alike will clearly accept smaller marginal returns in exchange for better outcomes. Rather, it illustrates, graphically, the fact that most of the change that occurs across these two scenarios results from a change in the system rather than from a change within the United States itself.

That said, we can see a *slight* change in the slope of the curve, indicating that there is in fact some change in the marginal rate of policy returns (which is in part a function of the degree to which the state's objectives have been satisfied, which in turn is a function of the state of the system). That change is indicative of a third conclusion: although the effects of immediate changes tend to be most noticeable, all of the inputs in the system are connected to all of the outputs, however remotely or tenuously. Any change has systemic repercussions. It is easy to overstate the magnitude of this point: Lorenzian, chaos-theoretic "butterfly effects" or dramatic differences in outcomes flowing from tiny differences in initial conditions, are not in evidence here.[18]

---

[18] Depending on one's perspective, this is an advantage or a disadvantage of the insensitivity of the model's equilibria to its starting values.

Nevertheless, the subtler implication of the butterfly story holds true: what happens in Tokyo or Brazil, however small, has an impact everywhere else.

The rise of China

When scholars of international relations focus on the issue of power in the future of the international system, it is generally not long before China is mentioned. The extent of China's rise is itself debatable: its impressive GDP growth in recent years is called into question by a host of other indicators – energy production, electricity output, imports, cargo traffic, air travel, floor area under construction, and the like – that suggest that it may well have been substantially overstated in recent years.[19] As a result, although China is presently the second-largest state in the world as measured by GDP, its exact placement in the ranks of the powers remains highly uncertain.[20]

Some conditional predictions of a general sort are, of course, possible. To the extent that America's security-related *desiderata* at the structural level coincide with those of China during the latter's rise (meaning, for example, that they emphasize ideological and *realpolitik* concerns to similar degrees), their preferences along those dimensions are diametrically opposed, and those preferences are strongly held,[21] the prediction would be for increasing levels of antagonistic security-related activity as China's relative power position increases – a new Cold War, perhaps, and possibly even a hot one.[22] To the extent that the two states' worldviews fail to overlap, their preferences are not entirely opposed, and they are indifferent across outcomes, however, little or no increase in activity should result.

These predictions follow in a straightforward manner in the short run. In the longer run, the question of willingness rather than opportunity – what China would wish to do on the world stage as its capabilities rise relative to those of the United States – may be the larger issue.[23] What the nested politics model suggests, and what the case studies in particular have shown, is that the reciprocal relationship of power between leaders and their constituencies in autocratic states makes long-range predictions about the intentions of autocracies highly contingent. Regardless of China's collective worldview today or tomorrow, the possibility that a Chinese Gorbachev (or a Chinese Hitler) could reach the pinnacle of Chinese politics tomorrow and then succeed in altering his constituency in order to consolidate power means that predictions about the implications of China's rise are fairly tenuous ones.

---

[19] Such indicators normally parallel GDP growth, and given the ease of misrepresenting the latter they are seen as reliable proxies when GNP data are questionable or absent. In China's case, they fall well short of official GDP figures, particularly during economic downturns. See *The Economist* (2009).

[20] See e.g., Chan (2005).

[21] By which I mean that outcomes near the state's ideal point are seen to be far lower, in terms of utility, than outcomes at the state's ideal point.

[22] The model itself cannot predict whether or not, or when, wars will erupt based solely on system-level characteristics. An extension (Braumoeller 2008) does so, however, by incorporating the logic of the spiral and deterrence models.

[23] These issues are explored at length in M. E. Brown (2000).

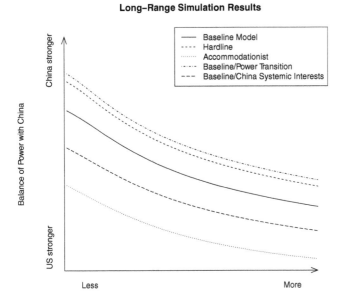

Figure 5.4. American salience and the balance of power with China.

That said, if we work these assumptions into a long-range forecast (Figure 5.4), we can at least begin to grasp their general outlines. First of all, the baseline model, which envisions a world in which the two states' relative latent capabilities remain constant, they have diametrically opposed interests in terms of power, and the intensity of the Chinese government's preferences are relatively moderate, the outcome varies, as we would expect, depending on the importance that the United States places on the issue – as that weight increases, the balance tilts toward the United States, again with diminishing marginal policy returns. A hardline Chinese regime (interpreted as one with more intense preferences or narrower indifference curves) shifts the outcome substantially toward a pro-Chinese balance, whereas a more moderate Chinese regime (one with less intense preferences) shifts the outcome substantially toward a pro-American balance. Interestingly, a power transition – that is, a shift to equality of latent capabilities, assuming that the Chinese government remains moderate rather than hardline – produces results that are nearly equivalent to those of a weaker regime with hardline preferences.

One implicit assumption in this exercise, and one that usually goes undiscussed, has to do with the implications of a Great Power's assumption of the task of managing the international system. In this simulation, it was assumed, for the sake of simplicity, that the United States was the sole Great Power in the system and that China was simply another actor without systemic concerns beyond the balance of power between itself and the United States. This is already a caricature, of course, and as China's capabilities

grow it is likely to take on an increasing role in the management of the system. Nevertheless, that simplification helps to illustrate a point. Robert Gilpin, among others, has argued that as states' capabilities grow, the costs to them of changing the system will decrease, and their incentives to do so will increase (Gilpin 1981, 95). To put it succinctly, "the appetite grows with the eating." As noted earlier (p. 57), the model is agnostic regarding this assumption, but an interesting twist develops when states are in the process of *becoming* aspiring hegemons or Great Powers. This model captures states' decreasing costs and (up to a point) their increased incentives, but it also captures the fact that, when states become Great Powers, they take on a growing portfolio of obligations that divides those capabilities among multiple tasks. In each of these simulations, American capabilities are divided among various tasks (fighting terrorism, countering proliferation, promoting democracy, etc.), whereas China's are devoted entirely to redressing the imbalance of power.

What happens if we divide China's attention as if it had a simulated portfolio of systemic interests that mirrors those of the United States? We can see the answer by examining the shift to the baseline simulation that occurs in the "China Global Governance" scenario: China's divided attention makes it, *de facto,* more accommodationist than it otherwise would have been and results in outcomes more favorable to the United States. The appetite may, indeed, grow with the eating, but so too do the number of courses on offer.

In any event, given that the nature of the U.S.–China relationship at the time of China's rise will likely be so dependent on China's worldview, and given that the Communist Party's top leadership retains a substantial degree of potential control over the composition of its constituency, it seems likely that little can be done by the United States to alter future developments other than to encourage progressive ideological development within China whenever the opportunity presents itself. Given the limited extent to which official Communist Party doctrine is capable of accommodating China's mixed economy and village- and town-level contested elections, and given the general need for words to match deeds when it comes to legitimating domestic regimes, it seems reasonable to conclude that a Chinese Gorbachev is the more likely of the two. Should one arrive on the scene, taking the risk of supporting his efforts early on, rather than waiting for another "Lost Year" to pass, would likely pay off.

Democracy

The Great Powers of the past two centuries have unfailingly focused on the distribution of political ideology as a structural dimension of the system, and indications so far are that the United States will continue to do so in the post–Cold War, post-September 11 world. Political elites in the 21st century seem poised to continue the tradition of their forebears from the 20th and 19th by arguing (rightly or wrongly) that the sources of international peace lie in the widespread acceptance of the political ideology that legitimates their own domestic governance and the unwillingness to wage war that such ideology produces.

The most succinct statements of these security logics can be found in the 2006 *National Security Strategy of the United States*.[24] The first goal listed in the 2006 *National Security Strategy* is "champion aspirations for human dignity":

> Championing freedom advances our interests because the survival of liberty at home increasingly depends on the success of liberty abroad. Governments that honor their citizens' dignity and desire for freedom tend to uphold responsible conduct toward other nations, while governments that brutalize their people also threaten the peace and stability of other nations. Because democracies are the most responsible members of the international system, promoting democracy is the most effective long-term measure for strengthening international stability; reducing regional conflicts; countering terrorism and terror-supporting extremism; and extending peace and prosperity.[25]

In short, if there is one overarching focus of the national security strategy of the United States, political ideology, specifically democratization, is it. The spread of democracy is a policy that is explicitly designed to produce a variety of attitudes among the peoples of the world that will be conducive to peace. Moreover, the embeddedness of democracy as a legitimating ideology at the domestic level seems likely to ensure that it remains an available and highly prominent dimension of American worldviews and therefore interests in the future. That said, as the Obama administration's increased emphasis on Afghanistan demonstrates, the relative weight placed on each of these dimensions will most likely continue to vary somewhat, sometimes within administrations, sometimes from one administration to the next.

We can, using simulations, assess the likely outcomes in the long run given a few different sets of assumptions. If we assume, as a baseline, that the United States is pursuing a policy of democratization against a cluster of uncoordinated antidemocratic movements worldwide, which collectively represent a relatively equally motivated force with considerably lesser capabilities, we again see (Fig. 5.5) a characteristic curvilinear relationship between salience and systemic outcomes – though this time, given that America's preference is for more rather than less of the good in question, the curve slopes upward rather than downward. Again, there are diminishing marginal policy returns to increasing the American focus on democratization, and increasing the intensity of the antidemocratic forces' preferences shifts the curve downward.

Another scenario worth exploring, at least hypothetically, is one in which Americans' commitment to democracy abroad dwindles – meaning not that it will become less intense, but rather, that they will come to advocate a form of societal organization abroad that is less democratic than the present ideal. In short, in this scenario, America's foreign policy ideology shifts toward a more moderate one. How might this outcome occur?

One possibility, derived from the literature on war and state-building, is that the present war on terror, or some future conflict, will engage Americans in war-making

---

[24] National Security Council (2006).   [25] National Security Council (2006, 3).

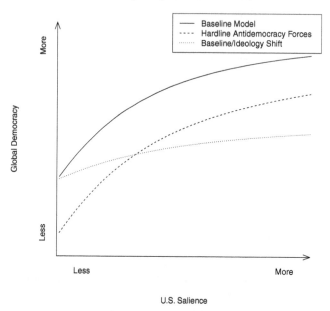

Figure 5.5. American salience and global democracy.

to such a degree that the American government itself will begin to take on more authoritarian characteristics as a result of its need to mobilize resources.[26] Given that a society's belief systems must typically be consistent with the basis of the leadership's claim to authority (Finer 1997, 29), it would not be unreasonable to expect that America's foreign policy worldview would evolve accordingly, perhaps toward a form of democracy with some authoritarian elements – restrictions on freedom of religion, perhaps, or speech, or *habeas corpus*.

Another possible reason for a shift in America's foreign policy ideology would be learning. After an impressive and exhaustive study of the subject, Hunt (1987, 198) suggests that a heavily ideological foreign policy has been quite costly to the country, especially in cases like Vietnam. Hunt suggests that, in the future, Americans might recognize this fact and realize that it is in their best interest to "accept as appropriate to some, perhaps even most, other societies, organizing principles that diverge from our own norms." In either case, the implication, as the third scenario (the Baseline/Ideology Shift line) in Figure 5.5 demonstrates, would be, not a downward shift in the curve, but rather a decrease in its slope – a logical result given that the American ideal point has shifted downward.

---

[26] See e.g., Thompson (1996); Hintze (1975). Lest this possibility seem fanciful, recall that no less ardent a democrat than Walter Lippmann advised President-elect Roosevelt that it might be best for the country if he were to assume dictatorial powers (Steel 1980, 300).

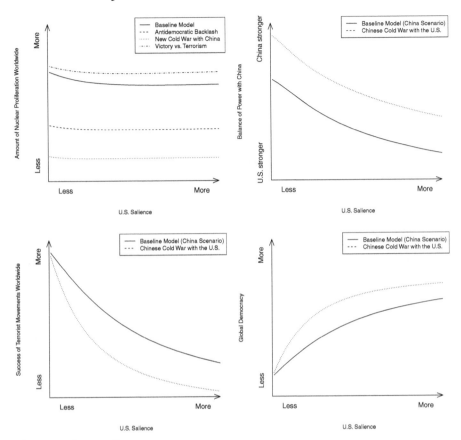

Figure 5.6. System effects.

System effects

It is also possible to illustrate the less direct impact of a change in one part of the system on outcomes in other parts of the system – the results of the flapping of the proverbial butterfly's wings – even though in this nonchaotic model those results may be attenuated rather than exaggerated by distance.

To illustrate this phenomenon, in Figure 5.6 I examine variation in the relationship between U.S. salience and one of the outcomes discussed earlier – the amount of nuclear proliferation worldwide – when parts of the model *not directly related to either one* are varied. The only effects in evidence here are system effects: a change in one part of the model has an impact on the structure of the system, and on the behavior of states, and then on the structure of the system along entirely different dimensions, until its ripples spread to every actor and every systemic dimension in the system. These are the effects described in $H_{Sys1}–H_{Sys4}$ (p. 45 and *passim*).

The graph in the upper left quadrant compares the results of the now-familiar baseline model to the results of three alternative scenarios. These scenarios represent

cases in which changes in the assumptions about developments in other spheres – democratization, the balance of power with China, and nuclear proliferation – eventually have an impact on worldwide proliferation. In each, the pathways to influence are multiple and complex.

The best way in which to illustrate them is to examine one of them – the new Cold War with China scenario – in detail. I do this in the illustrations in the remaining three quadrants. The existence of a new Cold War with China would, at first, be irrelevant to the American campaign against proliferation. As the confrontation with China heated up, however, the balance of power would shift in China's favor (represented by the graph in the upper right quadrant). That change, in turn, would exert upward pressure on the overall level of activity that the United States exerts to achieve all of its foreign policy goals and the resources that the United States devotes to foreign policy activity in general. Increased hostility with China would therefore increase the extent to which each of those goals is achieved: the most straightforward way to think of this effect is that the spillover from gearing up to take on China – in terms of additional manpower, improved military equipment, and so on – would constitute a net positive externality in other spheres.[27]

The expected result of this process, therefore, would be a greater degree of American success – however defined – in other spheres of activity. We can see this implication being played out in the lower left and lower right quadrants, where the increased activity resulting from the conflict with China "spills over" into positive externalities in the war against terror and in pro-democracy movements worldwide, respectively. Of course, it has an impact on the success of American anti-proliferation policy as well.

The impact of the conflict with China does not stop there, however. As the United States achieves its goals to a greater degree in each of the other spheres, its demand for foreign policy activity actually *decreases* to an extent. That decrease in activity dampens the original impetus toward greater activity spurred by the new confrontation with China. The effect of this change is to increase, marginally, the gains of would-be proliferators abroad and to cut into American antiproliferation gains to a modest extent.

The net effect is a new state of the world – a lower level of success for proliferators abroad – that is produced by a combination of the indirect effect of the initial condition (a new confrontation with China) via its impact on the structure of the system and the behavior of the actors, and even more indirect effects via all of the other dimensions of the international system.[28]

---

[27] It is important to note a key assumption in this line of reasoning – namely, that there will be no concurrent change in worldviews to a distribution so disproportionately focused on China that these externalities would all be directed toward China, rather than elsewhere. It may, in fact, be reasonable to expect one, and if it were to occur the model would take its effects into account as well, but such a change is not assumed *a priori*.

[28] The (probably rare, in practice) exception to this generalization would be the situation in which the two states' security priorities are so imbalanced – i.e., their distributions of salience are so dissimilar – that across-the-board American gains prompt an increase in Chinese activity that is focused in an area of relative American indifference, thereby producing a negative externality.

Systems and forecasts

The implications of systems for long-range forecasts, then, are actually fairly profound. The first, and most important, implication is that, as we have just seen, a change anywhere in the system resonates throughout the rest of the system: the interconnectedness of systems ensures that two independent spheres, or two discrete actors, will nevertheless influence one another via their common connections.

The second point is empirical rather than theoretical: systems are rarely entirely static for long. Something – the salience of one issue to one actor, the ideal point of another, a third actor's latent capabilities – is almost certain to change from one year to the next. In most years, quite a few things change. And given that the impact of each change has to be estimated empirically rather than assumed, the overall outcome of all of these changes, except in unusual cases in which one change far outweighs the rest, will most likely be indeterminate.

Simulations both allow us to grasp the enormity of these facts for forecasting and, in so doing, tacitly undermine their own practical value. The all-encompassing implications of a single change anywhere in the system, coupled with the fact that changes *somewhere* in the system are almost certain to happen quite regularly, render predictions highly uncertain, except for the very short term.[29] We have seen how the results of the model change from the baseline when we posit a new Cold War with China, which is simulated via a change in three parameters.[30] There are 23 others in the model that we must assume remain constant in order to derive these results. When we consider that, in the real world, the impact of a change in each depends on a parameter that must be estimated, with uncertainty, the inherent challenge of determinate long-range forecasting becomes clear: to put it succinctly, systems abhor forecasts.[31]

What is to be done?

Though long-range forecasts fire the popular imagination, systems theorists are well aware of the tradeoff between explanatory power and the ability to forecast. A simpler model, with less endogeneity, might be able to make more determinate predictions; yet the fact that it has less endogenity would mean that it explains less of the world, which after all is the primary goal of the exercise. We are nevertheless left with the question of what we, as analysts and citizens, can learn from the model that will be of use going forward.

The answer is "quite a bit." The immediate implications of a change in salience, or capabilities, or ideal points, on both the activities of actors and the status quo of the

[29] In more technical terms, the uncertainty of the forecast dominates the estimate in very short order. For a sense of the magnitude of the uncertainties involved in making forecasts using this model even one year ahead see Braumoeller (2010b, 172–176).

[30] The importance that the United States puts on the issue and that China puts on the issue are both increased, as are China's latent capabilities.

[31] Fearon (1996) comes to a similar conclusion based on similar thought experiments with cellular automata.

system (H_{A1} and H_{St1}) should be fairly intuitive: more capabilities tilts the system in one's favor, reducing levels of activity, and so on. A substantial part of the value of the theory lies in thinking in these terms and in thinking about the implications of changes in the world in terms of their direct impact on the system and on the behavior of the actors.

A much more profound benefit of the understanding of the system developed herein, however, lies in connecting those individual intuitions about connections among state and structure to form a holistic, systemic concept of the world – the understanding illustrated in the "System Effects" simulation earlier and developed in each of the case studies. The breadth and depth of the system's various interconnections, though far from intuitively obvious, are nevertheless crucial to understanding how the world works.

The "System Effects" scenario developed earlier is designed to illustrate precisely this point, by demonstrating how one change in the system – increased tension with China – resonates through to every other part of the system. The Soviet case detailed in the last chapter provides a good real-world example, especially because the failure to forecast the end of the Cold War has been discussed at some length.[32] If, as I have argued, the model is a reasonable representation of the process that led to the end of the Cold War, then that outcome *was* predictable – but not until Gorbachev had rid himself of the remnants of old thinking (or, more precisely, not until the new thinking came to dominate the old). At that point, given Gorbachev's ability to manipulate his constituency, the change in official Soviet worldviews became predictable, and given the change in official Soviet worldviews, the change in the structure of the system became predictable. Given the change in the system, America's reaction and therefore the end of the Cold War were all predictable outcomes.

As this discussion suggests, the best we can hope for in the international system are very short-run forecasts,[33] subject to *ceteris paribus* assumptions. Attempting to predict the end of the Cold War before the rise of Gorbachev is simply not a worthwhile goal.[34] By no means could anyone, using this model, have predicted the end of the Cold War before Gorbachev's ascent to office or probably even in his first year – and even doing so after that fact would require a remarkable degree of insight and access to information. It should, however, be reasonable to figure out what the implications of *a* Gorbachev would be, given his rise, an understanding of his worldview, and the preconditions of the Soviet system – and as I have demonstrated, the model helps us to do exactly that.

---

[32] See Gaddis (1992–1993) for a historian's critique – one that, I am happy to note, suggests as a remedy examining nonlinear causal relationships and structuralism; Hopf (1993) for a rejoinder that suggests that the failure was one of imagination, not theory; Wohlforth (1998) for a review of responses; and Bueno de Mesquita (1998) for a retroactive, and very ambitious, attempt to predict the Cold War's end starting from its initial conditions.

[33] This assessment, I should note, is hardly out of line with similar assessments in other social sciences; see Evans (1997) for a view that the stochastic components of macroeconomic models swamp the systematic terms, making long-term forecasting useless, and Hall (1995) for an only slightly more optimistic assessment.

[34] Here, again, the end of the Cold War must be distinguished from the dissolution of the Soviet state.

It is instructive to compare these relatively conservative conclusions to those of Bueno de Mesquita (1998), who argues that an American victory in the Cold War could have been predicted with reasonably high certainty using an expected utility model and data available in 1948. To make such a prediction, the expected utility model gains leverage from a few key assumptions about the processes of history – that coalitions will form among actors with similar alignment portfolios, for example – that were far more true in the 1950s than they were in (say) the more fluid 1870s and 1880s. It is also agnostic regarding the form that victory will take, which means that although it can predict an American victory in the Cold War, it cannot, technically, predict a *peaceful* one.

The expected utility model also assumes, critically, that the bargaining positions of the states – analogous to their ideal points here – are endogenous to their relative bargaining strength in the long run: states regularly reconsider their ideal points based on the relative capabilities of their coalitions, as well as salience, in a probabilistic manner. This assumption does produce predictions of concrete outcomes, though it is reasonable to wonder how well the mechanism by which they are produced maps to the one that produced the actual outcome. For one thing, as the author points out, the posited mechanism could have led to an American capitulation to Soviet values rather than the opposite (though this outcome occurs "infrequently" [p. 145] in the simulations). Moreover, if the mechanism is correct the timing of the end of the Cold War should be fairly improbable from the point of view of the model: the opposing coalitions had formed and relative capabilities were at their most imbalanced in the very early years of the Cold War. Khrushchev's liberalization is in some ways a better argument in favor of the model's internal logic than Gorbachev's – but it did not end the Cold War.

Such modeling choices reflect differences in emphasis (or perhaps interest, or taste) as much as anything else: there is no right or wrong answer to the question of how much weight should be placed on explanation versus prediction. The point is simply that the tradeoff is exceptionally difficult to avoid. Unfortunately, what this fact implies is that, although the model laid out here is satisfyingly descriptively rich, it is difficult to utilize it to know what the system will look like ten years down the road with a high degree of certainty. Its value does not lie in a static hundred-year forecast that would put Nostradamus to shame, because one of the fundamental implications of the complexity of the system that it describes is that no such forecast is possible. Rather, its value lies in the ability that it provides, once its logic has been fully internalized, to anticipate the systemic implications of new developments as they unfold, rather than to be surprised by them, as too many have been in the past.

Systems and international relations

Regardless of what we can and cannot say about the future direction of international politics, the larger point should not be lost: there is immense value to thinking about the international system, like the solar system, in systemic terms rather than piecemeal, one state or one pair of states at a time. The basis of that statement is both logical (given that a coherent, deductive systemic model of international politics has been described in detail here) and empirical (given that the model fits the known

facts, both broadly speaking over nearly two centuries and in depth in a few specific cases).

Absent such a perspective, I hope to have shown that state behavior and the evolution of the structure of the system are difficult to comprehend. If we were to examine a typical dyadic, data-based analysis of conflict in post-Napoleonic Europe literally, it would most likely portray the period as a series of unrelated conflicts in various places around the Continent. Nothing about the clashes in Spain, Portugal, Belgium, or Greece would give any indication that they were all part of a larger dynamic, propelled more than anything else by domestic liberalization within the United Kingdom, which drove it to revise the ideological structure of the international system, thereby creating a schism among the Great Powers that exacerbated those conflicts when they arose.

Similarly, many have argued that the United States in the latter part of the interwar period was oddly insular, protected by its oceans, or bound by a constitution designed for an isolationist state. The image of an isolationist ostrich, its head in the sand, is an enduring one to this day. Yet the facts of the case, when viewed in systemic perspective, are more complex: they start with the rise of Nazi Germany, which produced ideological and material changes within the country itself and eventually a substantial change in the structure of the system, and in so doing provoked an American reaction to that threat to the structure of the system. This portrayal suggest that, far from being a nonresponsive state, the United States actually responded fairly quickly once the threat to the system had manifested.

Finally, few cases lend themselves as well to "great man" theories of history as the end of the Cold War: some attribute it to an actor turned president, demanding that the Berlin Wall be torn down, whereas others attribute it largely to the actions of a stubborn and wily reformer from Stavropol. Although the latter interpretation is clearly more consistent with the evidence presented here, it is still far from complete: Gorbachev's "new thinking" was nothing if not inspired by, and designed to alter, the material and ideological structure of the system itself, with the long-range goal of improving the security of the state. And it was that change, rather than the substantial changes within the Soviet Union itself, that ultimately led the Americans to agree to an end to the Cold War.

In every case, the structure of the international system shapes and constrains the behavior of the actors – but that structure, itself, is also the product of their activity. In the end, Thomas Carlyle and Karl Marx were both right, but each one's fundamental insight was incomplete. Neither isolated agents nor impersonal structures wholly control outcomes in the world of international relations. Rather, there is a constant interplay between the most powerful states in the system and the structure that they collectively help to constitute. States both shape and respond to the structure of the international system; history constrains those who make it.

Theoretical details

The model

Let a_n ($n = \{i, j, k, \ldots\}$) denote the level of activity of country c and s_d ($d = \{r, y, \ldots\}$, for *realpolitik*, ideological, etc., spheres) denote the state of the system in dimension d. These are the endogenous variables – that is, the primary variables of interest in the model. The variable s contains multiple dimensions; one could be the balance of power, another could be the balance of ideology, and so forth, depending on the historical period in question. The actors exert effort (measured by the magnitude of a) to push and pull the status quo in this multidimensional space back and forth, until it reaches their constituencies' ideal points.

Let c_{nd} represent a frequency distribution of constituency ideal points for state n on dimension d; in concrete terms this might correspond to the constituency's answers to a poll asking what their preferred distribution of power, ideology, etc., would look like. Let $v_n(\cdot)$ represent state n's preference aggregation function (corresponding to the manner, in state n, that the answers to those poll questions are aggregated and transmitted to the leadership; are they simply averaged or weighted in some way?) and ω_{nd} represents the salience of issue area d to the constituency of n (in other words, the answer to the question, "How much are changes in d" – whatever d is – "relevant to our national security?").[1] The variable π_n represents the latent capabilities of state n or the resources it has available to convert actions into outcomes (scaled to $0 \leq \pi_n \leq 1$).

Of these, only $v_n(\cdot)$ is relatively complex. Debates have played out in the public choice literature for decades regarding how preferences can be aggregated without running the risk of deadlock or cycling, and many reasonable answers have been offered for specific legislatures or categories of legislatures, but few can reasonably be applied to governments as diverse as Reagan's America and Tsarist Russia. The most reasonable, and durable, general representation is one in which constituents support leaders with increasing probability as policies approach the constituents' ideal points,[2]

---

[1] Technically, ω_{nd} is a quantity that is aggregated from the constituency level to the level of the elite as well, so if we were being extremely explicit the notation would be $v_n(\omega_{nd})$ rather than ω_{nd}, or even $\xi_n(\omega_{nd})$ if we assumed a different aggregation function $\xi_n(\cdot)$. To avoid excess notation, and without loss of generality, I simply utilize ω_{nd}.

[2] The assumption of probabilistic support, rather than a deterministic model in which constituents support A over B with certainty if and only if their expected utility under A exceeds their expected utility under B, is fairly easy to justify in real-world terms. Constituents might be somewhat

ideal points along one dimension are unrelated to ideal points along another, and leaders act to maximize their support.

Under those conditions, and assuming that probability distribution functions are continuous and strictly concave, the leader's governance problem becomes the maximization of $\sum_{x=1}^{X} p_x$, where p_x is the probability that constituent x will support the leader. If all constituents are not weighted equally – if, for example, a skewed electoral system gives more weight to some votes than to others – the problem becomes the maximization of $\sum_{x=1}^{X} w_x p_x$, where w_x represents the weight accorded to constituent x. Similarly, if constituent 1 is more sensitive than constituent 2 to changes in policy, 1's preferences will carry more weight in determining the resultant policy than will 2's (Mueller 1989, 199–202). In the most generic case, that in which constituents are equally weighted, $\sum_{x=1}^{X} p_x$ is maximized at $\bar{c}_{nd}$, and because we assume for the sake of tractability that ideal points along one dimension are unrelated to ideal points along another, $v_n(c_{nd}) = \bar{c}_{nd} \ \forall d$, and $v_n(c_n) = \bar{c}_n$: the aggregated preferences of the constituency of n collapse to the multidimensional mean.

According to the theory, the constituency's worldview in state n determines both c_{nd} and ω_{nd}. Domestic politics determines both the size and nature of the subset of the citizenry that is defined as the constituency and the particulars of the preference aggregation function (e.g., the weight vector w). In the modern era the state's available (or latent) power resources determine π_n.[3] These variables determine the values of s_d and a_n in equilibrium in the following manner: ω_{nd} determines the extent to which dimension d matters to state n. Given that it is difficult and costly to change the state of the world, ω_{nd} captures the extent to which the state is willing to expend resources to bring about change in that dimension. Following Sargent (1978), the existence of costs of adjustment implies that adjustment will be partial rather than immediate (i.e., that constituents will not simply demand a jump to equilibrium in the manner of standard rational-expectations models).[4] If ω is high, the dimension in question is very important to the state, and costs will be low, in the sense that constituents will not object to very substantial expenditures of resources.[5] Accordingly, adjustment will be more rapid than it would be if ω were low.

$v_n(c_{nd})$ can be thought of as state n's collective "ideal point" along dimension d, and s_d constitutes the "state of the world" along that same dimension. Constituents demand action from the leadership in direct proportion to the extent that d matters to n *and* the state of the world diverges from their collective ideal point. Leaders maximize their domestic support by acting to satisfy their constituency. The demands

---

ignorant of the expected utilities of leaders' policies for them, or those policies might contain elements not captured by the model.

[3] As I discuss starting on page 75, this relationship is historically contingent: In the 19th century, states on balance were more concerned with the balance of latent capabilities and altered them utilizing realized capabilities. During that period, therefore, *realized* capabilities determine π_n and *latent* capabilities determine s.

[4] See Attfield, Demery, and Duck (1991) for an introduction to the rational-expectations literature.

[5] Implicit in this model is the assumption that states are rich enough to expend whatever their constituencies demand. Given that the states under study are exclusively Great Powers and they are not studied during wartime, it seems quite reasonable to assume that they are not exerting themselves to the absolute utmost.

of their constituency are based on the distance between the collective ideal point and the status of the system and the emphasis placed on that dimension of reality by the state's worldview, or ω_{nd}.

It is desirable to have the level of activity be the same whenever the state of the world s_d is a given absolute distance from state n's ideal point. Therefore, the simple distance between the ideal point and the state of the world, $v_n(c_{nd}) - s_d$, will not serve well as a component of the equation, simply because it does not possess this quality: it would produce "negative activity" whenever $v_n(c_{nd}) < s_d$, and aside from the conceptual unpalatability of such an outcome, empirically determining whether activity is designed to move the status quo upward or downward toward a state's ideal point would sometimes be very difficult. Using $|v_n(c_{nd}) - s_d|$ would ameliorate this problem, but absolute values possess undesirable mathematical qualities, especially as regards estimation. The most straightforward function that possesses the key qualities of $|v_n(c_{nd}) - s_d|$ – global concavity, nonincreasing when $v_n(c_{nd}) < s_d$, nondecreasing when $v_n(c_{nd}) > s_d$, and 0 when $v_n(c_{nd}) = s_d$ – is $[v_n(c_{nd}) - s_d]^2$.

Therefore, the action taken by the leadership is described by

$$a_{n(t+1)} = \sum_d \omega_{nd(t)} [v_{n(t)}(c_{nd(t)}) - s_{d(t)}]^2 \tag{A.1}$$

To illustrate this process in the case of specific states and specific systemic dimensions, imagine that state i's constituency is focused on two dimensions of the international system, the military (or *realpolitik*) and the ideological spheres, and is considerably more interested in the latter than in the former ($\omega_{ir} = 0.25$, $\omega_{iy} = 0.75$). In the ideological sphere, where 1 represents the spread of the state's domestic political regime throughout the globe and 0 represents its complete disappearance outside the borders of i itself, opinion in i is divided: a substantial group believes strongly that its own form of government is just and should be promoted, but a slightly larger group, although it has a mild preference for some governments of its own type, generally prefers to allow other peoples to choose their own path. In the *realpolitik* sphere, however, the majority believe that more power is unconditionally better and would therefore be happiest if i were to achieve hegemony. These constituency preferences could be represented by a bimodal c_{iy} distribution – perhaps with modes at 0.3 and 1, and a mean at 0.6 – and a c_{ir} distribution where the constituents are clustered at 1. At present, the structure of the system is not especially close to either of the state's ideal points: the state's political ideology has spread to about 20% of the globe, the state possesses 15% of the latent military capabilities in the system, and its allies possess a mere 5%. To determine the demand for activity on the part of the leadership we need only multiply weights by the distance between ideal points and the current status of the structure of the system and sum across dimensions, so

$$\begin{aligned} a_{i(t+1)} &= \sum_d \omega_{id(t)} [v_{i(t)}(c_{id(t)}) - s_{d(t)}]^2 \\ &= \omega_{iy(t)} [v_{i(t)}(c_{iy(t)}) - s_{y(t)}]^2 + \omega_{ir(t)} [v_{i(t)}(c_{ir(t)}) - s_{r(t)}]^2 \\ &= (0.75 \times (0.60 - 0.20)^2) + (0.25 \times (1 - 0.20)^2) \\ &= (0.75 \times 0.16) + (0.25 \times 0.64) \\ &= 0.28 \end{aligned}$$

Finally, we need to calculate the instantaneous rate of growth (or decrease) in the state's activity, $\dot{a}_i$, to characterize this as a dynamic system. This is done simply by subtracting the existing level of activity from the right-hand side of the equation:

$$\dot{a}_i = \sum_d \omega_{id}[v_i(c_{id}) - s_d]^2 - a_i \tag{A.2}$$

where $\dot{a}_i \equiv \dot{a}_{i(t)} \equiv a_{i(t+1)} - a_{i(t)}$ and the time subscripts are dropped for notational convenience.

Next, how should we model the impact of the state's actions on the structure of the international system? Three points are paramount. First, the level of the state's activity must be weighted by its capacity to produce change, which is proportional to its latent capabilities, π_i.[6] In the case of a complete absence of capabilities, the state's actions should have virtually no impact on the structure of the system. As capabilities increase, the impact of the state's activities should increase proportionally.

Second, the state will only seek to alter the structure of the international system to the extent that that structure is inconsistent with its security needs – and success in transforming the system will produce less, not more, ambition to change it. For example, a state that seeks security through democracy would exert less and less effort as its efforts succeed and the rest of the world approaches a fully democratic condition. This tendency – a simple logical necessity, really – could be captured in the term $[v_i(c_{id}) - s_d]^2$, earlier. Unfortunately, this quantity has an undesirable characteristic that is the mirror image of the one mentioned previously: in this case we *do* want to allow positive and negative changes to s, because states might act to move the status quo in either direction. The most straightforward quantity that retains this term's desirable qualities while allowing movements in both directions is $[v_i(c_{id}) - s_d]$.

It is worth noting a substantial difference between the assumptions of the nested politics model and those of Gilpin (1981, 18–23) regarding the relationship between power and preferences. Gilpin argues that the appetite grows with the eating: as the state becomes more powerful, it becomes more able, and therefore more willing, to expend resources in pursuit of security goals.[7] The argument of the nested politics model is a bit more complex. It argues that a different dynamic is implicated in the behavior of rising powers: as their latent capabilities (π) increase, so does the impact that their activity has on the structure of the system. In that sense, the model agrees with Gilpin that security is "easier" for a more powerful state to purchase than it is for a weaker one.

However, the nested politics model also argues, in line with standard utility-maximization models, that the closer the status quo gets to the state's ideal point (that is, as $[v_i(c_{id}) - s_d]$ approaches zero), the more satisfied it will be, and the less it will exert itself to achieve its goals. This tendency mitigates *against* increases in levels of state activity, producing a built-in moderating effect: as the state becomes more powerful and gets more of what it wants, it scales back its effort. Gilpin's argument

---

[6] Though see Footnote 3.
[7] I am grateful to Randall Schweller for bringing this point to my attention.

suggests that, as this occurs, the state's ideal point should shift as well, to such a degree that the state's level of dissatisfaction actually increases despite having received more of what it wants. It seems nearly impossible to evaluate this argument, given the many possible reasons for exogenous variation in state ideal points – but by permitting ideal points to be exogenous in the empirical section it is at least possible to allow for such variation to occur without constituting a threat to the model's conclusions.

Finally, salience also matters: a state's activity will have an impact in a given sphere only to the extent that this sphere is salient. If 90% of a state's attention is devoted to the *realpolitik* sphere and 10% is focused on the economic sphere, the state's activities should mostly produce outcomes in the military realm. More formally, the proportion of activity that state i will devote to changing the structure of the system in sphere d is given by $\frac{\omega_{id}}{\sum_d \omega_{id}}$. Because all of these values have the same denominator and only their magnitude relative to one another matters, we can eliminate the denominator and simply use ω_{id} to denote the salience of each dimension.

The following three principles – lead to a straightforward set of equations.

- The level of the state's activity must be weighted by its capacity to produce change, π_i.
- The state will only seek to alter the structure of the international system to the extent that that structure is inconsistent with its security needs, $v_i(c_{id}) - s_d$.
- A state's activity will have an impact in a given sphere only to the extent that that sphere is salient, ω_{id}.

For a single state i and a single systemic dimension d,

$$\dot{s}_d = a_i \pi_i \omega_{id} [v_i(c_{id}) - s_d]$$

Expanding to two states, i and j, can be done by simply summing their impact on the state variable s_d, so

$$\dot{s}_d = a_i \pi_i \omega_{id} [v_i(c_{id}) - s_d] + a_j \pi_j \omega_{jd} [v_i(c_{jd}) - s_d]$$

– or, in general,

$$\dot{s}_d = \sum_n a_n \pi_n \omega_{nd} [v_n(c_{nd}) - s_d] \tag{A.3}$$

Modeling multiple systemic dimensions follows in a straightforward way. For two dimensions, say, the ideological and *realpolitik* spheres, the equations would be

$$\dot{s}_y = \sum_{i=1}^{N} a_i \pi_i \omega_{iy} [v_i(c_{iy}) - s_y]$$

$$\dot{s}_r = \sum_{i=1}^{N} a_i \pi_i \omega_{ir} [v_i(c_{ir}) - s_r]$$

In this way, the impact of the actions of all of the states in the system on all of the dimensions deemed relevant by each can be modeled.

Relaxing the unidimensionality assumption

This characterization of the international system is based on the assumption that each *systemic* dimension is *conceptually* unidimensional – that the state of the system and the states' ideal points can be characterized as points along a single continuum. In the previous examples this characterization may be a plausible one: the ideological sphere can be characterized by a continuum with systemic democracy at one end and systemic autocracy at the other, and the *realpolitik* sphere can be characterized by a continuum with "*i*'s hegemony" at one end and "*j*'s hegemony" at the other ($c_{ir} = 1, c_{jr} = 0$). A potential problem arises, however, when an additional state, k, is added to the mix. The state k's *realpolitik* ideal point is not on the continuum just described; it might be happiest if i and j were rendered completely powerless, but such an outcome cannot be characterized by a point on the at continuum. One way to deal with the problem of multidimensional ideal points within a single systemic dimension is to break the state of the system down into multiple equations, one for each state:

$$\dot{s}_{ir} = a_i \pi_i \omega_{ir}(1 - s_{ir}) - a_j \frac{\pi_j}{N-1} \omega_{jr}(1 - s_{jr}) - a_k \frac{\pi_k}{N-1} \omega_{kr}(1 - s_{kr})$$

$$\dot{s}_{jr} = a_j \pi_j \omega_{jr}(1 - s_{jr}) - a_i \frac{\pi_i}{N-1} \omega_{ir}(1 - s_{ir}) - a_k \frac{\pi_k}{N-1} \omega_{kr}(1 - s_{kr})$$

$$\dot{s}_{kr} = a_k \pi_k \omega_{kr}(1 - s_{kr}) - a_i \frac{\pi_i}{N-1} \omega_{ir}(1 - s_{ir}) - a_j \frac{\pi_j}{N-1} \omega_{jr}(1 - s_{jr})$$

Note the subtraction of the effects of j's and k's activity from i's portion of the *realpolitik* sphere, and of its from theirs. Assuming that the various s_{ir} sum to unity when the simulation begins, this device ensures that they will continue to do so. The division of each player's capabilities by one less than the total number of players N indicates that each state's attention is divided equally among its potential foes – a reflection of the realist maxim that no one can be trusted in an anarchic world. Modifications of this assumption are, of course, possible. For example, a more sophisticated assumption, easily modeled, might be that states focus their energies against other states in direct proportion to their relative (latent) capabilities.

Sympathetic vs. antagonistic states

If it is possible to envision a change of the status quo point from s to s' such that $[v_i(c_{id}) - s_d'] < [v_i(c_{id}) - s_d]$ and $[v_j(c_{jd}) - s_d'] < [v_j(c_{jd}) - s_d]$, then joint gains for i and j are possible in d.[8] In a sphere in which joint gains are possible, a *sympathetic state* is a state whose ideal point lies on the same side of the status quo as one's own; therefore, in the area bounded by the sympathetic state's ideal point and the status quo point, joint gains are possible. An *antagonistic state* is a state whose ideal point lies on the other side of the status quo from one's own.

---

[8] Examples include ideological or religious spheres, in which two or more states with the same preferences over outcomes would both benefit more if a greater share of the system were organized according to their preferred belief system.

Finally, as the earlier equations make clear, states are assumed to react entirely to the changes that other states produce in the structure of the system rather than anticipating those changes and counteracting them ahead of time. Clearly, in reality states do both to some degree, but what explicitly justifies the assumption in this model? The partial-adjustment framework elaborated earlier provides an answer: although states possess accurate information about their own ideal points and capabilities and the extent to which different dimensions of the system matter to them, they are highly uncertain about these quantities in other states. The compounded uncertainty across all of these quantities means that the extent to which states will be proactive rather than reactive is exceedingly small. Because observation of the impact of states' actions is often difficult even years after the fact, moreover, contemporaneous learning is virtually impossible.

To illustrate this argument formally, Brainard (1967) has shown that uncertainty about the parameters of a model leads to partial adjustment, with the degree of "partial-ness" increasing with uncertainty, and Startz (2003) has applied this intuition to a dynamic setting. One finding is that even a modest amount of uncertainty can produce extremely minimal adjustment to the anticipated behavior of other states as an optimum. If adjustment of a were to produce results in s in a purely deterministic way, say, $s = \xi a$, but we are uncertain about the value of ξ, it is rational to adjust by a fraction λ_ξ of the optimal adjustment:

$$s = \lambda_\xi a$$

$$\lambda_\xi = \frac{\xi^2}{\xi^2 + \sigma_\xi^2}$$

To see how even a moderate amount of uncertainty dramatically reduces the state's degree of anticipatory adjustment, imagine that i wishes to counteract some fraction κ of j's activity (which, remember, will also be a partial adjustment because action is costly for j as well). Imagine also that i has a fairly good knowledge of the state of j, which we take to mean that it knows half of what it would need to know to carry out optimal adjustment in a perfect world: $\xi^2 = \sigma_\xi^2$. Given uncertainty about π_j, ω_{jd}, and $v_j(c_{jd})$, the latter two of which influence $\dot{s}_d$ twice (once immediately and a second time indirectly, via a), the fraction of j's activity that i would end up countering would be $\kappa \lambda_\pi \lambda_{v(c)}^2 \lambda_\omega^2$.

Multiplying out, we find that, in this simple example in which i knows half of what it needs to know to adjust to j's behavior, the compounding of its uncertainties leads to a far smaller coefficient of adjustment $-\frac{1}{32}\kappa$, a very small fraction indeed.

Analytical results

Realism implies a balance of power

To see this point, first assume a world of purely offensive realist states (though we relax the "offensive" part soon). That means, in terms of the equations, that $\omega_{nr} = 1$, $v_n(c_{nr}) = 1 \ \forall n$. Also assume that we are limiting the discussion to Great Powers whose latent capabilities are more or less equivalent ($\pi_i = \pi_j = \pi_k$), although their realized

capabilities might be quite different ($s_{ir} \neq s_{jr} \neq s_{kr}$ at time 0). The question then becomes, under which sets of initial conditions will they manage to achieve a balance of power?

The rather surprising answer is that they will *always* manage to achieve a balance of power in equilibrium ($s_{ir}^* = s_{jr}^* = s_{kr}^*$), regardless of the initial distribution of realized capabilities.

Begin with a system of three states competing solely over resources relevant to material power. Such a system can be derived from these equations:

$$\dot{a}_i = [1 - s_{ir}]^2 - a_i \tag{A.4}$$

$$\dot{a}_j = [1 - s_{jr}]^2 - a_j \tag{A.5}$$

$$\dot{a}_k = [1 - s_{kr}]^2 - a_k \tag{A.6}$$

$$\dot{s}_{ir} = a_i(1 - s_{ir}) - a_j \frac{s_{ir}}{s_{ir} + s_{kr}}(1 - s_{jr}) - a_k \frac{s_{ir}}{s_{ir} + s_{jr}}(1 - s_{kr}) \tag{A.7}$$

$$\dot{s}_{jr} = a_j(1 - s_{jr}) - a_i \frac{s_{jr}}{s_{jr} + s_{kr}}(1 - s_{ir}) - a_k \frac{s_{jr}}{s_{ir} + s_{jr}}(1 - s_{kr}) \tag{A.8}$$

$$\dot{s}_{kr} = a_k(1 - s_{kr}) - a_i \frac{s_{kr}}{s_{jr} + s_{kr}}(1 - s_{ir}) - a_j \frac{s_{kr}}{s_{ir} + s_{kr}}(1 - s_{jr}) \tag{A.9}$$

In equilibrium, none of the state variables will change over time; our first step, therefore, is to set $\dot{s}_{ir}$, $\dot{s}_{jr}$, and $\dot{s}_{kr}$ equal to zero and all of the $s = s^*$. We also know that $a_i = [1 - s_{ir}]^2$, $a_j = [1 - s_{jr}]^2$, and $a_k = [1 - s_{kr}]^2$; replacing the as with their respective $1 - s$'s, expanding, and simplifying gives

$$0 = [1 - s_{ir}^*]^3 - [1 - s_{jr}^*]^3 \frac{s_{ir}^*}{s_{ir}^* + s_{kr}^*} - [1 - s_{kr}^*]^3 \frac{s_{ir}^*}{s_{ir}^* + s_{jr}^*} \tag{A.10}$$

$$0 = [1 - s_{jr}^*]^3 - [1 - s_{ir}^*]^3 \frac{s_{jr}^*}{s_{jr}^* + s_{kr}^*} - [1 - s_{kr}^*]^3 \frac{s_{jr}^*}{s_{ir}^* + s_{jr}^*} \tag{A.11}$$

$$0 = [1 - s_{kr}^*]^3 - [1 - s_{ir}^*]^3 \frac{s_{kr}^*}{s_{jr}^* + s_{kr}^*} - [1 - s_{jr}^*]^3 \frac{s_{kr}^*}{s_{ir}^* + s_{kr}^*} \tag{A.12}$$

Also note that the latter two terms of each of these equations can be further reduced: because the s's sum to unity, $1 - s_{ir}^* = s_{jr}^* + s_{kr}^*$, $1 - s_{jr}^* = s_{ir}^* + s_{kr}^*$, and $1 - s_{kr}^* = s_{ir}^* + s_{jr}^*$,

$$0 = [1 - s_{ir}^*]^3 - s_{ir}^*[1 - s_{jr}^*]^2 - s_{ir}^*[1 - s_{kr}^*]^2 \tag{A.13}$$

$$0 = [1 - s_{jr}^*]^3 - s_{jr}^*[1 - s_{ir}^*]^2 - s_{jr}^*[1 - s_{kr}^*]^2 \tag{A.14}$$

$$0 = [1 - s_{kr}^*]^3 - s_{kr}^*[1 - s_{ir}^*]^2 - s_{kr}^*[1 - s_{jr}^*]^2 \tag{A.15}$$

From this,

$$[1 - s_{ir}^*]^3 - s_{ir}^*[1 - s_{jr}^*]^2 - s_{ir}^*[1 - s_{kr}^*]^2 = [1 - s_{kr}^*]^3 - s_{kr}^*[1 - s_{jr}^*]^2 - s_{kr}^*[1 - s_{ir}^*]^2 \tag{A.16}$$

which implies

$$s_{ir}^* = s_{kr}^* \tag{A.17}$$

Parallel calculations demonstrate that $s_{ir}^* = s_{jr}^*$; therefore, in equilibrium the capabilities of all states in the system are equal.

It should be clear that adding more states to the system does nothing to the conclusion that they will, in equilibrium, achieve a balance of power. The logic of the equilibrium solution would be precisely the same, except that an additional state would be added to the mix.

> The logic of offensive realism leads to the conclusion that balances of power recurrently form regardless of the number of Great Powers in the system and regardless of the initial distribution of power.

Defensive realism also implies a balance of power

For defensive realists, states do not typically seek to maximize power because they realize that doing so would constitute a threat to their neighbors. Their ideal point on the capabilities spectrum, therefore, is somewhere below complete hegemony, though we do not know exactly where: $v_n(c_{nr}) < 1$ for all states n.

The solution is straightforward: we begin with the system of equations outlined in A.4–A.9, and just as in that case we conclude A.13–A.15, but unlike that case $v_n(c_{nr}) \neq 1$. Therefore, these equations yield not A.16 but rather

$$[x - s_{ir}^*]^3 - s_{ir}^*[x - s_{jr}^*]^2 - s_{ir}^*[x - s_{kr}^*]^2 = [x - s_{kr}^*]^3 - s_{kr}^*[x - s_{jr}^*]^2 - s_{kr}^*[x - s_{ir}^*]^2 \tag{A.18}$$

where $x = v_i(c_{ir}) = v_j(c_{jr}) = v_k(c_{kr})$. A.18 also reduces to $s_{ir}^* = s_{jr}^*$, and we can demonstrate that $s_{ir}^* = s_{kr}^*$, so we end up with a balance of power in equilibrium in this situation as well.

Therefore, for any structural dimension d and state n, $s_{nd}^* = \frac{1}{N}$ in a system of N actors, *regardless* of the value of $v_n(c_{nd})$ – as long as $v_n(c_{nd})$ is constant across states. In substantive terms, this means that even though defensive realists assume that states' goals fall well short of domination of the system, the result of interstate interaction is precisely the same – a balance of realized capabilities – as it would be if all states were to seek universal domination.

> If we relax the assumption that states seek universal domination, the result is *still* a balance of power, regardless of the level of power that they seek – as long as that level is constant across states.

A balance of power does not imply realism

This is a simple existence proof, which relies on demonstrating that a balance of power can be brought about even under conditions in which the realist assumption

that states focus either entirely or primarily on the distribution of power is false. As such, the example in the text suffices to make the point.

Socialization implies a balance of power

What would constructivists who believe that the international system socializes the actors that constitute it expect to occur among Great Powers with disparate worldviews? (Wendt 1999, 326–335; Klotz 1995) Interestingly enough, such a process could facilitate a balance of power.

It is possible to model the constructivist notion that the international system socializes its actors by making worldviews into state variables rather than parameters and having them converge toward the systemic average over time, in the following manner[9]:

$$\dot{\omega}_{ie} = \frac{\omega_{ie} + \omega_{je}}{2} - \omega_{ie} \tag{A.19}$$

$$\dot{\omega}_{je} = \frac{\omega_{ie} + \omega_{je}}{2} - \omega_{je} \tag{A.20}$$

$$\dot{\omega}_{ir} = \frac{\omega_{ir} + \omega_{jr}}{2} - \omega_{ir} \tag{A.21}$$

$$\dot{\omega}_{jr} = \frac{\omega_{ir} + \omega_{jr}}{2} - \omega_{jr} \tag{A.22}$$

These equations produce path-dependent equilibria that can only be expressed in terms of the values of the variables at time 0:

$$\omega_{ie}^* = \omega_{je}^* = \frac{\omega_{ie(0)} + \omega_{je(0)}}{2} \tag{A.23}$$

$$\omega_{ir}^* = \omega_{jr}^* = \frac{\omega_{ir(0)} + \omega_{jr(0)}}{2} \tag{A.24}$$

The effects of socialization should also change the ideal points of the states' constituencies. If we relax the assumption that c_{nd} is constant across states but retain the assumption of a constant preference aggregation function $v_n(\cdot)$, it is fairly straightforward to specify a Markov process that describes transitions from one preference "state" to another in such a way that the various c_n variables converge to a common frequency distribution in precisely the same manner that the ω_n variables converge to a common scalar in the earlier equations.

To see this point, imagine five preference states, each corresponding to possession of an ideal point in a given fifth of the unit interval. Specify that, in each time period, citizens of n compare the relative frequencies of their own state and adjacent states across countries: if a given preference state is more popular abroad than at home,

---

[9] It would be possible to have one converge more slowly than the other simply by weighting the rates at which each converges; it would also be possible to have one state's worldview remain constant while the other moves toward it (though nothing in constructivist theory, to my knowledge, would explain such an outcome). The results would not differ.

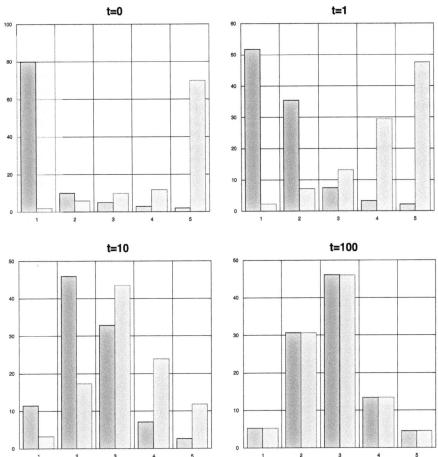

Figure A.1. Simulated Markov process describing effects of socialization on distributions of ideal points for constituencies in two states i and j.

citizens will gravitate toward it, whereas if it is less popular they will move away. (Denote the frequency of state p in country n as f_{cnp} and the frequency of adjacent states as f_{cnq}.) The process of socialization, then, involves being drawn away from citizens' existing states and toward adjacent preference states that are more popular in other states than they are in n. A reasonable transition rule for two states i and j would then be

$$\dot{f}_{cip} = \sum_{q} \left(1 - \frac{f_{cip}}{f_{cjp}}\right) - \left(1 - \frac{f_{ciq}}{f_{cjq}}\right) \tag{A.25}$$

Under those circumstances, as Figure A.1 illustrates, the frequency distributions c_{nd} of the various actors also converge. Given that the preference aggregation function is assumed to be the same for both states, the results regarding defensive realism apply, and a balance of power is assured, assuming equality of realized capabilities. The

balance will be upset in proportion to the extent to which the distribution of realized capabilities is unequal, but in a world of rough equality of realized capabilities, the socialization implied by constructivism should produce a balance of power.

It is worth noting that this result generalizes to any process that results in preference convergence over time. For example, Slaughter (2004, 61) argues that transnational networks can produce "convergence around a set of common ideas, approaches, and principles," a process that would mimic this one.

> **The existence of a balance of power need not be evidence in favor of realist theories. Balances of power are consistent with a wide range of theories.**

APPENDIX B
Empirical details

Nested politics and structural change

Having elaborated the theoretical model, we can now address the central question: the extent to which the dynamic model of nested politics and structural change maps to the real world in the three systems under consideration. Here, I focus on the more technical aspects of the investigation: ascertaining the probability that the data could plausibly be the product of random chance, as well as examining the correlations among the error terms of the actor-level equations (because these quantities can give us some clues as to whether or not states engage in contemporaneous coadjustment to within-period "shocks," or innovations)[1] and a moving sum of errors test to determine whether there are more than three systems in existence during the period under discussion.

Though what follows is couched in the standard language of hypothesis testing for the sake of convention,[2] I prefer to think of it as an exercise in ascertaining whether the reality implied by the model provides a reasonable match to the reality described by the data. In some cases the techniques used are the same: the question of whether zero falls within the 95% confidence intervals of the sampling distribution of a coefficient is an interesting one in both exercises, and standard frequentist statistical techniques provide the same answer. Nevertheless, interrogating the data is a fundamentally descriptive enterprise that admits a considerably wider range of questions, and potentially a richer set of descriptions, than standard hypothesis testing.[3]

---

[1] Such adjustments suggest that states are making some attempt to counter (or enhance) the impact of one another's actions on the structure of the system, rather than entirely waiting for that impact to play itself out.

[2] See Gill (1999) for a trenchant critique.

[3] My own sense is that, given observational data, all that we can do is describe. The position is summarized elegantly by Achen (1982, 77–78): "No matter how sophisticated, social science data analysis simply describes. That suffices. Given any satisfactory description, a provisional explanation can be constructed. Its validity is neither completely certain nor utterly dubious. Like almost all knowledge, its credibility depends, not on its resemblance to an idealized physics experiment, but on its competitiveness with other explanations. It will stand until another can be created that is equally simple, equally consistent with other knowledge, and more successful with the data."

Derivation

First, I demonstrate how the general theoretical model in Appendix A can be transformed into an empirical model suitable for estimation, given this information. Recall that the form of the model was derived from the structure of the system and the main actors – specifically,

$$\dot{s}_d = \sum_n \pi_n \omega_{nd} a_n [v_n(c_{nd}) - s_d] \tag{B.1}$$

and

$$\dot{a}_n = \sum_d \omega_{nd} [v_n(c_{nd}) - s_d]^2 - a_n \tag{B.2}$$

for all Great Powers $n = \{i, j, k, \ldots\}$ and all structural dimensions $d = \{r, y, \ldots\}$. These translate quite directly into estimable statistical equations. In fact, the equations resemble error-correction models of the sort described by Durr (1992), which leverage the strengths of differenced time series (namely, minimization of autocorrelation and unit root issues) while incorporating some information about levels in the adjustment term on the right-hand side.[4] The nonlinearity of the right-hand side makes them a bit more complex than a standard error-correction model, however. For example, once the right-hand side has been expanded and coefficients have been appended to each term for estimation, the equation for the United Kingdom in the 19th century would be

$$\dot{a}_{UK} = \beta_1 \omega_{UKBOP} v_{UK}(c_{UKBOP})^2 + \beta_2 \omega_{UKBOP}[2v_{UK}(c_{UKBOP})s_{BOP}]$$
$$+ \beta_3 \omega_{UKBOP} s_{BOP}^2 + \beta_4 \omega_{UKLIB} v_{UK}(c_{UKLIB})^2 + \beta_5 \omega_{UKLIB}[2v_{UK}(c_{UKLIB})s_{LIB}]$$
$$+ \beta_6 \omega_{UKLIB} s_{LIB}^2 + \beta_7 a_{UK}, \tag{B.3}$$

where a_{UK} denotes the level of activity of the UK, ω_{UKBOP} denotes the salience of the balance of power to the British, $v_{UK}(c_{UKBOP})$ represents the British ideal point with regard to the balance of power, s_{BOP} denotes the present balance of power, *LIB* subscripts refer to the balance of political ideology rather than to the balance of power, and the βs are coefficients to be estimated.[5] Four parallel equations describe the behavior of France, Austria/Austria-Hungary, Prussia/Germany, and Russia. Similarly,

---

[4] Normally the dependent variables, if nonstationary, are differenced to induce stationarity; in this case, the dependent variables are already differenced, and the resulting series demonstrate no evidence of serial correlation, moving averages, or unit roots.

[5] In principle, it is rarely desirable to estimate an interactive model without including all of the lower order terms as well. In this case, however, there are both theoretical objections (theory suggests these particular multiplicative terms and no others, not standard interaction terms with lower order coefficients) and practical ones (a mind-bogglingly large number of coefficients and insurmountable multicollinearity) to doing so.

the equation for the balance of power would be

$$
\begin{aligned}
\dot{s}_{BOP} = {} & \beta_1 \pi_{UK} \omega_{UKBOP} a_{UK} v_{UK} (c_{UKBOP}) + \beta_2 \pi_{UK} \omega_{UKBOP} a_{UK} s_{BOP} \\
& + \beta_3 \pi_{Fr} \omega_{FrBOP} a_{Fr} v_{Fr} (c_{FrBOP}) + \beta_4 \pi_{Fr} \omega_{FrBOP} a_{Fr} s_{BOP} \\
& + \beta_5 \pi_{Au} \omega_{AuBOP} a_{Au} v_{Au} (c_{AuBOP}) + \beta_6 \pi_{Au} \omega_{AuBOP} a_{Au} s_{BOP} \\
& + \beta_7 \pi_{Pr} \omega_{PrBOP} a_{Pr} v_{Pr} (c_{PrBOP}) + \beta_8 \pi_{Pr} \omega_{PrBOP} a_{Pr} s_{BOP} \\
& + \beta_9 \pi_{Ru} \omega_{RuBOP} a_{Ru} v_{Ru} (c_{RuBOP}) + \beta_{10} \pi_{Ru} \omega_{RuBOP} a_{Ru} s_{BOP},
\end{aligned} \tag{B.4}
$$

with two terms for each of the five Great Powers, and a second, parallel equation would describe the course of political liberalization on the continent. Dummy control variables were also added for exogenous "shocks" to ensure that these events did not distort the general trend.[6]

Because they are derived directly from the theoretical model, these equations represent direct tests of the actor-level and structural hypotheses from Chapter 2. A test of the significance of the coefficients in Equation B.3 is a test of the actor-level hypothesis,

H_{A1}: International structure prompts state security activity in proportion to the product of salience and dissatisfaction with the status quo,

in the case of Great Britain in the 19th century; tests of the significance of the coefficients in similar equations test the hypothesis for other Great Powers in other time periods. Similarly, a test of the significance of the coefficients in Equation B.4 is a test of the structural hypothesis,

H_{St1}: State security activity alters international structure in proportion to the product of state security activity, state latent capabilities, salience, and dissatisfaction with the status quo,

in the case of the balance of power in the 19th century.

---

[6] These include the Crimean War (in the equations for the UK, France, and Russia), the first year of World War I and of World War II, the first year of peace after each of these years, the first year of the Great Depression, and the first year after the fall of Eastern Europe and the end of the Cold War. These variables are included to ensure that these events do not distort the general trends that the model attempts to describe.

Detailed results

Table B.1. *Ratio of correct to incorrect predictions regarding coefficient sign, all estimators, all models. (Empty cell represents model with insufficient available information for estimation)*

		19th Century	Interwar Period	Cold War
	OLS	37 : 18	53 : 43	22 : 10
		(Pr = 0.0072)	(Pr = 0.1792)	(Pr = 0.0250)
Original	3SLS	38 : 17	65 : 31	28 : 4
		(Pr = 0.0032)	(Pr = 0.0003)	(Pr = 0.0000)
	FIML	37 : 18		29 : 3
		(Pr = 0.0072)		(Pr = 0.0000)

Table B.2. *Equation-level statistical significance, all estimators, all models. Numbers are F-statistics for OLS and 3SLS and χ^2 statistics for FIML*

	19th Century			Interwar Period			Cold War		
	OLS	3SLS	FIML	OLS	3SLS	FIML	OLS	3SLS	FIML
Bal. of Power	4.69 (0.000)	1.59 (0.104)	32.84 (0.000)	106.07 (0.000)	10.78 (0.000)		3.19 (0.023)	6.40 (0.000)	8.98 (0.062)
Bal. of Ideology	1.47 (0.166)	0.80 (0.632)	13.82 (0.181)	11.67 (0.003)	16.89 (0.000)		8.60 (0.000)	10.25 (0.000)	34.24 (0.000)
Arms Levels				2519.64 (0.000)	24.29 (0.000)		14.30 (0.000)	65.42 (0.000)	139.65 (0.000)
UK	3.03 (0.007)	3.62 (0.001)	20.10 (0.005)	57.81 (0.000)	22.99 (0.000)				
France	2.35 (0.030)	3.83 (0.000)	18.79 (0.009)	13.87 (0.001)	51.10 (0.000)				
Austria/A-H	4.87 (0.001)	4.59 (0.000)	24.65 (0.001)						
Prussia/Germany	1.60 (0.146)	6.38 (0.000)	18.56 (0.010)	2169.85 (0.000)	21.46 (0.000)				
Russia/USSR	2.18 (0.043)	4.29 (0.000)	21.40 (0.003)	235.72 (0.000)	109.56 (0.000)		5.29 (0.000)	2.42 (0.010)	32.37 (0.000)
Italy				770.75 (0.000)	19.25 (0.000)				
USA				61.16 (0.000)	75.21 (0.000)		1.77 (0.108)	1.01 (0.438)	11.62 (0.312)

Table B.3. *Correlations among error terms, 19th-century system*

	Balance of Power	Balance of Ideology	Activity of UK	Activity of Fr	Activity of Au	Activity of Pr
			3SLS			
BOI	0.0222					
aUK	−0.0745	0.113				
aFr	0.0266	0.1553	0.1642			
aAu	−0.0055	0.2701***	0.1682*	0.1511		
aPr	0.0316	0.1412	0.1628	0.2231**	0.2579**	
aRu	0.0639	0.0243	0.1506	0.0666	0.4892***	−0.1411
			FIML			
BOI	0.0274					
aUK	−0.0981	0.1647				
aFr	0.0259	0.2064**	0.1986*			
aAu	−0.0158	0.3268***	0.1863*	0.1663		
aPr	0.0516	0.205**	0.2226**	0.3077***	0.3171***	
aRu	0.0598	0.00024	0.1423	0.0774	0.4658***	−0.2013**

Table B.4. *Correlations among error terms, interwar system*

	Balance of Power	Balance of Ideology	Arms Levels	Activity of UK	Activity of Fr	Activity of Ge	Activity of It	Activity of Ru
				3SLS				
BOI	−0.6453***							
Arms	0.1825	−0.5343***						
aUK	−0.0091	0.0242	0.1171					
aFr	−0.464**	0.222	−0.2436	0.341				
aGe	−0.1352	−0.0296	−0.2279	0.2245	0.0458			
aIt	−0.079	−0.0856	−0.0933	0.0523	−0.1878	0.8384***		
aRu	0.2035	−0.3914*	−0.0798	−0.0169	0.0329	0.2922	0.3226	
aUS	0.1423	−0.0452	0.305	0.05	0.057	−0.7387***	−0.5407***	−0.2915

Table B.5. *Correlations among error terms, Cold War system*

	Balance of Power	Balance of Ideology	Arms Levels	Activity of US
			3SLS	
BOI	0.3918***			
Arms	−0.2804*	−0.1115		
aUS	0.0543	−0.1071	0.0102	
aSU	0.1342	0.1867	0.2086	−0.2819*
			FIML	
BOI	0.4424***			
Arms	−0.3546**	−0.1463		
aUS	0.0716	−0.1614	−0.0157	
aSU	0.1705	0.2343	0.3061**	−0.2769*

Table B.6. *Questions used from the Historians' Survey and the quantities that they inform*

All periods

Taking into account all forms of activity designed to increase national security, how active would you say the state's foreign policy was during this period? (1 = essentially isolationist, 4 = consistent with a normal Great Power during normal times, 7 = overwhelmingly aggressive or hyperactive) a

Vienna system

If political elites could have had their way, what would the distribution of power in Europe have looked like? What about the preferences of their constituency, if such a group existed? How did these answers change over time? (1 = all major states would have equal capabilities, 7 = even large inequalities of capabilities were fine as long as one state could still balance against threats) $v(c_{BOP})$

As a measure of the general importance of the distribution of power in Europe to the national security of the state, how wide or narrow was the range of outcomes considered acceptable by political elites and (if applicable) by their constituents? How did the answer to this question change over time? (1 = nearly any distribution of capabilities would have been acceptable from the point of view of national security, 7 = only an extremely narrow range of outcomes would have been acceptable; anything outside of that range would constitute a threat.) ω_{BOP}

If political elites could have had their way, how successful would movements for political liberalization have been throughout Europe? What about the preferences of their constituency, if such a group existed? How did these answers change over time? (1 = political power would have been concentrated at the very top; 7 = all citizens in all lands would have a voice in government.) $v(c_{LIB})$

As a measure of the general importance of political liberalization in Europe to the national security of the state, ... [rest of question parallels earlier importance question] ω_{LIB}

Interwar system

If political elites could have had their way, how closely would European reality have conformed to the military provisions of the Versailles settlement? What about the preferences of their constituency, if such a group existed? How did these answers change over time? (1 = Germany would be much, much weaker than other major states; 4 = Germany would be a normal state in terms of military power; 7 = Germany would be much, much stronger than other major states.) $v(c_{BOP})$

As a measure of the general importance of the military provisions of the Versailles settlement ... [rest of question parallels earlier importance question] ω_{BOP}

(continued)

Table B.6 *(continued)*

Interwar system (cont.)	
If political elites could have had their way, what would arms levels in Europe have looked like more generally? What about the preferences of their constituency, if such a group existed? How did these answers change over time? (1 = most major states would maintain only minimal armaments; 7 = most major states would maintain a strong military capable of projecting power.)	$v(c_{ARMS})$
As a measure of the general importance of arms levels in Europe ... [rest of question parallels earlier importance question]	ω_{ARMS}
If political elites could have had their way, what would the "balance of ideology" in Europe have looked like? What about the preferences of their constituency, if such a group existed? How did these answers change over time? (1 = far-right (Fascist) governments would dominate Europe, 4 = center (liberal democratic) governments would dominate Europe, 7 = far-left (communist) governments would dominate Europe.)	$v(c_{LIB})$
As a measure of the general importance of ideology in Europe ... [rest of question parallels earlier importance question]	ω_{LIB}
Cold War system	
If political elites could have had their way, what would the distribution of power in Europe have looked like? What about the preferences of their constituency, if such a group existed? How did these answers change over time? (1 = perfect balance between the two military blocs, 7 = overwhelming preponderance by one's own bloc over the other)	$v(c_{BOP})$
As a measure of the general importance of the distribution of power in Europe ... [rest of question parallels earlier importance question]	ω_{BOP}
If American (Soviet/Russian) political elites could have had their way, what would the superpowers' arms levels have looked like in general? What about the preferences of their constituency, if such a group existed? How did these answers change over time? (1 = superpowers would maintain only minimal armaments; 7 = essentially no arms limitations would be implemented)	$v(c_{ARMS})$
As a measure of the general importance of overall arms levels to the national security of the USA (USSR/Russia) ... [rest of question parallels earlier importance question]	ω_{ARMS}
If political elites could have had their way, what would the "balance of ideology" in Europe have looked like? What about the preferences of their constituency, if such a group existed? How did these answers change over time? (1 = all states would adopt Soviet-style communism; 7 = all states would adopt Western democratic capitalist forms of government.)	$v(c_{LIB})$
As a measure of the general importance of ideology in Europe ... [rest of question parallels earlier importance question]	ω_{LIB}

United Kingdom 1815–1864

As a measure of the general importance of the distribution of power in Europe to the national security of the state, how wide or narrow was the range of outcomes considered acceptable by political elites and (if applicable) by their constituents? How did the answer to this question change over time?

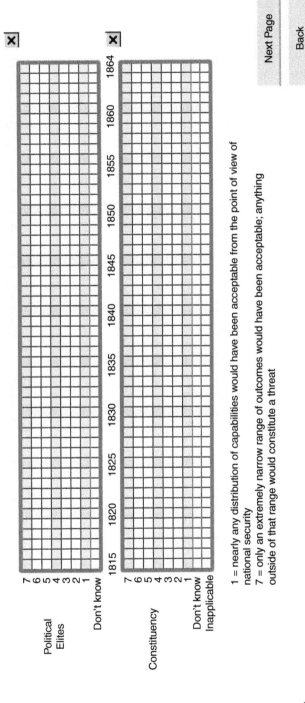

1 = nearly any distribution of capabilities would have been acceptable from the point of view of national security

7 = only an extremely narrow range of outcomes would have been acceptable; anything outside of that range would constitute a threat

Figure B.1. A sample question from the survey. Respondents were asked to indicate a starting value and points at which the value changed.

Table B.7. *Results of statistical tests*

1815–1914		
Balance of Power, OLS		
	β	se
L.term1UK	0.069	0.052
L.term1aUK	−0.196	0.343
L.term2Fr	−0.013	0.036
L.term2aFr	0.103	0.171
L.term3Pr	−0.075	0.066
L.term3aPr	0.026	0.446
L.term4Au	0.469	0.239
L.term4aAu	−0.860	0.432
L.term5Ru	0.009	0.018
L.term5aRu	0.010	0.057
constant	−0.005	0.004
Balance of Ideology, OLS		
	β	se
L.term1UK	−0.114	0.647
L.term1aUK	0.276	0.884
L.term2Fr	0.047	0.212
L.term2aFr	0.305	0.213
L.term3Pr	1.017	0.937
L.term3aPr	−0.402	0.432
L.term4Au	−0.011	0.393
L.term4aAu	−0.495	0.236
L.term5Ru	0.066	0.083
L.term5aRu	−0.074	0.082
constant	0.004	0.009
Activity of UK, OLS		
	β	se
L.term1aBOP	0.113	0.371
L.term1bBOP	−0.247	4.441
L.term1cBOP	−1.428	12.894
L.term2aLIB	−0.035	0.873
L.term2bLIB	−1.139	2.830
L.term2cLIB	1.480	2.344
L.activeUK	−0.366	0.105
crimeastUK	0.156	0.011
crimeaendUK	0.078	0.029
ww1	0.074	0.028
constant	0.215	0.057

Activity of France, OLS		
	β	se
L.term1aBOP	0.243	0.282
L.term1bBOP	−0.880	1.105
L.term1cBOP	2.258	1.697
L.term2aLIB	−0.904	0.514
L.term2bLIB	2.861	1.434
L.term2cLIB	−2.008	1.044
L.activeFr	−0.305	0.102
crimeastFr	−0.010	0.027
crimeaendFr	0.056	0.028
ww1	0.070	0.028
constant	0.103	0.040
Activity of Austria/A-H, OLS		
	β	se
L.term1aBOP	0.722	0.510
L.term1bBOP	−4.855	2.905
L.term1cBOP	8.869	4.400
L.term2aLIB	2.595	1.353
L.term2bLIB	−1.532	1.202
L.term2cLIB	0.506	0.377
L.activeAu	−0.288	0.071
ww1	0.151	0.011
constant	0.082	0.042
Activity of Prussia/Germany, OLS		
	β	se
L.term1aBOP	−0.255	0.410
L.term1bBOP	−0.739	0.824
L.term1cBOP	0.934	1.483
L.term2aLIB	0.971	1.654
L.term2bLIB	−2.912	2.514
L.term2cLIB	1.587	1.170
L.activePr	−0.159	0.132
ww1	0.034	0.019
constant	0.140	0.056
Activity of Russia, OLS		
	β	se
L.term1aBOP	−0.024	0.208
L.term1bBOP	0.190	0.725
L.term1cBOP	−0.852	0.879

Table B.7 *(continued)*

L.term2aLIB	1.501	0.460	LactiveUK	−0.383	0.095
L.term2bLIB	−2.516	0.822	crimeastUK	0.152	0.073
L.term2cLIB	0.922	0.362	crimeaendUK	0.092	0.075
L.activeRu	−0.061	0.033	ww1	0.130	0.077
crimeastRu	0.489	0.012	constant	0.216	0.063
crimeaendRu	−0.816	0.015	ActiveFr		
ww1	−0.063	0.014	L.term1aBOP	0.197	0.243
constant	0.031	0.040	L.term1bBOP	−0.842	1.244
3SLS Results			L.term1cBOP	3.521	2.557
	β	se	L.term2aLIB	−1.649	0.845
Power			L.term2bLIB	4.615	1.860
L.term1UK	0.084	0.069	L.term2cLIB	−2.767	1.238
L.term1aUK	−0.446	0.431	LactiveFr	−0.350	0.075
L.term2Fr	−0.082	0.052	crimeastFr	−0.031	0.075
L.term2aFr	0.047	0.115	crimeaendFr	0.070	0.071
L.term3Pr	0.023	0.134	ww1	0.092	0.073
L.term3aPr	−0.150	0.593	constant	0.092	0.044
L.term4Au	0.285	0.274	ActiveAu		
L.term4aAu	−0.490	0.492	L.term1aBOP	0.050	0.994
L.term5Ru	−0.013	0.041	L.term1bBOP	−1.572	5.185
L.term5aRu	0.054	0.066	L.term1cBOP	5.833	6.529
constant	−0.000	0.005	L.term2aLIB	2.386	1.059
Polity			L.term2bLIB	−1.334	0.949
L.term1UK	−0.516	0.571	L.term2cLIB	0.510	0.337
L.term1aUK	0.422	0.976	LactiveAu	−0.314	0.058
L.term2Fr	−0.167	0.249	ww1	0.226	0.060
L.term2aFr	0.587	0.539	constant	0.079	0.057
L.term3Pr	0.866	0.908	ActivePr		
L.term3aPr	−0.473	0.452	L.term1aBOP	−0.649	0.201
L.term4Au	−0.263	0.520	L.term1bBOP	0.849	0.838
L.term4aAu	−0.324	0.388	L.term1cBOP	−0.276	1.461
L.term5Ru	0.092	0.116	L.term2aLIB	1.635	1.575
L.term5aRu	−0.127	0.129	L.term2bLIB	−3.948	1.658
constant	0.014	0.007	L.term2cLIB	2.096	0.516
ActiveUK			LactivePr	−0.035	0.100
L.term1aBOP	0.068	0.370	ww1	0.146	0.036
L.term1bBOP	−0.175	4.408	constant	0.054	0.054
L.term1cBOP	−0.577	12.732	ActiveRu		
L.term2aLIB	0.290	0.907	L.term1aBOP	0.061	0.166
L.term2bLIB	−2.508	2.704	L.term1bBOP	−0.164	0.665
L.term2cLIB	2.752	2.123	L.term1cBOP	−0.580	0.788

(continued)

Table B.7 *(continued)*

	β	se		β	se
L.term2aLIB	1.472	0.331	crimeastUK	0.148	0.020
L.term2bLIB	−2.355	0.566	crimeaendUK	0.093	0.032
L.term2cLIB	0.778	0.220	ww1	0.148	0.041
LactiveRu	−0.066	0.026	constant	0.218	0.055
crimeastRu	0.504	0.039	ActiveFr		
crimeaendRu	−0.770	0.040	L.term1aBOP	0.162	0.263
ww1	−0.049	0.047	L.term1bBOP	−0.634	0.982
constant	0.032	0.028	L.term1cBOP	3.140	1.726
FIML, robust SEs			L.term2aLIB	−1.573	0.582
	β	se	L.term2bLIB	4.546	1.498
Power			L.term2cLIB	−2.774	1.024
L.term1UK	0.075	0.050	LactiveFr	−0.357	0.109
L.term1aUK	−0.389	0.302	crimeastFr	−0.029	0.037
L.term2Fr	−0.081	0.045	crimeaendFr	0.071	0.041
L.term2aFr	0.043	0.177	ww1	0.107	0.032
L.term3Pr	0.031	0.120	constant	0.099	0.040
L.term3aPr	−0.190	0.710	ActiveAu		
L.term4Au	0.292	0.234	L.term1aBOP	0.134	0.776
L.term4aAu	−0.496	0.421	L.term1bBOP	−2.067	4.017
L.term5Ru	−0.011	0.025	L.term1cBOP	6.530	5.146
L.term5aRu	0.054	0.050	L.term2aLIB	2.348	1.130
constant	−0.000	0.005	L.term2bLIB	−1.299	1.020
Polity			L.term2cLIB	0.494	0.349
L.term1UK	−0.572	0.461	LactiveAu	−0.324	0.076
L.term1aUK	0.495	0.797	ww1	0.240	0.035
L.term2Fr	−0.164	0.221	constant	0.086	0.047
L.term2aFr	0.589	0.486	ActivePr		
L.term3Pr	0.859	1.025	L.term1aBOP	−0.592	0.244
L.term3aPr	−0.473	0.525	L.term1bBOP	0.824	0.992
L.term4Au	−0.270	0.412	L.term1cBOP	−0.237	1.663
L.term4aAu	−0.361	0.276	L.term2aLIB	1.183	2.451
L.term5Ru	0.086	0.073	L.term2bLIB	−3.397	2.705
L.term5aRu	−0.131	0.125	L.term2cLIB	1.887	0.809
constant	0.015	0.009	LactivePr	−0.057	0.118
ActiveUK			ww1	0.148	0.028
L.term1aBOP	0.022	0.414	constant	0.062	0.056
L.term1bBOP	0.224	5.041	ActiveRu		
L.term1cBOP	−1.440	14.501	L.term1aBOP	0.080	0.182
L.term2aLIB	0.302	0.816	L.term1bBOP	−0.278	0.595
L.term2bLIB	−2.645	2.704	L.term1cBOP	−0.553	0.889
L.term2cLIB	2.914	2.293	L.term2aLIB	1.430	0.391
LactiveUK	−0.386	0.100	L.term2bLIB	−2.241	0.689

Table B.7 *(continued)*

	β	se			β	se
L.term2cLIB	0.731	0.236		Arms Levels, OLS		
LactiveRu	−0.067	0.028			β	se
crimeastRu	0.500	0.015		L.term1UK	37.440	40.343
crimeaendRu	−0.737	0.037		L.term1aUK	−0.000	0.000
ww1	−0.054	0.018		L.term2Fr	51.230	37.917
constant	0.035	0.033		L.term2aFr	−0.000	0.000
1918–1940				L.term3Ge	46.499	73.337
Balance of Power, OLS				L.term3aGe	−0.000	0.000
	β	se		L.term4It	−60.532	31.116
L.term1UK	12.704	31.626		L.term4aIt	0.000	0.000
L.term1aUK	−22.363	110.749		L.term5Ru	−105.432	174.121
L.term2Fr	4.212	28.959		L.term5aRu	0.000	0.000
L.term2aFr	−27.215	80.263		L.term6US	−119.681	34.019
L.term3Ge	2.321	3.302		L.term6aUS	0.000	0.000
L.term3aGe	−29.294	60.256		depression	0.002	0.069
L.term4It	−27.744	21.336		ww1	12.057	11.211
L.term4aIt	66.777	189.000		ww2	0.541	1.127
L.term5Ru	10.274	29.201		constant	0.982	1.007
L.term5aRu	17.881	17.148		Activity of UK, OLS		
L.term6US	−15.104	13.694			β	se
L.term6aUS	13.217	64.957		L.term1aBOP	0.324	0.884
depression	0.011	0.040		L.term1bBOP	12.070	12.605
ww1	1.510	3.503		L.term1cBOP	−3.034	4.977
ww2	0.164	0.294		L.term2aLIB	−0.591	11.338
constant	0.334	0.266		L.term2bLIB	−4.583	14.768
Balance of Ideology, OLS				L.term2cLIB	3.091	4.483
	β	se		L.term3aARMS	1.596	0.924
L.term1UK	−39.151	38.140		L.term3bARMS	−0.000	0.000
L.term1aUK	18.939	31.499		L.term3cARMS	0.000	0.000
L.term2Fr	6.851	8.528		L.activeUK	−0.735	0.314
L.term2aFr	−3.575	7.392		depression	0.006	0.013
L.term3Ge	−9.112	9.066		ww1	−0.012	0.331
L.term3aGe	8.210	6.663		ww2	0.056	0.093
L.term4It	−10.406	23.295		constant	0.273	0.220
L.term4aIt	−15.697	10.404		Activity of France, OLS		
L.term5Ru	5.428	8.193			β	se
L.term5aRu	−11.475	12.135		L.term1aBOP	5.925	3.961
L.term6US	11.009	7.604		L.term1bBOP	25.372	6.904
L.term6aUS	−6.002	6.163		L.term1cBOP	−7.055	1.820
depression	0.005	0.020		L.term2aLIB	4.754	4.142
ww1	−0.072	0.035		L.term2bLIB	−2.231	5.958
ww2	0.025	0.025		L.term2cLIB	1.689	2.079
constant	0.215	0.183		L.term3aARMS	2.490	0.320

(continued)

Table B.7 *(continued)*

L.term3bARMS	0.000	0.000		Activity of Russia/USSR, OLS		
L.term3cARMS	0.000	0.000			β	se
L.activeFr	−7.933	0.961		L.term1aBOP	−6.089	1.592
depression	0.024	0.012		L.term1bBOP	4.424	1.745
ww1	−0.319	0.081		L.term1cBOP	−2.235	2.650
ww2	−0.090	0.055		L.term2aLIB	3.102	1.791
constant	3.167	0.382		L.term2bLIB	−9.263	4.559
Activity of Germany, OLS				L.term2cLIB	6.021	3.266
	β	se		L.term3aARMS	−8.033	1.974
L.term1aBOP	1.611	2.270		L.term3bARMS	0.000	0.000
L.term1bBOP	4.979	10.023		L.term3cARMS	−0.000	0.000
L.term1cBOP	−13.825	27.665		L.activeRu	−0.526	0.264
L.term2aLIB	−29.097	32.319		depression	0.090	0.013
L.term2bLIB	38.816	40.998		ww1	−0.281	0.095
L.term2cLIB	−14.683	13.443		ww2	0.052	0.060
L.term3aARMS	−0.258	1.859		constant	0.915	0.227
L.term3bARMS	−0.000	0.000		Activity of USA, OLS		
L.term3cARMS	0.000	0.000			β	se
L.activeGe	−1.084	0.362		L.term1aBOP	1.012	0.786
depression	−0.032	0.075		L.term1bBOP	1.728	1.770
ww1	−0.234	1.750		L.term1cBOP	−0.895	2.076
ww2	0.026	0.309		L.term2aLIB	−2.141	2.521
constant	0.795	0.483		L.term2bLIB	2.303	3.608
Activity of Italy, OLS				L.term2cLIB	0.038	1.496
	β	se		L.term3aARMS	0.502	2.186
L.term1aBOP	−2.701	2.120		L.term3bARMS	−0.000	0.000
L.term1bBOP	36.422	13.059		L.term3cARMS	0.000	0.000
L.term1cBOP	−66.105	21.337		L.activeUS	−0.811	0.491
L.term2aLIB	7.235	5.304		depression	0.029	0.017
L.term2bLIB	−12.099	7.658		ww1	−0.699	0.233
L.term2cLIB	2.259	1.831		ww2	−0.038	0.017
L.term3aARMS	−1.012	0.746		constant	0.050	0.063
L.term3bARMS	0.000	0.000		3SLS Results		
L.term3cARMS	0.000	0.000			β	se
L.activeIt	−2.000	1.169		RpowGe		
depression	−0.015	0.019		L.term1UK	30.586	8.802
ww1	0.007	0.564		L.term1aUK	−28.862	28.168
ww2	−0.105	0.153		L.term2Fr	−3.057	8.195
constant	2.101	1.250		L.term2aFr	−15.180	11.454

Table B.7 *(continued)*

L.term3Ge	1.980	0.912	depression	−0.035	0.104
L.term3aGe	−47.065	16.365	ww1	−0.679	0.804
L.term4It	−33.552	12.431	ww2	−0.171	0.184
L.term4aIt	56.584	53.404	constant	1.897	0.433
L.term5Ru	11.535	7.786	ActiveUK		
L.term5aRu	28.325	8.439	L.term1aBOP	0.935	1.155
L.term6US	−13.782	4.090	L.term1bBOP	−9.783	5.161
L.term6aUS	16.490	18.582	L.term1cBOP	3.770	3.523
depression	0.010	0.025	L.term2aLIB	25.597	6.098
ww1	2.223	0.953	L.term2bLIB	−38.511	9.046
ww2	0.225	0.070	L.term2cLIB	14.482	3.317
constant	0.260	0.089	L.term3aARMS	1.597	0.891
Polity			L.term3bARMS	−1.403	0.513
L.term1UK	−47.734	11.691	L.term3cARMS	0.292	0.094
L.term1aUK	18.548	7.019	LactiveUK	−1.025	0.221
L.term2Fr	1.918	6.377	depression	0.028	0.025
L.term2aFr	1.381	5.168	ww1	−0.293	0.260
L.term3Ge	−9.033	2.146	ww2	0.086	0.037
L.term3aGe	9.951	1.396	constant	0.473	0.132
L.term4It	3.141	12.805	ActiveFr		
L.term4aIt	−11.765	3.395	L.term1aBOP	7.218	2.600
L.term5Ru	9.117	2.579	L.term1bBOP	2.012	2.779
L.term5aRu	−17.522	3.958	L.term1cBOP	−2.559	0.820
L.term6US	18.173	5.555	L.term2aLIB	25.856	2.449
L.term6aUS	−7.973	3.677	L.term2bLIB	−29.757	3.081
depression	0.004	0.017	L.term2cLIB	12.241	1.166
ww1	−0.023	0.031	L.term3aARMS	2.829	0.233
ww2	0.012	0.019	L.term3bARMS	−0.321	0.071
constant	−0.002	0.104	L.term3cARMS	0.110	0.022
ArmsLevel			LactiveFr	−9.991	0.671
L.term1UK	58.786	29.128	depression	0.041	0.010
L.term1aUK	1.016	11.356	ww1	−0.175	0.021
L.term2Fr	4.735	13.445	ww2	−0.042	0.013
L.term2aFr	−15.650	7.205	constant	3.994	0.267
L.term3Ge	−31.413	19.239	ActiveGe		
L.term3aGe	5.820	9.208	L.term1aBOP	1.747	0.851
L.term4It	−56.277	27.964	L.term1bBOP	−5.124	2.040
L.term4aIt	34.453	20.036	L.term1cBOP	15.283	5.142
L.term5Ru	94.039	49.975	L.term2aLIB	−43.354	7.626
L.term5aRu	−11.704	10.737	L.term2bLIB	56.924	9.842
L.term6US	−69.252	18.250	L.term2cLIB	−21.221	3.330
L.term6aUS	−4.165	4.285	L.term3aARMS	2.277	1.089

(continued)

Table B.7 *(continued)*

L.term3bARMS	−1.214	0.731
L.term3cARMS	0.104	0.147
LactiveGe	−1.035	0.211
depression	−0.023	0.057
ww1	1.510	0.321
ww2	0.108	0.068
constant	1.106	0.223
ActiveIt		
L.term1aBOP	−9.128	1.978
L.term1bBOP	−1.737	3.755
L.term1cBOP	6.389	6.729
L.term2aLIB	21.384	4.045
L.term2bLIB	−29.632	5.443
L.term2cLIB	4.122	1.294
L.term3aARMS	−0.379	0.570
L.term3bARMS	−0.662	0.340
L.term3cARMS	0.088	0.062
LactiveIt	−1.743	0.781
depression	−0.037	0.027
ww1	0.198	0.081
ww2	0.032	0.034
constant	3.593	0.713
ActiveRu		
L.term1aBOP	−5.753	0.547
L.term1bBOP	9.134	0.875
L.term1cBOP	−2.578	0.505
L.term2aLIB	−1.039	0.516
L.term2bLIB	1.240	1.449
L.term2cLIB	−0.676	0.963
L.term3aARMS	8.362	3.777
L.term3bARMS	−4.143	1.132
L.term3cARMS	0.426	0.088
LactiveRu	−0.447	0.058
depression	0.072	0.011
ww1	−0.054	0.057
ww2	0.096	0.013
constant	0.789	0.100
ActiveUS		
L.term1aBOP	2.974	0.505
L.term1bBOP	−7.702	1.266
L.term1cBOP	9.463	1.067

L.term2aLIB	6.875	2.153
L.term2bLIB	−10.057	2.999
L.term2cLIB	4.927	1.204
L.term3aARMS	−1.381	1.227
L.term3bARMS	−1.058	0.364
L.term3cARMS	0.115	0.040
LactiveUS	−1.335	0.279
depression	0.062	0.015
ww1	−0.340	0.051
ww2	−0.041	0.015
constant	0.110	0.061
1945–1991 Balance of Power, OLS		
	β	se
L.term1US	0.475	0.294
L.term1aUS	−0.502	0.294
L.term2SU	−0.103	0.630
L.term2aSU	−0.350	0.562
cwend	−0.006	0.014
constant	0.011	0.037
Balance of Ideology, OLS		
	β	se
L.term1US	0.172	0.068
L.term1aUS	−0.360	0.146
L.term2SU	3.108	0.877
L.term2aSU	−1.941	0.554
cwend	0.087	0.012
constant	0.090	0.037
Arms Levels, OLS		
	β	se
L.term1US	−1.668	0.683
L.term1aUS	−0.000	0.000
L.term2SU	4.451	2.737
L.term2aSU	−0.000	0.000
cwend	0.110	0.087
constant	0.593	0.154
Activity of USA, OLS		
	β	se
L.term1aBOP	1.790	1.294
L.term1bBOP	−3.600	2.848
L.term1cBOP	2.106	1.557

Table B.7 *(continued)*

	β	se		β	se
L.term2aLIB	2.639	1.598	L.term1aUS	−0.205	0.050
L.term2bLIB	−6.414	3.656	L.term2SU	4.302	1.428
L.term2cLIB	3.397	1.962	L.term2aSU	−0.454	0.098
L.term3aARMS	−0.097	0.108	cwend	0.099	0.123
L.term3bARMS	0.000	0.000	constant	0.610	0.071
L.term3cARMS	−0.000	0.000	ActiveUS		
L.activeUS	−0.460	0.202	L.term1aBOP	0.718	0.843
cwend	0.063	0.035	L.term1bBOP	−1.548	1.832
constant	0.387	0.168	L.term1cBOP	0.653	1.058
Activity of USSR, OLS			L.term2aLIB	1.079	0.952
	β	se	L.term2bLIB	−2.048	2.269
L.term1aBOP	1.885	1.786	L.term2cLIB	1.066	1.220
L.term1bBOP	−3.692	3.492	L.term3aARMS	0.027	0.312
L.term1cBOP	1.331	1.773	L.term3bARMS	−0.012	0.051
L.term2aLIB	15.045	8.004	L.term3cARMS	−0.001	0.002
L.term2bLIB	−11.852	6.426	LactiveUS	−0.381	0.145
L.term2cLIB	2.338	1.360	cwend	0.044	0.037
L.term3aARMS	0.248	0.183	constant	0.307	0.131
L.term3bARMS	0.000	0.000	ActiveSU		
L.term3cARMS	−0.000	0.000	L.term1aBOP	−0.080	1.940
L.activeSU	−0.366	0.132	L.term1bBOP	−0.121	3.580
cwend	0.038	0.013	L.term1cBOP	−0.213	1.747
constant	0.282	0.096	L.term2aLIB	7.753	7.925
3SLS Results			L.term2bLIB	−6.538	5.941
	β	se	L.term2cLIB	1.557	1.185
BOP			L.term3aARMS	0.791	0.676
L.term1US	0.482	0.262	L.term3bARMS	−0.042	0.069
L.term1aUS	−0.479	0.257	L.term3cARMS	−0.000	0.003
L.term2SU	0.315	0.659	LactiveSU	−0.338	0.104
L.term2aSU	−0.822	0.765	cwend	0.025	0.041
cwend	−0.009	0.033	constant	0.195	0.093
constant	0.009	0.035	**FIML, robust SEs**		
Polity				β	se
L.term1US	0.094	0.082	BOP		
L.term1aUS	−0.259	0.109	L.term1US	0.544	0.360
L.term2SU	3.561	0.688	L.term1aUS	−0.539	0.355
L.term2aSU	−2.215	0.412	L.term2SU	0.328	0.414
cwend	0.080	0.020	L.term2aSU	−0.826	0.593
constant	0.097	0.037	cwend	−0.010	0.017
ArmsLevel			constant	0.006	0.048
L.term1US	1.082	0.446	Polity		

(continued)

Table B.7 *(continued)*

L.term1US	0.095	0.129		L.term2cLIB	0.914	1.917
L.term1aUS	−0.243	0.213		L.term3aARMS	0.016	0.261
L.term2SU	3.746	1.311		L.term3bARMS	−0.011	0.042
L.term2aSU	−2.313	0.828		L.term3cARMS	−0.001	0.002
cwend	0.078	0.024		LactiveUS	−0.375	0.207
constant	0.094	0.028		cwend	0.041	0.022
ArmsLevel				constant	0.291	0.161
L.term1US	1.133	0.450		ActiveSU		
L.term1aUS	−0.207	0.041		L.term1aBOP	0.287	3.734
L.term2SU	4.200	1.818		L.term1bBOP	−0.678	6.723
L.term2aSU	−0.455	0.127		L.term1cBOP	−0.025	3.111
cwend	0.100	0.047		L.term2aLIB	9.065	7.680
constant	0.614	0.094		L.term2bLIB	−7.959	5.471
ActiveUS				L.term2cLIB	1.991	1.039
L.term1aBOP	0.712	1.085		L.term3aARMS	0.634	0.729
L.term1bBOP	−1.530	2.290		L.term3bARMS	−0.024	0.074
L.term1cBOP	0.650	1.313		L.term3cARMS	−0.001	0.002
L.term2aLIB	0.962	1.499		LactiveSU	−0.347	0.095
L.term2bLIB	−1.759	3.565		cwend	0.028	0.008

A note on variable names: It would take up too much space to reproduce the variable names in the tables directly from the model. Each cluster of independent variables has a set structure that can be easily inferred from the equations on page 226. For actor-level equations the variables are structured in clusters of three. For the UK in the 19th century, for example,

$$\text{term1aBOP} = \omega_{UKBOP} v_{UK} (c_{UKBOP})^2$$
$$\text{term1bBOP} = \omega_{UKBOP} [2v_{UK}(c_{UKBOP})s_{BOP}]$$
$$\text{term1cBOP} = \omega_{UKBOP} s_{BOP}^2$$
$$\text{term2aLIB} = \omega_{UKLIB} v_{UK} (c_{UKLIB})^2$$
$$\text{term2bLIB} = \omega_{UKLIB} [2v_{UK}(c_{UKLIB})s_{LIB}]$$
$$\text{term2cLIB} = \omega_{UKLIB} s_{LIB}^2$$

and for structural equations (in this case, the 19th-century balance of power), in clusters of two:

$$\text{term1UK} = \pi_{UK} \omega_{UKBOP} a_{UK} v_{UK} (c_{UKBOP})$$
$$\text{term1aUK} = \pi_{UK} \omega_{UKBOP} a_{UK} s_{BOP}$$
$$\text{term2Fr} = \pi_{Fr} \omega_{FrBOP} a_{Fr} v_{Fr} (c_{FrBOP})$$
$$\text{term2aFr} = \pi_{Fr} \omega_{FrBOP} a_{Fr} s_{BOP}$$
$$\text{term3Au} = \pi_{Au} \omega_{AuBOP} a_{Au} v_{Au} (c_{AuBOP})$$
$$\text{term3aAu} = \pi_{Au} \omega_{AuBOP} a_{Au} s_{BOP}$$
$$\text{term4Pr} = \pi_{Pr} \omega_{PrBOP} a_{Pr} v_{Pr} (c_{PrBOP})$$
$$\text{term4aPr} = \pi_{Pr} \omega_{PrBOP} a_{Pr} s_{BOP}$$
$$\text{term5Ru} = \pi_{Ru} \omega_{RuBOP} a_{Ru} v_{Ru} (c_{RuBOP})$$
$$\text{term5aRu} = \pi_{Ru} \omega_{RuBOP} a_{Ru} s_{BOP}$$

Bibliography

Abzug, Robert H. (1999). *America Views the Holocaust, 1933–1945: A Brief Documentary History*. Boston: Bedford/St. Martin's.

Achen, Christopher H. (1982). *Interpreting and Using Regression*. Thousand Oaks, CA: Sage.

Adler, Selig (1965). *The Uncertain Giant: 1921–1941*. London: Collier-Macmillan Ltd.

Alker Jr., Hayward R. (1970). Integration Logics: A Review, Extension, and Critique. *International Organization 24*(4), 869–914.

Allen, Grahame (2003, November 11, 2003). Inflation: The Value of the Pound 1750–2002. *House of Commons Library Research Papers* (03/82).

Allison, Graham T. (1988). Testing Gorbachev. *Foreign Affairs 67*(1), 18–32.

Allison, Roy (1992). Reasonable Sufficiency and Changes in Soviet Security Thinking. In Willard C. Frank and Philip S. Gillette (Eds.), *Soviet Military Doctrine from Lenin to Gorbachev, 1915–1991*, pp. 239–268. Westport, CT: Greenwood Press.

Almendingen, Edith Martha (1964). *The Emperor Alexander I*. New York: Vanguard Press.

Alperovitz, Gar (1994). *Atomic Diplomacy: Hiroshima and Potsdam: The Use of the Atomic Bomb and the American Confrontation with Soviet Power* (2nd expanded ed.). Boulder, CO: Pluto Press.

Altfield, Michael (1984). Measuring Issue-Distance and Polarity in the International System: A Preliminary Comparison of an Alliance and an Action Flow Indicator. *Political Methodology 10*(1), 29–66.

Ambrosius, Lloyd E. (1987). *Woodrow Wilson and the American Diplomatic Tradition*. Cambridge: Cambridge University Press.

Arbatov, Georgi A. (1992). *The System: An Insider's Life in Soviet Politics*. New York: Random House.

Archer, John E. (2000). *Social Unrest and Popular Protest in England, 1780–1840*. New Studies in Economic and Social History. New York: Cambridge University Press.

Aron, Raymond (1966). *Peace & War: A Theory of International Relations*. New York: Praeger.

Arrow, Kenneth (1951). *Social Choice and Individual Values*. New York: Wiley.

Artz, Frederick B. (1934). *Reaction and Revolution 1814–1832*. The Rise of Modern Europe. New York: Harper & Row.

Aspaturian, Vernon V. (1990). Gorbachev's "New Political Thinking" and Foreign Policy. In Jiri Valenta and Frank Cibulka (Eds.), *Gorbachev's New Thinking and Third World Conflicts*, pp. 3–44. New Brunswick, NJ: Transaction Books.

Attfield, C. L. F., D. Demery, and N. W. Duck (1991). *Rational Expectations in Economics.* Cambridge, MA: Blackwell.

Axelrod, Robert (Ed.) (1976). *Structure of Decision: The Cognitive Maps of Political Elites.* Princeton: Princeton University Press.

Axelrod, Robert (1984). *The Evolution of Cooperation.* New York: Basic Books.

Axelrod, Robert and D. Scott Bennett (1993). A Landscape Theory of Aggregation. *British Journal of Political Science 23*, 211–233.

Axelrod, Robert and Robert O. Keohane (1986). Achieving Cooperation under Anarchy: Strategies and Institutions. In Kenneth A. Oye (Ed.), *Cooperation under Anarchy,* pp. 226–254. Princeton, NJ: Princeton University Press.

Azar, Edward E (1982). *The Codebook of the Conflict and Peace Data Bank (COPDAB).* College Park, MD: Center for International Development, University of Maryland.

Bailey, Thomas A. and Paul B. Ryan (1979). *Hitler vs. Roosevelt: The Undeclared Naval War.* New York: Free Press.

Bankes, Steve (1993). Exploratory Modeling for Policy Analysis. *Operations Research 41*(3), 435–449.

Bariéty, Jacques (1977). *Les relations franco-allemandes après la Première-Guerre mondiale.* Paris: Editions Pedone.

Barnett, Vincent (1994). As Good as Gold? A Note on the Chervonets. *Europe-Asia Studies 46*(4), 663–669.

Bartels, Larry M. (2010). *Unequal Democracy: The Political Economy of the New Gilded Age.* Princeton, NJ: Princeton University Press.

Bartlett, Christopher (1979). Britain and the European Balance, 1815–48. In Alan Sked (Ed.), *Europe's Balance of Power, 1815–1848*, pp. 145–163. New York: Barnes & Noble.

Bartlett, C. J. (1993). *Defence and Diplomacy: Britain and the Great Powers 1815–1914.* New Frontiers in History. Manchester: Manchester University Press.

Bartlett, C. J. (1996). *Peace, War and the European Powers 1814–1914.* London: Macmillan.

Belanovsky, Sergei (1998). The Arms Race and the Burden of Military Expenditures. In Michael Ellman and Vladimir Kontorovich (Eds.), *The Destruction of the Soviet Economic System: An Insiders' History*, pp. 40–69. Armonk, NT: M. E. Sharpe.

Bell, P. M. H. (1997). *The Origins of the Second World War in Europe.* London and New York: Longman.

Bennett, Andrew (2005). The Guns That Didn't Smoke: Ideas and the Soviet Non-Use of Force in 1989. *Journal of Cold War Studies 7*(2), 81–109.

Benoit, Kenneth and Michael Laver (2007). Estimating Party Policy Positions: Comparing Expert Surveys and Hand-Coded Content Analysis. *Electoral Studies 26*(1), 90–107.

Bentham, Jeremy (1973[1823]). *An Introduction to the Principles of Morals and Legislation.* New York: Hafner Press.

Bergen, Peter (2002). *Holy War, Inc.: Inside the Secret World of Osama bin Laden.* New York: Free Press.

Bernhardi, Friedrich von (1914). *Germany and the Next War.* New York: Longmans, Green, and Co.

Bertalanffy, Ludwig von (1969). *General Systems Theory.* New York: Braziller.

Beschloss, Michael R. and Strobe Talbott (1993). *At the Highest Levels: The Inside Story of the End of the Cold War.* New York: Little, Brown and Company.

Bialer, Seweryn (1986). *The Soviet Paradox: External Expansion, Internal Decline*. New York: Alfred A. Knopf.

Binmore, Ken (1998). *Game Theory and the Social Contract II: Just Playing*. Cambridge, MA: MIT Press.

Black, Duncan (1958). *The Theory of Committees and Elections*. Cambridge: Cambridge University Press.

Blauberg, Igor Viktorovich, Vadim Nikolayevich Sadovsky, and Erik Grigoryevitch Yudin (1977). *Teoria System: Filosofskii i Metodologicheskie Problemi*. Moscow: Progress.

Bodkin, Ronald G., Lawrence R. Klein, and Kanta Marwah (1991). *A History of Macroeconometric Modelling*. Vermont: Edward Elgar Publishing.

Borges, Jorge Luis (1998). Of Exactitude in Science. In *Collected Fictions*. New York: Viking.

Bourne, Kenneth (1970). *The Foreign Policy of Victorian England 1830–1902*. Oxford: Clarendon Press.

Brainard, William C. (1967). Uncertainty and the Effectiveness of Policy. *American Economic Review 57*(2), 411–425.

Braumoeller, Bear F. (2008). Systemic Politics and the Origins of Great Power Rivalry. *American Political Science Review 102*(1), 77–93.

Braumoeller, Bear F. (2010a). The Myth of American Isolationism. *Foreign Policy Analysis 6*, 349.

Braumoeller, Bear F. (2010b). Understanding System Dynamics: Simple Models of Complexity. In Mathias Albert, Lars-Erik Cederman, and Alexander Wendt (Eds.), *New Systems Theories of World Politics*, pp. 158–191. Palgrave.

Bremer, Stuart (1977). *Simulated Worlds: A Computer Model of National Decision-Making*. Princeton, NJ: Princeton University Press.

Bremer, Stuart (1987). *The GLOBUS Model: Computer Simulation of Worldwide Political and Economic Developments*. Boulder, CO: Westview Press.

Bremer, Stuart and Michael Mihalka (1977). Machiavelli in Machina: Or Politics among Hexagons. In Karl W. Deutsch, Bruno Fritsch, Helio Jaguaribe, and Andrei S. Markovits (Eds.), *Problems of World Modeling: Political and Social Implications*, pp. 308–338. Cambridge: Ballinger Publishing.

Brewer, David (2001). *The Greek War of Independence: The Struggle for Freedom from Ottoman Oppression and the Birth of the Modern Greek Nation*. New York: Overlook Press.

Bridge, F. R. and Roger Bullen (1980). *The Great Powers and the European States System 1815–1914*. New York: Longman.

Broder, John M. (1998, May 2). Clinton Predicts a Safer and Richer Europe *New York Times*.

Brooks, Stephen G. and William Wohlforth (2007). Clarifying the End of Cold War Debate. *Cold War History 7*(3), 447–454.

Broszat, Martin (1981). *The Hitler State: The Foundation and Development of the Internal Structure of the Third Reich*. London: Longman.

Brovkin, Vladimir N. (1990). The Making of Elections to the Congress of People's Deputies (CPD) in March 1989. *Russian Review 49*(4), 417–442.

Brown, Archie (1996). *The Gorbachev Factor*. New York: Oxford University Press.

Brown, Archie (2007). *Seven Years that Changed the World: Perestroika in Perspective*. New York: Oxford University Press.

Brown, Courtney (1993). Nonlinear Transformation in a Landslide: Johnson and Goldwater in 1964. *American Journal of Political Science 37*(2), 582–609.

Brown, David (2002). Lord Palmerston. *Historian* (76), 33–36.

Brown, Mark (1978). The Comité Franco-Polonais and the French Reaction to the Polish Uprising of November 1830. *English Historical Review 93*(369), 774–793.

Brown, Michael E. (Ed.) (2000). *The Rise of China*. Cambridge, MA: MIT Press.

Bruner, Jerome S. (1944). *Mandate from the People*. New York: Duell, Sloan and Pearce.

Brutents, Karen (2006). Origins of the New Thinking. *Russian Social Science Review 47*(1), 73–102.

Budge, Ian (2001). Validating Party Policy Placements. *British Journal of Political Science 31*(1), 210–223.

Bueno de Mesquita, Bruce (1998). The End of the Cold War: Predicting an Emergent Property. *Journal of Conflict Resolution 42*(2), 131–155.

Bueno de Mesquita, Bruce, James D. Morrow, Randolph M. Siverson, and Alastair Smith (1999). An Institutional Explanation for the Democratic Peace. *American Political Science Review 93*(4), 791–807.

Bueno de Mesquita, Bruce, Alastair Smith, Randolph M. Siverson, and James D. Morrow (2003). *The Logic of Political Survival*. Cambridge, MA: MIT Press.

Bull, Hedley and Adam Watson (Eds.) (1984). *The Expansion of International Society*. Oxford: Oxford University Press.

Bullen, Roger (1977). France and the Problem of Intervention in Spain, 1834–1836. *Historical Journal 20*(2), 363–393.

Bulwer, Sir Henry Lytton (1871). *The Life of Henry John Temple, Viscount Palmerston: with Selections from his Diaries and Correspondence* (3rd ed.), Volume 3. London: Richard Bentley.

Bumiller, Elisabeth (2009). With Boots in Iraq, Minds Drift to Afghanistan. *New York Times*, A–1.

Bush, George H. W. and Brent Scowcroft (1998). *A World Transformed*. New York: Knopf.

Butterfield, Herbert (1966). The Balance of Power. In Herbert Butterfield and Martin Wight (Eds.), *Diplomatic Investigations: Essays in the Theory of International Politics*, pp. 132–148. Cambridge, MA: Harvard University Press.

Buzan, Barry, Charles Jones, and Richard Little (1993). *The Logic of Anarchy: Neorealism to Structural Realism*. New York: Columbia University Press.

Byman, Daniel L. and Kenneth M. Pollack (2001). Let Us Now Praise Great Men: Bringing the Statesman Back In. *International Security 25*(4), 107–146.

Cameron, A. Colin and Pravin K. Trivedi (2005). *Microeconometrics: Methods and Applications*. Cambridge: Cambridge University Press.

Campbell, David (1998). *Writing Security: United States Foreign Policy and the Politics of Identity* (revised ed.). Minneapolis: University of Minnesota Press.

Cantril, Hadley (1948). Opinion Trends in World War II: Some Guides to Interpretation. *Public Opinion Quarterly 12*(1), 30–44.

Cantril, Hadley (Ed.) (1951). *Public Opinion 1935–1946*. Princeton, NJ: Princeton University Press.

Caramani, Daniele (2000). *Elections in Western Europe since 1815: Electoral Results by Constituencies*. London: Macmillan.

Carlsnaes, Walter (1992). The Agency-Structure Problem in Foreign Policy Analysis. *International Studies Quarterly 36*(3), 245–270.

Carr, Edward Hallett (1939). *The Twenty Years' Crisis, 1919–1939: An Introduction to the Study of International Relations*. New York: Harper and Row.

Casey, Steven (2001). *Cautious Crusade: Franklin D. Roosevelt, American Public Opinion, and the War against Nazi Germany*. New York: Oxford University Press.

Cederman, Lars-Erik (1997). *Emergent Actors in World Politics*. Princeton, NJ: Princeton University Press.

Cederman, Lars-Erik (2001). Agent-Based Modeling in Political Science. *The Political Methodologist 10*(1), 16–22.

Cerny, Philip G. (1990). *The Changing Architecture of Politics*. London: Sage Publications.

Chafetz, Glenn, Michael Spirtas, and Benjamin Frankel (1999a). Introduction: Tracing the Influence of Identity on Foreign Policy. In Glenn Chafetz, Michael Spirtas, and Benjamin Frankel (Eds.), *The Origins of National Interests*, pp. vii–xxii. Portland, OR: Frank Cass.

Chafetz, Glenn, Michael Spirtas, and Benjamin Frankel (Eds.) (1999b). *The Origins of National Interests*. Portland, OR: Frank Cass.

Chan, Steve (2005). Is There a Power Transition between the U.S. and China? The Different Faces of National Power. *Asian Survey 45*(5), 687–701.

Checkel, Jeffrey (1993). Ideas, Institutions, and the Gorbachev Foreign Policy Revolution. *World Politics 45*(2), 271–300.

Checkel, Jeffrey T. (1997). *Ideas and International Political Change: Soviet/Russian Behavior and the End of the Cold War*. New Haven: Yale University Press.

Checkel, Jeffrey T. (1998). The Constructivist Turn in International Relations Theory. *World Politics 50*(2), 324–348.

Checkel, Jeffrey T. (Ed.) (2007). *International Institutions and Socialization in Europe*. New York: Cambridge University Press.

Chernyaev, Anatoly (2000). *My Six Years with Gorbachev*. University Park: Pennsylvania State University Press.

Chittick, William O., Kieth R. Billingsley, and Rick Travis (1995). A Three-Dimensional Model of American Foreign Policy Beliefs. *International Studies Quarterly 39*, 313–331.

Chollet, Derek and James M. Goldgeier (2003). Once Burned, Twice Shy? The Pause of 1989. In William C. Wohlforth (Ed.), *Cold War Endgame: Oral History, Analysis, Debates*, pp. 141–173. University Park: Pennsylvania State University Press.

Chu, Chia-Shang, Kurt Hornik, and Chung-Ming Kuan (1995). MOSUM Tests for Parameter Constancy. *Biometrika 82*(3), 603–617.

Churchill, Winston S. (1959). *Memoirs of the Second World War*. Boston: Houghton Mifflin.

Clarke, Kevin A. and David M. Primo (2005). Modernizing Political Science: A Model-Based Approach. Presented at the *Annual Meeting of the Midwest Political Science Association*, Chicago.

Claude, Inis L. (1962). *Power and International Relations*. New York: Random House.

Cobden, Richard (1867). *Political Writings, Volume 1*. London: William Ridgway.

Cohen, Warren I. (1987). *Empire without Tears: America's Foreign Relations, 1921–1933*. New York: McGraw-Hill.

Cole, H. S. D., Christopher Freeman, Marie Jahoda, and K. L. R. Pavitt (1973). *Models of Doom: A Critique of the Limits of Growth*. New York: Universe Books.

Coll, Steve (2004). *Ghost Wars: The Secret History of the CIA, Afghanistan, and bin Laden, from the Soviet Invasion to September 10, 2001*. New York: Penguin Press.

Conant, Jennet (2002). *Tuxedo Park: A Wall Street Tycoon and the Secret Palace of Science That Changed the Course of World War II*. New York: Simon & Schuster.

Condorcet, Marie-Jean-Antoine-Nicolas, Marquis de (1976/1785). Essay on the Application of Mathematics to the Theory of Decision Making. In Keith M. Baker (Ed.), *Condorcet: Selected Writings*, pp. 33, 48–50. Indianapolis, IN: Bobbs-Merrill.

Converse, Philip (1964). The Nature of Belief Systems in Mass Publics. In David Apter (Ed.), *Ideology and Discontent*, pp. 206–261. New York: Free Press.

Conybeare, John A. C. (1994). Arms versus Alliances. *Journal of Conflict Resolution 38*(2), 215–235.

Cooley, Francis Rexford (1998). From Isolationism to Interventionism in Maine, 1939–1941. *Maine History 37*(4), 210–225.

Copeland, Dale C. (2000). *The Origins of Major War*. Ithaca: Cornell University Press.

Costigliola, Frank (1984). *Awkward Dominion: American Political, Economic, and Cultural Relations with Europe, 1919–1933*. Ithaca: Cornell University Press.

Craig, Gordon A. and Alexander L. George (1983). *Force and Statecraft: Diplomatic Problems of Our Time*. New York: Oxford University Press.

Croco, Sarah E. and Tze Kwang Teo (2005). Assessing the Dyadic Approach to Interstate Conflict Processes: A.k.a. "Dangerous" Dyad-Years. *Conflict Management and Peace Science 22*(1), 5–18.

Cusack, Thomas R. and Richard Stoll (1990). *Exploring Realpolitik: Probing International Relations Theory with Computer Simulation*. Boulder, CO: Lynne Rienner.

Dangerfield, George (1997). *The Strange Death of Liberal England*. Stanford: Stanford University Press.

Danilovic, Vesna (2002). *When the Stakes Are High: Deterrence and Conflict among Major Powers*. Ann Arbor: University of Michigan Press.

Davis, Richard W. (1999). The House of Lords, the Whigs and Catholic Emancipation 1806–1829. *Parliamentary History 18*(1), 23–43.

Deist, Wilhelm (1990). The Rearmament of the Wehrmacht. In Wilhelm Deist, Manfred Messerschmidt, Hans-Erich Volkmann, and Wolfram Wette (Eds.), *Germany and the Second World War*, Volume I, pp. 375–540. Oxford: Clarendon Press.

Dessler, David (1989). What's at Stake in the Agent-Structure Debate? *International Organization 43*(3), 441–473.

Deutsch, Karl W. (1966). *The Nerves of Government: Models of Political Communication and Control*. New York: Free Press.

Deutsch, Karl W. (1978). *The Analysis of International Relations*. Englewood Cliffs, NJ: Prentice-Hall.

Deutsch, Karl W. and J. David Singer (1964). Multipolar Power Systems and International Stability. *World Politics 16*, 390–406.

Diamond, Jared (1997). *Guns, Germs, and Steel: The Fates of Human Societies.* New York: W. W. Norton.

Dinwiddy, J. R. (1990). English Radicalism before the Chartists. *Modern History Review 2*(2), 2–4.

Divine, Robert A. (1979). *The Reluctant Belligerent: American Entry into World War II.* New York: John Wiley & Sons.

Dobrynin, Anatoly (1995). *In Confidence: Moscow's Ambassador to America's Six Cold War Presidents (1962–1986).* New York: Random House.

Doty, Roxanne Lynn (1993). Foreign Policy as Social Construction: A Post-Positivist Analysis of U.S. Counterinsurgency Policy in the Philippines. *International Studies Quarterly 37,* 297–320.

Doyle, Michael W. (1986). *Empires.* Ithaca: Cornell University Press.

Duch, Raymond M. (1993). Tolerating Economic Reform: Popular Support for Transition to a Free Market in the Former Soviet Union. *American Political Science Review 87*(3), 590–608.

Duroselle, Jean-Baptiste (1963). *From Wilson to Roosevelt: Foreign Policy of the United States 1913–1945.* Cambridge, MA: Harvard University Press.

Durr, Robert H. (1992). An Essay on Cointegration and Error Correction Models. *Political Analysis 4,* 185–228.

Easton, David (1965). *A Framework for Political Analysis.* Englewood Cliffs, NJ: Prentice-Hall.

The Economist (2009, May 23). The Art of Chinese Massage, p. 72.

Ellis, Harold A. (1979). Aristocratic Influence and Electoral Independence: The Whig Model of Parliamentary Reform 1792–1832. *Journal of Modern History (On Demand Supplement) 51*(4), D1251–D1276.

Ellis, John (1993). *World War II: A Statistical Survey: The Essential Facts and Figures for All the Combatants.* New York: Facts on File.

Enelow, James M. and Melvin J. Hinich (1984). *The Spatial Theory of Voting: An Introduction.* Cambridge: Cambridge University Press.

English, Robert D. (2000). *Russia and the Idea of the West: Gorbachev, Intellectuals, and the End of the Cold War.* New York: Columbia University Press.

Erikson, Erik H. (1968). *Identity: Youth and Crisis.* New York: Norton.

Ermarth, Fritz W. (1990, May). The Russian Revolution and the Future Threat to the West. Central Intelligence Agency memorandum written for senior Bush administration officials concerned with the USSR.

Evangelista, Matthew (2001). Norms, Heresthetics, and the End of the Cold War. *Journal of Cold War Studies 3*(1), 5–35.

Evangelista, Matthew (2002). *Unarmed Forces: The Transnational Movement to End the Cold War.* Ithaca, NY: Cornell University Press.

Evangelista, Matthew (2004). Turning Points in Arms Control. In Richard K. Herrmann and Richard Ned Lebow (Eds.), *Ending the Cold War: Interpretations, Causation, and the Study of International Relations,* pp. 83–106. New York: Palgrave Macmillan.

Evans, Robert (1997). Soothsaying or Science? Falsification, Uncertainty, and Social Change in Macroeconometric Modelling. *Social Studies of Science 27*(3), 395–438.

Fearon, James D. (1995). Rationalist Explanations for War. *International Organization 49*(3), 379–414.

Fearon, James D. (1996). Counterfactuals and Causation in Social Science: Exploring an Analogy between Cellular Automata and Historical Processes. In Philip Tetlock and Aaron Belkin (Eds.), *Counterfactual Thought Experiments in World Politics*, pp. 39–67. Princeton, NJ: Princeton University Press.

Fearon, James D. (1998). Domestic Politics, Foreign Policy, and Theories of International Relations. *Annual Review of Political Science 1*, 289–313.

Feis, Herbert (1970). *From Trust to Terror: The Onset of the Cold War, 1945–1950*. New York: Norton.

Finer, Samuel E. (1997). *The History of Government from the Earliest Times*. Oxford: Oxford University Press.

Finkelstein, Norman G. and Ruth Bettina Birn (1998). *A Nation on Trial: The Goldhagen Thesis and Historical Truth*. New York: Henry Holt.

Fleming, Denna Frank (1961). *The Cold War and its Origins*. Garden City, NY: Doubleday.

Fraser, Peter (1961). Public Petitioning and Parliament before 1832. *History 46*(158), 195–211.

Frieden, Jeffrey A. (1999). Actors and Preferences in International Relations. In David A. Lake and Robert Powell (Eds.), *Strategic Choice and International Relations*, pp. 39–76. Princeton, NJ: Princeton University Press.

Friedman, Milton (1953). The Methodology of Positive Economics. In Milton Friedman (Ed.), *Essays in Positive Economics*, pp. 3–43. Chicago: University of Chicago Press.

Gaddis, John Lewis (1982). *Strategies of Containment: A Critical Appraisal of Postwar American National Security Policy*. New York: Oxford University Press.

Gaddis, John Lewis (1983). The Emerging Post-Revisionist Synthesis on the Origins of the Cold War. *Diplomatic History 7*(summer), 171–190.

Gaddis, John Lewis (1992–1993). International Relations Theory and the End of the Cold War. *International Security 17*(3), 5–58.

Gaddis, John Lewis (1997). *We Now Know*. New York: Oxford University Press.

Garthoff, Raymond L. (1994). *The Great Transition: American-Soviet Relations and the End of the Cold War*. Washington, DC: Brookings.

Geertz, Clifford (1973). *The Interpretation of Cultures*. New York: Basic Books.

Geller, Daniel S. and J. David Singer (1998). *Nations at War: A Scientific Study of International Conflict*. Cambridge: Cambridge University Press.

Gelpi, Christopher F. and Michael Griesdorf (2001). Winners or Losers? Democracies in International Crisis, 1918–94. *American Political Science Review 95*(3), 633–647.

Gerlach, Christian (1998). The Wannsee Conference, the Fate of German Jews, and Hitler's Decision in Principle to Exterminate All European Jews. *Journal of Modern History 70*(4), 759–812.

Gerring, John (2007). *Case Study Research: Principles and Practices*. New York: Cambridge University Press.

Gervasi, Tom (1986). *The Myth of Soviet Military Supremacy*. New York: Harper & Row.

Gholz, Eugene, Daryl G. Press, and Harvey M. Sapolsky (1997). Come Home, America: The Strategy of Restraint in the Face of Temptation. *International Security 21*(4), 5–48.

Giddens, Anthony (1979). *Central Problems in Social Theory: Action, Structure, and the Contradiction in Social Analysis.* Berkeley: University of California Press.

Giddens, Anthony (1984). *The Constitution of Society.* Berkeley: University of California Press.

Gill, Jeff (1999). The Insignificance of Null Hypothesis Significance Testing. *Political Research Quarterly 52*(3), 647–674.

Gillespie, John V., Dina A. Zinnes, G. S. Tahim, Philip A. Schrodt, and Michael Rubison (1977). An Optimal Control Model of Arms Races. *American Political Science Review 71*(1), 226–244.

Gilpin, Robert (1981). *War and Change in World Politics.* Cambridge: Cambridge University Press.

Goldhagen, Daniel Jonah (1996). *Hitler's Willing Executioners: Ordinary Germans and the Holocaust.* New York: Random House.

Goldstein, Joshua S. and John R. Freeman (1990). *Three-Way Street: Strategic Reciprocity in World Politics.* Chicago: University Of Chicago Press.

Goldstein, Judith and Robert O. Keohane (1993). Ideas and Foreign Policy: An Analytical Framework. In Judith Goldstein and Robert O. Keohane (Eds.), *Ideas and Foreign Policy: Beliefs, Institutions, and Political Change*, pp. 3–30. Ithaca: Cornell University Press.

Goodlad, Graham (2002). Liberal Toryism. *Modern History Review 14*(2), 4–8.

Gorbachev, Mikhail (1987). *Perestroika: New Thinking for Our Country and the World.* New York: Harper and Row.

Gordon, Michael R. (December 8, 1988). The Gorbachev Visit; Western Officials Term Troop Cuts Significant. *New York Times*, A–1.

Gourevitch, Peter (1978). The Second Image Reversed: The International Sources of Domestic Politics. *International Organization 32*(4), 881–912.

Grachev, Andrei (2008). *Gorbachev's Gamble: Soviet Foreign Policy and the End of the Cold War.* New York: John Wiley & Sons.

Grieco, Joseph M. (1997). Realist International Theory and the Study of World Politics. In Michael W. Doyle and G. John Ikenberry (Eds.), *New Thinking in International Relations Theory*, pp. 163–201. Boulder, CO: Westview Press.

Guetzkow, Harold and Joseph J. Valadez (Eds.) (1981). *Simulated International Processes: Theories and Research in Global Modeling.* Beverly Hills: Sage Publications.

Gulick, Edward Vose (1955). *Europe's Classical Balance of Power.* New York: W. W. Norton and Co.

Gurley, John G. (1976). *Challengers to Capitalism: Marx, Lenin, and Mao.* San Francisco: San Francisco Book Co.

Haas, Ernst B. (1953). The Balance of Power: Prescription, Concept, or Propaganda? *World Politics 5*, 442–477.

Haas, Mark L. (2007). The United States and the End of the Cold War: Reactions to Shifts in Soviet Power, Policies, or Domestic Politics? *International Organization 61*(1), 145–179.

Hahn, Gordon M. (1997). The first Reorganisation of the CPSU Central Committee Apparat under Perestroika. *Europe-Asia Studies 49*(2), 281–302.

Haight Jr., John McVickar (1970). *American Aid to France, 1938–1940.* New York: Atheneum.

Halévy, Élie (1926). *A History of the English People 1815–1830*. New York: Harcourt, Brace and Company.

Hall, Peter (1986). *Governing the Economy: The Politics of State Intervention in Britain and France*. New York: Oxford University Press.

Hall, Stephen (1995). Macroeconomics and a Bit More Reality. *Economic Journal 105*(431), 974–988.

Harris, David (1955). European Liberalism in the Nineteenth Century. *American Historical Review 60*(3), 501–526.

Harris, Jonathan (1992). Vadim Andreevich Medvedev and the Transformation of Party Ideology, 1988–1990. *Russian Review 51*(3), 363–377.

Harrison, Mark (1988). Resource Mobilization for World War II: The U.S.A., U.K., U.S.S.R., and Germany, 1938–1945. *Economic History Review 41*(2), 171–192.

Hart, Jeffrey (1974). Symmetry and Polarization in the European International System, 1870–1879: A Methodological Study. *Journal of Peace Research 11*(3), 229–244.

Harty, Martha and John Modell (1991). The First Conflict Resolution Movement, 1956–1971: An Attempt to Institutionalize Applied Interdisciplinary Social Science. *Journal of Conflict Resolution 35*(4), 720–758.

Hartz, Louis (1955). *The Liberal Tradition in America*. New York: Harcourt, Brace and World.

Hay, William Anthony (2005). *The Whig Revival, 1808–1830*. New York: Palgrave Macmillan.

Hayes, Paul (1975). *The Nineteenth Century 1814–80*. London: Adam & Charles Black.

Hazan, Baruch A. (1987). *From Brezhnev to Gorbachev: Infighting in the Kremlin*. Boulder: Westview Press.

Healy, Brian and Arthur Stein (1973). The Balance of Power in International History. *Journal of Conflict Resolution 17*(1), 33–61.

Heinrichs, Waldo (1988). *Threshold of War: Franklin D. Roosevelt and American Entry into World War II*. New York: Oxford University Press.

Hero, Alfred O. (1973). *American Religious Groups View Foreign Policy: Trends in Rank-and-File Opinion, 1937–1969*. Durham, NC: Duke University Press.

Herrmann, Richard K. and Richard Ned Lebow (Eds.) (2004). *Ending The Cold War: Interpretations, Causation, and the Study of International Relations*. New York: Palgrave Macmillan.

Herz, John H. (1951). *Political Realism and Political Idealism: A Study in Theories and Realities*. Chicago: University of Chicago Press.

Hickman, Bert G. (1991). Project LINK and Multi-Country Modelling. In Ronald G. Bodkin, Lawrence R. Klein, and Kanta Marwah (Eds.), *A History of Macroeconometric Modelling*, pp. 482–506. Vermont: Edward Elgar Publishing.

Hinsley, F. H. (1963). *Power and the Pursuit of Peace: Theory and Practice in the History of Relations between States*. Cambridge: Cambridge University Press.

Hintze, Otto (1975). Military Organization and the Organization of the State. In Felix Gilbert (Ed.), *The Historical Essays of Otto Hintze*, pp. 178–215. New York: Oxford University Press.

Holmes, Jack E. (1985). *The Mood/Interest Theory of American Foreign Policy*. Lexington: University Press of Kentucky.

Holmes, Stephen (1982). Two Concepts of Legitimacy: France after the Revolution. *Political Theory 10*(2), 165–183.

Holsti, Kalevi J. (1991). *Peace and War: Armed Conflicts and International Order 1648–1989*. Cambridge: Cambridge University Press.

Holsti, Ole R. (1962). The Belief System and National Images: A Case Study. *Journal of Conflict Resolution 6*, 244–252.

Holsti, Ole R. (1979). The Three-Headed Eagle: The United States and System Change. *International Studies Quarterly 23*, 339–359.

Holsti, Ole R. (1996). *Public Opinion and American Foreign Policy*. Ann Arbor: University of Michigan Press.

Homer-Dixon, Thomas F. (1994). Environmental Scarcities and Violent Conflict: Evidence from Cases. *International Security 19*(1), 5–40.

Hopf, Ted (1991). Polarity, the Offense-Defense Balance, and War. *American Political Science Review 85*(2), 475–493.

Hopf, Ted (1993). Getting the End of the Cold War Wrong. *International Security 18*(2), 202–08.

Hopf, Ted (2002). *Social Construction of International Politics: Identities and Foreign Policies, Moscow, 1955 & 1999*. Ithaca: Cornell University Press.

Hopf, Ted (2006). Moscow's Foreign Policy, 1945–2000: Identities, Institutions and Interests. In Ronald Grigor Suny (Ed.), *The Cambridge History of Russia Volume III: The Twentieth Century*, pp. 662–705. Cambridge University Press.

Hough, Jerry F. (1987). Gorbachev Consolidating Power. *Problems of Communism 36*(4), 21–43.

Hough, Jerry (1990). *Russia and the West: Gorbachev and the Politics of Reform* (2nd ed.). New York: Touchstone.

Hough, Jerry F. and Merle Fainsod (1979). *How the Soviet Union Is Governed*. Cambridge, MA: Harvard University Press.

Hunt, Michael H. (1987). *Ideology and U.S. Foreign Policy*. New Haven: Yale University Press.

Huntington, Samuel P. (1993). The Clash of Civilizations? *Foreign Affairs 72*, 22–49.

Huntington, Samuel P. (1996). *The Clash of Civilizations and the Remaking of World Order*. New York: Simon and Schuster.

Ikenberry, G. John (2000). *After Victory: Institutions: Strategic Restraint, and the Rebuilding of Order after Major Wars*. Princeton, NJ: Princeton University Press.

Imbens, Guido W. and Paul R. Rosenbaum (2005). Robust, Accurate Confidence Intervals with a Weak Instrument: Quarter of Birth and Education. *Journal of the Royal Statistical Society A 168*(1), 109–126.

Ingebritsen, Christine, Iver B. Neumann, Sieglinde Gstöhl, and Jessica Beyer (Eds.) (2006). *Small States in International Relations*. Seattle: University of Washington Press.

Jäckel, Eberhard (1972). *Hitler's* Weltanschauung: *Blueprint for Power*. Middletown, CT: Wesleyan University Press.

Jäckel, Eberhard (1984). *Hitler in History*. Hanover, NH: Brandeis University Press.

Jacobson, Jon (1983). Is There a New International History of the 1920s? *American Historical Review 88*(3), 617–645.

Jervis, Robert (1970). *The Logic of Images in International Relations*. Princeton, NJ: Princeton University Press.

Jervis, Robert (1976). *Perception and Misperception in International Politics*. Princeton, NJ: Princeton University Press.

Jervis, Robert (1978). Cooperation under the Security Dilemma. *World Politics 30*, 167–214.

Jervis, Robert (1997). *System Effects: Complexity in Political and Social Life*. Princeton, NJ: Princeton University Press.

Johnson, Donald Bruce (1960). *The Republican Party and Wendell Willkie*. Urbana: University of Illinois Press.

Johnston, Alastair Iain (1995). *Cultural Realism: Strategic Culture and Grand Strategy in Chinese History*. Princeton, NJ: Princeton University Press.

Jonas, Manfred (1966). *Isolationism in America 1935–1941*. Ithaca: Cornell University Press.

Jones, Bradford, Benjamin Radcliff, Charles Taber, and Richard Timpone (1995). Condorcet Winners and the Paradox of Voting: Probability Calculations for Weak Preference Orders. *American Political Science Review 89*(1), 137–144.

Jones, Kenneth Paul (1981). Alanson B. Houghton and the Ruhr Crisis: The Diplomacy of Power and Morality. In Kenneth Paul Jones (Ed.), *U.S. Diplomats in Europe, 1919–1941*, pp. 25–39. Santa Barbara, CA: ABC-Clio.

Kaiser, David (1990). *Politics and War: European Conflict from Philip II to Hitler*. Cambridge, MA: Harvard University Press.

Kaplan, Morton (1957). *System and Process in International Politics*. New York: John Wiley and Sons.

Katzenstein, Peter (1985). *Small States in World Markets: Industrial Policy in Europe*. Ithaca: Cornell University Press.

Katzenstein, Peter J. (Ed.) (1996). *The Culture of National Security: Norms and Identity in World Politics*. New York: Columbia University Press.

Keegan, John (1993). *A History of Warfare*. New York: Vintage Books.

Keeney, Ralph L. and Howard Raiffa (1993). *Decisions with Multiple Objectives: Preferences and Value Tradeoffs*. Cambridge: Cambridge University Press.

Kennedy, Paul (1987). *The Rise and Fall of the Great Powers: Economic Change and Military Conflict from 1500 to 2000*. New York: Random House.

Kennedy, Peter (1985). *A Guide to Econometrics* (2nd ed.). Cambridge, MA: MIT Press.

Keohane, Robert (1984). *After Hegemony: Cooperation and Discord in the World Political Economy*. Princeton, NJ: Princeton University Press.

Keohane, Robert (1989). *International Institutions and State Power*. Boulder, CO: Westview Press.

Keohane, Robert O. (1983). The Demand for International Regimes. In Stephen D. Krasner (Ed.), *International Regimes*, pp. 141–171. Ithaca: Cornell University Press.

Keohane, Robert O. and Joseph S. Nye (1989). *Power and Interdependence* (2nd ed.). New York: Harper Collins.

Kifner, John (2006). Hezbollah Leads Work to Rebuild, Gaining Stature. *New York Times*, A–1.

Kimura, Masato and David A. Welch (1998). Specifying "Interests": Japan's Claim to the Northern Territories and Its Implications for International Relations Theory. *International Studies Quarterly* 42(2), 213–244.

Kissinger, Henry (1957). *A World Restored.* London: Weidenfeld and Nicolson.

Kissinger, Henry (1994). *Diplomacy.* New York: Simon and Schuster.

Klare, Michael T. (2001). *Resource Wars: The New Landscape of Global Conflict.* New York: Henry Holt and Co.

Klingberg, Frank L. (1952). The Historical Alternation of Moods in American Foreign Policy. *World Politics* 4(2), 239–273.

Klingberg, Frank L. (1983). *Cyclical Trends in American Foreign Policy Moods: The Unfolding of America's World Role.* New York: University Press of America.

Klotz, Audie (1995). Norms Reconstituting Interests: Global Racial Equality and U.S. Sanctions against South Africa. *International Organization* 49(3), 451–478.

Knock, Thomas J. (1992). *To End All Wars: Woodrow Wilson and the Quest for a New World Order.* Princeton, NJ: Princeton University Press.

Knorr, Klaus and Sidney Verba (Eds.) (1961). *The International System: Theoretical Essays.* Princeton, NJ: Princeton University Press.

Kokoshin, Andrei A. (1998). *Soviet Strategic Thought, 1917–91.* Cambridge, MA: MIT Press.

Kolb, Eberhard (1988). *The Weimar Republic.* London: Unwin Hyman.

Krasner, Stephen D. (Ed.) (1983). *International Regimes.* Ithaca: Cornell University Press.

Krasner, Stephen D. (1993). Westphalia and All That. In Judith Goldstein and Robert O. Keohane (Eds.), *Ideas and Foreign Policy: Beliefs, Institutions, and Political Change,* pp. 235–264. Ithaca: Cornell University Press.

Krasner, Stephen D. (1999). *Sovereignty: Organized Hypocrisy.* Princeton, NJ: Princeton University Press.

Kratochwil, Friedrich (1982). On the Notion of "Interest" in International Relations. *International Organization* 36(1), 1–30.

Kydd, Andrew (2005). *Trust and Mistrust in International Relations.* Princeton, NJ: Princeton University Press.

LaFeber, Walter (1985). *America, Russia, and the Cold War 1945–1984* (5th ed.). New York: Alfred A. Knopf.

Laitin, David (1998). *Identity in Formation: The Russian-Speaking Populations in the Near Abroad.* Ithaca: Cornell University Press.

Lake, David A. (1992). Powerful Pacifists: Democratic States and War. *American Political Science Review* 86(1), 24–37.

Langer, William L. (1966). *European Alliances and Alignments 1871–1890* (2nd ed.). New York: Alfred A. Knopf.

Langer, William L. and S. Everett Gleason (1952). *The Challenge to Isolation: The World Crisis of 1937–1940 and American Foreign Policy.* New York: Harper and Brothers.

Lasky, Melvin J. (1973). The English Ideology. *Encounter* 40(1), 19–34.

Ledeneva, Alena V. (1998). *Russia's Economy of Favours: Blat, Networking, and Informal Exchanges.* Cambridge: Cambridge University Press.

Leffler, Melvyn P. (2000). Bringing it Together: The Parts and the Whole. In Odd Arne Westad (Ed.), *Reviewing the Cold War: Approaches, Interpretations, Theory*, pp. 43–63. New York: Frank Cass.

Leffler, Melvyn P. (2008). *For the Soul of Mankind: The United States, the Soviet Union, and the Cold War*. New York: Hill and Wang.

Legro, Jeffrey W. (2000). Whence American Internationalism. *International Organization 54*(2), 253–289.

Lenin, V. I. (1939). *Imperialism: The Highest Stage of Capitalism*. New York: International Publishers.

Lévesque, Jacques (1997). *The Enigma of 1989: The USSR and the Liberation of Eastern Europe (1989, la fin d'un empire)*. Berkeley: University of California Press.

Lévesque, Jacques (2004). The Emancipation of Eastern Europe. In *Richard K. Herrmann* and *Richard Ned Lebow (Eds.) Ending the Cold War: Interpretations, Causation, and the Study of International Relations*, pp. 107–129. New York: Palgrave Macmillan.

Lewis, Jeffrey B. and Keith T. Poole (2004). Measuring Bias and Uncertainty in Ideal Point Estimates via the Parametric Bootstrap. *Political Analysis 12*(2), 105–127.

Li, Richard P. Y. and William R. Thompson (1978). The Stochastic Process of Alliance Formation Behavior. *American Political Science Review 72*(4), 1288–1303.

Lincoln, W. Bruce (1978). *Nicholas I: Emperor and Autocrat of All the Russias*. Bloomington: Indiana University Press.

Livermore, Gordon (Ed.) (1990). *Soviet Foreign Policy Today: Reports and Commentaries from the Soviet Press*. Columbus, OH: Current Digest of the Soviet Press.

Lobanov-Rostovsky, Andrei (1954). *Russia and Europe, 1825–1878*. Ann Arbor, MI: G. Wahr.

Lohmann, Susanne (1994). The Dynamics of Informational Cascades: The Monday Demonstrations in Leipzig, East Germany, 1989–91. *World Politics 47*(1), 42–101.

Lukacs, John (1998). *The Hitler of History*. New York: Alfred A. Knopf.

Lundestad, Geir (2000). How (Not) to Study the Origins of the Cold War. In Odd Arne Westad (Ed.), *Reviewing the Cold War: Approaches, Interpretations, Theory*, pp. 64–80. New York: Frank Cass.

Lynch, Allen (1987). *The Soviet Study of International Relations*. New York: Cambridge University Press.

Mandler, Peter (1990). *Aristocratic Government in the Age of Reform. Whigs and Liberals, 1830–1852*. New York: Oxford University Press.

Mansfield, Edward D. (1988). Distributions of War over Time. *World Politics 41*(1), 21–51.

Maoz, Zeev and Bruce Russett (1993). Normative and Structural Causes of Democratic Peace, 1946–1986. *American Political Science Review 87*(3), 624–638.

Martin, Andrew D. and Kevin M. Quinn (2002). Dynamic Ideal Point Estimation via Markov Chain Monte Carlo for the U.S. Supreme Court, 1953–1999. *Political Analysis 10*(2), 134–153.

Matlock, Jack F. Jr. (2004). *Reagan and Gorbachev: How the Cold War Ended*. New York: Random House.

May, Ernest R. (2000). *Strange Victory: Hitler's Conquest of France*. New York: Hill and Wang.

Mazower, Mark (1998). *Dark Continent: Europe's Twentieth Century*. New York: Vintage Books.

McClelland, Charles A. (1966). *Theory and the International System*. New York: The Macmillan Company.

McClosky, Herbert (1964). Consensus and Ideology in American Politics. *American Political Science Review 58*(2), 361–382.

McCloskey, Herbert (1967). Personality and Attitude Correlates of Foreign Policy Orientation. In James N. Rosenau (Ed.), *Domestic Sources of Foreign Policy*, pp. 51–109. New York: Free Press.

McDonald, H. Brooke and Richard Rosecrance (1985). Alliance and Structural Balance in the International System: A Reinterpretation. *Journal of Conflict Resolution 29*(1), 57–82.

McFaul, Michael A. (2001). *Russia's Unfinished Revolution: Political Change from Gorbachev to Putin*. Ithaca: Cornell University Press.

McGee, Michael C. (1977). The Fall of Wellington: A Case Study of the Relationship between Theory, Practice, and Rhetoric in History. *Quarterly Journal of Speech 63*(1), 28–42.

McKelvey, Richard D. (1976). Intransitivities in Multidimensional Voting Models and Some Implications for Agenda Control. *Journal of Economic Theory 12*(3), 472–482.

Meadows, Donella H., Dennis L. Meadows, Jorgen Randers, and William W. Behrens (1972). *The Limits to Growth*. New York: Potomac Associates.

Mearsheimer, John J. (2001). *The Tragedy of Great Power Politics*. New York: W. W. Norton & Co.

Mendelson, Sarah E. (1998). *Changing Course: Ideas, Politics and the Soviet Withdrawal from Afghanistan*. Princeton, NJ: Princeton University Press.

Merritt, Richard L., Robert G. Muncaster, and Dina A. Zinnes (Eds.) (1994). *Management of International Events: DDIR Phase II*. Ann Arbor: University of Michigan Press.

Messerschmidt, Manfred (1990). Foreign Policy and Preparation for War. In Wilhelm Deist, Manfred Messerschmidt, Hans-Erich Volkmann, and Wolfram Wette (Eds.), *Germany and the Second World War*, Volume I, pp. 541–717. Oxford: Clarendon Press.

Milosz, Czeslaw (1953). *The Captive Mind*. New York: Alfred Knopf.

Milton, Giles (2000). *Nathaniel's Nutmeg: or, The True and Incredible Adventures of the Spice Trader Who Changed the Course of History*. New York: Penguin.

Mitchell, Austin (1965). The Whigs and Parliamentary Reform before 1830. *Historical Studies. Australia and New Zealand 12*(45), 22–42.

Mitchell, Austin (1967). *The Whigs in Opposition 1815–1830*. Oxford: Clarendon Press.

Mitchell, L. G. (1999). The Whigs, the People, and Reform. *Proceedings of the British Academy 100*, 25–41.

Mommsen, Hans (1996). *The Rise & Fall of Weimar Democracy*. Chapel Hill: University of North Carolina Press.

Moravcsik, Andrew (1997). Taking Preferences Seriously: A Liberal Theory of International Politics. *International Organization 51*(4), 513–553.

Morgenthau, Hans J. (1948). *Politics among Nations: The Struggle for Power and Peace*. New York: Alfred A. Knopf.

Morgenthau, Hans J. (1952). *In Defense of the National Interest: A Critical Examination of American Foreign Policy.* New York: Alfred A. Knopf.

Morrow, James D. (1993). Arms versus Allies: Trade-offs in the Search for Security. *International Organization 47*(2), 207–233.

Morrow, James D. (1994). *Game Theory for Political Scientists.* Princeton, NJ: Princeton University Press.

Most, Benjamin and Harvey Starr (1989). *Inquiry, Logic, and International Politics.* Columbia: University of South Carolina Press.

Mueller, Dennis C. (1989). *Public Choice II.* Cambridge: Cambridge University Press.

Mueller, John (2004–2005). What Was the Cold War About? Evidence from Its Ending. *Political Science Quarterly 119*(4), 609–631.

Mueller, John (2009). *Atomic Obsession: Nuclear Alarmism from Hiroshima to Al-Qaeda.* New York: Oxford University Press.

Mullins, Willard A. (1972). On the Concept of Ideology in Political Science. *American Political Science Review 66*(2), 498–510.

Muncaster, Robert G. and Dina A. Zinnes (1983). A Model of Inter-Nation Hostility Dynamics and War. *Conflict Management and Peace Science 6*(2), 19–37.

Murray, Shoon Kathleen (1996). *Anchors against Change: American Opinion Leaders' Beliefs after the Cold War.* Ann Arbor: University of Michigan Press.

Murray, Williamson (1984). *The Change in the European Balance of Power, 1938–1939: The Path to Ruin.* Princeton, NJ: Princeton University Press.

Nation, R. Craig (1992). *Black Earth, Red Star: A History of Soviet Security Policy, 1917–1991.* Ithaca: Cornell University Press.

National Security Council (2002). *The National Security Strategy of the United States of America.* Washington, DC: U.S. Government Printing Office.

National Security Council (2006). *The National Security Strategy of the United States of America.* Washington, DC: U.S. Government Printing Office.

Nicolson, Harold (1946). *The Congress of Vienna: A Study in Allied Unity, 1812–1822.* New York: Harcourt, Brace and Co.

Nierop, Tom (1994). *Systems and Regions in Global Politics.* New York: John Wiley and Sons.

Nincic, Miroslav (1996). Domestic Costs, the U.S. Public, and the Isolationist Calculus. Presented at the *Annual Meeting of the International Studies Association*, San Diego, CA.

Niou, Emerson M.S., Peter C. Ordeshook, and Gregory F. Rose (1989). *The Balance of Power: Stability in International Systems.* Cambridge: Cambridge University Press.

Niou, Emerson M. S. and Peter Ordeshook (1994). "Less Filling, Tastes Great": The Realist-Neoliberal Debate. *World Politics 46*(2), 209–234.

Nordlinger, Eric (1995). *Isolationism Reconfigured: American Foreign Policy for a New Century.* Princeton, NJ: Princeton University Press.

Norris, Robert S. and William M. Arkin (1997, November/December). Global Nuclear Stockpiles, 1945–1997. *Bulletin of the Atomic Scientists 53*(06), 67.

North, Douglass C. (1981). *Structure and Change in Economic History.* New York: W. W. Norton and Co.

Nye, Joseph S. (1991). *Bound to Lead: The Changing Nature of American Power*. New York: Basic Books.

Oberdorfer, Don (1998). *From the Cold War to a New Era: The United States and the Soviet Union, 1983–1991*. Baltimore: Johns Hopkins University Press.

Office of Assistant Secretary of Defense, Public Affairs (1998, February 2). Department of Defense Budget for FY 1999. News release.

Olson, Mancur (1965). *The Logic of Collective Action: Public Goods and the Theory of Groups*. Cambridge, MA: Harvard University Press.

Olson, Mancur and Richard Zeckhauser (1966). An Economic Theory of Alliances. *Review of Economics and Statistics 48*(3), 266–279.

Organski, A. F. K. and Jacek Kugler (1980). *The War Ledger*. Chicago: University of Chicago Press.

Ouimet, Matthew J. (2003). *The Rise and Fall of the Brezhnev Doctrine in Soviet Foreign Policy*. Chapel Hill: University of North Carolina Press.

Overy, Richard J. (1984). German Air Strength 1933 to 1939: A Note. *Historical Journal 27*(2), 465–471.

Oye, Kenneth (Ed.) (1986). *Cooperation under Anarchy*. Princeton, NJ: Princeton University Press.

Palmer, Alan Warwick (1974). *Alexander I: Tsar of War and Peace*. London: Weidenfeld and Nicolson.

Palmer, Glenn (1990). Alliance Politics and Issue-Areas: Determinants of Defense Spending. *American Journal of Political Science 34*(1), 190–211.

Parrott, Bruce (1988). Soviet National Security under Gorbachev. *Problems of Communism 6*, 1–36.

Parssinen, T. M. (1972). The Revolutionary Party in London, 1816–20. *Bulletin of the Institute of Historical Research [Great Britain] 45*(112), 266–282.

Pepinsky, Thomas B. (2005). From Agents to Outcomes: Simulation in International Relations. *European Journal of International Relations 11*(3), 367–394.

Peress, Michael (2009). Small Chamber Ideal Point Estimation. *Political Analysis 17*(3), 276–290.

Perkins, Bradford (1993). *The Cambridge History of American Foreign Relations, Volume I: The Creation of a Republican Empire, 1776–1865*. Cambridge: Cambridge University Press.

Persson, Torsten and Guido Tabellini (2002). *Political Economics: Explaining Economic Policy*. Cambridge, MA: MIT Press.

Peterson, Genevieve (1945). Political Inequality at the Congress of Vienna. *Political Science Quarterly 60*(4), 532–554.

Pevehouse, Jonathan C. and Joshua S. Goldstein (1999). Serbian Compliance or Defiance in Kosovo? Statistical Analysis and Real-Time Predictions. *Journal of Conflict Resolution 43*(4), 538–546.

Pilbeam, Pamela (1970). The Emergence of Opposition to the Orleanist Monarchy, August 1830–April 1831. *English Historical Review 85*(334), 12–28.

Pilbeam, Pamela (1982). The Growth of Liberalism and the Crisis of the Bourbon Restoration, 1827–1830. *Historical Journal 25*(2), 351–366.

Pinkney, David H. (1987). The French Revolution of 1830 Reconsidered. *Proceedings of the Annual Meeting of the Western Society for French History 14*, 215–222.

Plott, Charles R. (1967). A Notion of Equilibrium and Its Possibility under Majority Rule. *American Economic Review 57*(4), 787–806.

Pollins, Brian M. and Randall L. Schweller (1999). Linking the Levels: The Long Wave and Shifts in U.S. Foreign Policy, 1790–1993. *American Journal of Political Science 43*(2), 431–464.

Poole, Keith T. and Howard Rosenthal (1997). *Congress: A Political Economic History of Roll Call Voting.* New York: Oxford University Press.

Powell, Robert (1999). *In the Shadow of Power: States and Strategies in International Politics.* Princeton, NJ: Princeton University Press.

Pulzer, Peter (1997). *Germany, 1870–1945: Politics, State Formation, and War.* New York: Oxford University Press.

Putnam, Robert (1988). Diplomacy and Domestic Politics: The Logic of Two-Level Games. *International Organization 42*, 427–460.

Quinault, Roland (1994). The French Revolution of 1830 and Parliamentary Reform. *History 79*(257), 377–393.

Ragsdale, Hugh (1988). *Tsar Paul and the Question of Madness: An Essay in History and Psychology.* New York: Greenwood Press.

Rasmusen, Eric (1989). *Games and Information: An Introduction to Game Theory.* Cambridge: Cambridge University Press.

Reinerman, Alan J. (1995). England and Italian Reform: The Seymour Mission of 1832. *Consortium on Revolutionary Europe 1750–1850: Selected Papers*, 701–708.

Reiter, Dan and Allan C. Stam III (2002). *Democracies at War.* Princeton, NJ: Princeton University Press.

Remnick, David (1994). *Lenin's Tomb: The Last Days of the Soviet Empire.* New York: Vintage Books.

Resnick, Mitchel (1994). *Turtles, Termites, and Traffic Jams.* Cambridge, MA: MIT Press.

Reynolds, David (1982). *The Creation of an Anglo-American Alliance, 1937–41: A Study in Competitive Cooperation.* Chapel Hill: University of North Carolina Press.

Riasanovsky, Nicholas V. (1959). *Nicholas I and Official Nationality in Russia, 1825–1855.* Berkeley: University of California Press.

Rich, Norman (1992). *Great Power Diplomacy 1814–1914.* Boston: McGraw Hill.

Richardson, Lewis F. (1960). *Statistics of Deadly Quarrels.* Chicago: Quadrangle Books.

Richter, James (1996). Russian Foreign Policy and the Politics of National Identity. In Celeste A. Wallander (Ed.), *The Sources of Russian Foreign Policy after the Cold War*, pp. 69–93. Boulder, CO: Westview Press.

Risse-Kappen, Thomas (1994). Ideas Do Not Float Freely: Transnational Coalitions, Domestic Structures, and the End of the Cold War. *International Organization 48*(2), 185–214.

Roeder, Philip G. (1984). Soviet Policies and Kremlin Politics. *International Studies Quarterly 28*, 171–193.

Roeder, Philip G. (1993). *Red Sunset: The Failure of Soviet Politics.* Princeton: Princeton University Press.

Rogowski, Ronald (1999). Institutions as Constraints on Strategic Choice. In David A. Lake and Robert Powell (Eds.), *Strategic Choice and International Relations*. Princeton, NJ: Princeton University Press.

Rooney, John W. (1984). Palmerston and the Revolutions of 1830–1833. *Consortium on Revolutionary Europe 1750–1850: Proceedings 14*, 406–413.

Rose, Guideon (1998). Neoclassical Realism and Theories of Foreign Policy. *World Politics 51*(1), 144–172.

Rosecrance, Richard (1963). *Action and Reaction in World Politics*. Boston: Little, Brown and Co.

Rosecrance, Richard (1986). *The Rise of the Trading State: Commerce and Conquest in the Modern World*. New York: Basic Books.

Rosenberg, Shawn W. and Gary Wolfsfeld (1977). International Conflict and the Problem of Attribution. *Journal of Conflict Resolution 21*(1), 75–103.

Rubinstein, Ariel (1982). Perfect Equilibrium in a Bargaining Model. *Econometrica 50*(1), 97–109.

Ruggie, John Gerard (1998). What Makes the World Hang Together? Neo-utilitarianism and the Social Constructivist Challenge. *International Organization 52*(4), 855–885.

Rush, Myron (1993). Fortune and Fate. *National Interest 31*, 19–25.

Russett, Bruce (1993). *Grasping the Democratic Peace: Principles for a Post-Cold War World*. Princeton, NJ: Princeton University Press.

Sack, James J. (1980). The House of Lords and Parliamentary Patronage in Great Britain, 1802–1832. *Historical Journal 23*(4), 913–937.

Said, Abdul Aziz (1977). *Ethnicity and U.S. Foreign Policy*. New York: Praeger.

Saperstein, Alvin M. (1992). Alliance Building versus Independent Action: A Nonlinear Modeling Approach to Comparative International Stability. *Journal of Conflict Resolution 36*(3), 518–545.

Saperstein, Alvin M (1999). *Dynamical Modeling of the Onset of War*. River Edge, NJ: World Scientific.

Sargent, Thomas J. (1978). Estimation of Dynamic Labor Demand Schedules under Rational Expectations. *Journal of Political Economy 86*(6), 1009–1044.

Schelling, Thomas C. (1966). *Arms and Influence*. New Haven: Yale University Press.

Schelling, Thomas C. (1978). *Micromotives and Macrobehavior*. New York: W. W. Norton.

Schlesinger Jr., Arthur (1967). Origins of the Cold War. *Foreign Affairs 46*(October), 22–52.

Schlesinger Jr., Arthur (1986). *The Cycles of American History*. Boston: Houghton Mifflin.

Schneider, William (1983). Conservatism, Not Interventionism: Trends in Foreign Policy Opinion, 1974–1982. In Kenneth Oye, Robert J. Lieber, and Donald Rothchild (Eds.), *Eagle Defiant: United States Foreign Policy in the 1980s*, pp. 33–64. Boston: Little, Brown and Co.

Schrodt, Philip A. (1994). Event Data in Foreign Policy Analysis. In Laura Neack, Jeanne A. K. Hey, and Patrick J. Haney (Eds.), *Foreign Policy Analysis: Continuity and Change*, pp. 145–166. New York: Prentice-Hall.

Schroeder, Paul (1994a). Historical Reality vs. Neo-realist Theory. *International Security 19*(1), 108–148.

Schroeder, Paul W. (1994b). *The Transformation of European Politics.* Oxford: Clarendon Press.

Schwartzberg, Steven (1988a). The Lion and the Phoenix – 1: British Policy toward the Greek Question, 1821–32. *Middle Eastern Studies 24*(2), 139–177.

Schwartzberg, Steven (1988b). The Lion and the Phoenix – 2: British Policy toward the Greek Question, 1821–32. *Middle Eastern Studies 24*(3), 287–311.

Schweller, Randall L. (1998). *Deadly Imbalances: Tripolarity and Hitler's Strategy of World Conquest.* New York: Columbia University Press.

Scott, Ivan (1972). Counter Revolutionary Diplomacy and the Demise of Anglo-Austrian Cooperation, 1820–1823. *Historian 34*(3), 465–484.

Seliger, Martin (1976). *Ideology and Politics.* London: Allen & Unwin.

Semeyko, Lev (1989). Instead of Mountains of Weapons: On the Principle of Reasonable Sufficiency. In Isaac J. Tarasulo (Ed.), *Gorbachev and Glasnost: Viewpoints from the Soviet Press,* pp. 248–253. Wilmington, Del.: SR Books.

Sestanovich, Stephen (1988). Gorbachev's Foreign Policy: A Diplomacy of Decline. *Problems of Communism 37*(1), 1–15.

Seton-Watson, Robert William (1937). *Britain in Europe 1789–1914: A Survey of Foreign Policy.* Cambridge: Cambridge University Press.

Shepardson, Whitney H. and William O. Scroggs (1941). *The United States in World Affairs: An Account of American Foreign Relations, 1940.* Harper & Brothers.

Shevardnadze, Eduard (1991). *The Future Belongs to Freedom.* New York: The Free Press.

Shlapentokh, Vladimir (1998). Standard of Living and Popular Discontent. In Michael Ellman and Vladimir Kontorovich (Eds.), *The Destruction of the Soviet Economic System: An Insiders' History,* pp. 30–39. Armonk, NY: M. E. Sharpe.

Shoptaugh, Terry L. (1993). Borderline Neutrality: The Transport of Military Aircraft near Pembina, North Dakota, 1940. *North Dakota History 60*(2), 2–13.

Shuster, Richard J. (2006). *German Disarmament after World War I: The Diplomacy of International Arms Inspection, 1920–1931.* New York: Routledge.

Sims, Christopher A. (1980). Macroeconomics and Reality. *Econometrica 48*(1), 1–48.

Singer, J. David (1961). The Level-of-Analysis Problem in International Relations. *World Politics 14*(1), 77–92.

Singer, J. David, Stuart Bremer, and John Stuckey (1972). Capability Distribution, Uncertainty, and Major Power War, 1820–1965. In Bruce M. Russett (Ed.), *Peace, War, and Numbers,* pp. 19–48. Beverly Hills: Sage Publications.

Sked, Alan (Ed.) (1979a). *Europe's Balance of Power, 1815–1848.* New York: Barnes & Noble.

Sked, Alan (1979b). The Metternich System, 1815–48. In Alan Sked (Ed.), *Europe's Balance of Power, 1815–1848,* pp. 98–121. New York: Barnes & Noble.

Skocpol, Theda (1979). *States and Social Revolutions: A Comparative Analysis of France, Russia, and China.* Cambridge: Cambridge University Press.

Slaughter, Anne Marie (2004). *A New World Order.* Princeton, NJ: Princeton University Press.

Smith, Anthony D. (1991). *National Identity.* Reno: University of Nevada Press.

Smith, Hedrick (1976). *The Russians.* New York: Ballantine Books.

Snyder, Jack (1985). Civil-Military Relations and the Cult of the Offensive, 1914 and 1984. In Steven E. Miller (Ed.), *Military Strategy and the Origins of the First World War*, pp. 108–146. Princeton, NJ: Princeton University Press.

Snyder, Jack (1991). *Myths of Empire: Domestic Politics and International Ambition*. Ithaca: Cornell University Press.

Sontag, Raymond J. (1933). *European Diplomatic History 1871–1932*. New York: Appleton-Century-Crofts.

Sontag, Raymond J. (1971). *A Broken World: 1919–1939*. New York: Harper and Row.

Sorokin, Gerald L. (1994). Arms, Alliances, and Security Tradeoffs in Enduring Rivalries. *International Studies Quarterly 38*, 421–446.

Southgate, Donald (1966). *"The Most English Minister..."*: The Policies and Politics of *Palmerston*. London: Macmillan.

Spechler, Dina (1982). *Permitted Dissent in the USSR: Novy Mir and the Soviet Regime*. New York: Praeger.

Spiezio, Kim Edward (1990). British Hegemony and Major Power War, 1815–1939: An Empirical Test of Gilpin's Model of Hegemonic Governance. *International Studies Quarterly 34*(2), 165–181.

Sprout, Harold and Margaret Sprout (1951). Form of Government as a Factor in National Strength. In Harold Sprout and Margaret Sprout (Eds.), *Foundations of National Power*, pp. 28–62. New York: D. Van Nostrand Company, Inc.

Spruyt, Hendrik (1994). *The Sovereign State and Its Competitors: An Analysis of Systems Change*. Princeton, NJ: Princeton University Press.

Spykman, Nicholas John (1942). *America's Strategy in World Politics*. New York: Harcourt, Brace and Company.

Stapleton, Edward J. (Ed.) (1887a). *Some Official Correspondence of George Canning*, Volume I. London: Longmans, Green, and Co.

Stapleton, Edward J. (Ed.) (1887b). *Some Official Correspondence of George Canning*, Volume II. London: Longmans, Green, and Co.

Starr, Harvey (1978). "Opportunity" and "Willingness" as Ordering Concepts in the Study of War. *International Interactions 4*(4), 363–387.

Startz, Richard (2003). Partial Adjustment as Optimal Response in a Dynamic Brainard Model. *Manuscript, University of Washington, September*.

Steel, Ronald (1980). *Walter Lippmann and the American Century*. London: Bodley Head.

Stegemann, Bernd (1991). Germany's Second Attempt to Become a Naval Power. In Klause A. Maier, Horst Rohde, Bernd Stegemann, and Hans Umbreit (Eds.), *Germany and the Second World War*, Volume II, pp. 60–66. Oxford: Clarendon Press.

Stein, Janice Gross (1994). Political Learning by Doing: Gorbachev as Uncommitted Thinker and Motivated Learner. *International Organization 48*(2), 155–183.

Steinmo, Sven and Kathleen Thelen (1992). Historical Institutionalism in Comparative Politics. In Sven Steinmo, Kathleen Thelen, and Frank Longstreth (Eds.), *Structuring Politics: Historical Institutionalism in Comparative Analysis*, pp. 1–32. Cambridge: Cambridge University Press.

Stephens, Jerone (1972). An Appraisal of Some System Approaches in the Study of International Systems. *International Studies Quarterly 16*(3), 321–349.

Sterling-Folker, J. (2000). Competing Paradigms or Birds of a Feather? Constructivism and Neoliberal Institutionalism Compared. *International Studies Quarterly* 44(1), 97–119.

Stoakes, Geoffrey (1986). *Hitler and the Quest for World Dominion.* Leamington Spa: Berg Publishers Ltd.

Stone, Norman (1984). *Europe Transformed 1878–1919.* Cambridge, MA: Harvard University Press.

Suri, Jeremi (2002). Explaining the End of the Cold War: A New Historical Consensus? *Journal of Cold War Studies* 4(4), 60–92.

Tarasulo, Isaac J. (Ed.) (1989). *Gorbachev and Glasnost: Viewpoints from the Soviet Press.* Wilmington, DE: SR Books.

Taylor, A. J. P. (1957). *The Trouble Makers: Dissent over Foreign Policy, 1792–1939.* London: H. Hamilton.

Temperley, Harold (1966). *The Foreign Policy of Canning 1822–1827: England, the Neo-Holy Alliance, and the New World.* London: Frank Cass & Co. Ltd.

Temperley, Harold and Lillian M. Penson (Eds.) (1938a). *A Century of Diplomatic Blue Books 1814–1914.* Cambridge: Cambridge University Press.

Temperley, Harold and Lillian M. Penson (1938b). *Foundations of British Foreign Policy from Pitt (1792) to Salisbury (1902).* Cambridge: Cambridge University Press.

Thelen, Kathleen (2004). *How Institutions Evolve: The Political Economy of Skills in Germany, Britain, the United States, and Japan.* New York: Cambridge University Press.

Therry, Roger (1836). *The Speeches of the Right Honourable George Canning. With a Memoir of His Life.* London: J. Ridgway & Sons.

Thompson, William R. (1986). Polarity, the Long Cycle, and Global Power Warfare. *Journal of Conflict Resolution* 30(4), 587–615.

Thompson, William R. (1996). Democracy and Peace: Putting the Cart before the Horse? *International Organization* 50(1), 141–174.

Thomson, David (1978). *Europe since Napoleon.* New York: Penguin Books.

Tilly, Charles (Ed.) (1975). *The Formation of National States in Western Europe.* Princeton, NJ: Princeton University Press.

Tsebelis, George (1990). *Nested Games: Rational Choice in Comparative Politics.* Berkeley: University of California Press.

Tuchman, Barbara W. (1985). *The March of Folly: From Troy to Vietnam.* New York: Ballantine Books.

Ulam, Adam B. (1974). *Expansion and Coexistence: Soviet Foreign Policy 1917–73.* New York: Praeger.

Valdez, Jonathan C. (1993). *Internationalism and the Ideology of Soviet Influence in Eastern Europe.* New York: Cambridge University Press.

Van Evera, Stephen (1985). The Cult of the Offensive and the Origins of the First World War. In Steven E. Miller (Ed.), *Military Strategy and the Origins of the First World War,* pp. 58–107. Princeton, NJ: Princeton University Press.

Volgy, Thomas J. and John E. Schwartz (1994). Foreign Policy Restructuring and the Myriad Webs of Restraint. In Jerel A. Rosati, Joe D. Hagan, and Martin W. Sampson III (Eds.), *Foreign Policy Restructuring: How Governments Respond to Global Change,* pp. 22–39. Columbia: University of South Carolina Press.

Von Neumann, John and Oskar Morgenstern (1944). *Theory of Games and Economic Behavior*. Princeton, NJ: Princeton University Press.

Wagner, R. Harrison (1986). The Theory of Games and the Balance of Power. *World Politics 38*(4), 546–576.

Walker, Martin (1995). *The Cold War: A History*. New York: Holt.

Wallerstein, Immanuel (1979). *The Capitalist World Economy*. Cambridge: Cambridge University Press.

Walt, Stephen M. (1992). Revolution and War. *World Politics 44*(3), 321–368.

Waltz, Kenneth N. (1959). *Man, the State and War: A Theoretical Analysis*. New York: Columbia University Press.

Waltz, Kenneth N. (1979). *Theory of International Politics*. New York: Random House.

Waltz, Kenneth N. (1986). Reflections on Theory of International Politics. A Response to My Critics. In Robert Keohane (Ed.), *Neorealism and Its Critics*, pp. 322–346. New York: Columbia University Press.

Waltz, Kenneth N. (1988). The Origins of War in Neorealist Theory. In Robert I. Rotberg and Theodore K. Rabb (Eds.), *The Origin and Prevention of Major Wars*, pp. 39–52. Cambridge: Cambridge University Press.

Waltz, Kenneth N. (1996). International Politics Is Not Foreign Policy. *Security Studies 6*(1), 54–57.

Ward, Adolphus William and George Peabody Gooch (Eds.) (1923). *The Cambridge History of British Foreign Policy 1783–1919*. New York: Macmillan.

Wasson, E. A. (1977). The Coalitions of 1827 and the Crisis of Whig Leadership. *Historical Journal 20*(3), 587–606.

Webster, Charles (1951). *The Foreign Policy of Palmerston 1830–1841: Britain, the Liberal Movement, and the Eastern Question*, Volume 1. London: G. Bell & Sons, Ltd.

Webster, C. K. (1931). *The Foreign Policy of Castlereagh 1812–1815: Britain and the Reconstruction of Europe*. London: G. Bell and Sons, Ltd.

Webster, C. K. and Harold Temperley (1924). British Policy in the Publication of Diplomatic Documents under Castlereagh and Canning. *Cambridge Historical Journal 1*(2), 158–169.

Weibull, Jörgen W. (2002). *Evolutionary Game Theory*. Cambridge, MA: MIT Press.

Weinberg, Gerhard L. (1970). *The Foreign Policy of Hitler's Germany: Diplomatic Revolution in Europe 1933–36*. Chicago: University of Chicago Press.

Weinrod, W. Bruce (1988). Soviet "New Thinking" and U.S. Foreign Policy. *World Affairs 151*(2), 59–65.

Weiss, Seymour (1989). U.S.-Soviet Detente: The Collision of Hope and Experience. *Strategic Review 17*(1), 16–24.

Weltman, John J. (1973). *Systems Theory in International Relations: A Study in Metaphoric Hypertrophy*. Lexington, MA: D. C. Heath & Co.

Wendt, Alexander (1987). The Agent-Structure Problem in International Relations Theory. *International Organization 41*, 335–370.

Wendt, Alexander (1999). *Social Theory of International Politics*. Cambridge: Cambridge University Press.

Westad, Odd Arne (Ed.) (2000). *Reviewing the Cold War: Approaches, Interpretations, Theory*. New York: Frank Cass.

Williams, John T. and Michael D. McGinnis (1988, November). Sophisticated Reaction in the U.S.-Soviet Arms Race: Evidence of Rational Expectations. *American Journal of Political Science 32*(4), 968–995.

Williams, William Appleman (1972). *The Tragedy of American Diplomacy* (3rd ed.). New York: W.W. Norton and Co.

Wiskemann, Elizabeth (2007). *Italy.* Asbury Park, NJ: Schuyler Press.

Witkiewicz, Stanislaw Ignacy (1977). *Insatiability.* Urbana: University of Illinois Press.

Wittkopf, Eugene (1986). On the Foreign Policy Beliefs of the American People: A Critique and Some Evidence. *International Studies Quarterly 30*, 425–445.

Wittkopf, Eugene R. (1990). *Faces of Internationalism: Public Opinion and American Foreign Policy.* Durham, NC: Duke University Press.

Wohlforth, William Curti (1993). *The Elusive Balance: Power and Perception during the Cold War.* Ithaca: Cornell University Press.

Wohlforth, William C. (1998). Reality Check: Revising Theories of International Politics in Response to the End of the Cold War. *World Politics 50*(4), 650–680.

Wohlforth, William C. (2000). A Certain Idea of Science: How International Relations Theory Avoids Reviewing the Cold War. In Odd Arne Westad (Ed.), *Reviewing the Cold War: Approaches, Interpretations, Theory*, pp. 126–148. New York: Frank Cass.

Wohlforth, William C. (Ed.) (2003). *Cold War Endgame: Oral History, Analysis, Debates.* University Park: Pennsylvania State University Press.

Wohlforth, William C. (2009). Unipolarity, Status Competition, and Great Power War. *World Politics 61*(1), 28–57.

Wolfers, Arnold (1962). *Discord and Collaboration: Essays on International Politics.* Baltimore: Johns Hopkins Press.

Wolfers, Arnold (1966). *Britain and France between the Two Wars: Conflicting Strategies of Peace from Versailles to World War II.* New York: W. W. Norton.

Wolfson, Murray, Patrick James, and Eric Solberg (1998). In a World of Cannibals Everyone Votes for War: Democracy and Peace Reconsidered. In Murray Wolfson (Ed.), *The Political Economy of War and Peace*, pp. 155–176. Boston: Kluwer Academic Publishers.

Wolfson, Murray, Anil Puri, and Mario Martelli (1992). The Nonlinear Dynamics of International Conflict. *Journal of Conflict Resolution 36*(1), 119–149.

Wright, Quincy (1942). *A Study of War.* Chicago: University of Chicago press.

Yurchak, Alexei (2006). *Everything Was Forever, until It Was No More: The Last Soviet Generation.* Princeton, NJ: Princeton University Press.

Zakaria, Fareed (1998). *From Wealth to Power: The Unusual Origins of America's World Role.* Princeton, NJ: Princeton University Press.

Zaller, John (1992). *The Nature and Origins of Mass Opinion.* New York: Cambridge University Press.

Zaslavskaia, Tatiana I. (1989). *A Voice of Reform: Essays by Tatiana I. Zaslavskaia.* Armonk, NY: M. E. Sharpe.

Zimmerman, William (1969). *Soviet Perspectives on International Relations, 1956–1967.* Princeton, NJ: Princeton University Press.

Zinnes, Dina A. and Robert Muncaster (1987). Transaction Flows and Integrative Processes. In Claudio Cioffi-Revilla, Richard L. Merritt, and Dina A. Zinnes (Eds.),

Communication and Interaction in Global Politics, pp. 23–48. Beverly Hills: Sage Publications, Inc.

Zinnes, Dina A. and Robert G. Muncaster (1988). The War Propensity of International Systems. *Synthese 76*(2), 307–331.

Zubok, Vladislav (2003). Gorbachev and the End of the Cold War: Different Perspectives on the Historical Personality. In William C. Wohlforth (Ed.), *Cold War Endgame: Oral History, Analysis, Debates*, pp. 207–242. University Park: Pennsylvania State University Press.

Zubok, Vladislav and Constantine Pleshakov (1996). *Inside the Kremlin's Cold War*. Cambridge, MA: Harvard University Press.

Index

Cambridge Studies in International Relations